MW01140848

Welding Technology for Engineers

Welding Technology
for Engineers

Editors
Baldev Raj
V Shankar
A K Bhaduri

Narosa Publishing House
New Delhi   Chennai   Mumbai   Kolkata

The Materials
Information Society

Editors
Baldev Raj
Director

V Shankar
Scientific Officer
Materials Technology Division

A K Bhaduri
Head, Material Joining

Indira Gandhi Centre for Atomic Research
Kalpakkam, India

Copyright © 2006 Narosa Publishing House Pvt. Ltd.
22 Daryaganj, Delhi Medical Association Road, New Delhi 110 002, India

All rights reserved. No part of this publication may be reproduced, stored in a retrieval system or transmitted in any form or by any means, electronic, mechanical, photocopying, recording or otherwise, without prior written permission of the publisher.

ISBN-13: 978-0-87170-831-1
ISBN-10: 0-87170-831-0

Printed in India.

Foreword

Manufacturing technology worldwide is constantly evolving towards better quality and competitiveness. The technology needs of mass produced low-cost goods are vastly different from highly engineered technologically advanced products that deliver state-of-the-art performance. The industry has transformed itself to meet the challenges of our internal needs in the areas of conventional and nuclear power industries, chemical and petrochemical plants, high performance components for defence and aerospace industries, and the automobile sector. In many of these areas our capabilities are among the most competitive on a global level and goods manufactured in India are now sought after. Indian manufacturing technology is poised to play a major role worldwide in the next few years and beyond. However, technological leadership places stringent demands on knowledge upgradation and innovation, requiring continuous feedback between these two processes. **"Welding Technology for Engineers"** is a major contribution towards knowledge upgradation of welding personnel.

Materials joining technologies are the key to manufacturing, since most often joining is the vital link between raw material and finished component. Welding appears in the manufacturing cycle at such locations that are crucial to the quality and functionality of the component. Materials, manufacturing processes and quality assessment are but different facets of quality management in an organisation. Continuous innovation and knowledge upgradation are part of any effective strategy for quality management. **"Welding Technology for Engineers"** covers a variety of topics of interest to every manufacturing sector in this country, such as weldability of carbon and low alloy steels, stainless steels, nonferrous alloys, welding processes, selection of welding consumables, advanced non-destructive testing and quality concepts. Also covered are topics such as welding of aluminium and titanium alloys, nickel and copper alloys, corrosion of weldments, leak and pressure testing, etc. With the manufacturing sector becoming more broad-based, the use of a wide variety of materials becomes inevitable. This book is a key source of expertise in these specialised topics.

The various chapters in the book are written by recognised experts in the subject and are comprehensive in the treatment of the subject. Moreover, the material presented includes some of the latest work in the respective fields that are not readily available for reference elsewhere. The book would prove to be an asset to all welding professionals and a valuable reference source for academia and industry.

A. Srinivasulu

Preface

At the undergraduate level, there are few programs of study leading to a formal engineering degree in welding both in India and abroad. Even post-graduate programs in welding are very few and many of the programmes do not have direct industry linkages that would add value and credibility to the curriculum. In this scenario, mechanical engineers and metallurgists employed by industry usually have to transform themselves into welding engineers. To do this effectively, they need basic knowledge presented in a focused way to absorb and competently deal with advanced welding technologies and highly engineered materials encountered today. Topics such as welding design, choice of welding consumables, welding equipment, welding procedures for various metals, quality assurance methods and quality assessment during manufacturing represent the foundation of more advanced topics.

Welding Technology for Engineers was first conceived as a module of instruction at the Indira Gandhi Centre for Atomic Research in 1996 and has been offered as a course several times in the past few years. This book is intended to fulfil the need to disseminate the latest developments in welding to the industry. The material presented in this book has been refined over the years through interaction with the nearly two hundred professionals who have attended the programme from various industries all over India. The faculty for the course have been drawn from premier research and academic institutions and from the nuclear, conventional power and manufacturing industries.

This volume contains twenty chapters covering three broad areas, viz. welding metallurgy and basic concepts, welding processes, welding design and welding consumables, and weld quality assessment and advanced NDT. After an introduction to basic concepts of welding covering arc physics, polarity, weld heat and fluid flow, topics such as weldability of carbon and low alloy steels, stainless steels, dissimilar welding and cladding, weldability of aluminium and titanium alloys, nickel and copper alloys are covered. In the welding processes and related subjects, arc welding processes, resistance and solid state welding processes, welding design, residual stresses and distortion and selection of welding consumables have been featured. The last part of the book starts with basic quality requirements, qualification, quality control requirements for various materials, followed by mechanical testing, corrosion of welds and welded components, basic and advanced non-destructive testing techniques, leak and pressure testing, and quality management in welding.

The above topics are intended to provide knowledge towards meeting the stringent demands of many key sectors in Indian industry such as heavy engineering and fabrication, aerospace and transport industries, chemical, petrochemical and fertilizer industries, conventional and nuclear power industries, and any other industry using advanced welded fabrication. The book is a focused module of instruction that would prepare welding professionals to face up to the demands of these vital areas of interest to the welding technologists. The editors of this volume have been involved designing the course content, in the choice of experts and in streamlining the order of presentation for better understanding. The editors and all the faculty have had the benefit of active interactions with all the participants from various industries and institutes and the editors are thankful to them for their valuable feedback that has gone on to enrich the content of this volume.

We look forward to your feedback for further improvements in the contents and the style of communication of the knowledge from experts to students, budding researchers and industry, which generates wealth on the merits of welding science and technology.

Baldev Raj
V Shankar
A K Bhaduri

Acknowledgements

The authors gratefully acknowledge the various primary sources in the literature for some of the figures and tables used in this text. In Chapter 1, Fig. 5 and 6, and Table 1 have been reproduced from AWS Welding Handbook vol. 1. In Chapter 4, Fig. 2 and 3 are from F.B. Pickering's Physical Metallurgy and the Design of Steels, Applied Science, 1978. Tables 1-5 from Chapter 4 are reproduced from A.J. Sedriks: Corrosion of Stainless Steels, John Wiley, 1996. In Chapter 5, Tables 2, 4, 5 and 6 are reproduced from www.azom.com, while Table 1 is reproduced from www.luskmetals.com. Figure 5 in Chapter 11 is reproduced from D.J. Kotecki and D.G. Howden, WRC Bulletin 184, 1973. In Chapter 13, Fig. 1 and Table 2 and Fig. 9 of Chapter 16 are reproduced courtesy of ASME BPVC 2004. Fig. 5 of Chapter 16 is reproduced from Design Data Book, PSG Tech. publications, Coimbatore, 1995. Numerous other sources in the literature have also been cited wherever information has been drawn from published work.

We thank the contributors for their earnest efforts to improve the quality of the manuscript by extending all help in bringing out this volume.

Baldev Raj
V Shankar
A K Bhaduri

Contents

Foreword   *v*

Preface   *vii*

Acknowledgements   *ix*

1. Basic Concepts and Physical Metallurgy of Welding   1
   A.K. Bhaduri and V. Shankar

2. Welding Metallurgy of Steels   22
   Shaju K. Albert

3. Weldability of Austenitic Stainless Steels   37
   V. Shankar

4. Welding of Ferritic, Martensitic and Duplex Stainless Steels   48
   S. Sundaresan

5. Weldability of Aluminium and Titanium Alloys   67
   S. Sundaresan

6. Weldability of Nickel and Copper Base Alloys   79
   B.G. Muralidharan

7. Dissimilar Metal Welding and Cladding   97
   A.K. Bhaduri

8. Arc Welding Processes   116
   S. Manoharan

9. Resistance and Solid State Welding Processes   157
   K.G.K. Murthy

10. Residual Stresses in Weldments   172
    S. Suresh

11. Corrosion of Steel and Stainless Steel Weldments   183
    Hasan Shaikh

12. Non-Destructive Testing of Welded Components   224
    C.V. Subramanian

13. Quality Assurance and Welding Qualifications   248
    B.S.C. Rao

14. Leak and Pressure Testing of Welds and Field NDT Experience   253
    M. Palaniappan

15. Quality Control in Production Welding of Different Metals and their Alloys   278
     M. Gopalakrishna and B.S.C. Rao

16. Weld Joint Design   289
     T.K. Mitra

17. Challenges in Meeting Reliability Requirements in Welding   304
     Baldev Raj and T. Jayakumar

18. Selection of Welding Consumables   342
     R.D. Pennathur

19. Mechanical Testing of Weldments   355
     S.K. Ray

20. Advanced Non-destructive Testing Techniques for Inspection of Weldments   368
     T. Jayakumar, G.K. Sharma and Baldev Raj

     Index   403

1. Basic Concepts and Physical Metallurgy of Welding

A.K. Bhaduri and V. Shankar

Materials Joining Section, Materials Technology Division

Indira Gandhi Centre for Atomic Research, Kalpakkam 603 102

1 BASIC CONCEPTS

Welding in its broadest sense can be defined as the process by which materials can be joined through the action of interatomic or intermolecular forces. Thus welding, brazing, soldering and adhesive bonding can be considered welding processes. Soldering is a joining method that uses lead or tin based filler with a melting temperature not exceeding 450°C, and bonding is achieved by wetting of the base materials by the filler (solder). Brazing refers to joining using filler metals that have a melting point above 450°C, but well below the melting temperature of either base material being joined. A welded joint is produced, (a) in the solid state by intimate direct contact under heat and/or pressure between the two materials being joined, or (b) by melting and fusion of either side of the joint with or without a filler metal of melting point close to that of the base materials. In adhesive joining, use is made of polymeric adhesives that wet the mating surfaces and bonding is achieved by "setting" through crosslinking or polymerisation. Having a large surface area over which joining takes place compensates for the relatively weak bonding of non-metallic adhesives. Next to mechanical fastening, welding is the oldest and the most reliable joining method. The earliest known welding process is probably the hammer or forge welding process. Over the years, several new ways of joining materials have evolved necessitated primarily by the stringent demands put on materials and their joints. Table 1 presents a complete list of the various welding processes available today.

1.1 Fundamentals of Welding

A weld joint can be made by bringing two clean surfaces into intimate contact with each other. Depending on the state of the surface either pressure or heat or both may be applied to obtain a bond. From the atomistic point of view, when two neutral atoms are brought together from infinite separation, an electrostatic or Coulombic attractive force comes into play between the negatively charged electron cloud of one atom and the positively charged nucleus of the other atom. The repulsive forces between the two electron clouds and the nuclei, though present, are weak when the separation between the atoms is large. The attractive force increases with decreasing distance between the two atoms. The system's potential energy also decreases as the atoms come

Table 1 Classification of welding processes

Group	Welding Process	Group	Welding Process
Arc welding	Carbon arc Electrogas Flux-cored arc Gas metal arc	Oxyfuel gas welding	Oxyacetylene welding Oxyhydrogen welding Air acetylene welding Pressure gas welding
	Gas tungsten arc Plasma arc Shielded metal arc Stud arc Submerged arc	Resistance welding	Flash welding Projection welding Resistance seam welding Resistance spot welding Upset welding
Solid-state welding	Cold welding Diffusion welding Explosion welding Forge welding Friction welding Hot pressure welding Roll welding Ultrasonic welding	Other welding processes	Electron beam Electroslag Flow Induction Laser beam Percussion Thermit

close, as illustrated schematically in Fig. 1. When the distance between the atoms is reduced further, the repulsive force between the two electron clouds begins to increase more rapidly than the attractive force. At a critical distance, the attractive and repulsive forces just balance each other and the system's potential energy attains a minimum value. The atoms are said to have bonded. The tendency for atoms to bond is the fundamental basis for welding. The key to all welding is interdiffusion between materials being joined, whether that diffusion occurs in the liquid, solid, or mixed state.

The metals are joined in welding through the formation of metallic bonds. Thermoplastic polymers are joined through the formation of some covalent bonds and substantially secondary bonds like van der Waals or permanent dipole forces, as well as by substantial molecular tangling. Glasses can be welded with primary covalent bond formation, while in ceramics the bonding is through the formation of ionic, covalent, or mixed bonds depending on the type of ceramic. According to the above, dissimilar welding between materials having different type of bonding cannot be achieved. For example, in metal to ceramic welding, metal has metallic bonding while ceramic has ionic, covalent, or mixed ionic-covalent bonding. In such situations, joining can be achieved by modification of one of the surfaces, brazing, and soldering or adhesive bonding.

1.2 Role of Interfaces in Welding

In an ideal situation, if two perfectly flat and clean surfaces are brought together, bonding between the surface atoms takes place and the two pieces are welded perfectly, as illustrated in Fig. 2 for two materials A and B. After welding there is no remnant of a physical interface and no disruption in the atomic structure across the interface. The joint efficiency is 100% and its strength equals that of the base metal.

However, real surfaces are not perfectly smooth. Therefore, a perfect joint is never achieved

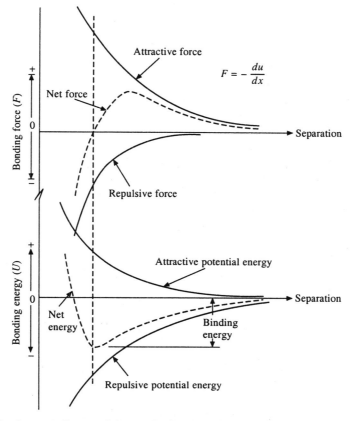

Fig. 1 The forces and potential energies involved in bond formation leading to welding

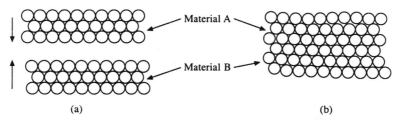

| (a) | (b) |

Fig. 2 Two ideal surface brought together to form a weld (a) before and (b) after welding

in practice. Real materials have surfaces that are highly irregular with peaks and valleys tens to thousands of atoms high and deep. When such surfaces are brought together for welding, only a few points of intimate contact, where atomic bonding can take place, can be achieved as shown in Fig. 3(a). The joint strength therefore, is only a fraction of the theoretical strength that can be achieved. In addition to surface irregularities, real surfaces are not perfectly clean and often are contaminated with adsorbed moisture, oxide film, grease layer, etc. as shown in Fig. 3(b). To achieve welding these contaminants have to be removed to bring most, if not all, of the atoms of those surfaces into intimate contact. This can be achieved by two ways; one is to apply heat and the other is to apply pressure. In actual practice both heat and pressure are applied to obtain a sound joint. The application of heat helps in driving off the adsorbed layers, breaking the oxide films through differential thermal expansion or through thermal decomposition and lowering the yield strength of the base materials and allowing plastic deformation (under pressure) to bring more atoms to the mating surfaces. Even after removal of contaminants from the surfaces by heat, welding can only take place between areas of intimate contact, as shown in Fig. 3(c). Another important function of heat is to melt the members of the joint thus allowing atoms to come together by fluid flow and form bonds. A filler material of the same or different type, but compatible with the base material, may be added to form a joint. This is shown schematically in Fig. 3(d). In some welding processes pressure, with or without heat, can be applied to create a bond between two surfaces. It helps to deform or break the intervening layers and plastically deform the asperities to bring together clean surfaces for bonding. Fig. 3(e) shows a near perfect weld made by the application of heat and pressure.

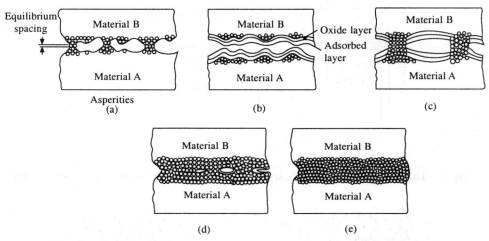

Fig. 3   **Two real surfaces brought together to form a bond (a) bonding at the points of intimate contact, (b) surface contamination hinders bond formation, (c) heat removes contaminants, (d) increased pressure increases contact and (e) near perfect weld**

The relative amount of heat and pressure to join two materials varies from one extreme to the other. In many welding processes only heat is employed to achieve a bond and pressure is required only to keep the elements to be joined in place, e.g. GTAW, SMAW, SAW, etc. However, in some processes, like cold welding, roll welding, ultrasonic welding, etc., only pressure is employed to force atoms together by plastic deformation. In between these two extremes, there are several other welding processes, such as resistance welding, friction welding, etc., where both heat and pressure are applied. Therefore, each welding process requires energy in some form, usually heat, to join two materials. The heat may be generated by a flame, an arc, resistance to electric current, radiant energy or by mechanical means. Most commercial welding processes use electric current as a source of heat and among these electric arc is by far the most popular.

1.3 The Welding Arc

The welding arc is an electric discharge between two electrodes that takes place through ionized gas known as plasma. In an arc there is a voltage drop at the anode as well as at the cathode and these are referred to as anode and cathode fall voltages, respectively (Fig. 4). These voltage drops occur over very short distances from the electrode surfaces and the cooling effect of the electrodes

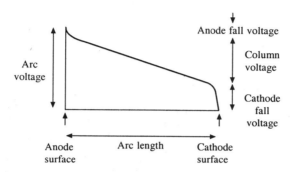

Fig. 4   Voltage distribution along an arc

makes the potential gradients very steep. The central region of the arc, with a uniform potential gradient, is called the arc column. Extremely high temperatures, varying from 5000 to 50000 K, can exist in the arc column. A typical case of isothermal distribution in an argon shielded tungsten arc is shown in Fig. 5. From the central core the temperatures drop rapidly to the outer layers of the arc plasma and in a given atmosphere both the temperature and diameter of the central core depend on the current passed by the arc. The relationship between arc current and potential is not according to Ohm's law but takes the non-linear form shown in Fig. 6. At low currents, the arc voltage falls sharply with increasing current and then remains flat or slightly, rising until high currents are reached. Figure 6 also shows the difference in the arc voltage-current characteristics as a function of normal mode and cathode spot mode of operation. In normal mode, the tungsten cathode tip is rounded and the arc root covers the whole tip, and in cathode spot mode, the end of the tungsten electrode is ground to a conical form and a well-defined cathode spot forms at the tip of the cone.

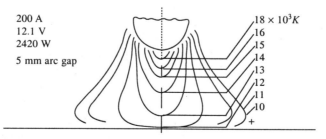

Fig. 5   Temperature distribution in a tungsten arc
Source: AWS Welding Handbook vol. 1, p. 69

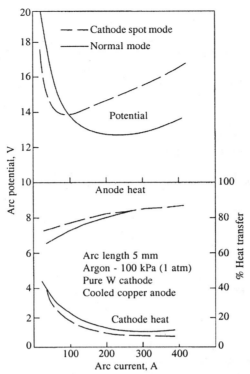

Fig. 6 **Typical volt-ampere and percent heat transfer characteristics of GTAW**
Source : AWS Welding Handbook vol. 1, 2001, p. 71

Welding arcs are generally operated in the high current region so that there is a tendency to a marked radial temperature gradient which, combined with the influence of the magnetic field created by the flow of current through the arc, exerts a constricting effect on the arc column – the pinch effect.

1.3.1 Effect of Electrode Polarity

When the work piece is connected to the positive terminal of a DC power supply and the electrode to the negative terminal, the operating mode is referred to as direct current straight polarity (DCSP) or direct current electrode negative (DCEN). When the electrode is connected to the positive terminal of the DC power supply and the work piece to the negative terminal, it is termed as direct current reverse polarity (DCRP) or direct currenty electrode positive (DCEP).

In the DCEN mode, electrons are emitted from the tungsten electrode and travel at high speeds and kinetic energies through the arc column and give up their energy to the workpiece on collision. The electrons carry most of the arc heat and deliver it to the workpiece thus producing deep penetrating narrow welds (Fig. 7). On the other hand, in DCEP mode where tungsten is positive, the electrons deliver most of the arc heat to the tungsten electrode which may melt. Therefore, in the DCEP mode of operation the tungsten electrode should be cooled with water. The welds produced in the DCEP mode are shallow (Fig. 7). This mode is preferred for welding of thin sections. The most important advantage of DCEP mode is the scrubbing action which is

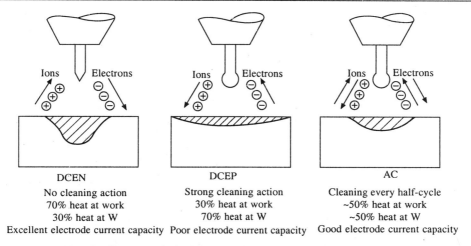

Fig. 7 **Characteristics of the various operating modes of GTAW**

achieved by the bombardment of positive ions on the workpiece surface thus removing the oxide films on materials like Al and Mg. In addition to the DCEN and DCEP modes of operation, welding can also be carried out in the AC mode which gives some of the characteristics of both the modes. In AC mode, reasonably good penetration is achieved coupled with surface cleaning action (Fig. 7).

1.3.2 Effect of Magnetic Field

The welding arc interacts with magnetic fields and the effect may be detrimental or beneficial. The usual effect of magnetic fields on the welding arc is manifested in arc deflection and is determined by Fleming's left-hand rule, as shown in Fig. 8. If the deflection of the arc is in the direction of travel i.e. forward deflection, a shallow weld with less penetration can be made. The forward deflection, therefore, can be employed to weld thin sheets. However, in case of backward deflection of the arc, defective welds with undercutting and reinforcements are produced. The imposition of alternating magnetic fields makes the arc oscillate and is used to advantage in hot wire GTAW and also in refining weld microstructures.

Under certain conditions, the arc is deflected away from the point of welding and produces unacceptable quality of welds. This is called arc blow. One of the main reasons for arc blow is the placement of the ground return to the welding machine very close to the end of the weld run, and the interaction of the induced

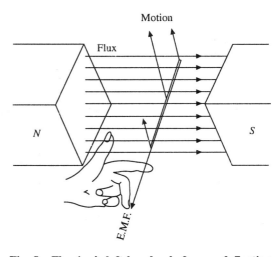

Fig. 8 **Fleming's left-hand rule for arc deflection**

magnetic field with the arc produces arc blow as shown in Fig. 9. Welding away from the ground connection can be adopted to take advantage of the forward deflection of the arc. Alternatively, a system of return leads can be designed to overcome the arc blow problems. In some other situations, the workpiece may have residual magnetism which also results in arc blow. The best solution to the problem is to demagnetize the material.

1.4 Energy Input and Distribution

The energy supplied by the welding arc in a fusion welding process is called arc energy and is calculated from current, voltage and welding speed. However, all the arc energy is not utilized

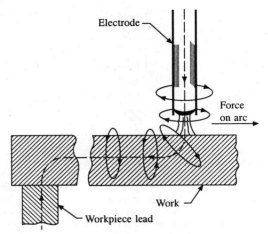

Fig. 9 Force on the arc by an induced magnetic field

for welding; some of it is invariably lost, as shown in Fig. 10. The extent of energy loss varies with the welding process, welding parameters, type of material, preheat temperature, etc. To

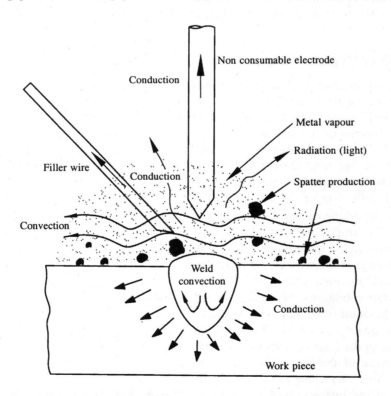

Fig. 10 Sources of energy loss affecting the heat transfer efficiency of fusion welding processes

account for the energy loss and estimate the actual energy given to the workpiece, a term known as heat input is employed. The heat input of a single pass weld is calculated by multiplying the efficiency of the welding process and arc energy. Table 2 lists some typical energy transfer efficiencies of various welding processes. The efficiency is not invariant with arc energy and decreases with arc energy as shown in Fig. 11. Therefore, heat input at best can serve as a rough guide to the amount of heat supplied to the workpiece.

Table 2   Typical energy transfer efficiencies for various welding processes

Welding Process	Transfer Efficiency	Welding Process	Transfer Efficiency
Gas-tungsten arc		Gas	0.25 – 0.80
Low current DCEN	0.40 – 0.60	Submerged arc	0.85 – 0.9
High current DCEN	0.60 – 0.80	Electroslag	0.55 – 0.82
DCEP	0.20 – 0.40	Electron beam	
AC	0.20 – 0.60	Melt-in	0.70 - 0.85
Gas-metal arc		Keyhole	0.80 – 0.95
Globular or short-arc	0.70 – 0.85	Laser beam	
Spray	0.65 – 0.75	Reflective	< 0.005
Shielded metal arc	0.65 – 0.85	Keyhole	0.50 – 0.70

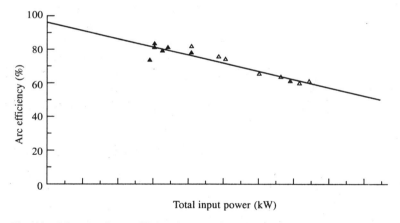

Fig. 11   Measured arc efficiencies as a function of total power generated

The heat supplied to a workpiece also depends on the distribution of energy density of the arc, as shown in Fig. 12 for a tungsten arc. The power-density distribution decides the weld bead characteristics such as penetration. In the case of GTAW, vertex angle of the conical tip of the tungsten electrode influences the weld depth-to-width ratio. The presence of certain impurity elements in materials and the nature of the shielding gas also have critical influence on the weld bead penetration.

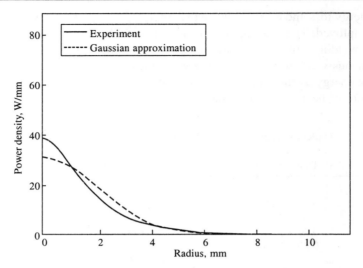

Fig. 12. Power density distribution in GTAW

1.5   DISSIPATION OF WELDING HEAT

The energy applied to create a weld joint is dissipated by conduction to the base metal, welding fixtures and the environment. That part of the base metal experiencing various thermal cycles is called the heat affected zone (HAZ). During welding, the HAZ does not undergo melting but experiences complex thermal and stress alterations. The imposition of welding thermal cycles on the base material causes changes in the properties of the HAZ. A welding thermal cycle is characterised by heating rate, peak temperature and cooling rate; Fig. 13 presents a typical family of thermal cycles for arc welding. The following three characteristics are apparent:

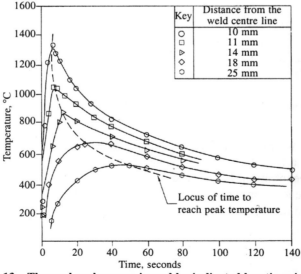

Fig. 13   Thermal cycles experienced by indicated locations in the HAZ

1. Peak temperature decreases rapidly with increasing distance from the weld centre line
2. Time required to reach peak temperature increases with increases distance from the weld centre line.
3. Rates of heating and cooling decrease with increasing distance from the weld centre line

Thermal cycles are also affected by heat input, preheating temperature, plate thickness and joint geometry

1.6 Weld Joint

A weld joint consists of several zones - (1) weld metal or mixed zone which is essentially a solidified structure, (2) unmixed zone in the base metal adjacent to the fusion line where the base metal has melted but is not mixed with the filler material, (3) partially melted zone which has seen thermal cycles with peak temperatures lying between the solidus and liquidus temperatures, and (4) heat affected zone which has not melted but is exposed to thermal cycles with temperatures less than the solidus temperature. Each zone because of its characteristic microstructural features has different properties.

2 PHYSICAL METALLURGY ASPECTS

During welding, a small volume of metal is molten by a heat source which is moved along the line in which a joint is sought. In comparison with casting, welding processes involve cooling rates several orders of magnitude higher than that in conventional casting and the growth rates are correspondingly higher. Further, weld puddles are subject to vigorous mixing by various forces acting on the molten metal. Since the base metal must necessarily melt back for good fusion to occur, there is considerable dilution into the weld puddle. As the heat source moves away, the heat conduction starts the solidification process and the weld metal starts solidifying epitaxially at the fusion line, and nucleation is not required to initiate the growth of the solid. In pure metals, the melting takes place at a constant temperature by absorption of latent heat from the heat source, which must be conducted away during solidification. In this case, the melting and solidification is a pure heat flow problem. However, engineering alloys solidify over a temperature range. The temperature above which the alloy is completely molten is called the liquidus, and the temperature below which the alloy is completely solid is called solidus. The difference between these two temperatures is called the equilibrium melting (or solidification) temperature range. The composition of the solid phase in equilibrium with the liquid phase is a function of temperature. Hence, in addition to heat flow, alloy solidification involves the redistribution of solutes or alloying elements. An understanding of weld solidification requires a consideration of both heat and mass transfer phenomena. The solidification and fluid flow phenomena are affected greatly by the weld metal composition and welding parameters, which govern weldability aspects such as hot cracking, grain structure and weld puddle shape.

2.1 Development of the Weld Puddle Shape

When a stationary welding arc is directed at a metal surface, a circular melt forms since the heat spreads equally in all directions. When the arc is moved, melting takes place preferentially at the leading edge of the arc, while at the trailing edge the weld metal starts solidifying. Thus, the circular shape gets elongated into an ellipse, as shown in Fig. 14. Surrounding the weld puddle in Fig. 14 is a slightly larger region bounded by a dotted line, which indicates the partially melted zone. In this region the grain boundaries melt partially and many welding defects originate from here. This region will be discussed subsequently.

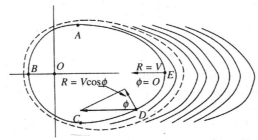

Fig 14   Schematic of a moving weld pool showing the relation between welding speed and local growth rate

Considering the arc to move with a welding speed V, the melting front is located along the leading edge ABC while the solidification front is located along the trailing edge CDEA. Heat flows perpendicular to the contour while crystal growth is fastest at 180° to this direction. The local growth rate R is related to the welding speed by the relation $R = V \cos \phi$, where ϕ is the angle between the welding direction and the growth direction. Thus, growth is fastest at E, where $R = V$. At points A and C where the melting and solidification fronts meet, the growth rate is zero.

The elliptical shape of the weld puddle is affected by welding speed. At slow speeds, the puddle is slightly elliptical, which becomes more and more elongated as speed is increased, finally becoming tear-drop shaped at very high welding speeds. This is illustrated in Fig. 15, where experimentally observed growth rates are shown as a function of welding speed, A tear-

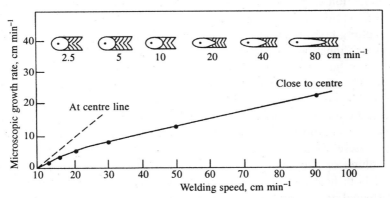

Fig. 15   Change in microscopic growth rate R as a function of welding speed. Change in weld puddle shape with welding speed is indicated in the top of the figure (after T. Ganaha and H.W. Kerr, Metals Technology vol. 5, 1978, p. 62)

drop shape means that the grains grow almost parallel to each other without much change in growth direction (Fig. 16a). The parallel grains impinge at the centre line where the final liquid to solidify is located and this becomes a line of weakness. Such a grain structure is not preferred,

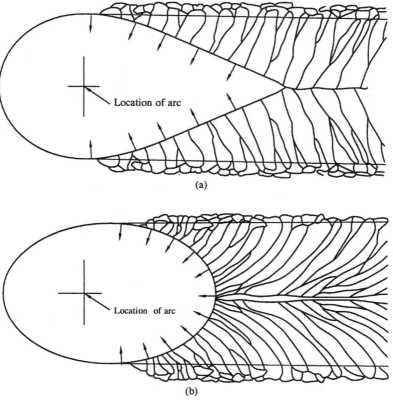

Fig. 16 **Change in shape of fusion zone grains formed under different weld puddle shapes (a) tear drop-shaped puddle and (b) elliptically shaped puddle**

as it makes the weld prone to cracking by enrichment of impurities towards the centre line (centre line cracking) and generally promotes poor weld properties. Therefore, welding processes and procedures are oriented to produce grain refinement in the microstructure.

2.2 Fusion Zone

2.2.1 Various Zones in a Weldment

When filler metal is added to a weld, its composition is modified by mechanical mixing with material melted from the base metal. This region, which constitutes the majority of the weld bead, is of a composition intermediate between that of the base metal and filler metal and depends upon the degree of dilution with base metal. This zone is known as the composite zone.

Close to the fusion line, a small boundary layer exists at the fusion line where the melting front has just touched. This layer is called the unmixed zone, since it has essentially no dilution. The unmixed zone is not only located in the boundary layer, but is sometimes found well inside the fusion zone. The unmixed zone has been found to be subject to corrosion attack and to be a favoured site for failures.

2.2.2 Microsegregation

During solidification of an alloy, the morphology of the emerging solid is determined by thermal gradient G and growth rate R, besides the composition (solute content C and partition coefficient k). Partitioning of solute into the liquid during solidification leads to a region ahead of the solid-liquid (S-L) interface, which has cooled to below its solidification temperature, by virtue of solute diffusion. This is illustrated for a binary alloy of A and B in Fig. 17. This region of constitutional supercooling makes the moving S-L interface unstable and the growth front develops

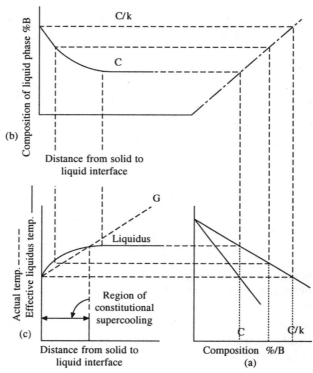

Fig. 17   **Schematic illustration of constitutional supercooling in a binary alloy: (a) binary phase diagram showing portion of alloy, (b) variation of liquid phase composition with distance from the S-L interface and (c) variation of effective liquidus temperature showing constitutionally supercooled zone**

into elongated cells or dendrites, depending on the solidification parameters and composition. This is illustrated in Fig. 18, where the growth morphologies have been mapped as a function of C_0/k and G/R. It is observed that for higher solute contents or partitioning tendency ($k < 1$), the structures are more dendritic. More refined microstructures are obtained at high growth rates and thermal gradients associated with high energy density process such as EBW or LBW, while increasing the heat input increases segregation and dendrite arm spacing.

Due to solute partitioning between the solid and the remaining liquid, which takes place according to the equilibrium phase diagram, the cell/dendrite cores have a different composition

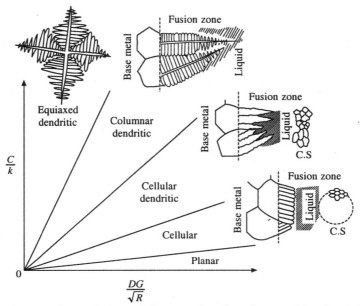

Fig. 18 **Solidification growth morphology of alloys as a function of compositional and thermal parameters**

than the intercellular regions. This microsegregation, which can be quite severe during welding of alloys because of the high solidification rates, can lead to deviations from the design composition in localised regions, with implications on the strength and corrosion behaviour of the weld. For estimating microsegregation, a volume element at the tip of a columnar dendrite/secondary arm is usually considered. The solute profiles that can result depend upon the extent of convective mixing in the weld pool and diffusion in the solid state which equalises the composition behind the S-L interface, as given in Fig. 19. In complete equilibrium solidification, a liquid of composition

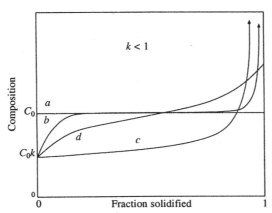

Fig. 19 **Schematic diagram of compositional variation in a volume element solidified under (a) equilibrium conditions, (b) diffusion in the liquid considered, (c) full convective mixing in the liquid considered and (d) actual case where full conventional mixing in the liquid and diffusion in the solid influnce composition C_0 is the initial composition of the alloy and k the partition coefficient**

C_0 emerges as a solid of the same composition (case *a*). When diffusion in the solid is neglected and only diffusion in the liquid is taken into account, profile *b* is obtained, while profile *c* results for complete mixing in the liquid and no diffusion in the solid. Actual weld solidification falls somewhere between the two extremes represented by *b* and *c*, as the diffusion in the solid is not negligible and the profile approximately follows that of *d*, which is closer to profile *c* than that of *b*.

Segregation of solute and impurity elements during welding is undesirable as it introduces inhomogeneity in mechanical properties and decreases corrosion resistance of the weld metal. The other important deleterious effect of segregation is the enhanced tendency for cracking and microfissuring. The segregation of impurity elements such as S and P is particularly strong during welding since they exhibit poor solubilities in the solid and have low partition coefficients (*k* between 0.01 and 0.1). This strong segregation leaves the intercrystalline regions in the last solidifying pockets highly enriched in solute. This leads to the formation of low melting eutectics which may solidify as much as a few hundred degrees below the solidus temperature of the alloy.

2.2.3 Hot Cracking

Under the action of shrinkage stresses in a restrained weld, the already solidified part can crack when wetted by low melting eutectic liquid. The ratio of interfacial energies of the solid and liquid phases is an important determinant of hot cracking during welding. The effect of this ratio on wetting angle is given by:

$$\gamma_{SL}/\gamma_{SS} = 1/(2 \cos (\theta/2))$$

where γ_{SS} and γ_{SL} are the interfacial energies of the S-L and S-S boundaries respectively, and θ is the wetting angle. When θ is nearly 0, wetting of the *S-S* boundary is enhanced and cracking is promoted. The variation of wetting angle with change in the interfacial energy ratio is shown in Fig. 20. The wetting angle has been found to be sensitive to the segregation of highly surface-active elements such as S, O and Se.

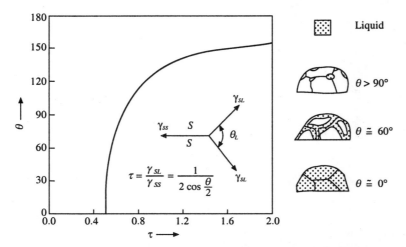

Fig. 20 **Variation of dihedral contact angle θ with interfacial energy ratio τ. Change in wetting of solidified grains with contact angle is illustrated**

The conditions conducive to hot cracking in a particular alloy system are not easy to predict, since the characteristics of the liquid films and their interaction behaviour with the solid are not readily available parameters. This places emphasis on actual weldability testing for establishing the composition limits and welding conditions to avoid cracking.

2.2.4 Partially Melted Zone: Liquation Cracking

Completely surrounding the moving weld pool is a region where the peak temperatures experienced fall between the liquidus and the effective solidus. This zone was shown earlier in Fig. 14. The segregation invariably present in commercial alloys ensures that the effective solidus is always below the equilibrium solidus for the nominal alloy composition. In addition, interactions between precipitates, inclusions and the matrix cause a depression of the solidus. At the high temperatures experienced near the fusion line, rapid grain boundary migration would occur as a result of natural grain growth. However, the liquated regions, since they would have a composition similar to that of the matrix, readily wet the intercepting boundaries and form molten films which arrest further grain boundary migration. During the migration process, the grain boundaries are said to "sweep" along with them impurity elements such as S, P, Si, etc., which are very effective in depressing the melting point of the grain boundary. Under these conditions, any restraining force would lead to cracking, as shown in Fig. 21, which illustrates liquation cracking in a nitrogen-bearing type 316L stainless steel. The thickened grain boundaries along the partially melted zone are clearly visible. However, the cracking has extended quite deeply into the HAZ.

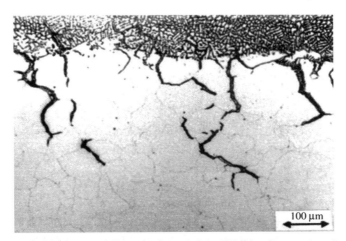

Fig. 21   Liquation cracking in the partially melted zone of the HAZ in nitrogen-bearing 316L stainless steel

2.2.5 Weld Pool Convection – Weld Penetration

Convection is responsible for the shape of the weld puddle and ensures uniform distribution of heat and solutes within the melt zone. Convection currents are set up in the weld pool by (i) surface-tension induced flows, (ii) electromagnetic forces created by the arc current and magnetic fields, (iii) buoyancy forces created by density differences between hot and cold metal, and (iv) aerodynamic drag forces by gas flow on the surface of the weld pool. Of these forces, surface tension forces are dominant in giving shape to the penetration profile during welding. The origin of surface tension-driven forces is illustrated in Fig. 22. The variation of surface tension with temperature is a strong function of the concentration of surface-active elements in the weld pool. When the coefficient of surface tension is negative, as in Fig. 22(a), the centre of the weld pool directly under the arc experiences a lower surface tension by virtue of its higher temperature. As the cooler peripheral regions have greater surface tension, the surface flow of liquid sets up an outward current. Such a movement, which produces weak convection currents, results in shallow weld puddles, poor and inconsistent weld penetration and occurs when there is insufficient concentration of surface-active elements. The inconsistency in penetration profile occurs in the absence of a dominant factor among the various convective forces. When elements such as S or O are present above a critical concentration, a positive coefficient of surface tension prevails (Fig. 22b) and the direction of convection is reversed. Now the surface flow is inward towards the centre of the weld puddle. The hot liquid under the arc is pushed down, which results in a digging action, increasing the depth/width ratio and providing consistent weld profiles.

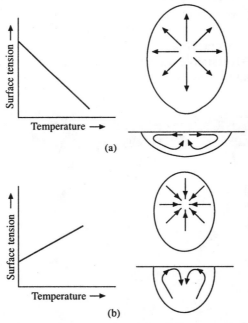

Fig. 22   Different convective flow patterns produced by different temperature coefficients of surface tension: *a* negative; *b* positive

The problem of inconsistent weld penetration has been found in stainless steels, particularly under autogeneous GTA welding conditions. It has also been found in non-ferrous materials like nickel-base alloys and zircaloy. Some recommended welding procedures to improve weld penetration and obtain more consistent penetration for heats with varying S contents are given in Table 3. The methods recommended differ with sulphur content and range from changes in arc length and electrode preparation to admixture of gases such as He, H_2, O_2 or SO_2 to the shielding gas.

Table 3 **Recommended welding procedures to improve weld penetration and obtain more consistent weld penetration for casts with varying S contents***

Objectives	High S casts (S > 70 ppm)		Low S casts (S < 50 ppm)	
	Changes in fluid flow required	Changes in welding procedure required	Changes in fluid flow required	Changes in welding procedure required
Improved weld penetration	High E, High M(+), Low A	Short arc length, Pointed electrode, Reasonably high current, Inclined electrode, Slower welding speed, Add He, H_2, O_2 or N_2 to shielding gas	High E, Low M(−), Low A	Short arc length, Wedge electrode ⊥ to wd, Optimum I [balance between high E and low M(−)], Inclined electrode, Slower welding speed, Add SO_2 to torch gas
More consistent weld penetration for casts with varying S	High E, Low/medium M (+), Low A	Short arc length, Wedge electrode ⊥ to wd	High E, Low M(−), Low A	Short arc length, Wedge electrode ⊥ to wd, Medium or low I, Inclined electrode, Slower weding speed, Add SO_2 to torch gas

A: aerodynamic drag force; E: electromagnetic force;
I: welding current; M: thermocapillary force [(+) or (−) indicating the sign of dr/dT;
⊥ to wd: perpendicular to welding direction
* after K.C. Mills and B.J. Keene, Int. Mater. Rev. 35(4) (1990) 185–216.

2.3 Heat Affected Zone Microstructure

The relevant portion of the iron-carbon phase diagram along with a schematic sketch of a weld and HAZ is shown in Fig. 23. During heating part of the weld thermal cycle, the peak temperature to which base metal is heated varies with distance from the fusion line as shown in the figure. If the peak temperature exceeds the lower critical temperature A_1, ferrite (stable at room temperature with a bcc crystal structure) transforms into austenite (high temperature phase with fcc crystal structure). In the region of the HAZ where the temperature exceeds the upper critical temperature A_3, this transformation will be complete and an austenitic microstructure is formed. At temperatures higher than 1300°C, extensive growth of the austenite grains takes place. The region of the HAZ where extensive grain growth of the weld metal takes place is referred to as coarse grained HAZ (CGHAZ). The region of the HAZ next to it, where peak temperature is in the range of 900-1200°C and austenite grain size remains small, is called fine grained HAZ (FGHAZ). The region of the HAZ heated to the temperature range in between the two critical temperatures A_1 and A_3 is often referred to as intercritical HAZ (ICHAZ).

During the cooling cycle, the austenite formed at high temperatures transforms back to ferrite or other metastable phases, and this transformation is best represented with the help of a continuous cooling transformation (CCT) diagram. A typical CCT diagram is shown in Fig. 24. The lines shown in the figure are the boundaries which define the start and finish of transformation of austenite into various phases like, ferrite, pearlite (a mixture of ferrite and carbides), bainite or

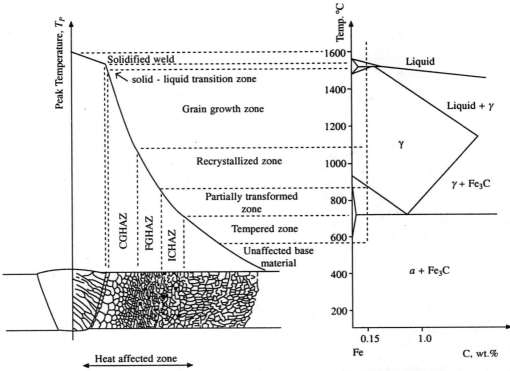

Fig. 23   **Schematic diagram of various sub-zones of the heat affected zone approximately corresponding to the alloy of 0.15 wt% C indicated on Fe-Fe$_3$C equilibrium diagram**

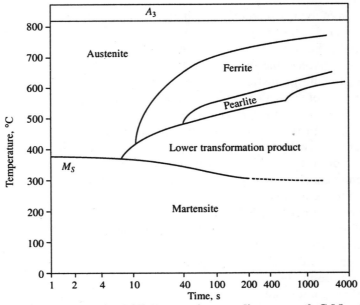

Fig. 24   **Example of a CCT diagram for a medium strength C-Mn steel**

martensite. An actual welding cooling curve can be inserted into this diagram and the phases formed in that region of the weld to which the cooling curve corresponds can be obtained. It can be seen that for low cooling rate, as experienced in high heat input welding i.e., submerged arc welding, electroslag welding, etc., or in welds produced with sufficient preheat, austenite transforms predominantly into a mixture of ferrite and carbides. If the cooling rate is very high, this transformation is prevented and low temperature transformation products like bainite or martensite are formed.

As the cooling rate in the different regions of the HAZ varies with distance from the fusion zone of the weld, the phases formed from transformation may also vary with distance. Further, CCT curves defining start and finish of ferrite transformation shift towards the right with increase in alloy content and prior austenite grain size. As both grain size and cooling rate experienced are maximum for CGHAZ, the probability of this region transforming into bainite or martensite is very high. This explains why CGHAZ is having maximum hardness and poor toughness properties compared to the rest of the HAZ.

As indicated above, the effect of alloying elements on the CCT diagram is to shift the ferrite transformation curves towards the right. Thus, for a given cooling rate, the HAZ of an alloy steel contains higher volume fraction of bainite than that of mild steel with low C content and without any significant alloying elements. This property of the steel to produce a hard microstructure when cooled from austenite phase is often referred to as hardenability and this increases with alloy content and austenite grain size. Hence, in high carbon or high alloyed steel welds, HAZ microstructure is fully martensitic irrespective of the weld heat input or the preheat temperature used to reduce the cooling rate. For example, in the case of SMAW, HAZ microstructure of mild steel is a mixture of carbides and ferrite, while that of 2.25Cr-1Mo steel is fully bainitic and that of 9Cr-1Mo steel is fully martensitic even though welding is carried out without any preheating in the case of the first and with preheating in the other two.

BIBLIOGRAPHY

1. Welding Handbook-, Vols. 1 and 2, American Welding Society, Miami, USA, 1987.
2. The Physics of Welding, International Institute of Welding, Paris, France, 1986.
3. R.W. Messler Jr., Joining of Advanced Materials, Butterworth-Heineman, Boston, USA, 1993.
4. P.T. Houldcroft, Welding Process Technology, Cambridge University Press, Cambridge, UK, 1977.
5. S.A. David and J.M. Vitek, The Correlation Between Solidification Parameters and Weld Microstructures, International Materials Reviews, 1992, p. 37.
6. W.F. Savage, Solidification, segregation and weld imperfections, Welding in the World, 18(5/6), 1980, pp. 89–113.
7. J.G. Garland and G.J. Davies, Solidification structure and properties of fusion welds, International Metallurgical Reviews, 1975, p. 83.
8. J.F. Lancaster, Metallurgy of Welding, 4th Edn., Allen and Unwin, London, 1987.
9. Easterling, Introduction to the Physical Metallurgy of Welding, 2nd Edn., Butterworth Heinemann, Oxford, 1992.

2. Welding Metallurgy of Steels

Shaju K. Albert

Materials Technology Division, Indira Gandhi Centre for Atomic Research, Kalpakkam 603 102

1 INTRODUCTION

Steels are the most widely used structural materials. Properties that make the steels ideally suitable as a structural material are closely linked with the solid-state transformations that steels undergo during heat treatment. Both the HAZ and the weld metal are subjected to these transformations during the weld thermal cycle. However, heating and cooling rates in the weld thermal cycle are much faster than in a normal heat treatment and hence the final transformation products formed in the HAZ and weld metal could be different from those present in the unaffected base metal. This has been briefly explained in the first chapter in the section dealing with HAZ microstructure. These transformations, coupled with formation of residual stresses, segregation in the weld metal, liquation near the fusion zone, absorption of hydrogen by the molten metal from the arc atmosphere, etc. make the steel weldments susceptible to cracking. Cracking can occur during welding, or after the weldment is cooled to room temperature or during post weld heat treatment (PWHT). Similarly, location of cracking can also vary like toe cracking, under-bead cracking, HAZ cracking, weld metal cracking etc. Most of the codes and standards for welded fabrication do not permit any form of cracking and hence it is essential that welds should be free of cracks before they are put to service. Based on the mechanism, cracking can be broadly classified as *hot cracking, cold cracking (hydrogen assisted cracking or delayed cracking), lamellar tearing and reheat cracking*. A brief description of these different types of cracking and the methods to prevent them are presented here.

2 HOT CRACKING

This cracking occurs during solidification and subsequent cooling of the weld and the mechanism has been briefly described in the first chapter. It can be further divided into solidification cracking, liquation cracking and ductility dip cracking. Austenitic stainless steels are more susceptible to this form of cracking than steels and detailed description of mechanism of hot cracking is given in the next chapter. In steels, hot cracking is of concern only if the impurity levels in the weld metal are high and high heat input welding processes like submerged arc welding are employed. Various criteria available in literature to assess the susceptibility of hot cracking in steels are presented here.

Hot cracking sensitivity (HCS) is a parameter to assess susceptibility of steels to cracking during welding and this is defined as follows:

$$HCS = \frac{\left(S + P + \frac{Si}{25} + \frac{Ni}{100} \right) 10^3}{3Mn + Cr + Mo + V}$$

In general, if HCS < 4, the susceptibility is low. However, high strength steels are susceptible to cracking even if HCS is 1.6-2.

Submerged arc welds are the more prone to solidification cracking than welds by other processes and an empirical relation was developed based on the results obtained from transvarestraint cracking test in units of crack susceptibility (UCS).

$$UCS = 230C + 190S + 75P + 45Nb - 12.3Si - 4.5\,Mn - 1$$

Significance of the values calculated by the above formula is that, with submerged arc welding, values up to 10 UCS represent a very low risk of cracking and values of 30 or greater, a high risk. Influence of C and S is the maximum in promoting solidification cracking, while Mn provides maximum resistance to cracking. In steels cracking occurs mainly due to the formation of low melting FeS and the effect of Mn is to replace FeS by a mixed sulphide (Mn, Fe)S which melts at a higher temperature.

3   COLD CRACKING OR HYDROGEN ASSISTED CRACKING

This is probably the most widely encountered cracking problem in steel welds. It occurs mainly in the CGHAZ, though in high alloy steels, where welding is carried out using consumables of matching composition, weld metal is also susceptible to this form of cracking. Further, in steels of very low carbon content like HSLA steels, weld metal is more susceptible to cracking than the HAZ. As the name suggests, it is caused by hydrogen that is introduced into the molten metal during the welding process and retained in the weld at ambient temperatures even after many hours or even days of welding. For the cracking to occur the following three conditions are to be met.

(a) Sufficient amount of hydrogen
(b) A susceptible microstructure and
(c) Presence of sufficient restraint

The main source of hydrogen in the weld metal is the moisture in the electrode coating (in the case of SMAW process) or in the powder flux (in SAW process). Thus, this type of cracking is less severe in other welding processes like GTAW and GMAW where no flux is used. However, moisture can either be present as an impurity in the shielding gas or gain entry into the arc from the atmosphere due to poor shielding. Other sources of hydrogen are the organic material used in cellulose-coated electrodes, grease or other organic products that may be present in the dirty joint surfaces or even corrosion products.

Hydrogen enters the weld metal through the welding arc where gaseous hydrogen, moisture or other compounds containing hydrogen dissociate to form atomic hydrogen that dissolves in the weld metal. As the weld solidifies, the hydrogen in the weld metal becomes supersaturated (the solubility of hydrogen in iron is very low and it decreases with temperature). However, due to high cooling rate, not all supersaturated hydrogen can diffuse out of the weld metal during cooling. Some of these hydrogen atoms get trapped at various defects like grain boundaries, inclusions etc. where they recombine to form hydrogen molecules. Hydrogen thus trapped is called residual hydrogen and this does not contribute to cracking. The atomic hydrogen that diffuses through the matrix is called diffusible hydrogen. Hydrogen in this form assists plastic deformation in the regions of stress concentrations like notches and root of the welds etc. thus leading to cracking.

Susceptibility to cracking is strongly influenced by the microstructure. In general, martensitic microstructure is the most susceptible and ferritic, the least. Structure of the HAZ depends on both alloy composition and heat input (cooling time $t_{8/5}$). Composition is represented by a parameter called carbon equivalent (CE) which normalizes the effect of different alloying elements on the structure into a single parameter. A large number of equations are available to determine CE of steels, which are valid for different ranges of alloy composition. CE_{IIW}, formulated by the International Institute of Welding, and P_{CM}, originated in Japan, which are used in the discussion that follows are defined below.

$$CE_{IIW} = C + \frac{Mn}{6} + \frac{Cu + Ni}{15} + \frac{Cr + Mo + V}{5}$$

$$P_{CM} = C + \frac{Si}{30} + \frac{Mn + Cu + Cr}{20} + \frac{Ni}{60} + \frac{Mo}{15} + \frac{V}{10} + 5B$$

Welding heat input is best represented by cooling rate of the weld, as the efficiency of different welding processes differs significantly. Time required for the weld to cool from 800°C to 500°C ($t_{8/5}$) is the most widely used parameter to represent the cooling rate as the austenite to ferrite transformation takes place in this temperature range. Another parameter employed is t_{100}, the time required for weld to cool down to 100°C; this in addition to time available for transformation also accounts for the time for hydrogen to diffuse out of the weld metal.

Hardness of the HAZ, which can be measured very easily, varies with microstructure, and is also used as a parameter that indicates the susceptibility of the welds to cracking. As a thumb rule, it is assumed that steel is not susceptible to cracking if its CE_{IIW} is < 0.4 and if its HAZ hardness is < 350 VHN.

Restraint imposed by different parts of a component during fabrication can significantly influence the stress state in the actual weld joints. Restraint of the joint increases with increase in thickness of the weld and hence thickness is often used as a parameter in empirical equations that are available to determine the critical preheat temperature to avoid cracking.

Prevention of cold cracking: It was initially believed that cold cracking could be prevented in the steel if the maximum hardness of the steel HAZ was kept below a critical value. This critical hardness was considered as independent of CE or the alloy composition. In many C-Mn steels, maximum hardness decreases with cooling rate, and hence the main emphasis was to reduce the cooling rate to obtain hardness below the critical value. This was achieved by preheating the job before welding, so that after welding it cools slowly, thus resulting in a microstructure of lower hardness. This approach was often referred to as the hardness control approach in the literature and was developed by The Welding Institute, UK. A nomogram based on this approach is shown in Fig. 1. It considers four factors, namely, *combined thickness, diffusible hydrogen content of the electrode (HD), carbon equivalent (CE_{IIW})* and *weld heat input*. The weld metal hydrogen

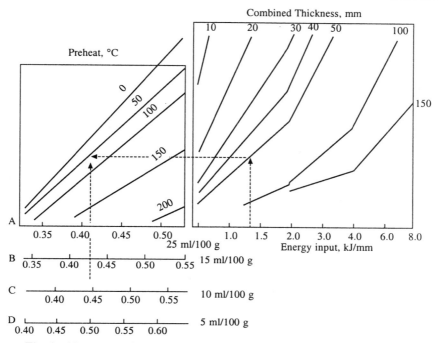

Fig. 1   Nomogram for choosing safe preheat temperature to avoid HAC

content is divided into four groups: A with *HD levels* > 15 *ml/100 g (high)*, B with 15 > *HD* > 10 (medium) C with *10 > HD > 5 (low)* and D *HD < 5 (very low)*. CE values valid for these four levels of HD are shown separately in the nomogram. However, later it was shown by Graville that this approach is valid only for steels of limited alloy content. He divided the steels into three broad categories based on carbon content and CE and proposed a diagram as shown in Fig. 2. According to this diagram, steels falling in Zone I (low carbon and low alloy content) are least susceptible to cracking, which occurs only under conditions of high hydrogen content and restraint. For alloys falling in Zone II, hardness varies with cooling rate, and hardness control approach can be applied to determine the preheat temperature to prevent cracking. For high alloy and high carbon steels falling in Zone III, their hardenability will be too high to alter their hardness by varying the cooling rate in normal welding conditions.

For steels falling in Zone I and Zone III, preheat temperatue is determined by hydrogen control approach. In this approach, it is assumed that cracking can be avoided by reducing the diffusible hydrogen content in the weld. In addition to reducing HAZ hardness, preheating helps in lowering the diffusible hydrogen content of the steel by giving more time for removal of hydrogen at high temperatures where diffusion is much faster than the ambient temperature. The time taken by the weld to cool down to 100°C, is also considered in determining the preheat temperature. Based on this approach, Ito and Bessyo defined a cracking parameter P_w, which considers the effect of composition, hydrogen content and restraint separately.

$$P_{W.} = P_{CM} + \frac{H_{JIS}}{60} + \frac{R_F}{40 \times 10^4}$$

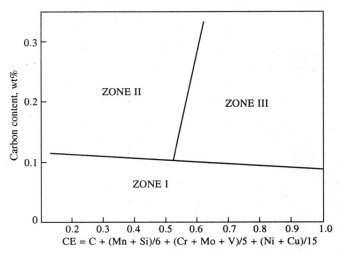

Fig. 2   Graville diagram for classifying steels acording to their cracking susceptibility

P_{CM} has been defined earlier. H_{JIS} is the diffusible hydrogen content as measured by glycerin method and R_F is the restraint factor (N mm^{-1} mm^{-1}), which is defined as force/unit length of weld required to contract or expand a gap by unit length in the direction perpendicular to the weld. R_F is given by

$$R_F = \eta r_f h$$

where r_f is a restraint coefficient (< 400 Nmm^{-2}mm^{-1} for normal welds), h is the plate thickness in mm and η a correction factor for the plate thickness. The correction factor η varies with the plate thickness and for thickness in the range of 5 – 100 mm, it is estimated using the following equation

$$\eta = \exp [(5.6 - h)/80.3]$$

The critical preheat temperature (T_{critical}) above which no cracking take place can be estimated from the parameter P_w using the following equation

$$T_{\text{critical (°C)}} = 1440 \, Pw - 392$$

Minimum cooling time for the weld to cool down to 100 °C to avoid cracking (t_{100}) can also be calculated from P_w using the following relation.

$$t_{100}(s) = 14 \times 10^4 (P_w - 0.28)^2$$

There are many more equations available in the literature to determine either the preheat temperature or time for cooling down to 100°C. Most of them are determined using the data derived from different cracking tests which determine the preheat temperature in severe restraint conditions and hence are conservative in nature. However, any reduction in preheat temperature lead to substantial reduction in energy consumption and hence research is in progress to develop low hydrogen welding consumables and to determine the minimum preheat temperature more accurately for specific welding conditions.

Cracking susceptibility of the steels can be assessed and the minimum preheat temperature or minimum cooling rate required to avoid cracking can be determined from various cracking tests also. These tests generally fall in two categories; external restraint tests in which stress is applied externally to promote cracking as in implant test and self restraint test, in which restraint is introduced in the joint design used for testing as in Y-groove test. For a detailed description of these tests, paper by Yurioka and Suzuki given in the bibliography listed at the end of the chapter may be referred.

Hydrogen Assisted Cracking in Weld Metal: Though hydrogen assisted cracking is mainly associated with CGHAZ, it can also take place in the weld metal if favourable conditions exist. One such condition is the very high hydrogen levels in the welds. This is the case when electrodes with cellulose coatings are used for welding. It has been found that cracking can take place in weld even if its hardness is as low as 200 VHN. Another condition that favours weld metal hydrogen cracking is the use of welding electrodes of composition matching that of base metal, especially in the case of alloy steels. Unlike in C-Mn steel welds, both microstructure and hardness of the weld metal and HAZ would be similar, making both HAZ and weld metal susceptible to cracking.

Cracking in weld metal can also occur if the C content in the base metal is very low. This is the situation encountered in the welding of HSLA steels where C content is kept low and strengthening is achieved by precipitation and grain refinement. CE and hardness of the weld metal is often higher than that of the base metal thus weld metal becomes more prone to cracking.

Chevron cracking is a special type of cracking observed in submerged arc welds. It is transverse to the weld line, but at 45° to the surface. It is usually observed in multipass welds. It is assumed that due to a large bead size, diffusion distance for hydrogen becomes so large that sufficient time is not available to allow hydrogen to diffuse out before the weld cools. Presence of this type of crack in high heat input welds indicates that although increasing heat input slows down weld cooling and allows more time for hydrogen diffusion, this beneficial effect is negated by the harmful effect of the greater diffusion distances resulting from the larger weld bead size. Chevron cracking can be prevented in the weld metal if the hydrogen level is kept below 5 ml/100 g.

4 LAMELLAR TEARING

This is a cracking problem associated mainly with plates, and to a certain extent with extrusions that are welded in such a way that the weld fusion zone is parallel to the surface. It is caused by the presence of elongated inclusions, mainly sulphides of Mn and Fe, which are deformed in the direction of rolling or extrusion. The stresses formed during welding lead to de-bonding of these inclusions from the matrix resulting in the formation of microcracks. During subsequent passes, the microcracks thus formed join up leading to cracking. This cracking takes place only in the base metal, often even away from the HAZ and can be prevented only by controlling the weld metal composition or modifying joint design in such a way that stresses formed in the though-thickness direction of the plate are reduced.

In the modern structural steels like HSLA steels, this type of cracking is not a serious problem as sulphur content is significantly reduced by current steel making practices. Further, addition of small quantities of Ca or rare earth metals modifies the composition of the inclusions and makes them more resistant to deformation thus preventing elongated inclusions from forming. The property, which is indicative of the susceptibility of steel to lamellar tearing is the through-thickness ductility. It is determined from a through-thickness tension test or short transverse tension test. Steels having short transverse reduction in area (STRA) of more than 15% are considered not susceptible to cracking and those having less than 5% are considered highly susceptible.

As indicated above, welding parameters have little influence in controlling lamellar tearing. However, joint geometry can be suitably designed in such a way that stresses are reduced in the through thickness-direction. Another option is buttering of the plate surfaces before welding. Figure 3 shows the practices employed in welding to reduce lamellar tearing.

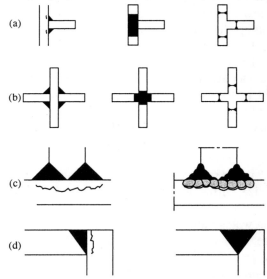

Fig. 3 **Different types of joint design employed to minimize lamellar tearing; joint designs for overcoming lamellar tearing tendency are shown to the right**

5   REHEAT CRACKING

This cracking occurs mainly in the CGHAZ during PWHT, in the welds of steels containing at least two of the alloying elements such as Cr, Mo, V, Nb and B. It is also known as stress relief cracking or post weld heat treatment cracking. *It is interesting to note that it occurs by stress relaxation at high temperatures (creep deformation) in creep resistant steels! Cracking occurs along the grain boundary regions at elevated temperatures, as these regions are less ductile and/ or slightly weaker than the grain interiors.* If the grain boundary is weak, any local deformation that accompanies the release of residual stresses occurs predominantly at the grain boundaries. A coarse grained HAZ has fewer grain boundaries to share this deformation so that ductility is soon exhausted in this region than in the fine-grained region. Low ductility of grain boundaries by impurity segregation can make an otherwise heat treatable steel liable to crack. A coarse grain size is harmful in this respect also because it provides less grain boundary area over which such impurities can be distributed.

The relative strengths of the HAZ and weld metal also influences cracking. If the HAZ is appreciably stronger than the weld metal, the weld metal would start deforming first and the HAZ would not strain plastically. If the weld metal is stronger than the HAZ, plastic deformation is forced on the HAZ, and this makes it susceptible to cracking. This situation is particularly likely when ferritic steels are clad with stainless steels (underclad cracking), because stainless steels are stronger at high temperature than the ferritic steels.

Strengthening of grain interiors in preference to grain boundaries occurs by intragranular precipitation of alloy carbides. Carbides of Mo and V that precipitate uniformly throughout the grains during PWHT are more harmful than that of Cr which precipitates preferentially along the grain boundaries. Based on the effect of various alloy carbides, in strengthening grains, two susceptibility indices have been proposed.

$$\Delta G = Cr + 3.3\ Mo + 8.1\ V + 10C - 2$$

$$P_{sr} = Cr + Cu + 2Mo + 10V + 7Nb + 5Ti - 2$$

when the value of parameter ΔG or P_{sr} is equal to or greater than zero, the steel is said to be susceptible to reheat cracking. Later it was reported that P_{sr} formula cannot be applied to low-carbon (C < 0.1%) or high Cr (Cr > 1.5) steels. Application of the crack susceptibility equation to experimental data has revealed several deficiencies in the use of these equations. They are (a) the equations were useful only over the range of compositions for which they were developed, (b) the applicability of the P_{sr} parameter depends on the stress relieving temperature, and (c) both these relations do not account for the effect of trace elements, which are believed to play an important role in the reheat cracking. In view of these limitations, the two equations should be used only as a general guide to assess the susceptibility of various materials to reheat cracking.

The effect of impurity elements in promoting reheat cracking is given by the following empirical equation

$$MCF = Si + 2Cu + 2P + 10As + 15Sn + 20Sb$$

Like P_{sr} and ΔG, this parameter also can be used only to find out the order of embrittlement. As cracking occurs mainly in the CGHAZ where segregation of impurity elements at the grain boundaries is high, using steels with low impurity content is the best option to reduce this type of cracking. Another option is to reduce or even eliminate CGHAZ using suitable welding techniques. One of the methods to achieve this is buttering of the susceptible alloys by depositing weld metal on the surfaces to be joined with low heat input welding process so that grain growth in the HAZ is kept to a minimum. It is also possible to increase the grain refinement by overlapping the HAZ of two successive passes. Another method is to use temper beads; small stringer beads placed over the last pass to refine grain structure of the HAZ.

All the methods described above discuss how careful welding procedures help in reducing reheat cracking. Similarly, careful control of heat treatment procedures also can minimise cracking. It is now well known that there is a temperature range in which impurity segregation takes place in the as-welded structure. *For* Cr-Mo *steels this temperature range is 550-650°C.* Chances of cracking are high if tempering and stress relaxation also occur in this temperature range. Hence, if the time to which the weldment is exposed to this temperature range is minimised during heat treatment, then cracking can be avoided. In some cases intermediate PWHT for 2 hours at 500°C has been found to be beneficial as this would bring down the residual stresses substantially.

Another option is to carry out the heat treatment in two stages allowing sufficient soak at a lower temperature, which is below the susceptible temperature range and then heating rapidly to the final temperature so that time spent within the susceptible range is reduced.

6   STRAIN AGE EMBRITTLEMENT AND TEMPER EMBRITTLEMENT

These two forms of embrittlement take place during service (some times during PWHT) and are different from the four types of cracking described above which take place during either welding or PWHT. Strain ageing is caused by the presence of any free nitrogen or carbon in solid solution in the ferritic lattice and interacting with the movement of dislocations. Nitrogen is more important than carbon and base metal or weld metal is susceptible to this embrittlement if 'free' Al content (i.e., Al not in the form of Al_2O_3) is less than twice the nitrogen content. If free Al content is not known, the following approximation can be used to ensure that the steel is not susceptible.

$$(Al_{total} + 0.010) > 2N_{total}$$

Weld metal (that is not subjected to any stress relieving treatment) is more prone to this form of embrittlement than the base metal, as some nitrogen is picked up from the arc atmosphere. it takes place only in a specific temperature range where strain ageing occurs and can be prevented by carrying out PWHT, if permitted.

Temper embrittlement is a serious form of embrittlement occurring in certain alloy steels containing impurity elements such as P, Sb, Sn, when they are exposed to temperatures within the range of 350-600°C. These elements segregate to the prior austenite boundaries at temperatures below 600°C and thus make the steel brittle by raising the ductile to brittle transition temperature. The embrittlement is fully reversible if the steel is re-heat treated at temperatures above 600°C. Cr-Mo steels (especially 2.25Cr-1Mo steel) are susceptible to this type of embrittlement. A parameter called J factor has been defined to assess the susceptibility of 2.25 Cr-1Mo steel to such an embrittlement.

$$J = (Si + Mn) \times (P + Sn) \times 10^4$$

The value of J should be kept below a predetermined value (~180) to avoid cracking. A more general parameter proposed for weld metal is given below

$$P_E = C + Mn + Mo + Cr/3 + Si/4 + 3.5(10P + 5Sb + 4Sn + As)$$

The value of P_E should be maintained below 2.8-3 to avoid embrittlement. In addition to Cr-Mo steels, Ni-Cr-Mo steels and Ni steels are also susceptible to this type of embrittlement. Separate equations to assess the susceptibility of these steels are also available in the literature.

7   WELDABILITY OF DIFFERENT FE-C ALLOYS

7.1   Cast Iron

Though cast iron is an alloy of iron and carbon, its C content is so high (typically 2–3.5%) that it is not considered in the family of steels. In cast iron, most of the carbon is present as graphite. During the heating cycle of welding, the matrix transforms into austenite and graphite particles partially dissolve in it. Some cementite is also formed. During cooling, the regions of austenite containing high carbon transform into martensite and the regions with low carbon to pearlite. The cementite particles remain untransformed. Hence at the end of a weld thermal cycle, the microstructure is a mixture of undissolved graphite, cementite, martensite, pearlite and some ferrite. This structure is very hard and brittle and if such a weld is tested in tension or bending, it fails through the weld boundary. Typical microstructure of the HAZ of grey cast iron welded using nickel base welding consumable is shown in Fig. 4.

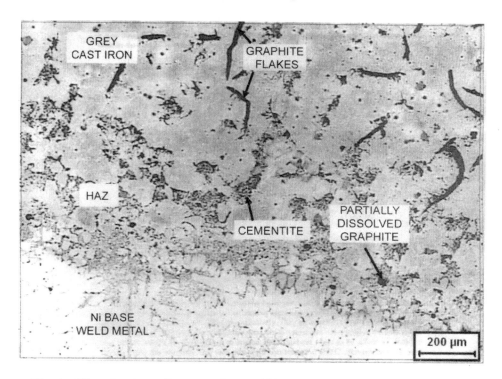

Fig. 4   Microstructure of grey cast iron weld in the HAZ near the fusion boundary

Welding of cast iron is carried out using low hydrogen coated electrodes of 55% Ni-45% Fe alloy. This alloy has the advantage of low melting point and yield strength, which minimise the hardening effect and degree of restraint respectively. They are relatively tolerant to sulphur and the metal transfer is in the form of large droplets, which reduces the dilution from the base metal. Cast iron is welded by preheating it to around 300°C and the edges to be joined are buttered initially using this electrode, and then post-weld heat treated at 650°C. Subsequently the joint may be completed using the same electrodes with or without preheat or PWHT. Where preheat is not used, it is desirable to reduce the heat input to the lowest practicable level by making short runs and allowing the metal to cool between each run. This minimises the width of the HAZ and reduces the extent to which graphite is dissolved and precipitated as carbide. When correctly applied, this technique is capable of producing load bearing joints.

7.2 Carbon and C-Mn Steels

Most of the aspects related to the metallurgy of welding discussed above are based on C and C-Mn steels. These steels can be welded without any serious problems. Carbon steels for welded construction have carbon content up to 0.35%, Mn up to 0.15 and Si up to 0.35%. In these steels, the steel making route influences the weldability. It is better for killed steels in which sufficient deoxidants are added during steel making, than for semi killed or rimmed steels. Similarly, steels produced by Bessemer converter in which air is blown for decarburisation exhibit poor weldability compared to those produced by open hearth, electric arc or oxygen converter processes. This is due to strain age embrittlement and high ductile to brittle transition temperature of these steels because of their high nitrogen content.

Most carbon steels used in welded construction have low CE and are not crack sensitive and hence welding can be carried out without any preheat. However, when sections of thickness higher than 25 mm are welded, preheating up to 100°C may be necessary if the restraint is high or the carbon content is near the upper limit.

Manganese is added in C-Mn steels to improve the strength and toughness. Toughness of the steel is also increased by reducing the grain size and this is achieved by minor additions of Al. These steels are susceptible to cold cracking and CE is used as an index of the weldability. This along with HD content in the weld and section thickness can be used to predict the minimum preheat temperatue to avoid cracking of the weld.

C-Mn steel weldments are normally given a stress relieving heat treatment if the section thickness is large, typically above 30 mm. Stress relieving temperature is around 600°C and time depends on the thickness, usually 1h per 25 mm of thickness.

7.3 Microalloyed or HSLA Steels

Microalloyed steels or HSLA steels are defined as steels possessing yield strength of at least 300 MPa, achieved by micro alloying or special thermo-mechanical processing or both. Microalloying elements, usually added to the steel include niobium, vanadium, titanium, aluminum and boron. Nitrogen and sulphur content in these steels are carefully controlled. Grain refinement is achieved by strain induced precipitation of AlN and Ti(C,N) during rolling in the temperature range of 900-1000°C, which prevents grain growth of recrystallised austenite grains and promotes inter-phase precipitation of NbC, VC or Ti(C,N) during transformation of the austenite, that in turn prevents the grain growth of ferrite. In order to achieve this, rolling temperatures should be carefully controlled within a narrow range of temperatures. Grain refinement thus achieved results in a marked improvement in both the strength and toughness of these steels.

Fine ferritic grain structure can also be achieved by carrying out the finish rolling at a lower temperature than the initial rolling passes and thus causing ferrite to form at a lower temperature (550°C). Ferrite thus produced is similar to acicular ferrite formed in the weld metal. Steels with such a microstructure possess high strength and toughness properties. They are known as thermo-mechanically controlled processed (TMCP) steels. Another route employed to increase the strength of this class of steels is precipitation strengthening through the addition of copper.

It can be seen that, in microalloyed steels, the strengthening is achieved by reducing the grain size, controlled rolling, precipitation of carbides, carbonitrides etc., and not by producing martensite and its subsequent tempering to improve toughness. Hence, carbon content in these steels is lower than in C-Mn steels and this does not translate into lower mechanical properties. This, in turn, means that the weldability of the steels is not adversely affected due to their higher strength as in the C-Mn steels. Hence these steels are replacing conventional C-Mn steels in offshore structures and large diameter pipes in petrochemical industries where extensive welding fabrication is unavoidable.

One of the problems associated with welding of these steels is the dilution of weld metal especially in the case of submerged arc welding. This can increase Nb, Ti or V content in the weld metal resulting in a reduction in toughness. Another problem is the grain growth in the CGHAZ. Though the presence of carbides prevents grain growth up to 1000°C, temperatures the experienced close to the fusion zone are higher than this and hence large prior austenite grains are formed in this zone. As the toughness and strength of these steels depend on the grain size, grain coarsening leads to loss of toughness in this region. Local brittle zones (LBZs), observed in multipass welds, also occur in this region. In the case of TMCP steels, welding can lead to the softening of the HAZ.

In predicting susceptibility of the steels to hydrogen assisted cracking, CE values derived based on conventional C-Mn steels have been found to be inadequate as C content in these steels is low and their strength is high. Further, cracking often occurs in the weld metal instead of the HAZ. Prediction of minimum preheat temperatue to avoid cold cracking is one of the current areas of research related to weldability of these steels.

7.4   Cr-Mo Steels

These steels are used mainly in high temperature applications like steam pipes and heat exchangers in power plants and petrochemical industries. They contain Cr in the range of 1-12% and Mo 0.5-1% and welding is carried out with Cr-Mo steel consumables of matching composition. In the as-welded condition the microstructure of both the weld and the HAZ varies from ferritic to fully martensitic as the Cr content increases from 1 to 12%. Weld may also contain a small volume fraction of delta-ferrite in steels with Cr content above 9%. Hardenability of these steels is sufficiently high that preheating has only a marginal influence on the HAZ or weld metal hardness, that too in the case of the lower alloyed versions. High hardenability of these steels makes them susceptible to cold cracking both in the weld metal and the HAZ and use of preheat, post heat and low hydrogen welding consumables are all necessary to prevent cracking. In certain alloys such as, 12Cr-1Mo steel it is required to carry out PWHT before the weldment is brought to ambient temperature to prevent this type of cracking.

Steels containing below 3% Cr are susceptible to reheat cracking during PWHT. One of the carbides formed during PWHT is Mo_2C, which nucleates uniformly throughout the prior austenite grains thus making it stronger than the grain boundaries leading to grain boundary sliding during stress relaxation. Impurity segregation at the grain boundaries also assists the cracking. Susceptibility to cracking is higher in the steels containing Nb or V as their carbides also strengthen the grain interior. Susceptibility of steels to such cracking can be assessed from their composition with the help of the appropriate cracking parameter.

Another problem associated with welding of these steels is temper embrittlement. 2.25Cr-1Mo steel is specifically susceptible to this type of embrittlement. Its susceptibility can be assessed from J-factor or P_E values that can be determined from the composition. In any case embrittlement can be removed by heat treating the steel above 600°C.

As the microstructure in the as welded condition is predominantly bainitic or martensitic in both the HAZ and the weld metal, it is required to carry out PWHT to temper the microstructure and thus improve the toughness. It is usually carried out in the temperature range of 650–750°C. Higher the alloy content, higher the temperature of PWHT, with the Ac_3 temperature as the upper limit. Time of heat treatment varies with thickness of the job and is usually taken as 1h/25 mm of thickness.

Creep strength of the weld joints of Cr-Mo steels and other ferritic steels meant for high temperature application is lower than that of the base metals. This is due to Type IV cracking, fracture of the weld joints in the FG/ICHAZ during creep with rupture life significantly lower than that of the base metal or weld metal. This is attributed to poor creep strength of the FG/ICHAZ and complex stress–strain state developed in the weld joints due to existence of different zones like base metal, FG/ICHAZ, CGHAZ and weld metal that differ vastly in their creep properties. In fact, the performance of Cr-Mo and other ferritic steels are limited by Type IV cracking and efforts are on to develop steels which are resistant to this form of cracking so that the maximum temperature range of application can be pushed up from the present 550-600°C to 650°C and beyond.

7.5 Ni Steels

These steels are mainly used for cryogenic applications. Nickel content in this class of steels varies from 0.7 to 12%. These steels should have a high degree of purity (low S + P content), careful control of C and N, addition of small quantity of Al or other elements like Ti to bind the interstitial elements including O and small additions of Mo and Mn to increase the strength and toughness at low temperatures. The C content in these steels has been progressively reduced with increasing Ni contents. Steels containing less than 2.5% Ni are generally used in quenched and tempered condition. For other steels the heat treatment given is quite complex including austenitising, quenching, tempering, reverse annealing and/or thermal cycling in the transformation temperature range to produce fine grain size. At the end of these heat treatments, the microstraucture is a mixture of fine ferrite, carbides and austenite.

For steels containing up to 1% Ni, weldability is similar to that of C-Mn or microalloyed steels. Welding can be carried out without preheating in the case of steels of lower strength and small section thickness. For thickness greater than 30 mm, multipass welds may lead to softening of the HAZ. Further, it may be difficult to achiever the base metal toughness in the CGHAZ. Hence during welding, heat input should be controlled to reduce the size of CGHAZ. Welding consumables with 1-2.5% Ni are used to produce a weld metal of toughness matching that of the base metal even at subzero temperatures. As the alloy content is high, preheating may be required to produce the desired microstructure.

For steels containing 1-3.5% Ni, welding consumables containing up to 3.5% Ni or austenitic steel consumables are used. The structure of the HAZ in the as welded condition is predominantly martensitic and hence low hydrogen consumables should be used for welding. As no PWHT is carried out, temper bead technique is used to refine the microstructure in the CGHAZ and to reduce residual stresses. If the S content is high, the weld will be susceptible to hot cracking. In order to prevent grain growth in the CGHAZ, low heat input welding is recommended.

In the case of steels with higher Ni content, the HAZ microstructure is fully martensitic and toughness of the HAZ is highly inferior to that of the base metal. However, due to the presence of large volume fraction of retained austenite in the HAZ, these steels are not susceptible to

HAC and hence welding can be carried out without any preheat. Austenitic stainless steel consumables or Ni base consumables are recommended for welding steels with more that 3.5% Ni. This is also a reason why no preheat is required for welding. Toughness of the HAZ can be improved by PWHT at 650°C, followed by rapid quenching. Welding is carried out at low heat input to reduce the width of HAZ.

7.6 Maraging Steels

Maraging steels are low carbon Ni-Co-Mo steels with small additions of Ti and Al. They have been developed to combine high yield strength with good fracture strength. High strength of these steels is obtained by martensitic transformation followed by age hardening in the temperature range about 500°C. The steel is initially solution annealed at 820°C, air-cooled and then age hardened. Due to very low carbon content (< 0.03%), the martensite formed is not hard and the strengthening is achieved mainly by precipitation of intermetallics like Ni_3Ti, Ni_3Mo and Fe_2Mo during ageing.

Welding is carried out using consumables of matching composition. In the CGHAZ, coarse martensitic structure is formed as a result of welding. Regions of HAZ heated to 600–700°C transform into a mixture of fine martensite and residual austenite. No further ageing takes place in this zone during subsequent annealing, which has the lowest strength. In the as-welded condition, the mechanical strength of the weld is equal to that of the parent metal in the solution annealed condition, but post weld ageing at 480°C for 3 h gives properties that match that of the fully treated alloys.

These steels are not susceptible to cold cracking. However, due to very low Mn content, they are prone to hot cracking if the sulphur content is high. No preheating is required and interpass temperature is maintained below 100°C. Welding is carried out using GMAW or GTAW processes; SAW and SMAW are usually avoided due to the poor toughness of the weld metal and the increased susceptibility to cracking.

8 SUMMARY

The first part of the chapter dealt with cracking susceptibility of steel welds. Cold cracking is the most important form of cracking in steels and preheating is the most widely used method to prevent this. Empirical relations are available to determine the preheat temperature from the composition of the steel and welding parameters; but they are of limited validity and preheat temperature is chosen more by experience in most of the cases. However, a better understanding of metallurgical changes in welding and use of low hydrogen welding consumables and welding processes can certainly assist in choosing safe lower preheat temperatures than the current practice and this could lead to considerable savings in terms of money and energy. This is one area in welding metallurgy where considerable research is going on. Steels are also susceptible to other types of cracking such as hot cracking, reheat cracking, lamellar tearing etc., if the impurity content is high. It is possible to find out the susceptibility of steels to various forms of cracking, from their composition.

The second part of this chapter dealt with specific problems associated with welding of different types of steels. With a proper understanding of the steel microstructure and prudent choice of welding consumables and processes, it is possible to weld most of the steels without any defects and to ensure satisfactory performance of the weld joints in service.

BIBLIOGRAPHY

1. N. Yurioka and H. Suzuki "Hydrogen Assisted Cracking in C-Mn and Low Alloy Steel Weldments" Int. Materials Reviews (35)4 1990 pp. 217–247.
2. J.F. Lancaster "Metallurgy of Welding" Abington Publishing, Cambridge UK 1999.
3. K. Easterling "Introduction to the Physical Metallurgy of Welding" 2nd Ed. Butterworth Heinemann, Oxford, UK 1992.
4. N. Bailey "Weldability of Ferritic Steels" Abington Publishing Cambridge UK 1994.
5. J.F. Lancaster "Handbook of Structural Welding" Abington Publishing Cambridge UK 1992.
6. N. Bailey, F.R. Coe, T.G. Gooch, P.H.M. Hart, N. Jenkins and R.J. Pargeter "Welding Steels Without Hydrogen Cracking" ASM International and Abignton Publishing Cambridge, 1992.
7. G.E. Linnert "Welding Metallurgy of Carbon and Alloy Steels V. 1 Fundamentals" American Welding Society, Miami, Florida, USA, 1994.
8. Ivan Hrivnak "Theory of Weldability of Metals and Alloys" Elsevier, Amsterdam, 1992.

3 Weldability of Austenitic Stainless Steels

V. Shankar

Materials Joining Section, MTD, IGCAR, Kalpakkam 603 102

1 INTRODUCTION

Stainless steels are extensively used in a variety of applications where corrosion resistance is required in combination with good strength and toughness. Of the various classes of stainless steels, namely the austenitic, martensitic, ferritic, precipitation-hardenable and duplex stainless steels, the most easily welded are the austenitic steels. These steels contain typically 16–25% Cr, 7–20% Ni, and less than 0.08% C. For improved corrosion resistance, 2–6%Mo, 0.1–0.2% N and niobium or titanium in the stabilized varieties are added. Standard welding practices for austenitic stainless steels focus on selection of appropriate filler metals to control microstructure of the weld metal and on post-treatment of the welded component to ensure corrosion resistance. The major metallurgical problem encountered during welding is hot cracking. Other problems encountered are localized corrosion or intergranular stress corrosion cracking, that may occur during service. The scope of this article includes welding metallurgy of austenitic stainless steels including solidification and solid state phase transformation, control of delta ferrite, origin, classification and assessment of hot cracking and post-weld heat treatment of components. Weldability recommendations are made for some specific grades, including super-austenitic stainless steels.

2 WELDING OF AUSTENITIC STAINLESS STEELS

2.1 Welding Metallurgy of Austenitic Stainless Steels

2.1.1 The Iron-Chromium-Nickel System:

Although welding produces microstructures far away from equilibrium, a consideration of the equilibrium phase diagram provides a basis for the understanding the phase composition and subsequent solid state transformations in stainless steel welds. The 70% Fe section of the Fe-Ce-Ni ternary phase diagram shown in Fig. 1 is commonly used to analyse the solidification and microstructure of austenitic stainless steels. As shown in Fig. 1, a ternary eutectic transformation occurs during solidification, with simultaneous formation of austenite and delta-ferrite from the liquid, the relative proportions of which are a function of the composition (Cr_{eq}/Ni_{eq} ratio[1]). The

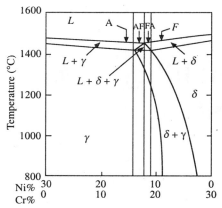

Fig. 1 **The 70% Fe section of the Fe-Cr-Ni phase diagram showing the solidification modes as a function of composition**

various transformations that occur in the solid state are that of delta-ferrite to sigma phase, carbides and austenite. The sigma phase appears at temperatures below about 900°C on the primary ferritic side of the diagram. Transformation to sigma phase occurs in weld microstructures on ageing in the temperature range 600–950°C. In the presence of carbon, the chromium carbide $M_{23}C_6$ precipitates rapidly on exposure in the temperature range 550–850°C. These transformations are of interest if heat-treatment of welded structures is envisaged.

2.1.2 Solidification Mode and Weld Microstructure

The various solidifying modes occurring in stainless steels welds are also indicated in Fig. 2. In

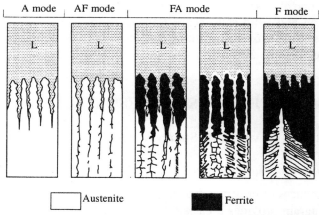

Fig. 2 **Schematic appearance of solidifying phases and room temperature microstructure as a function of solidification mode**

---

[1]Cr_{eq}/Ni_{eq} ratio as defined by Suutala. $Cr_{eq} = Cr + 1.37\ Mo + 1.5Si + 2Nb + 3Ti$, $Ni_{eq} = Ni + 22C + 14.2\ N + 0.31\ Mn + Cu$. These formulae will be used in the rest of this paper.

the fully austenitic solidification mode (Cr_{eq}/Ni_{eq} < 1.5) austenite crystals form from the melt and there is no change in the structure after solidification. In the austenitic-ferritic mode ($Cr_{eq}/Ni_{eq} \cong 1.5$), austenite is the primary phase and a part of the remaining liquid solidifies as eutectic ferrite. The ferritic-austenitic mode results for Cr_{eq}/Ni_{eq} ~ 1.6 and fully ferritic modes result for Cr_{eq}/Ni_{eq} > 1.9. In the primary ferritic compositions, there may be considerable amounts of ferrite (50 to 100%) just after solidification, which transforms partially to austenite depending on the composition and cooling rate during welding. In austenitic stainless steels, only a small amount of ferrite is retained in the form of vermicular or intercellular ferrite.

Weld metal ferrite morphologies are a function of Cr_{eq}/Ni_{eq} ratio and the transformation temperature. Eutectic ferrite is present as small particles of retained ferrite occurring between primary austenite dendrites (Cr_{eq}/Ni_{eq} < 1.5, FN < 1). Vermicular ferrite occurs by primary ferritic solidification in which the dendritie cores being rich in Cr, remain as ferrite while the rest of the microstructure transforms to austenite at fairly high temperatures (1100–1300°C). Vermicular ferrite is found as a continuous or semi-continuous network. A continuous network of vermicular ferrite (7–10 FN) is highly undesirable, since it provides an easy path for propagation of brittle fracture. For higher Cr_{eq}/Ni_{eq} ratios (> 1.6), the structure becomes more elongated and finer as the transformation occurs at lower temperatures. Acicular and Widmanstatten type ferrite structures occur in welds of duplex stainless steels.

2.1.3 *Prediction of Delta Ferrite in Weld Metal*

The Schaeffler and DeLong diagrams are widely used to estimate the amount of ferrite expected to be present after welding. However, these diagrams do not give information on the solidification mode, which is essential to identify the risk of hot cracking in various compositions. Also, the prediction range of these diagrams is limited. The WRC-92 FN diagram shown in Fig. 3 has been developed to improve the predictability of weld metal ferrite contents up to 100% ferrite and includes solidification mode boundaries. This diagram has been shown to be statistically more

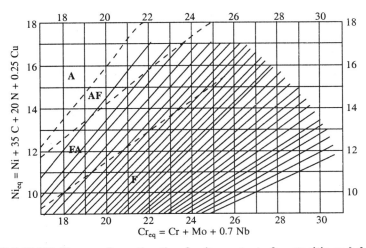

Fig. 3　**The WRC-92 FN diagram for estimating ferrite content of austenitic and duplex stainless steel welds; solidification mode boundaries are also shown**

accurate than the DeLong diagram and is indispensable in the welding of duplex stainless steels. The effects of Mn and Si are found to be mutually counteractive and no coefficients have been assigned to both these elements, besides the changes in weightage for C, N, Cu and Nb with respect to the DeLong diagram. The WRC-92 diagram is not applicable to high Mn, N and Mo stainless steels (> 3% Mo and > 2% Mn).

2.2 Weldability Problems in Austenitic Stainless Steels

2.2.1 Hot Cracking

Hot cracking occuring during welding of stainless steels is known to be of three types:
   (1) Solidification cracking, 2) HAZ liquation cracking and 3) Ductility dip cracking

Solidification cracking occurs in the interdendritic regions of fully austenitic microstructures as A) gross cracking, occurring at the junction of grains with differing orientation, detectable by visual and liquid penetrant testing, or B) microfissuring in the interdendritic regions which is revealed only under magnification or after applicaton of strain. Solidification cracking depends on two factors, namely the mechanical restraint and the metallurgical susceptibility, which is a function of composition. *Hot cracking of stainless steels is caused by the formation of low melting eutectics at the grain boundaries during welding, which cause failure under the action of shrinkage stresses associated with solidification.*

HAZ liquation cracking occurs intergranularly due to localised melting of the base metal grain boundaries adjacent to the fusion line where temperatures are close to the weld metal solidus. The liquation is associated with the formation of low melting eutectic phases caused by segregation of elements such as niobium and titanium along with impurities such as phosphorus and silicon. HAZ liquation cracking mainly occurs in highly restrained welds encountered in thick section joints.

Ductility dip cracking occurs at the HAZ grain boundaries without liquation at temperatures much below the lowest solidus. This cracking is ascribed to a variety of factors including creep and precipitation phenomena not involving the liquid phase. Ductility dip cracking occurs in multipass welds of type 347 stainless steel either during welding, or even after several years of service exposure. This phenomenon is also responsible for the stress relief cracking observed during heat treatment or service exposure of heavy section type 347 and 321 stainless steel welds.

   The elements involved in causing both types of cracking however, are similar. Both the types of cracking can occur in the base metal or in the previously deposited passes in thick-section welds. Dissolution of carbides of the NbC type are responsible for grain boundary liquation cracking in the type 347 stainless steel. On the other hand, in a fully austenitic 310 and 316 stainless steels not containing titanium or niobium, HAZ cracking occurs by segregation to the grain boundaries, and cracking is minimized by lowering the levels of P, S and Si.

2.2.2 Effect of Composition on Hot Cracking Resistance

It has been found that primary ferritic solidification mode greatly reduces hot cracking during welding, rather than the residual ferrite content. Several reasons have been attributed to the

be ~~rite~~ in reducing hot cracking. Delta-ferrite has a higher solubility for
i' ~~reduces~~ the concentration of P and S at the grain boundaries, making
' ~~s~~ difficult. Further, the solidifying weld structure which retains
~~om~~ temperature, is composed of ferrite-austenite interfaces during
r hand, in fully austenitic solidification, only austenite-austenite interfaces
boundaries are easily wetted by the remaining liquid, increasing cracking.
nust be used to ensure that primary ferritic solidification occurs, to avoid
e noted from Fig. 3 that the amount of retained ferrite to ensure primary
ncreases with alloy addition. This is reflected in the following table:

rrite Number Required in Various Weld Metals to Prevent Fusion Zone Cracking

Designation (ASTM/AISI)	Nominal Composition	WRC FN
16-8-2	16Cr-8Ni-2Mo-0.1C	2
301	17Cr-7Ni-0.1C	2
304, 304L	19Cr-10Ni-0.06C, (0.02C)	3
316, 316L	17Cr-12Ni-2.5Mo-0.06C, (0.02C)	3
309	23Cr-13Ni-0.1C	4
347	18Cr-10Ni-0.06C-8 × C ≤ Nb + Ta ≤ 1%	6

To obtain more detailed information, correlation between composition and hot cracking behaviour
was attempted by Suutala, who mapped compositions in terms of Cr_{eq}/Ni_{eq} ratio versus P + S, as
shown in Fig. 4. It is observed in Fig. 4 that even with primary ferritic solidification the cracking
susceptibility could be high for compositions in the range Cr_{eq}/Ni_{eq} 1.5–1.6, if the P + S content
is high. Further, there is a steep drop in the tolerance for impurity elements in the weld metal in

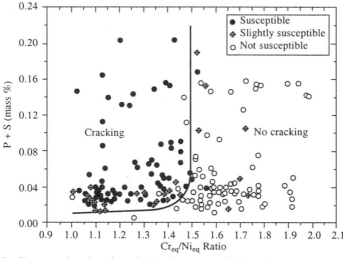

Fig. 4 **The Suutala diagram showing the relation between solidification mode and cracking susceptibility
in austenitic stainless steels**

this range of ratios. This diagram can be used to provide a rough estimate of weldability from the composition.

2.2.3 *Evaluation of Hot Cracking Susceptibility*

Tests for weldability can be classified as self-restraint tests, and versatile cracking tests. Self-restraint tests in which wold beads are laid on a plate under various welding conditions, such as Y-groove test, circular patch test, etc. are the simplest type of test. The versatile (variable restraint) tests such as Varestraint test and PVR test are laboratory tests that give a quantitative measure of cracking susceptibility of materials. These laboratory tests are performed when a comprehensive evaluation of weldability is required in situations such as welding consumable development or evaluation of autogenous weldability for critical applications.

The Varestraint Test:

The Varestraint test consists of applying a known strain on to the specimen during deposition of a GTA weld bead. The application of strain subjects the solidifying weld puddle to a controlled restraint. A sketch of the Varestraint test setup is shown in Fig. 5. The specimen of dimensions $127 \times 25 \times 3$ mm, is subjected to strain by conforming over a die block of known radius. The strain is applied by pneumatic force within a very short time, so that the position of the weld puddle is essentially frozen at the instant of strain application. Cracking is measured by noting the lengths of the individual cracks and their locations, viz. fusion zone or HAZ. The data is then analysed using the following criteria.

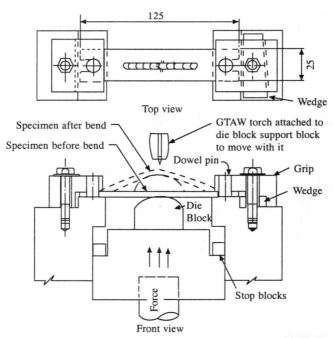

Fig. 5   The Varestraint test equipment showing specimen and test procedure

Cracking Threshold: The cracking threshold is the minimum strain at which cracking occurs.

Total Crack Length: The total crack length is obtained by adding together the lengths of cracks found in the weld puddle or in the HAZ. An average value from several specimens is used. This criterion is considered to give the best quantitative estimate of cracking susceptibility for a material.

The Varestraint test is extremely useful for evaluation of filler metals and electrodes, to assess heat-to heat variations in weldability and for welding consumable selection and development.

Field Weldability Tests:

Frequently, it is required to assess the weldability of certain material and geometrical combinations when quick decisions must be made regarding material selection. Such field weldability tests rely on simulating the material, geometric and thermal conditions prevailing in the actual joint. A few examples of field weldability tests are given in Table 2. From among those listed, the one closely representing the actual geometry can be used. Evidently, a more severe test would automatic qualify a less severe geometry. The welding engineer could evolve his own procedure for such tests, using more complex geometries as required.

Table 2   Self-Restraint Tests Recommended for Qualifying Filler Metals for Hot Cracking

Geometry	Restraint	Reference	Applicable Configurations
I. Bead-On-Edge	Low		Butt Welds
II. Fillet Weld Test	Moderate	Din 50129	Fillets, Butt Welds
III. Circular Fillet Weld Test	High		Nozzles, Fillets, Butt Welds
IV. Circular Groove Test	Severe	Ref. 6	Standard Qualification Test
V. Tubing Weld Cracking Test	Severe	Ref. 7	Pipe Welds (Fig. 6)

I   II   III   IV

2.3   Welding Recommendations for Specific Grades of Stainless Steels

2.3.1   *Welding of Stabilized Stainless Steels:*

The stabilized grades of stainless steel such as 347 and 321 usually contain niobium or titanium to stabilize carbon and prevent intergranular corrosion, in addition to providing higher strength than the unstabilized grades. Stabilized stainless steels are however, more prone to solidification and liquation cracking. Titanium is similar to Nb in its effect on hot cracking, though it is slightly less harmful.

Niobium containing stainless steels are usually welded with matching consumable. For titanium stabilized steels, welding is carried out with niobium containing fillers if high temperature strength is required in the weldment. A low carbon unstabilized filler metal is used if a lower service temperature range is acceptable. The general recommendations for welding these types of stainless steels include:

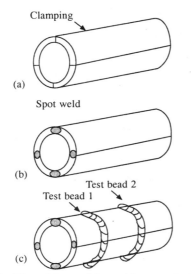

Fig. 6   The tubing weld cracking test (ref. 7)

(a) ensuring sufficient amount of δ ferrite in the weld metal to prevent cracking, (i.e., at least 6 FN).

(b) restricting the amount of Nb or Ti to the appropriate amount required for stabilization (maximum of 10 times and 5 times % C respectively) and

(c) sufficient care during post weld heat treatments to ensure intergranular corrosion resistance. Particular attention must be paid to the risk of PWHT cracking or **stress relief cracking** in stabilized stainless steel welds. The measures proposed to reduce the risk of this type of cracking include (a) reduction of stress concentration at the toe of fillet welds, (b) rapid heating in the temperature range 600–950°C, and (c) the use of molybdenum-containing filler metals which are resistant to carbide precipitation in the grain interiors. The use of 16-8-2 type of filler metal has been found particularly useful, since it produces sound welds with a strain-tolerant microstructure.

2.3.2   Welding of Fully Austenitic Stainless Steels:

Fully austenitic compositions must be welded in several applications such as for urea service, for high temperature service, cryogenic magnets, etc. Alloys such as type 310 are susceptible to hot cracking, which calls for certain composition controls. It must be ensured that the filler material contains at least 0.1% carbon, less than 0.015% P and S, and not more than 0.5% Si. Carbon and nitrogen are beneficial additions in fully austenitic stainless steels as regards hot cracking. However, an exception is for urea service, where the carbon content is limited to 0.02% for maintaining excellent corrosion resistance while maintaining resistance to cracking.

2.3.3   Welding of Nitrogen-Added Stainless Steels:

The nitrogen-added grades 304LN and 316LN have gained usage in view of their better resistance to intergranular corrosion as well as excellent high temperature properties. These steels contain up to 0.16% nitrogen without additions of chromium or manganese. Other grades containing higher additions of Cr or Mn can have as much as 0.4% N. Welding is carried out with 1-2% nitrogen addition to argon gas to prevent loss of nitrogen. With weld metal nitrogen levels above 0.6% N in the low Mn grades, porosity can be a problem.

Further, addition of nitrogen increases the fusion zone and HAZ cracking, particularly in the weld metal HAZ. It is recommended that a FN of at least 3 is maintained both in the base metal (ferrite potential) and in weld metal. Since these grades are greatly resistant to sensitization, stress relieving at low temperatures (600°C) appears to be a feasible option.

2.4 Embrittlement of Stainless Steel Welds

Austenitic stainless steel welds intended for elevated service temperatures suffer embrittlement during service exposure by the transformation of δ-ferrite which is retained to avoid hot cracking, into deleterious phases such as σ, χ, α' etc. The formation of these phases is influenced by a number of factors such as weld composition, ferrite content and morphology, in addition to temperature and time of transformation. The carbon content of the weld metal plays a crucial role in retarding the ferrite to sigma transformation. It has been proposed that the ferrite decomposition process proceeds by two stages in high carbon type 316 weld metal. In the first stage, at shorter aging times, ferrite to austenite transformation assisted by the rapid precipitation of $M_{23}C_6$ particles at the delta/gamma interface. In the second stage, the transformation of the remaining δ-ferrite either to sigma or gamma or both was sluggish. On the other hand, in low carbon welds, δ-ferrite transformed rapidly to sigma and gamma. This mechanism is valid in the temperature range 600–750°C. Based on regression analysis of actual weld data, a nomogram has been derived to estimate the amount of sigma phase formed after 90% of the δ-ferrite has transformed, which is shown in Fig. 7. It is observed that the sigma phase content increases with increasing Cr and Mo content, with Mo being nearly 4 times as effective as Cr in promoting sigma formation. On the other hand, sigma percentage decreases with increasing carbon content. Nitrogen additions also have a retarding effect on sigma phase formation.

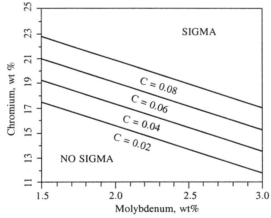

Fig. 7 Nomogram for estimation of sigma phase formation tendency in austenitic stainless steel welds intended for high temperature service

2.5 Autogenous Welding of Stainless Steels

Autogenous welding of stainless steel sheet using gas tungsten arc welding is a special case where welding defects caused by poor penetration could reduce weldability, apart from cracking. This problem has been largely overcome by the recent introduction of special flux coatings in very thin layers to the sheets to be autogenously welded. These flux layers which are applied using a brush to the surface prior to welding, give consistent and improved penetration depth by 200–300% with respect to that without the flux. This has led to the possibility of joining by welding without either filler metal addition or edge preparation (i.e., with square edges) thickness up to 6 mm in a single pass and up to 12 mm in two passes.

2.6   Post-Weld Heat Treatment of Stainless Steel Welded Components

Fabricated stainless steel components are rarely heat treated, except where there is a definite risk of stress corrosion cracking in service or when repair welding is envisaged after service exposure. Heat treatments are classified as low temperature treatments (below 550°C) carried out to ensure *dimensional stability that* reduces peak stresses. True *stress relief occurs* at temperatures above 600°C when the yield stresses drop sufficiently for this to occur. *Solution annealing* in the temperature range 1050–1100°C is used to dissolve second phases such as carbides and delta-ferrite, which aids in recovery of corrosion resistance in the weldment, in addition to reducing residual stresses substantially. Anticipated problems during heat treatment include stress relief cracking and formation of embrittling phases such as carbides, sigma and other intermetallic phases. These problems are solved by selecting an appropriate cooling cycle to avoid precipitation, or by water quenching. Water quenching should be used with caution, since non-uniform quenching could reintroduce residual stresses in the component.

The lower alloyed grades of stainless steel are solutionized at 1040–1100°C. Heat treatments in the higher range 1100–1200°C are used to dissolve carbides and other phases formed during service exposure of 25Cr20Ni-O.4C catalytic reformer tubes before repair welding. Higher annealing temperatures have been found to reduce cracking during welding.

2.7   Welding of Super Austenitic Stainless Steels

Super austenitic stainless steels are those grades that are highly alloyed and possess high resistance to corrosive attack in various media. Specifically, the term is applied to those steels that have a pitting resistance equivalent number (PREN = C + 3.3Mo + 16N) greater than 40. Many of these grades have been in use as proprietary compositions before being incorporated into various standards. Further, these materials are very expensive and are often intended for highly specific applications. Welding for corrosive service is recommended using filler wire appropriately overmatched for corrosion resistance and autogenous welding may be permissible only in some cases. Typical compositions of some grades are given in Table 3. Filler material recommended for welding these alloys are given in Table 4. Wherever possible, the original manufacturer or supplier must be contacted for carrying out critical fabrication. In the absence of such support, information on material suitability for particular service conditions is useful in material substitution or repair of existing plant and equipment.

Table 3   Designations and Chemical Compositions (wt. %) of some Super Austenitic Stainless Steels

Designation	Cr	Ni	Mo	N	Mn	C	Cu	PREN
X1 CrNiMoCuN 20 18 7	20	18	7	0.2	1	0.02	0.75	43.8
X1 NiCrMoCuN 31 27 4	27	31	4	0.1	2	0.02	1.0	40
X1 NiCrMoCuN 32 28 7	28	32	7	0.2	2	0.015	1.2	52
X1 NiCrMoCuN 25 20 5	20	25	5	0.1	2	0.02	1.5	38
X1 NiCrMoCuN 25 20 6	21	25	6.5	0.2	2	0.02	1	45
NA 16	21	42	3	–	1	0.05	2.5Ti	–

Table 4 Recommended Filler Metals for Welding Superaustenitic Stainless Steels

Designation	Filler Metals	Comments
X1 CrNiMoCuN 20 18 7		Resistant to seawater, acids
X1 NiCrMoCuN 31 27 4		Seawater piping, pulp and paper plant, phosphoric and sulphuric acid plants
X1 NiCrMoCuN 32 28 7	ENiCrMo-3,	-do-
X1 NiCrMoCuN 25 20 5	ERNiCrMo-3, NA43, ERNiCr20Mo9Nb	Chemical plant, refinery, bleaching tanks
X1 NiCrMoCuN 25 20 6		Seawater condensers, flue gas desulphurisation plant, high pressure piping for desalination plant
NA 16	ERNiCr26Mo, ERNiFeCr1, NA 41, NA 43	Resistant to chloride SCC, sulphuric acid plant, sour gas application

REFERENCES

1. E. Folkhard, "Welding Metallurgy of Stainless Steels", 1992.
2. "Welding of Stainless Steels and Other Joining Methods", American Iron & Steel Institute, distributed by Nickel Development Institute.
3. K. Easterling, "An Introduction to the Physical Metallurgy of Welding".
4. DIN 50129 – 1973, "Testing of Metallic Materials – Testing of Welding Filler Metals for Liability to Cracking."
5. J.F. Lancaster, "Handbook of Structural Welding" Abington Publishing, Cambridge, England, 1992.
6. T.W. Nelson, J.C. Lippold, W. Lin and W.A. Baeslack III, Weld. J. March 1997, p 110-s.
7. C.D. Lundin and C.Y.P. Qiao, 'Tubing Weld Cracking Test', in Proc. 2nd Intl. Conf. on Heat-Resistant Materials, Gatlinburg, Tennessee, September 1995, ASM Publication.
8. P.J. Cunat, in "Stainless Steels," eds. P. Lacombe *et al*, Les Editions de Physique Les Ulis, 1993, Cedex A, France.

4. Welding of Ferritic, Martensitic and Duplex Stainless Steels

S. Sundaresan

Professor Emeritus, Dept of Metallurgical Engineering, Indian Institute of Technology Chennai

WELDING OF FERRITIC STAINLESS STEELS

In the absence of nickel the ferritic stainless steels are cheaper than the austenitic grades and perform quite satisfactorily under milder service conditions. The ferritic stainless steels possess a greater resistance to stress corrosion cracking, and a higher yield strength. However, on account of the bcc crystal structure, the ferritic steels undergo the ductile-brittle transition when temperature is lowered.

In principle, ferritic stainless steels (FSS) are straight Fe-Cr alloys containing chromium exceeding 12% and C restricted to a maximum of 0.1%. While higher Cr contents confer greater corrosion resistance, they also result in embrittlement and an inhanced tendency to form intermetallic phases such as σ on thermal exposure. An upper limit of 26% Cr is therefore common in commercial FSS. Other alloying elements are often added for specific functions: Mo to increase corrosion resistance, Al for grain refinement and Nb (or Ti) to stabilise against chromium carbide precipitation and also reduce dissolved C and N and thereby increase toughness.

From the Fe-Cr-C phase diagram (Fig. 1), it may be seen that, depending on composition, some austenite may be formed above 800°C before the fully ferritic region is re-entered at temperatures exceeding 1150°C. On cooling, the ferrite first transforms to austenite, often in Widmanstatten fashion, before forming martensite on further cooling. The martensite may be tempered up to 760°C when austenite re-forms. The martensite then transforms during tempering to ferrite and carbide, the latter corresponding Cr_7C_3 for lower chromium and $Cr_{23}C_6$, for higher chromium contents. It nitrogen is present, Cr_2N forms on heating, but both carbide and nitride re-dissolve at temperatures greater than 850°C.

The standard ferritic stainless steels are: AISI Type 446 (25%Cr), Type 430 (17% Cr) and Types 405 (13% Cr) and 409 (11.5% Cr). Some typical compositions are given in Table 1.

Type 405 is ferritic because it has maximum C at 0.08% and contains an average of 0.20% Al, which is a strong ferrite-former. Type 409 is ferritic because it also has a low C level (0.08% C max) and a minimum Ti content equal to $6 \times$ %C.

It has been realised that interstitial elements raise the impact transition temperature (Fig. 2a). However, if the C and N can be bound as compounds, say with Ti or Nb, the toughness can be improved. An added advantage of these compounds is the reduction of grain growth. Modern steel-making aims at producing ferritic stainless steels with low interstitials. Since an oxidation

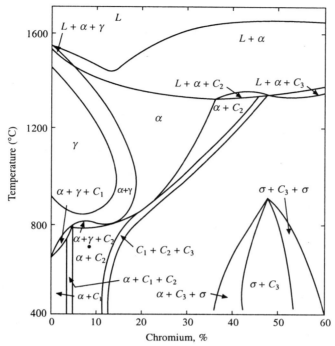

Fig. 1 **Vertical section of the Fe-Cr-C phase diagram at 0.1% C; C1 – M$_3$C, C2 – M$_7$C$_3$, C3 – M$_{23}$C$_6$**

Table 1 **Compositions of some common ferritic stainless steels (wt.%)**

UNS No.	Name	Cr	C	Mn	Si	Others
S40500	405	11.5–14.75	0.08	1.0	1.0	Al 0.10–0.30
S40900	409	10.5–11.7	0.08	1.0	1.0	Ti > 6x %C, 0.75 max.
S43000	430	16–18	0.12	1.0	1.0	–
S43035	439	17.75–18.75	0.07	0.6	0.6	Ti > 12x%C, 1.1 max.; Ni 0.5
S44600	446	23–27	0.20	1.5	1.0	N 0.25; also Nb, Al, Ti optional
S44626	26–15	25–27	0.06	0.75	0.75	Ti > 7(%C + %N); Mo 0.75–1.5 N 0.04; Cu 0.2; Ni 0.5
S44660 (Super ferritic)	Sea-Cure	25–27	0.025	1.0	1.0	(Ti + Nb) > [0.2 + 4(%C + %N)]; Ni 1.5–3.5; Mo 2.5–3.5; N 0.035

Note: Single values one maximum values.
[Source: A. John Sedriks: Corrosion of Stainless Steels, IInd Ed. Wiley-Interscience Publication, John Wiley A sons Inc.]

route removes chromium as well as carbon, the method adopted is to reduce the partial pressure of oxygen as C is gradually eliminated. Known as argon oxygen decarburization (AOD), a mixture of argon and oxygen is blown and, as carbon level decreases, the proportion of argon in the mixture is raised. More recently, electron beam refining and vacuum melting techniques provide an even better alternative to AOD as still lower interstitial levels can be realised.

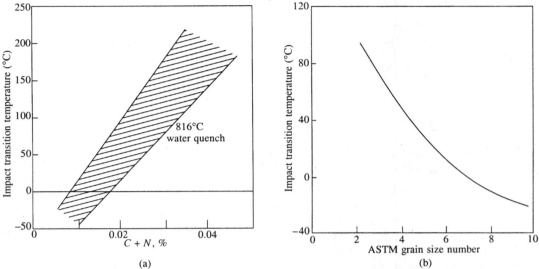

(a)   (b)

Fig. 2 **Effect of (a) interstitial content and (b) ferritic grain size, on impact transition temperature of ferritic stainless steels (after F.B. Pickering, "Physical Metallurgy and the Design of Steels" Applied Science, New York, 1978)**

Table 2 **Mechanical properties of ferritic stainless steels**

Type	Yield strength (MPa)	UTS (MPa)	Elongation (%)
405	280–380	400–510	20–30
430	280–450	450–580	20–30

Ferritic stainless steels have a yield strength greater than that of the austenitic type, being 280–460 MPa compared with 230 MPa for the latter. However, the ductility and impact resistance are lower. Mechanical property ranges for two important ferritic stainless steels are given in Table 2.

On account of the single-phase microstructure and the greater atomic mobility, FSS suffer from rapid grain growth on heating. The grain-coarsening temperature is lower at 600°C in relation to 900°C for the austenitic steels. Grain refinement increases the yield and tensile strengths according to the Petch relationship (strength varies as $d^{-1/2}$). The impact transition temperature of FSS is higher than that of mild steel due to the embrittling effect of Cr dissolved in ferrite. Grain size control is imperative from this point of view (Fig. 2b).

Formation of increasing amounts of austenite on heating results in a greater percentage of martensite on cooling. This raises strength and reduces toughness, in the first instance. The effect is, however, complicated by the presence of internal stresses and the grain refining influence of martensite (Fig. 3).

Chromium-rich ferrite is basically brittle but, in addition, 17–25% Cr steels suffer from '475°C embrittlement' when heated to temperatures in the range 400–550°C. This is due to the precipitation of coherent chromium-rich alpha-prime particles by spinodal decomposition in the miscibility gap in the Fe-Cr system. The embrittlement can be reduced by lowering chromium and interstitial contents. The higher chromium ferritic steels may form sigma-phase and get embrittled. The presence Mo and Ti aids sigma formation.

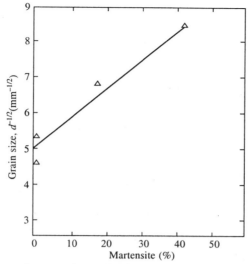

Fig. 3   Effect of martensite on ferritic grain size (after F.B. Pickering, 1978)

In general, the FSS are less weldable than the austenitic types and welded joints have lower toughness. The phenomena described above directly influence the behaviour of ferritic stainless steels during welding:

1. *Grain coarsening* is perhaps the most serious problem in welding of FSS as it results in reduced ductility and toughness. It can be controlled somewhat by (a) minimizing heat input during welding; and (b) additions of Ti, Nb and/or Al, which form undissolved compounds.

2. *Martensite formation* depends on composition. Primarily it reduces ductility and may necessitate subsequent annealing. However, annealing is costly and may result in excessive distortion, particularly in joints that were previously formed by a cold working process. The formation of martensite however, has occasionally been used to advantage. Provided that the workpiece can be annealed after welding, some martensite may be allowed as it inhibits ferritic grain growth. In such a case it is necessary to preheat and also select a steel of lower %C in order to guard against HAZ cracking. When postweld annealing is not feasible, martensite formation must be avoided by selecting a base metal containing a substantial amount of strong ferrite former, such as A1, Nb or Ti.

3. *475°C embrittlement* will have to be reckoned with in steels with chromium greater than 17%. Steels with less than 17% Cr are generally regarded insensitive. The phenomenon is usually not significant during welding, as the dwell-time is short. It assumes importance, however, during cooling after post-weld annealing, where in the range 550–400°C slow cooling must be avoided. Heavy sections may require forced cooling or a spray quench to bring them safely through the embrittlement range. If the embrittlement has occurred, it can be removed by a short-time heat treatment at 700–800°C followed by rapid cooling.

4. *Sigma-phase formation* that may occur on exposure in the range 650–850 °C makes the material brittle (hardness 1000 H_v) and may also lead to intergranular corrosion. Heat treatment at temperatures higher than 900°C is required to redissolve sigma if it has formed. Time during welding is insufficient, but annealing may lead to sigma formation

in susceptible compositions. Annealing, however, may be indispensable for overcoming the other difficulties.

5. *Intercrystalline corrosion* may occur in the HAZ as a result of chromium carbide precipitation at the ferrite grain boundaries which produces local chromium depletion and preferential corrosive attack. The conditions under which these events occur are, however, different from those in austenitic stainless steels. The FSS sensitise on heating to beyond 900°C and cooling rapidly. The carbon dissolves on heating and forms $M_{23}C_6$ carbide with chromium on cooling. The formation of the Cr-rich carbide occurs much faster in ferritic stainless steels than in the austenitic grades on account of (a) the greater degree of supersaturation resulting from the reduced carbon solubility in ferrite, and (b) the faster diffusion through the more open bcc lattice. The rapid cooling inherent in welding is thus unable to suppress chromium carbide precipitation. The problem can be overcome by annealing at 650–850°C, which allows chromium diffusion into the chromium-impoverished regions, or by stabilising the steel with Nb or Ti. The latter is not desirable for service in oxidising acids which vigorously attack TiC and TiN.

6. Notch toughness of FSS is relatively low and decreases further with increasing %Cr. For the 17% Cr steels, the transition temperature could lie just above room temperature, depending on interstitial content and section thickness. This is important, in the selection of joint design and welding conditions. Multi-axial residual stresses may be developed during welding, especially in thick sections. Annealing will then be necessary for stress relief. Notches and other stress concentrations must be scrupulously avoided by careful welding practice. Since a relatively small rise of temperature greatly increases impact toughness, preheating is often useful in preventing cracking in weldments.

7. Preheating will be required for avoiding cracks, particularly when dealing with higher Cr contents and larger thickness. The recommended temperature range is 150–250°C.

8. Post-weld annealing at 700–850°C is required for transforming any martensite formed, removing the 475 °C embrittlement, overcoming susceptibility to intercrystalline corrosion, stress relief, etc. The temperature of annealing must be below that for austenite formation and grain coarsening. However, annealing has three disdvantages: (a) the time and cost of treatment; (b) scale formation and (c) distortion, especially for light sections.

To minimize distortion from handling, weldments often are allowed to cool to about 600°C in the annealing furnace before they are removed to further cool in air. Slow cooling through the range 550–440°C must be avoided as described earlier..

Selection of filler material

The choice is between similar (ferritic) and dissimilar (austenitic) filler materials. FSS filler metals offer the advantages of having the same colour and appearance, coefficient of thermal expansion and corrosion resistance as the base metal. Annealing after welding, as seen above, is necessary to improve ductility.

Austenitic stainless steel filler metals (308, 309, 310) have the advantage of excellent ductility. Note, however, that grain coarsening, etc., in the HAZ will not be prevented. Also, austenitic steels have a coefficient of expansion ($19 \times 10^{-6} K^{-1}$) much higher than that of FSS (12×10^{-6}. K^{-1}). This leads to thermal stresses and possibly fatigue cracks if the weldment is subjected to temperature fluctuations in service. One suggested alternative is to use duplex stainless steel (say 25Cr-4Ni) filler metal that has an expansion coefficient quite close to that of FSS. Austenitic fillers do not require annealing; in fact, annealing may lead to sensitization.

Where temperature changes are not likely in service and where the joint does not require annealing, austenitic filler metals can be used to advantage - the possibility also exists of making the inner layers with austenitic and outer layers with ferritic filler materials.

WELDING OF MARTENSITIC STAINLESS STEELS

Properties and Applications: Martensitic stainless steels contain about 11–18% chromium and up to 1.2% carbon, with minor additions of nickel (up to 3%). Typical compositions and properties of some martensitic stainless steels are given in the following tables:

Table 2   Compositions of some martensitic stainless steels

UNS No.	Name	Cr	C	Mn	Si	Others
S40300	403	11.5–13.0	0.15	1.0	0.5	–
S41000	410	11.5–13.5	0.15	1.0	1.0	–
S41400	414	11.5–13.5	0.15	1.0	1.0	Ni 1.25–2.50
S42000	420	12–14	0.15	1.0	1.0	–
S42200	422	11–13	0.20–0.25	1.0	0.75	Ni 0.40–1.0, Mo 0.75–1.25 W 0.75–1.25, V 0.15–0.30
S44002	440A	16–18	0.60–075	1.0	1.0	Mo 0.75
S44003	440B	16–18	0.75–0.95	1.0	1.0	Mo 0.75
S44004	440C	16–18	0.95–1.20	1.0	1.0	Mo 0.75

Note: Single values are maximum values.
[Source: A. John Sedriks: Corrosion of Stainless Steels, IInd Ed. Wiley-Interscience Publication, John Wiley & Sons Inc.]

Table 3   Typical mechanical properties of martensitic stainless steels

Name	Condition	YS (MPa)	UTS (MPa)	Elongation (%)	Hardness
403, 410	Annealed	276	517	30	B 82
420	H + T at 316 C	1345	1586	8	C 50
422	H + T at 427 C	1282	1627	10	–
	H + T at 649 C	862	1000	14	C 32
440A	H + T at 316 C	1655	1393	5	C 55
440B	H + T at 316 C	1862	1930	3	C 55
440C	H + T at 316 C	1896	1965	2	C 57

H : Hardened; T: Tempered
[Source: A. John Sedriks: Corrosion of Stainless Steels, IInd Ed. Wiley-Interscience Publication, John Wiley & Sons Inc.]

Since the Cr content is relatively low, corrosion resistance is only moderate. The alloy content is restricted so that M_s is not depressed to too low a value. Note that the relatively high C content is necessary for martensite formation, but corrosion problems may arise due to sensitization on slow cooling from high temperature.

Due to the high creep strength in the 550°C range, these steels find wide application in steam generators of conventional and nuclear power plants. The use of this material permits lower wall thickness and greater flexibility in design (typically 65 mm for 125 mm of P22), apart from higher start-up velocities in operation. In relation to austenitic grades, the higher thermal conductivity and lower thermal expansion provide better transient start-up conditions.

The major difficulty in welding these steels is the possibility of hydrogen-assisted cracking in the HAZ. The martensitic stainless steels are used in the quenched and tempered or normalised and softened condition. They solidify first as ferrite, enter the austenite loop of the Fe-Cr-C phase diagram, before retransforming to a martensitic structure. Martensite starts to form below ~300°C (M_s) and goes to completion on cooling to ~150°C (M_f).

Consumables: Welding can either be done using matching filler or austenitic grades such as 309L or 308L. However, in the latter case, PWHT cannot be done for reason of sensitization or embrittlement of the weld metal and to avoid carbon migration from the base metal towards the deposit. Pure argon or argon-helium mixtures can be used in gas-shielded welding. However, hydrogen and nitrogen additions are not permissible either for shielding or purging.

Welding procedures for these steels are similar to those for normal quenched and tempered ferritic steels:

% C	Preheat/Interpass	PWHT
<0.1	none	none required
0.1–0.2	200–300°C	920–1050°C SA, Q + 500–750°C T

With carbon contents less than 0.1%, the weld and HAZ are soft enough so that no PWHT is required. In general, welding is carried out in either the austenitic (above M_s) or semi-transformed condition (between M_s and M_f). The latter procedure has the advantage that the subsequent passes have the effect of tempering the previous ones where 50–60% martensite would have formed. Furthermore, the untransformed austenite can deform and serve as a cushion for the stresses enduced by the transformation in each pass. Finally, the weld is cooled to about 50°C to ensure full transformation to martensite (see Fig. 4) and heat-treatment is given as above.

Since these steels are meant for corrosion-resistant applications or for high temperature service, some special precautions are called for, depending on the carbon content, as given below:

1. Cooling after welding must be done to about 50°C to ensure complete martensitic transformation. Otherwise SCC resistance will be affected, as the amount of retained austenite increases. On the other hand, cooling to room temperature may induce quench-cracking in some steels.

2. Fast cooling from solutionising temperature to room temperature is required to avoid sensitization in the HAZ and weld metal.

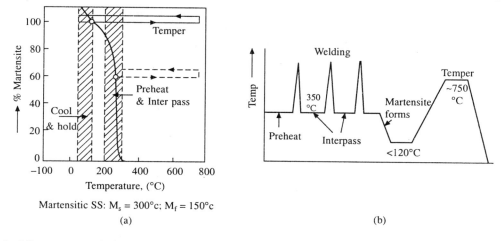

Martensitic SS: $M_s = 300°c$; $M_f = 150°c$

(a)   (b)

Fig. 4 **Microstructural changes (a), and schematic temperature cycle (b) for martensitic stainless steel welds**

WELDING OF DUPLEX STAINLESS STEELS

Duplex stainless steels (DSS), in comparison with the conventional austenitic or ferritic grades, have a two-phase microstructure containing approximately equal amounts of austenite and ferrite. In relation to the normal austenitic steels, the DSS have higher Cr and Mo contents and a lower Ni content. The composition is generally in the range 18–26% Cr, 4–8% Ni and 0–4% Mo, often with nitrogen and copper additions. Compositions and mechanical properties of some duplex stainless steels are listed in the tables below:

Interest in the DSS stems from the high yield strength and excellent resistance to stress corrosion cracking (SCC) and pitting corrosion. In these respects they are superior to the austenitic grades. In addition, they have a lower toughness transition temperature than that of the ferritic grades. They have considerable potential for use in chemical process equipment, pollution control devices, marine applications and particularly tubing for oil and gas wells. The application of DSS is generally restricted to the temperature range –20 to +300°C.

Table 4 **Compositions of some duplex stainless steels**

UNS No.	Name	C	Cr	Ni	Mo	N	Others
S32900	329	0.20	23–28	2.5–5	1–2	–	
J93370	CD-4MCu	0.04	24.5–26.5	4.75–6	1.75–2.25	–	Cu 2.75–3.25
S31500	3RE60	0.03	18–19	4.25–5.25	2.5–3	–	
S31803	2205	0.03	21–23	4.5–6.5	2.5–3.5	0.08–0.2	–
S32550	Ferr.255	0.04	24–27	4.5–6.5	2–4	0.1–0.25	Cu 1.5–2.5
S32750	SAF2507	0.03	24–26	6–8	3–5	0.24–0.32	–
S32760	Zeron100	0.03	24–26	6–8	3–4	0.2–0.3	Cu 0.5–1, W 0.5–1

Table 5   Typical mechanical properties[a] of duplex stainless steels

Name	Tensile strength (MPa)[b]	Yield strength (0.2% offset) (MPa)	Elongation (%)	Hardness (Rockwell B or C)
CD-4MCu[c]	745	558	25	C26
329	724	551	25	B98
7Mo Plus	779	579	36	–
SAF 2304	600[d]	400[d]	25[d]	B97[e]
3RE60	617	482	48	B92
44LN	800	450	25	–
IN-744	689	517	35	B95
NAS 64	820	620	22	C24
2205	760	520	27	–
Uranus 50	600	386	25	C8
DP-3W	862	568	42	C25
Ferralium 255	869	676	30	B100
SAF 2507	800[d]	550[d]	25[d]	C28[e]
Zeron 100	750[d]	550[d]	25[d]	C28[e]

[a]Mill-annealed condition.   [b]1 MPa = 145.03 psi.
[c]Cast material.   [d]Minimum.
Source : A. John Sedriks: Corrosion of stainless Steels IInd Edition Wiley-Interscience Publication John Wiley and Sons, Inc.

The austenitic 18–9 steels are widely used and are easy to form and weld, but suffer from an important weakness, viz., that they are sensitive to stress corrosion cracking (SCC) - a defect that imposes severe limitations on their use as materials in the process industries. Fig. 5 summarises the different types of corrosive attack on an 18–9 steel in Japanese process industries. It may be seen that SCC is the most frequent cause of failure. Ferritic stainless steels, on the other hand, are resistant to SCC and have higher yield strength, but they are difficult to form and weld. Also, their ductile-brittle transition temperature is high, giving a much greater risk of brittle fracture during service.

Edeleanu was one of the first to observe, in the early 1950s, the beneficial effect on stress corrosion resistance through the introduction of ferrite into austenitic stainless steels (Kiessling, 1984). However, no significant development occurred for many years subsequently. It was only recently that interest has been revived. On the one hand, this activity has been spurred by the requirement of materials with high resistance to SCC; on the other, it

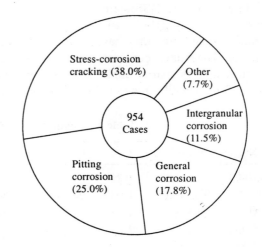

Fig. 5   **Types of corrosion attack on AISI 304 (18Cr-9Ni) steels in Japanese process industries (Kiessling, 1984)**

has been facilitated by developments in process metallurgy that have made it possible to produce extra low-carbon steels economically.

The principal merit of introducing ferrite into austenitic steel is to reduce susceptibility to SCC: the threshold stress level for SCC is increased drastically. In addition, the ferrite component raises the yield strength over that of the unmodified austenitic steels (Fig. 6). At the same time the austenite component lowers the ductile-brittle transition temperature compared with the ferritic steels (Fig. 7).

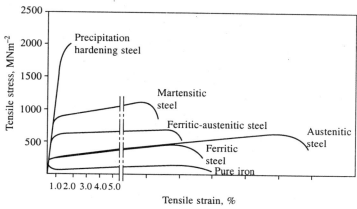

Fig. 6   Tensile behaviour of various stainless steels and pure iron (Kiessling 1984)

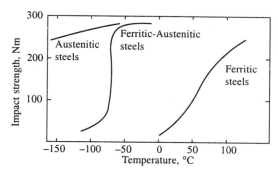

Fig. 7   Variation of Charpy impact strength of various stainless steels with temperature

The control of the relative ferrite and austenite fractions is most easily understood from the Schaeffler diagram, shown in Fig. 8. It is clear that, in order to produce compositions corresponding to nearly equal proportions of ferrite and austenite, the Ni equivalent must be less and the Cr equivalent more than in fully austenitic stainless steel. Thus duplex stainless steels typically have chromium greater than 18% and nickel less than 7%. They also contain Mo and, optionally, small amounts of Cu or W as well as 0.1 – 0.2% N. The carbon content has to be kept low, below about 0.04%, in order to discourage some undesirable precipitation reactions, which will be described later. Compositions of a few typical commercial duplex stainless steels are given in Table 4. Some of these compositions are also located in Fig. 8.

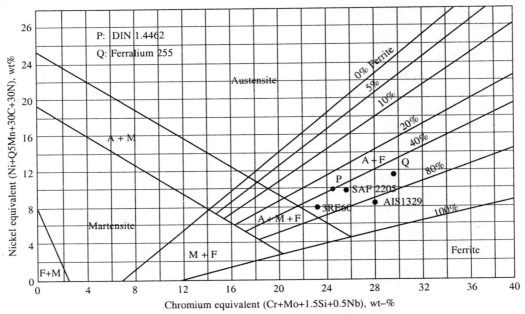

Fig. 8   Modified Schaeffler diagram for duplex stainless steels

The ferrite/austenite balance has a critical influence on the properties of DSS. With increasing austenite both strength and SCC resistance are reduced; while increase in ferrite reduces fracture toughness and is detrimental to corrosion resistance due to increased susceptibility to hydrogen-assisted cracking and pitting. In order to further improve the pitting resistance, superduplex stainless steels with still higher Cr and Mo contents have been developed. However, in order to restrict the ferrite level for ensuring low-temperature toughness, an increase in the austenite stabilisers such as Ni, N and Mn is also necessary.

WELDING OF DSS

Experience in the welding of duplex stainless steels over the past few years has shown that they possess adequate weldability, that a number of conventional welding processes can be used and that problems due to cracking are not more severe than in other types of stainless steels. However, the realisation of weldment properties matching those of the parent material causes more serious concern. This aspect is discussed in greater detail in the remaining part of this paper.

Structural Changes During Welding

It is to be expected that the mechanical, chemical and electrochemical properties of duplex stainless steel weldments will be strongly dependent on the ferrite/austenite ratio and other features of the microstructure. In order to consider these relationships in detail, it is necessary to understand the structural transformations that could occur as the steel is heated and cooled during welding. The iron-chromium-nickel ternary equilibrium diagram serves as a convenient point of departure. Fig. 9 shows a constant-iron section of this diagram drawn schematically to represent about 65% iron. Alloys with compositions in zone 1 will start solidification as austenite; they will be either fully austenitic or have a low residual ferrite content and will be prone to hot cracking during welding. Alloys with compositions in zones 2, 3 and 4 will begin to solidify as ferrite; on further cooling part of the ferrite transforms to austenite at temperatures below the ferrite solvus. In zone 2 about 20–30% of vermicular ferrite is retained at room temperature. In zone 3 about 50% of the ferrite can be retained, the morphology of which is more acicular. In the high chromium-equivalent zone 4 most of the ferrite will be retained (up to the range 80–100%). Duplex stainless steels have compositions predominantly in zone 3. It may be noticed that in these steels the structure is completely ferritic on completion of solidification. The transformaton sequence on cooling form the liquid state can be represented as follows:

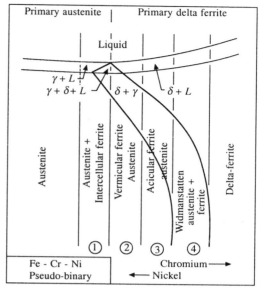

Fig. 9 Schematic constant iron section at 65% iron of the Fe-Cr-Ni ternary diagram, showing variation of solidification mode and ferrite morphology with composition

$$L \rightarrow L + \delta \rightarrow \delta \rightarrow \delta + \gamma$$

The duplex stainless steels are preferably welded after solution treatment in the range 1000–1100°C, the temperature and time being decided by steel composition and section size, respectively. It may be seen from Fig. 9 that this heat treatment would result in nearly equal proportions of austenite and ferrite in a typical duplex stainless steel.

During welding, in the heat-affected zone (HAZ) austenite is transformed to ferrite on heating whenever the ferrite solvus temperature is exceeded. One consequence of the austenite dissolution is the growth of ferrite grains. Coarse-grained regions are commonly noticed adjacent to the fusion line, The phenomenon is, of course, similar to that encountered in ferritic stainless steels. During cooling the austenite forms again along the prior ferrite grain boundaries and at intragranular sites. The extent of reversion to austenite is a function of composition, temperature and time. A high density of dark-etching precipitates also characterizes the HAZ microstructure (Baeslack, 1988). Like the austenite these precipitates form along the ferrite boundaries or within the ferrite grains. Regions surrounding either grain boundary or intragranular austenite are free from precipitation. The precipitates include carbides, carbonitrides, nitrides, alpha prime and other hardening phases such as the intermetallics sigma, chi and eta (Kiessling, 1984). The precipitate-free zone is believed to occur because the austenite acts as a sink for the fast-diffusing interstitial elements carbon and nitrogen, thus inhibiting precipitation in the vicinity of the austenite crystal. The formation of the precipitates is time-dependent and follows the usual C-type reaction rate curve (Fig. 10).

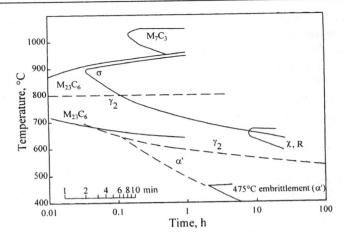

Fig. 10 **Time-temperature-diagram for intermetallic and other phases in duplex stainless steel (after H.D. Solomon and T.M. Devine, Jn., ASTM STP-672, 1979, p. 430–461)**

During multi-pass welding the HAZ experiences additional thermal cycles. Dissolution as well as precipitation may occur depending on temperature and time, but the net effects usually are an increase in the austenite fraction and growth of precipitate phases (Stephenson, 1987).

In the weld metal, solidification occurs as ferrite and the solidification pattern, as in other weld metals, tends to be columnar and epitaxial through multi-run weld deposits. On further cooling, the ferrite transforms partially to austenite which forms continuous networks at the prior-ferrite grain boundaries. The austenite forms also, particularly when its percentage is high, as Widmanstatten side-plates nucleating from the grain boundary austenite and growing along specific crystallographic orientations in the ferrite matrix (Southwick and Honeycombe 1980). Precipitation reactions and structural changes during multi-pass welding are similar to those in the HAZ.

High weld heat inputs and high preheat and interpass temperatures promote coarse-grained weld deposits and heat-affected zones, extend the width of the HAZ and encourage precipitation. These structural changes may affect adversely the properties of the weldment. On the other hand, low heat inputs lead to rapid cooling that restricts grain growth and precipitation effects; however, the fast cooling suppresses the delta-gamma transformation and the consequent reduction in austenite content may also be undesirable in many respects.

Ferrite-Austenite Balance

As in the unwelded duplex stainless steel, the ferrite/austenite ratio in the weld metal and the heat-affected zone is an important parameter. However, control of the ferrite/austenite balance in DSS welds is not as straightforward as in the base metal. It is evident that it is a function of composition, peak temperature and the cooling rate. In the HAZ, on the other hand, the cooling rate is the primary factor. As a consequence, the ferrite/austenite balance in the weld metal and HAZ can vary considerably from that of the base metal. This variation often compromises the performance of welded duplex stainless steels under service conditions (Baeslack 1988).

It is to be expected that the transformation of ferrite to austenite on cooling will be retarded under high cooling rates. Fig. 11 shows a typical CCT diagram for this reaction. It has been reported that, in extreme cases, resistance, electron beam and laser welds may virtually be fully ferritic and, as welded, will display poor toughness and corrosion resistance (Stephenson, 1987).

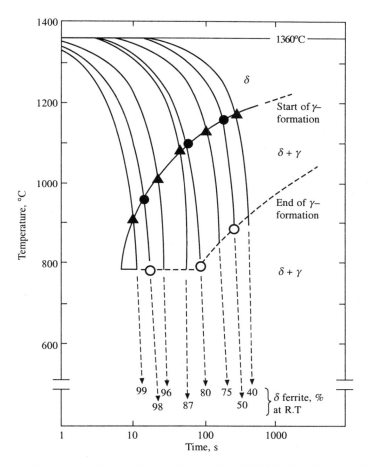

Fig. 11   CCT diagram for cast-duplex stainless steel containing 0.02%C, 23% Cr and 7.6% Ni (Stephenson, 1987)

Depending on the composition of the steel and section size, it is usual to restrict the preheat and interpass temperatures and to control weld heat input. Often, multipass welds are made to encourage austenite formation in the earlier passes and in their heat-affected zones and to restrict the degree of grain coarsening. Nevertheless, the required properties generally cannot be obtained from the weld metals having compositions strictly matching those of the parent material. Therefore, nickel-enhanced welding consumables have been developed to ensure adequate austenite contents and to compensate for adverse effects of grain coarsening and precipitation. The weld metals may thus contain 6–10% Ni, the composition being otherwise similar to that of the base metal. The use of nitrogen in addition to nickel to increase reversion to austenite in the weld metal has also been reported (Bonnefois et al., 1986). The nitrogen may be introduced either through the weld metal or through the shielding gas.

It is pertinent at this stage to mention that the ferrite content in duplex stainless steels is usually expressed in terms of an extended ferrite number (EFN). This new system is necessary because in the conventional WRC ferrite number system the calibration range ends at 28 FN. It has been shown that the familiar WRC system can be extended to cover DSS weld metals by the addition of counterweights to a MagneGage and extrapolation of the calibration line (Kotecki, 1982). This EFN system was shown to provide good laboratory-to-laboratory reproducibility on duplex stainless steel weld metals. A normalized ferrite number (NFN) has also been proposed by devising a correcting factor into the EFN. The correcting factor is obtained using the EFN of a fully ferritic sample of the same iron content. Good agreement has been reported between the NFN and volume percent ferrite determined by metallographic means.

It has been shown that variation in weld metal ferrite content may occur depending upon the relative proportion of ferrite-stabilizing and austenite-stabilizing elements in the steel (Baeslack, 1988). At compositions near the left-hand limit of the composition range for DSS shown in Fig. 8, the ferrite-to-austenite transformation starts at temperatures only slightly below the solidification range where diffusion is relatively rapid. As a result the transformation to austenite occurs readily and the resultant microstructure contains a large fraction of austenite. As the chromium equivalent in the steel increases at the expense of the nickel equivalent, the transformation begins at lower temperatures and is limited by the rate of diffusion. This effect is of course, in addition to the fact that the equilibrium amount of ferrite increases on moving from left to right in the diagram.

In the as-welded multi-run welds made with increased Ni, the ferrite contents of the root runs and capping passes tend to be somewhat higher than in the body of the weld. This has been attributed to the greater dilution of the root run by the base metal and the lower extent of reversion to austenite in the capping passes. The ferrite content may increase by 10–20% in this manner. It has been suggested that this can be counteracted with controlled root gaps and nitrogen addition to the shielding gas. The possible use of shaped consumable root inserts has also been mentioned.

As a further step in the continuing development in this field, DSS of improved weldability have been designed, in which reversion to austenite is promoted through nitrogen addition and precipitation of carbide and alpha prime is inhibited through decrease of carbon and control of chromium contents (Stephenson, 1987).

The effect of weld metal ferrite content on the mechanical properties of duplex weld deposits has been investigated by Kotecki (1986) using flux-cored open arc electrodes of varying composition so that a rnge of ferrite contents could be studied. It was found that the tensile and yield strengths are scarcely affected by EFN variation from as low as 32 to as high as 117. These two properties are similar to those of the base metal as long as the ferrite content exceeds 30 EFN. However, the ductility and notch toughness are markedly affected by the EFN of the deposit. A ferrite content of less than 60 EFN is apparently necessary for ensuring sufficient ductility and toughness. Regarding composition an increase in the electrode nickel content promotes austenite formation and improves the mechanical properties, more nickel being required if the DSS has higher chromium equivalent. Titanium has a very potent effect in retaining the ferrite, presumably through nitride formation, which removes the austenitizing effect of nitrogen in solution. Molybdenum enrichment as an approach to enhancing weld metal corrosion resistance raises the distinct possibility of embrittlement, even at low ferrite levels.

Welding Consumables

The development of welding consumables has kept pace with that of the parent duplex stainless steels. Consumables are available now which can meet the increasingly onerous requirements of the offshore and land-based oil and petrochemical industries. These weld metals are designed to have adequately low carbon levels, optimum Cr-Ni ratios, controlled nitrogen additions and reduced oxygen potential owing to improved deoxidation practices. These features combine to give excellent properties including toughness at temperatures down to −50°C (Marshall and Farrar, 1986). Although the emphasis has been on manual arc welding electrodes, there have been developments in the area of welding consumables for mechanised and automatic welding as well.

Welding Processes

Duplex stainless steels can be welded using most welding processes that are applicable to conventional stainless steels. Manual metal arc welding and gas tungsten-arc welding are widely employed. However, it has been mentioned that the flux-shielded processes deposit weld metals that can contain oxide and slag particles that reduce toughness and also probably impair corrosion resistance. While the toughness could be improved by selection of basic rather than acidic fluxes, the use of basic flux-coated electrodes may pose problems concerned with operability and slag detachment in some instances (Stephenson, 1987). Gas tungsten-arc welding is often used for root pass welds in combination with a non-oxidising backing gas in order to prevent local corrosion, in particular crevice corrosion, which can be a result of slag formation and oxidation (Rademakers and Stephens, 1986).

The coefficient of thermal expansion and thermal conductivity of DSS lie between those of the ferritic and austenitic stainless steels. The fusion and penetration characteristics of DSS are in general comparable with those of the austenitic steels and conventional techniques of joint preparation, cleaning, fit-up and welding are applicable to DSS also (Blumfield et al, 1981)

Post-Weld Heat Treatment

If appropriate filler metals and welding procedures are used, the properties of as-welded joints are usually adequate for most purposes. Nevertheless, for thick-section heavy-restraint joints and those likely to encounter severally corrosive environments in service, a post-weld heat treatment may be necessary. Ideally, from a metallurgical viewpoint, a solution heat treatment in the usual range of 1000–1100°C followed by quenching may be employed to ensure, among other things, satisfactory ferrite/austenite balance in the weldment. However, such a treatment is impracticable for large structures, site welds and offshore constructions. For improving stress corrosion resistance and for dimensional stability, a stress relieving heat treatment may be appropriate. It must be remembered, however, that the DSS are susceptible to the 475°C embrittlement (precipitation of alpha prime) and if heated in the temperature range 700–900°C may also be embrittled by formation of the sigma phase. Thus a heat treatment at 600°C or slightly less than 600°C followed by rapid cooling through the 475°C embrittlement range may be satisfactory. Nevertheless, usual DSS welding practice does not include postweld heat treatment.

Hot Cracking

Weld solidification cracking does not appear to be a serious problem with DSS in actual welding practice but a few instances of hot cracking have been reported (Blumfield et al, 1981). In general, the DSS have been found to be more sensitive to cracking than austenitic stainless steel welds which solidify as ferrite and exhibit a microstructure with 5–10 FN, but less susceptible than alloys with fully austenitic microstructures (Baeslack, 1988).

It was postulated by Hull (1967) more than 20 years ago that grain boundary wetting by liquid films occurs more readily along like-phase boundaries than along ferrite-austenite boundaries; cracking tendency is thus reduced along interphase interfaces. According to Suutala et al (1979), the cracking susceptibility of a stainless steel could be correlated with the ratio of Cr- to Ni- equivalents. When this ratio is low, primary solidification is as austenite and hot cracking occurs extensively. Above a critical value of the ratio, primary crystallization occurs as ferrite and cracking tendency is reduced. When the Cr_{eq}/Ni_{eq} ratio increases further to a range where the weld metal ferrite content exceeds 30%, the cracking propensity increases once more. It has been argued that, with ferrite less than 30%, some austenite forms between the primary ferrite dendrites and this inhibits interdendritic wetting; cracking susceptibility is reduced as proposed by Hull. Where welds contain more than 30% ferrite, as in DSS, primary freezing is entirely ferritic and interdendritic liquid films can more easily wet the ferrite-ferrite boundaries.

Nelson, Baeslack and Lippold (1987) have quantitatively investigated weld hot cracking in a number of DSS using the Varestraint test. Their results substantiated the above arguments. It was further observed that elements such as Cu and P have a tendency to segregate to the ferrite grain boundaries in commercial DSS welds and cause hot cracking; the cracking was much reduced in experimental DSS alloys where these elements were absent.

Corrosion Resistance

The corrosion behaviour of DSS is influenced by the ferrite/austenite ratio, the distribution of alloying elements in the two phases and other microstructural features such as precipitate phases, elemental segregation, etc. When the ferrite content of DSS is less than about 35%, its SCC resistance will be less than optimum. Ferrite contents in excess of about 60% are detrimental to cracking resistance due to reduced toughness and increased susceptibility to hydrogen-assisted cracking and pitting (Laing et al, 1986).

The superior SCC resistance of DSS has been confirmed by Madsen et al (1987) who performed long-and short-term tests on three DSS both in the welded and unwelded conditions. Based on the corrosion and mechanical properties they found the material and the joints acceptable for a major Alaskan offshore project.

Empirical formulae have been suggested for estimating the pitting resistance of DSS, e.g., pitting resistance equivalent PRE = (%Cr) + 3.3 (%Mo) + 16(%N) (Clark et al, 1986). It is therefore clearly desirable to increase Cr, Mo and N contents. It has also been shown that Cu and

N can enhance the corrosion resistance of DSS with respect to temperature, pH and chloride content in acidic sulphate solutions (Simpson, 1986).

The effect of welding parameters on the pitting resistance of a DSS has been investigated by Sridhar et al (1984). A higher heat input was found to be beneficial on account of the lower cooling rate. This was not through increasing the volume fraction of austenite alone, but also through distributing the various alloying elements between the two phases. Corrosion of the weld metal was observed to occur preferentially in the ferrite along the austenite-ferrite boundaries. In conventional austenitic stainless steels, such as type 304, containing small percentages of ferrite, segregation of the ferritizing elements Cr and Mo occurs during solidification. Pitting corrosion of weldments in these austenitic stainless steels has been shown to occur in the Cr- and Mo-depleted austenite phase. In contrast, solidification in the DSS welds occurs completely as ferrite, which later undergoes a solid-state transformation to austenite. Since the diffusion of Cr and Mo is much faster in the ferrite than in the austenite, no significant segregation results and the ferrite phase remains enriched in Cr and Mo. The preferential localised corrosion in the ferrite thus cannot be explained on the basis of segregation.

It is generally believed that chromium nitride precipitates at the grain boundaries on cooling creating depletion regions adjacent to them. Such precipitation has been known to occur even on quenching from high temperatures. In fact the beneficial effect of slower cooling is to provide sufficient time for Cr to diffuse and heal the Cr-depletion zones surrounding the Cr nitride particles (Tamaki, 1986). By the same token, a higher heat input would be advantageous as the increased austenite content serves to dissolve a greater amount of nitrogen. It is interesting to note that chromium carbide precipitation does not lead to this kind of denudation because it is found to occur mainly on moving austenite-ferrite interphase boundaries (Stephenson, 1987).

The effect of heat input on corrosion performance has also been studied by Ume et al (1987) who established that the pitting resistance improves with increase of heat input and that the pitting itself was due to chromium nitride precipitation. However, it was noticed that excess heat input also led to degradation by causing precipitation farther away from the fusion line where the reduced ferrite content alters the time-temperature conditions appropriate to sensitization. An imporant result was that post-weld solution annealing very effectively improves corrosion resistance in the HAZ.

CONCLUSION

It is seen that the DSS offer many advantages over the traditional austenitic and ferritic stainless steels. They can be satisfactorily welded using conventional welding processes and near-matching filler materials. Their weldability mut be considered to be not inferior to that of the austenitic stainless steels.

The unique properties of the DSS have resulted in their use in a variety of industrial applications. Understanding and development of the steels has proceeded to an extent that a substantial increase in their utilization is envisaged, particularly in the oil and gas industry. The duplex stainless steels constitute a class of alloys from which it is possible to select the best compromise regarding mechanical and chemical properties. If these steels cannot quite replace the high-grade and high-cost Ni-base alloys, they can practically always be used instead of current austenitic stainless steels of similar cost but lower properties.

REFERENCES

1. Baeslack, W.A. and Lippold, J.C. (1988). Phase Transformation Behaviour in Duplex Stainless steel Weldments. Metal Const., 20(1), p.p. 26R–31R.
2. Blumfield, D. et al (1981). Welding Duplex Austenitic-ferritic Stainless Steel Metal Const,, 13(5), pp. 269–273.
3. Bonnefois, B. et al (1986). Control of the Ferrite Level in Duplex Stainless Steel Welds. Proc. Of the Intern. Conf. On 'Duplex Stainless Steel', The Hague, Oct. 1986.
4. Bul, F.C. (1967). Effect of Delta Ferrite on the Hot Cracking of Stainless Steel. Welding J., 46(9), pp. 339-s to 409-s.
5. Kiessling, R. (1984). Stainless Steels-Materials in competetion Metals Tech., 11(5), pp. 169–180.
6. Kotecki, D. (1982). Extension of the WRC Ferrite Number System Welding J., 61(11), pp. 352-s to 361-s.
7. Laing, B. et al (1986). Effec of Heat Input During Pulsed Gas Metal Arc Welding on Austenite. Ferrite Balance in Duplex Stainless Steel pipe Welds. Proc. Of the Intern. Conf. On 'Duplex Stainless Steel', The Hague, Oct. 1986.
8. Madsen, A.C. et al (1987). Duplex Stainless Steel pipelines and piping on the North Slope. Materials Performance, Feb. 1987, pp. 49–55.
9. Marshall, A.W. and Farrar J.C. (1986). The Development of Welding Consumables for Duplex Stainless Steels. Proc. Of the Intern. Conf. On 'Duplex Stainless Steel', The Hague, Oct. 1986.
10. Nelson, D.E. et al (1987). An Investigation of weld Hot Cracking in DSS. Welding J., 66(8) pp. 241-s to 250-s.
11. Rademakers, P.L.F. and Stephens, C.P. (1986). DSS—An introduction. Proce. Of the Intern. Conf. On 'Duplex Stainless Steel'. The Hague, Oct. 1986.
12. Simpson, H.P. (1986). Corrosion Behaviour of Duplex Steels in Sulphuric Acid containing Chloride. Ibid.
13. Sridhar, N. et al (1984). Effect of Welding Parameters on Localized Corrosion of a DSS. Materials Performance. Dec. 1984, pp. 52–55.
14. Stephenson, N. (1987). Welding status of Duplex Stainless Steels for offshore Applications-part I. Welding and Metal Fab., 55(4), pp. 159–164.
15. Southwick, P.D. and Honeycoombe, R.W.K. (1980). Decomposition of Ferrite to Austenite in 26 Cr-5 Ni Stainless Steel. Metal Science, 4(7) pp. 253–261.
16. Suutala, N. et al (1979). Single Phase Ferritic solidification Mode in Austenitic-Ferritic Stainless Steel Welds. Met. Trans., 10A(8), pp. 1183–1190.
17. Tamaki, K et al (1986). Metallurgical Characteristics of the Weld Metals and corrosion Performance of a Girth Weld Joint. Proc. Of the Intern. Conf. On 'Duplex Stainless Steels'. The Hague, Oct. 1986.
18. Ume, K. et al (1987). Influence of Thermal History on the Corrosion Resistance of Duplex Stainless Steel Linepipe. Materials performance, August 1987, pp. 25–31.

5. Weldability of Aluminium and Titanium Alloys

S. Sundaresan

Professor Emeritus, Department of Metallurgical Engineering
Indian Institute of Technology Madras, Chemai 600 036

WELDING OF ALUMINIUM AND ITS ALLOYS

Introduction

The most important properties that warrant the widespread use of aluminium and its alloys are their high electrical conductivity, high strength-to-weight ratio (especially in some heat-treated tempers), absence of a transition temperature and good corrosion resistance. They are therefore used for electrical purposes, for transportation by land, water and air, for cryogenic pressure vessels and storage tanks, for military bridges, armoured vehicles, missile and space craft tankage, etc.

For many decades only commercially pure aluminium was welded, with gas, arc and atomic hydrogen processes. After the introduction of gas-shielded welding, there has been a spurt in the welding of high-strength Al alloys. Indeed, one contributory cause for the increased use of aluminium and its alloys is the successful development of welding techniques for their fabrication.

Special characteristics of aluminium alloys

Whatever the process employed, the welding procedure has to take into account the special properties of Al-base materials. Some of the physical characteristics of aluminium are listed in Table 1.

Table 1   Physical properties of aluminium

Melting point	660°C
Density at 20°C	2.70 g/cc
Coefficient of thermal expansion in the range 0–100°C	23.5×10^{-6}/°C
Specific heat in the range 0–100°C	0.92 kJ/kg/°C
Thermal conductivity in the range 0–100°C	240 W/m/°C
Electrical resistivity	0.0269 Ω mm^2/m
Elastic modulus at 20°C	71,900 MPa

1. The high conductivity calls for a concentrated heat input in welding, though the melting temperature is low. Otherwise, the HAZ becomes wide and softening results in cold-worked and

age-hardened materials. The process with the fastest energy input is the best suited. The high conductivity, especially of pure Al, can lead to porosity on account of rapid cooling.

2. Coefficient of thermal expansion and liquid-to-solid shrinkage are higher than for steel: thus enhanced cracking tendency, stresses and distortion. To some extent this is counteracted by the shorter cooling range and smaller elastic modulus.

3. The almost impervious oxide skin (which confers, incidentally, the corrosion resistance) has a high melting point (2050°C compared to 660°C for the metal). In the presence of the oxide layer, the individual droplets of filler metal get covered with an oxide film which interferes with satisfactory mixing during welding. The oxide therefore must be removed and prevented from reforming. Apart from careful mechanical or chemical cleaning of the edges before welding, flux (usually made up of halides of alkali and alkali earth metals) is needed in gas welding and open-arc welding, as also a reducing flame in the former and DC with electrode positive polarity in the latter. One of the greatest drawbacks in these processes is that the flux must be removed scrupulously after welding, otherwise it might absorb moisture and lead to corrosion problems later on. In fact, it is the absence of flux that spurred the development of the inert gas techniques, first for aluminium alloys and later for other materials.

The high hardness of the oxide in relation to that of the metal has been exploited in the pressure (especially cold pressure) welding processes. The high electrical and thermal conductivity of aluminium, however, makes resistance welding difficult but not impracticable. Machines designed for steel are in general not applicable to aluminium since higher currents, shorter time periods and finely-adjustable electrode force (because the softening temperature range is narrow) are necessary. Usually only up to 3 mm sheet is satisfactorily welded using up to 60,000 A current, 10 cycles welding time, 300 kg electrode force.

Types of aluminium alloys

There are basically two kinds of Al alloys: age-hardenable and non-heat-treatable. The latter usually derive their strength from cold working: half-hard, hard, etc.). The important materials in this group are:

Commercially pure Al (greater than 98%);
Al with 1% Mn;
Al with 1,2,3 and 5% Mg;
Al with 2% Mg and 1% Mn;
Al with 4.5% Mg and 1% Mn.

The strengths range from 40 to 240 MPa (soft) and 100 to 320 MPa (hard). The cast alloys contain Si, Mg or both. Al-Mg alloys are often used for welded construction.
Elements like Cu, Mg, Zn and Li confer the tendency to age-harden after suitable heat-treatment: solutionizing, quenching and aging. The important alloys in this group are:

Al-Cu-Mg type with 2.5 to 4.3% Cu, 0.5 to 1.5% Mg;
Al-Mg-Si type with 0.7 to 1.0% Mg, 0.5 to 1.1% Si;
Al-Zn-Mg type with 4.0 to 7.4% Zn, 1.2 to 3.0% Mg;
Al Cu-Mg-Li type with for example 3% Cu, 2% Li, 1% Mg, 0.2% Zr.

The age-hardenable alloys can be heat-treated to strengths ranging from 250 to 550 MPa. The

Al -Zn-Mg alloys are the most easily welded, but must then be free of copper. Another element that drastically reduces weldability is lead. The lithium-containing alloys are more recent and have been developed as a result of efforts to produce high-strength, high-modulus, low-density materials for aircraft and other applications.

Tables 1 and 2 list the compositions and mechanical properties of selected aluminium alloys, both heat-treatable and non-heat-treatable.

Table 1   Chemical composition limits for some aluminum alloys

Alloy	Si	Fe	Cu	Mn	Mg	Cr	Ni	Zi	Ti	Each	Total	Aluminum
1100	.095	Si + Fe	0.05–0.20	0.05	..	..	..	0.10	..	0.05	0.15	99.00
2011	0.40	0.7	5.0–6.0	..	..	..	..	0.30	..	0.05	0.15	Remainder
2024	0.50	0.50	3.8–4.9	0.30–0.9	1.2–1.8	0.10	..	0.25	0.15	0.05	0.15	Remainder
3003	0.6	0.7	0.05–0.20	1.0–1.5	..	..	..	0.10	..	0.05	0.15	Remainder
5005	0.30	0.7	0.20	0.20	0.50–1.1	0.10	..	0.25	..	0.05	0.15	Remainder
5052	0.25	0.40	0.10	0.10	2.2–2.8	0.15–0.35	..	0.10	..	0.05	0.15	Remainder
5083	0.40	0.40	0.10	0.40–1.0	4.0–4.9	0.05–0.25	..	0.25	0.15	0.05	0.15	Remainder
5086	0.40	0.50	0.10	0.20–0.7	3.5–4.5	0.05–0.25	..	0.25	0.15	0.05	0.15	Remainder
6061	0.40–0.8	0.7	0.15–0.40	0.15	0.8–1.2	0.04–0.35	..	0.25	0.15	0.05	0.15	Remainder
6063	0.20–0.6	0.35	0.10	0.10	0.45–0.9	0.10	..	0.10	0.10	0.05	0.15	Remainder
7075	0.40	0.50	1.2–2.0	0.30	2.1–2.9	0.18–0.28	..	5.1–6.1	0.20	0.05	0.15	Remainder

Composition (in percent) by weight maximum unless shown as a range or a minimum.
Source: www.luskmetals.com

Table 2   Mechanical properties of selected aluminum alloys.

Alloy	Temper	Proof Stress 0.2% (MPa)	Tensile strength (MPa)	Shear strength (MPa)	Elongation A5(%)	Hardness vickers (HV)
AA1050A	H16	120	130	80	7	–
AA4015	H14	135	160–200	–	3	–
AA5083	H32	240	330	185	17	95
	0/H111	145	300	175	23	75
AA6063	0	50	100	70	27	85
	T4	90	160	11	21	50
	T6	210	245	150	14	80
AA7075	0	105–145	225–275	150	9	65
	T6	435–505	510–570	350	5	160

Source: www.azom.com

Welding processes

Through gas welding and manual metal-arc welding have been used, these have been largely superseded by the gas-shielded techniques. The former is capable of handling only small parts and its use today is restricted to these and the repair welding of castings. SMA welding is occasionally still preferred for open-air welding, but it is rarely applied for critical joints

Inert gas-shielded welding is the most widely employed process for aluminium alloys, gas tungsten-arc welding for thin sheet and gas metal-arc welding for thicker sections. In both, argon of at least 99.95% purity is used for shielding; argon is heavier (hence less gas needed) and cheaper than helium. For special purposes, argon-helium mixtures are used.

Gas tungsten-arc welding

Since aluminium gets oxidised rapidly, there must be provision for removing the oxide film formed between pre-weld cleaning and welding. This is conveniently ensured by keeping the workpiece negative, when electron emission and ion bombardment will break up the oxide layer. However, with the positive pole on the electrode, it gets overheated, requiring large electrode diameters and decreasing arc efficiency. As a compromise, the usual practice is to use AC polarity.

A secondary difficulty with AC is the problem of "inherent rectification" due to the imbalance caused by differences in electron emission from the tungsten and the aluminium. This results in a decrease in cleaning action and hence a rise in argon consumption by about 20%. Compensation must therefore be provided through suitable circuitry: common is to use a bank of capacitors in series, the unit being called a DC suppressor. A battery would also serve the same purpose, but is not usually employed. The arc is started by using a high-voltage impulse generator operating at high frequency. For sustaining a stable arc during welding, the HF unit is left on throughout the operation, unlike in DC welding.

Possible defects are tungsten inclusions (avoided by careful practice, reduction in current density), incomplete fusion (use higher current, reduce speed); porosity (raise current, reduce speed, increase argon flow rate, use better prior cleaning practice) and instability of arc (purify electrode tip, increase current density, raise HF current).

Welding speeds can be increased, HAZ narrowed and bead appearance improved by automatic welding, which is especially useful for welding long, straight seams. Feeding of filler wire. where required, is mechanized, but the wire carries no current. Preheating is generally necessary only when the thickness exceeds 10 mm, a situation where GTA welding itself is usually regarded commercially unattractive. Recommended welding conditions are indicated in Table 3.

Table 3   Manual and automatic GTA welding of Al alloys

Sheet thickness (mm)	Current (A)		Speed (m/min)		Argon flow (1/min)	
	Manual	Automatic	Manual	Automatic	Manual	Automatic
1.5	70	130	0.32	1.5	7	9
2.0	80	325	0.30	1.5	7	9
3.0	140	460	0.29	0.4	8	11
6.0	280	–	0.25	–	10	–
10.0	360	–	0.13	–	14	–

Gas metal-arc welding

The efficiency of heat utilisation is much greater than in GTA welding, heat concentration is hence more effective. Welding speeds are higher, penetration deeper, HAZ narrower and distortion less. Thicker material (borderline around 6-7mm) is hence more conveniently handled by GMA welding. Even for thinner sheet, GMA welding offers some advantages: easy metal transfer, absence of separate filler, easier out-of-position welding. With thickness greater than 25 mm. argon-helium mixtures perform better.

The polarity is always DCEP, since quick electrode melting and work cleaning are both achieved throughout. Spray transfer is the preferred mechanism and calls for enhanced current densities. A problem arises for thin sections where the current must be low. This requires the use of small-diameter electrode wires. In fully-automatic welding such wires present no difficulty, but in semiautomatic welding it is troublesome to push thin wire of soft aluminium through long distances without kinking or snarling. Solutions like increasing the electrode stick-out have been suggested, but eventually, one has to think in terms of employing other transfer types such as dip transfer and pulsed transfer.

GMA welds generally exhibit very fine porosity: caused by hydrogen or moisture absorbed on the wire surface, unclean plate edges, insufficient argon flow rate, etc. Apart from improving the cleaning practice, one could also encourage slower cooling by adjusting welding conditions. Semi-automatic GMA welding is widely used, but fully-automatic GMA welding with a voltage-controlled arc is popular for joining thick-walled tubes and all flat-position jobs.

Other Processes

Electron beam welding

The most significant advantage is the narrow and deep penetration resulting in a high depth/width ratio for the weld. The intense concentration of heat is attractive in many ways as it limits the extent of metallurgical reactions and reduces residual stresses and distortion. The vacuum takes care of contamination, which is useful for reactive metals like aluminium.

In the case of non-heat-treatable Al alloys, the restriction of the softened HAZ leads to a higher yield strength for the joint. In heat-treated materials, the strengths are higher due to accelerated cooling; also the weld and HAZ respond better to natural or artificial aging and one may often dispense with solution treatment. Crack-sensitive Al alloys present problems, especially in heavily restrained or thick sections, since the more crack-resistant high-Si or high-Mg filler materials cannot be added in conventional electron beam welding. In thin sheet material in such alloys cracking is much less likely.

Plasma arc welding poses problems because any polarity other than DCEN is difficult and arc cleaning does not occur under DCEN operation. Laser welding entails a different kind of drawback: the reflectivity of aluminium and its thermal diffusivity militate against the build-up of the required heat concentration.

Pressure welding

Aluminium alloys are perhaps the most amenable to pressure welding, in view of the softness of the metal and the hardness/brittleness of the oxide. Some applications have been reported in the electrical industry for connections in foil and wire and joints between Al and Cu. Pre-weld cleaning, e.g., by wire brushing after degreasing, is essential for producing sound and strong joints.

Some variants of the basic pressure welding process offer much scope for greater usage: explosive, friction and ultrasonic welding. These are particularly useful for dissimilar welds involving aluminium, because the rapidity of the thermal cycle reduces the extent of formation of brittle intermetallic compounds.

Welding of heat-treatable aluminium alloys

The development of high joint mechanical properties in precipitation-hardened materials depends upon obtaining suitable aging reactions in the weld metal and HAZ. With some heat-treatable materials, matching filler compositions tend to produce severe weld metal cracking; this is usually overcome with the use of non-heat-treatable fillers like Al-5% Si and Al-5% Mg. In such cases, the weld metal has a lower strength than the parent material. This cannot be rectified even when a full heat treatment (solutionizing followed by aging) is applied after welding, since the weld metal composition responds less to heat treatment. On the other hand, with Al-Zn-Mg alloys, weld metal compositions can be similar to that of the parent metal and hence hardening response is not much reduced. In addition, joint properties can be improved by a simple precipitation treatment (not full heat treatment) after welding.

The HAZ of a weld in a fully heat-treated material can be divided into three regions. Adjacent to the weld, the temperature exceeds the solvus temperature of the alloy and the material gets re-solution treated. On the other edge of the HAZ the maximum temperature reached only just exceeds the previous aging temperature if at all and structural and property changes are marginal. Between these two, the heat of welding usually causes overaging and softening. A simple post-weld artificial aging treatment further coarsens the precipitate and reduces strength.

While these reactions are common to other age-hardenable Al alloys, the behaviour is different with Al-Zn-Mg alloys. In the re-solutionised region next to the weld, some precipitation may occur during cooling after welding in a quench-sensitive material, in which case the tendency to harden during post-weld aging is reduced. It is sometimes argued that Al-Zn-Mg alloys are less quench-sensitive, so that they respond better to aging after welding. However, it is now known that weld cooling rates are faster than oil quenching so that, in the region adjacent to the weld, the behaviour will be the same in all aluminium alloys.

It is in the zone beyond, viz., 'overaging' region, that Al-Zn-Mg alloys are different and superior. The aging rates in these materials are so slow that overaging is not likely during the rapid weld thermal cycle. On the other hand, the Al-Zn-Mg alloys are susceptible to reversion where the precipitate re-dissolves on heating to a temperature higher than the previous aging temperature but lower than the re-solution temperature. The dissolution is due to thermodynamic instability on heating. A simple post-weld artificial aging treatment thus leads to precipitation and hardening.

Since the weld metal and the entire HAZ thus respond to aging after welding, the Al-Zn-Mg alloys are considered more easily weldable than the other types. Natural aging is also possible so that the welded joints regain their properties by being simply left to age as shown in Fig. 1. It is, however, more common to use artificial aging.

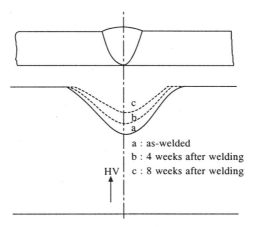

Fig. 1 **Effect of natural ageing on Al-Zn-Mg alloy welds (schematic)**

WELDING OF TITANIUM ALLOYS

Titanium and its alloys, in view of their high strength-to-weight ratio, creep strength, fracture toughness and ductility, are essential materials in the development of present and future aerospace systems. Their excellent corrosion and stress corrosion resistance make them attractive also for chemical and marine applications. In overall combination of these characteristics, the merits of titanium and its alloys vis-à-vis their competitors, viz., steels and aluminium alloys, are being increasingly recognised.

Properties of titanium

Titanium has a density of about 4.5 g/cc- between that of aluminium and steel-and is considered a light metal. It undergoes an allotropic transformation from cph (alpha) to bcc (beta) at 880°C on heating.

Commercially pure titanium usually contains as impurities Fe, C, N, O and H. Depending on the impurity content, it has a tensile strength varying from 300-700 MPa in the annealed condition. The addition of suitable alloying elements increases the strength to the range 800–1000 MPa without decreasing the ductility too much. Some of the alloys can be age-hardened to still higher strength levels in the vicinity of 1400-1500 MPa. One of the most attractive features of Ti alloys is thus their high strength-to-weight ratio. The coefficient of thermal expansion (8.5×10^{-6}/K) is somewhat lower than that of ferritic steels and much smaller than that of austenitic steels and aluminium alloys. This is of some advantage in welding, especially in complex assemblies, when distortion and internal stresses are minimized. The electrical and thermal conductivities of unalloyed Ti are about the same as those of 18-8 stainless steel, Ti alloys are more resistive. Titanium and its alloys can therefore be resistance welded easily. Titanium has excellent corrosion resistance in the unalloyed state. Alloying decreases it to some extent, but a small addition of palladium (0.15%) improves it in reducing environments.

Principal titanium alloys

Alloying elements stabilize either the alpha or the beta form of titanium, depending on whether they raise or lower the transformation temperature. The elements Al, O, N, C and B are alpha-stabilizers while Cr, Fe Mn, Mo, V and H stabilize the beta form. Titanium alloys are thus classified as alpha, near-alpha, alpha-beta and metastable beta alloys depending on the nature and level of alloying elements rolled.

Compositions and minimum strungth levels of important titanium alloys are listed in Tables 4 and 5, respectively. Since strength to wright ratio is most signficant to the utility of titanium alloys, a comparison is made in Table 6 of the normalized strength levels of titanium alloys vis-a-vis some high-strength steels.

Table 4   Titanium alloys classified by metallurgical structure

Alloy	Example
Alpha Alloys	Commercially Pure–ASTM grades 1,2,3, and 4
	Ti/Pd Alloys–ASTM grades 7 and 11
Alpha + Compound	Ti-2.5Cu–IMI 230
Near Alpha Alloys	Ti-8Al-1Mo-1V
	Ti-6Al-5Zr-0.5Mo-0.2Si–IMI 685
	Ti-6Al—2Sn-4Zr-2Mo-0.08Si
	Ti-5.5Al-3.5Sn-3Zr-1Nb-0.3Mo-0.3Si–IMI 829
	Ti-5.8Al-4Sn-3.5Zr-0.7NB-0.5Mo-0.3Si–IMI 834
	Ti-6Al-3Sn-4Zr-0.5Mo-0.5Si–Ti 1100
Alpha-Beta Alloys	Ti-6Al-4V
	Ti-4Al-4Mo-2Sn-0.5Si
	Ti-4Al-4Mo-4Sn-0.5Si–IMI 551
	Ti-6Al-6V-2Sn
	Ti-6Al-2Sn-4Zr-6Mo
Metastable Beta Alloys	Ti-3Al-8V-6Cr-4Zr-4Mo–Beta C
	Ti-15Mo-3Nb-3Al-0.2Si–Timetal 21 S
	Ti-15V-3Cr-3Sn-3Al

Source: www.azom.com

Welding

The main difficulty is the high reactivity of titanium. Especially at elevated temperatures it reacts strongly with most elements like, oxygen, hydrogen, nitrogen, etc. Even if small amounts of impurity are picked up during welding the material is noticeably embrittled. Thus stringent protection from the atmosphere is called for.

Welding of Ti is especially successful in protected chambers and by using the electron beam process but these present difficulties in the case of larger components. In EBW there is the additional problem of porosity due to the narrowness of the bead and the rapid cooling. Resistance welding is also possible, favoured by the high electrical resistivity of titanium.

Most widely employed, however, are the processes using an inert gas shield, viz., GTA, GMA and plasma arc welding. Several precautions, as listed below, are required on account of the reactivity of titanium.

Table 5   Classification of titanium alloys by strength

Category	Min strength (MPa)	Composition
Low Strength	500	ASTM grades 1,2, 3,7 and 11
Moderate Strength	500–900	ASTM grades 4,5, and 9 Ti-2.5Cu Ti-8Al-1Mo-0.1V
Medium Strength	900–1000	Ti-6Al-2Sn-4Zr-2Mo Ti-5.5Al-3.5Sn-3Zr-1Nb-0.3Mo-0.3Si
High Strength	1000–1200	Ti-3Al-8V-6Cr-4Zr-4Mo Ti-4 Al-4Mo-2Sn-0.5Si Ti-6Al-6V-2.5Sn Ti-15V-3Cr-3Sn-3Al Ti-5Al-2Sn-4Mo-2Zr-4Cr Ti-6Al-5Zr-0.5Mo-0.2Si Ti-6Al-2Sn-4Zr-6Mo Ti-11Sn-5Zr-2.5Al-1Mo Ti-5.8Al-4Sn-3.5Zr-0.7Nb-0.5Mo-0.3Si
Very High Strength	1200	Ti-10V-2Fe-3Al Ti-4Al-4Mo-4Sn-0.5Si

Source: www.azom.com

Table 6   Strength of some titanium alloys at room temperature, normalised by density, compared with other structural metals.

Material		Yield str/density ($\times 10^6$N.m.kg^{-1})	Tensile Str/density ($\times 10^6$N.m.kg^{-1})	10^7 Cycle fatigue Str/Density ($\times 10^6$N.m.kg^{-1})
Commercially Pure	ASTM Grade 2	78	107	54
Ti-6Al-4V	ASTM Grade 5	206	226	135
Ti-6Al-2Sn-4Zr-2Mo		202	223	123
Ti-4Al-4Mo-2Sn-0.5Si	IMI 550	225	247	136
Ti-10V-2Fe-3Al		264	282	155
Maraging Steel		170	202	121
FV 520 B Steel	153	165	105	
13 Cr Stainless Steel		95	105	68
18/8 Stainless Steel		68	75	40

Source: www.azom.com

(a) During edge preparation, attention must be paid to the scrupulous removal of all foreign matter like oil, grease, grinding debris, oxide or other compounds, etc. Degreasing with acetone and pickling in a solution containing HCl and HNO$_3$ is usually recommended. Filler rods must also be so cleaned and must be handled only with a pair of clean gloves. It will be good practice to remove the oxidised end of the wire prior to welding.

(b) The purity of the argon (or helium if it is used) must be at least 99.95%. The gas should also be dry to avoid porosity and embrittlement.

(c) If protected chamber welding is not possible, effective protection can be obtained by providing argon not only with the welding torch but also on the trailing side through a separate feed-tube and nozzle attached to the torch. Argon is also supplied on the underside through a longitudinal groove in a copper backing plate. Argon shielding must be provided till the HAZ has cooled to below about 300°C.

(d) It is generally advisable to use a wider nozzle and get better coverage.

(e) It is not advisable to employ higher gas flow rates more than the recommended 3-5 1/min, as they may result in turbulence and air entrapment.

(f) The arc length must be held as short as possible.

(g) Wherever possible, filler addition must be avoided; job becomes simpler, one source of impurity is eliminated. When filler becomes necessary (for thickness exceeding 2.5 mm), the melting end of the wire must remain within the gas shield all the time. Machine feeding of the wire eliminates this difficulty.

Weldability

The weldability of titanium alloys is closely related to the type of alloy (alpha, alpha-beta or beta) under consideration. Unalloyed and alpha-Ti alloys are usually welded in the annealed condition and appear to present no particular difficulty.

During the last two decades considerable attention has been given to addressing the problems associated with the welding of advanced alpha-beta titanium alloys. These investigations have resulted in a better understanding of the microstructure-mechanical property relationships in such materials. In the as-welded condition the yield and ultimate tensile strengths typically exceed those of the annealed base materials. Unfortunately, however, those strengths are normally accompanied by low fusion zone ductilities, particularly with increasing amounts of beta-stabilizers. In the first instance it is possible to obtain the required mechanical properties by the use of post-weld heat treatments which control the decomposition and precipitation reactions responsible for the poor weld performance. Nevertheless attempts to develop heat treatments which restore ductility in such weldments have not always met with complete success.

The structural changes during welding are best illustrated by referring to the relevant portion of the phase diagram shown in Fig. 2. Prior to welding the base material consists of small equiaxed alpha grains within a beta matrix. During welding the weld metal and adjoining heat-affected zone are taken to temperatures beyond the beta transus. The cooling rates from these temperatures and the resulting microstructures depend upon the welding process and procedure. The extremely rapid cooling experienced in processes like laser and electron beam welding are likely to result in a fine, acicular, entirely màrtensitic microstructure. As cooling rates become reduced, as in automatic gas tungsten arc welding, and still further as in manual GTAW, there is an increasing amount of diffusion-controlled alpha precipitation at prior-beta grain boundaries. Some beta may also be retained as the weldment cools to room temperature. Thus the as-welded microstructure may consist of alpha, alpha-prime (martensite) and metastable beta phases.

These are explained in terms of the continuous cooling transformation diagram (CCT) for the

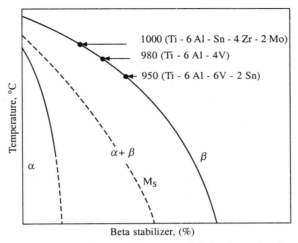

Fig. 2 **Schematic phase diagram of alpha-beta titanium alloys**

alloy in question. A schematic CCT diagram is shown in Fig. 3. Cooling at a rate faster than CR_1 converts the beta entirely to martensite, while with cooling slower than CR_2 the transformation occurs entirely by diffusional nucleation and growth. At rates between CR_1 and CR_2, the diffusional transformation is interrupted by the martensitic reaction. With increasing beta stabilisation the CCT curve is shifted to lower temperatures and longer time periods, with a corresponding decrease also in the M_s temperature. For the cooling rates normally associated with gas tungsten-arc weldments (20 to 80°C/s), the nose of the CCT curve is crossed for many alpha-beta titanium alloys. Thus some transformation to alpha should occur by nucleation and growth before the remaining beta transforms to martensite by shear or is retained. A cooling rate of 9°C/s has been quoted for Ti-6 Al-4V welds below which no alpha-prime is formed.

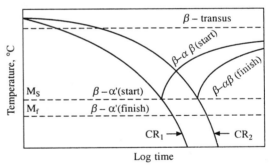

Fig. 3 **Typical continuous cooling transformation diagram for alpha-beta titanium alloys**

Post-weld heat treatment at sub-transus temperatures ages the martensite in the fusion and near HAZ regions by a mechanism that involves either a spinodal decomposition or a direct reversion to the beta phase. This reduces the concentration of the beta-stabilizing elements in the super-saturated martensite until its composition ultimately approaches that of equilibrium alpha. Precipitation of fine alpha in the retained metastable beta is another reaction occurring during ageing. Higher the heat treatment temperature, coarser will be the resulting microstructure.

Typically, the as-welded condition is characterised by high strength but low ductility. The latter is attributed to the coarse prior-beta grain size and the largely martensitic microstructures mentioned above. Efforts to improve the ductility through post-weld heat treatment have been the subject of numerous investigations. In general, such treatments are meant to increase the ductility at some sacrifice in strength levels. However, many studies have shown that high ageing temperatures of about 900°C or even higher are required if ductility is to be sensibly improved. In fact there is some evidence that lower-temperature heat treatment may even reduce ductility in some of the alloys. Apparently, overageing and structural coarsening occurring at the higher ageing temperatures are required for restoring to a certain degree fusion zone ductility. A high-temperature heat treatment under vacuum may also be beneficial by eliminating small amounts of contaminating elements such as hydrogen in the weld region.

It has been demonstrated many times that processes such as electron beam and laser welding that are characterised by rapid cooling would be advantageous on account of the small fusion zone grain size. Any such advantage, however, must be weighed against possible detrimental effects of rapid cooling on non-equilibrium transformation behaviour and the resulting microstructural characteristics. This would suggest that slow weld cooling rates may avoid brittle transformation products and thus may actually enhance ductility. Evidence for such an influence is also available and it has been shown in the case of Ti-6Al-6V-2Sn weldments that slower cooling rates promote the nucleation and growth of larger alpha plates; this enriches the beta phase with beta-stabilizers so that the M_s temperature is lowered and the beta tends to be retained at room temperature; such microstructures have better toughness.

Metastable beta-Ti alloys exhibit properties highly desirable in a formable sheet material Despite an elastic modulus slightly lower than that of the alpha-beta alloys, good fabricability in the solution heat-treated condition and an excellent ageing response to high strength levels render these alloys ideal candidates for a variety of aerospace structural applications.

The fusion and near-HAZ in metastable beta alloys are characterised by a ductile, low-strength retained beta structure. The weldments contain large columnar grains in the fusion zone and smaller nearly equiaxed grains in the HAZ. As might be expected, the rapid cooling rates associated with welding and the high proportion of beta-stabilizing elements (such as Mo, V, Cr. Fe) combine to promote the retention of beta in those regions in the joint which were taken above the beta-transus temperature during welding. Post-weld heat treatment promotes both heterogeneous and homogeneous alpha precipitation in all regions of the weldments. Increased ageing temperatures render the alpha coarser.

As-welded, the material has low yield and tensile strengths and high ductility compared to solution heat treated base material. Ageing of the weldments significantly increases strength and corresponsingly decreases ductility. In general, higher ageing temperatures result in decreased yield strength and increased ductility as well as a trend from transgranular to intergranular fracture.

Hot Cracking

Titanium alloys are relatively less susceptible than other materials to hot cracking, on account of the generally narrow freezing range, especially in dilute alloys. They, however, exhibit a loss of ductility at elevated temperatures, which is manifested by cracking as the beta phase is cooled through the transformation range. This is attributed to features associated with the beta-to-alpha transformation. For example, it is found that more rapid cooling lowers the temperature of cracking.

Of the many forms of alpha phase that could nucleate, the lamellar side-plate alpha is believed to be harmful and basketweave alpha beneficial. Faster cooling is known to promote the latter and has been found to reduce cracking tendency. Similarly, for a given cooling rate, an increase in beta stabilizer content lowers crack susceptibility. The cracking is intergranular and follows prior-beta grain boundaries. Some compositions are particularly susceptible, e.g., Ti-6Al-2Nb-1Ta-0.8 Mo, an alloy developed for marine applications Niobium is often believed to enhance crack sensitivity.

6. Weldability of Nickel and Copper Base Alloys

B.G. Muralidharan

L&T Powai Works, Mumbai 400 072

WELDABILITY OF NICKEL-BASE ALLOYS

Nickel-base alloys are often utilized at a higher proportion of their melting temperature than any other group of engineering materials, on account of their excellent creep, fatigue and oxidation resistance. Though these alloys were primarily intended to meet the demands of aerospace engineering, where the need for such attributes is the most acute, they are also extensively used in the fields of food processing, petrochemical processing, thermal processing, power generation including nuclear reactor systems and marine engineering. As all these applications involve welding as a fabrication step, it is important to achieve good-quality welded joints that can perform as well, when subjected to similar strenuous service and environmental conditions, as the base metal.

This paper reviews the weldability of some wrought nickel and nickel-base alloys, which are grouped, as under:

1. Nickel 200 (99.5% Ni)
2. Monel 400 (Ni-Cu)
3. Solid-solution strengthened alloys

   (a) Inconels®, 600 and 625 (Ni-Cr-Fe)
   (b) Hastelloys® (Ni-Cr-Mo)

4. Precipitation-hardenable alloys

   (a) Waspaloy® and Udimet® (Ni-Cr-Co)
   (b) Inconels, 718 and X-750 and Custom Age 625 Plus® (Ni-Cr-Fe-Nb)

The nominal compositions of these alloys are provided in Table 1. These alloys have been picked up as suggestive examples and this grouping is not comprehensive. Fe-base alloys such as Incoloy 800 and Incoloy 900 are not in the scope of this paper though they contain about 35% Ni. Besides, the discussions are limited to arc welding processes only as the priority of this paper is to provide an understanding of the various factors which influence the weldability of these alloys.

The major persistent problem encountered during the welding of Ni-base alloys, particularly those that are precipitation-hardenable, is hot cracking. Both the weld metal and the HAZ are susceptible to such type of cracking under conditions of moderate constraint. The cracking is not only attributed to tramp elements, as in the case of fully austenitic stainless steels, but also to some crucial alloying elements which often directly conflict with weldability requirements. Thus, for several critical applications

Table 1   Nominal compositions of some commercial nickel alloys

	Nickel 200	Monel 400	Inconel 600	Inconel 625	Hastelloy C-4	Hastelloy C-22	Hastelloy C-276	Udimet 500	Waspaloy	Inconel X-750	Inconel 718	Custom age 625 plus
Ni	99.5	66.5	76	61	67	57	55	54	58	73	52.5	61
C	0.08	0.15	0.08	0.05	0.01	0.01	0.01	0.01	0.08	0.04	0.04	0.01
Cr	–	–	15.5	21.5	16	21	16	18	19.5	15.5	19	21
Mo	–	–	–	9	15	13.5	15.5	4	4	–	3	8
Fe	0.2	1.25	8	2.5	0.5	3.2	5.5	–	–	7	18.5	13.5
Co	–	–	–	–	0.1	0.9	0.9	18.5	13.5	–	–	–
Cu	0.13	31.5	0.2	–	–	–	–	–	1.3	–	–	–
Al	–	–	–	0.2	–	–	–	2.9	–	0.7	0.5	0.2
Ti	–	–	–	0.2	0.2	–	–	2.9	3	2.5	0.9	1.3
Nb	–	–	–	3.6	–	–	–	–	–	1	5.1	3.5
Mn	0.18	1.0	0.5	0.2	0.2	0.3	0.5	0.5	–	0.5	0.2	0.05
Si	0.18	0.25	0.2	0.2	0.05	0.05	0.05	0.5	–	0.5	0.2	0.05
W	–	–	–	–	0.1	3.25	4	–	–	–	–	–
B	–	–	–	–	–	–	–	0.006	0.006	–	0.003	0.003

involving nuclear and aerospace engineering, it is not unusual to employ filler metals with a chemistry vastly different from the base metal to reduce the extent of hot cracking.

In case of solid solution alloys like Nickel 200 and Monel 400, which are prone to weld metal porosity, welding can be carried out without any problem using filler metals of matching composition modified with deoxidizers and/or denitriders. Table 2 lists the filler metals available for welding Ni-base alloys. On the other hand, some of the practical difficulties that are posed by the poor fluidity of the molten metal can be overcome with a proper combination of joint design and weaving. Firstly, the problems related to the weldability of Nickel 200 and Monel 400 are addressed.

Nickel 200 and Monel 400

Nickel 200 has about 99.5% Ni with small additions of Fe, Mn, Si, C and Cu forming the rest. Monel 400 series alloys belong to Ni-Cu system containing 30-45% Cu; alloying with Cu improves toughness and ductility. Both these alloys are prone to the formation of weld metal porosity due to the absence of strong N_2 fixing elements such as Al or Ti. The threshold values of N_2 that can induce porosity in pure Ni during Ar-gas shielded welding has been measured be about 30 ppm and it increases with the addition of H_2. The contribution to porosity from H_2 has been found insignificant and as high as 50% H_2-Ar mixtures can be tolerated by nickel. Porosity due to CO evolution is also possible in commercial grade nickel (specific max. content for C is 0.08%) due to the oxygen pick-up during GTA welding (usually in the range of 0.005 to 0.02 mass %). Pure nickel and Monel are also susceptible to hot cracking caused by sulphur contamination to a greater extent than Ni-Cr-Fe alloys. However, all these problems can be overcome using welding consumables containing Al or Ti and adopting good welding practice.

For GTAW of Monel 400, ERNiCu-7, with a composition matching the parent metal modified with A1, Ti and increased amounts of Mn is used. They are also produced in layer-wound reels for GMAW. For SMAW, ENiCu-7, with a similar composition is employed.

Solid-solution Strengthened Alloys

Inconel 600 is a solid-solution strengthened Ni-Cr-Fe alloy (Ni-72% min., Cr- 14-17%, Fe - 6- 10%).

Table 2 Filler metals for welding nickel alloys

AWS or trade name	C	Mn	Fe	S	Si	Cu	Ni	Co	Al	Ti	Cr	Nb+Ta	Mo	Other
ERNiCr-3	0.1	2.5–3.5	3.0	0.015	0.5	0.5	67 min	–	–	0.75	18–22	2–3	–	0.5
ERNiCrFe-5	0.08	1.0	6–10	0.015	0.35	0.5	70 min	–	–	–	14–17	1.5–3.0	–	1.0
ERNiCrFe-6	0.08	2.0–2.7	10.0	0.015	0.35	0.5	67 min	–	–	2.5–3.5	14–17	–	–	0.5
ERNiCrFe-7	0.08	1.0	5–9	0.01	0.5	0.5	70 min	–	0.4–1.0	2.0–2.75	14–17	0.7–1.2	–	0.5
ERNiCrMo-3	0.1	0.5	5.0	0.015	0.5	–	rem	1.0	0.4	0.4	20–23	3.15–4.15	8–10	–
GMR-235	0.16	0.25	9–11	0.03	0.6	–	rem	2.5	1.75–2.25	2.25–2.75	14–17	–	4.5–6.5	0.009B
ERNiCrMo-2	0.05–0.15	1.0	17–20	0.03	1.0	–	rem	0.5–2.5	–	–	20.5–23	–	8–10	0.2–1.0 W
Hastelloy S	0.01	0.2	1.0	0.005	0.2	–	67	–	0.2	–	15.5	–	15.5	0.009B, 0.02La
ERNiCrMo-7	0.007	0.5	1.5	0.005	0.04	–	65	1.0	–	–	16	–	15.5	–
Haynes 556	0.1	1.5	–	0.005	0.4	–	20	20	0.3	–	22	0.1	3	0.9Ta, 0.2N, 2.5W
ERNiCrMo-4	0.01	0.5	5.5	0.005	0.04	–	62	1.2	–	–	16	–	16	3.5W, 0.35V
Inconel 601	0.05	0.5	14.1	0.007	0.25	0.25	60.5	–	1.35	0.24	23.0	–	–	–
Inconel 617	0.07	0.02	0.4	0.005	0.14	–	54	12.5	1.0	–	22	–	9	–
Inconel 718	0.08	0.35	rem	0.015	0.35	0.3	50–55	1.0	0.2–0.8	0.65–1.15	17–21	4.75–5.5	2.8–5.5	–
Rene 41	0.12	0.1	5.0	0.015	0.5	–	rem	10–12	1.4–1.6	3.0–3.3	18–20	–	9–10.5	–
Waspaloy	0.07	0.1	0.75	–	0.1	–	rem	13.5	1.4	3.0	19.75	–	4.45	–
ENiCrFe-1	0.08	1.5	11.0	0.015	0.75	0.5	68 min	–	–	–	13–17	1.5–4.0	–	0.5
ENiCrFe-2	0.1	1.0–3.5	6–12	0.02	0.75	0.5	rem	–	–	–	13–17	0.5–3.0	0.5–2.5	0.5
ENiCrFe-3	0.1	5.0–9.5	6–10	0.015	1.0	0.5	rem	–	–	1.0	13–17	1.0–2.5	–	0.5
ENiMo-1	0.12	1.0	4–7	0.03	1.0	–	rem	2.5	–	–	1.0	–	26–30	–
ENiMo-3	0.12	1.0	4–7	0.03	1.0	–	rem	2.5	–	–	2.5–5.5	–	23–27	–
ENiCrMo-3	0.1	0.5	5.0	0.015	0.5	–	rem	1.0	0.4	0.4	20–23	3.15–4.15	8–10	–
ENiCrMo-2	0.1	0.5	18.5	0.005	0.5	–	47	1.5	–	–	22	–	9	0.005 B
ENiCrMo-7	0.007	0.5	1.5	0.005	0.1	–	65	1.0	–	–	16	–	15.5	–
ENiCrMo-4	0.01	0.5	5.5	0.005	0.04	–	62	1.2	–	–	16	–	16	3.5W, 0.35V
Inconel 117	0.01	0.6–1.4	1.7	0.008	0.5	0.2	52	12	0.2	–	23.5	0–0.5	9	–

One of the several notable attributes of this alloy is its immunity to chloride assisted stress corrosion cracking (SCC) due to its high Ni content. Cr offers resistance to oxidizing conditions at high temperatures and in corrosive solutions.

The weldability of Inconel 600 is adversely affected by the presence of even small amounts of impurity elements such as S and P (0.015%). Though it can be autogenously welded in sheet-metal thickness, it is not useful as a GMA filler for welding thicker sections on account of its poor weld metal cracking resistance. Inconel 62 (AWS ERNiCrFe-5) and Inconel 82 (AWS ERNiCr-3) filler metals are often used to weld this alloy to reduce the extent of hot cracking. Covered electrodes such as Inconel 182 (AWS ENiCrFe-3) and Inconel 132 (AWS ENiCrFe-1) can also be used to join Inconel 600 to itself or to a different alloy. SMAW and SAW processes are not usually recommended as the presence of even small amounts of residual slag can lead to problems of corrosion at high temperatures due to moisture pick-up.

Inconel 625 is a solid-solution strengthened Ni-Cr-Fe-Nb alloy (Ni-58% min. Cr-20-23, Fe-5.0 max, Mo-8- 10%, Nb-3-4. 15%) and it exhibits similar weldability characteristics. Mention should be made here about the formation of a low melting γ/Laves constituent which extends the solidification range of the alloy promoting weld metal cracking susceptibility. Detailed discussions on the Laves phase are provided later. Matching filler metal is available (ERNiCrMo-3) which is also frequently used to join Ni-Cr-Mo alloys.

Hastelloys are also solid-solution strengthened alloys derived from Ni-Cr-Mo system. Among these alloys, hastelloy C-4 shows the best weld metal cracking resistance, which is comparable to 304 SS with 3-4% delta ferrite. Studies have shown that this alloy does not form any low melting phase upon solidification and thus possesses a much narrower solidification range. On the other hand, both Hastelloy C-22 and Hastelloy C-276, terminate their solidification with low melting phases like P, μ and σ which are similar to Laves in their crystal structure. The tendency to form such low melting phases is associated with the segregation of alloying elements such as Mo and, in particular, W during solidification. Hastelloy C-4, because of its lower content of W, exhibits better weld metal cracking resistance.

Precipitation-Hardenable Alloys

Ni-base alloys containing aluminium and titanium (with a combined content of at least 1%) are age-hardenable. The hardening phase that is usually contained in the Ni-Cr-Mo alloys and Ni-Cr-Fe alloys such as Inconel X-750 is $Ni_3(AlTi)$ (γ') and is precipitated from a supersaturated solid-solution obtained by quenching after a homogenization treatment. The precipitation of γ' occurs rapidly during the stage of quenching itself and thus is very effective in strengthening the alloy. However, this rapid precipitation adversely affects the weldability of these alloys as it leads to cracking (which occurs at a subsolidus temperature) either during welding or in the subsequent heat treatment as explained below.

Though the alloys containing are welded in the solution annealed condition (1065 – 1150′°C followed by water quenching) to dissolve the phases like γ' during cooling through the range of about 825 °C, significant hardening results within a few seconds in the HAZ due to the rapid precipitation of γ'. Subsequently, such regions lack sufficient ductility to resist the microstresses developed due to the thermal stresses accompanying the welding cycle thus leading to the formation of cracks. They can also occur during PWHT, which accompanies stress-relief with precipitation hardening, especially if the heating rate is slow enough to cause significant hardening before stress-relief. Such type of cracking is referred to as strain-age cracking (SAC) or reheat cracking and is seen along clean grain boundaries that are not immediately adjacent to the fusion line.

The strain-age cracking tendency of precipitation-hardenable Ni-base alloys is dependent on the total Al and Ti content. Fig. 1 shows the effect of Al and Ti content on strain-age cracking in various alloys. As it can be seen from this figure, Inconel 718 has the greatest resistance to this type of cracking among all the alloys because of its lower Al and Ti content. But more importantly, this attribute arises from a unique hardening constituent, γ'' ($Ni_3(NbTi)$), which requires an incubation

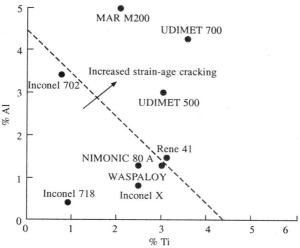

Fig. 1 **Effect of Al and Ti content on strain-age cracking tendency of various nickel alloys (after Owczarski 1980)**

period to nucleate. As it can be seen from the Fig. 2, which is the TTT diagram for Inconel 718, the precipitation of γ'' is quite sluggish and thus it cannot form during welding cycles in the HAZ and stress relief can also be achieved before γ'' precipitation.

Though the Nb addition has helped to avoid SAC, it has made the alloy to inherit hot cracking. The HAZ cracking has been primarily attributed to the constitutional liquation of NbC and the events leading to such cracking are schematically shown in Fig. 3. However, the extent of such cracking in the HAZ can be minimized by welding in the solution-treated condition (925°C/1 h, followed by water quenching). On the other hand, the poor weld metal cracking resistance exhibited by this alloy accrues from its wider solidification range due to the formation of a low melting γ/Laves eutectic in the interdendritic regions, which solidifies at a much lower temperature than the bulk solidus of the alloy. Laves phase is a size effect intermetallic of general formula A_2B, where A elements are Ni, Cr or Fe which are about 20-30% smaller than the B elements such as Nb, Mo, Ti or Si. This phase forms when the B elements segregate to the interdendritic regions during solidification and exceed their solubility limit in the austenitic matrix. It has also been reported that the presence of boron in amounts more than 0.003%, diminishes drastically the resistance to cracking.

While filler metal of a matching composition (ERNiFeCr-2) can be used to weld Inconel 718 to achieve good mechanical properties, the risk of solidification cracking and its influence on mechanical properties cannot be ignored. Such cracks are fine and not revealed by NDT. The presence of these cracks can degrade mechanical properties and especially under creep and fatigue conditions of service, they can grow leading to failures in the welded joint. Hence a filler metal has to be chosen carefully keeping in view the fabrication and service weldability requirements. The effect of filler metals with non-matching composition on specific properties of Inconel 718 welds is not well

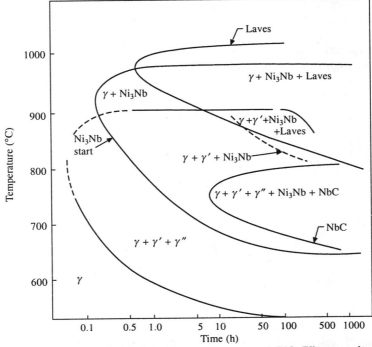

Fig. 2 Time-temperature-transformation diagram for Inconel 718 (Vincent, cited by Thompson and Genculu 1983)

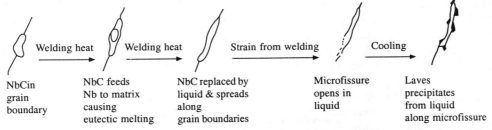

Fig. 3 Schematic illustration showing the formation the formation of hot cracks in the HAZ due to constitutional liquiation of NbC particles (after Thompson et al., 1985)

documented. Inconel filler metal 82 (ERNiCr-3) is a better choice for welding alloy 718. Fig. 4 compares the weld metal cracking susceptibility of Alloy 718 with Alloy 600 and filler metal Inconel 82. ErNiCrFe-6 and ErNiCrFe-7 (contain Al, Ti, Nb and Ta) filler metals can also be used and the weld deposits respond to age-hardening treatment. However, filler metals which cannot be age-hardened, bring in fewer welding problems.

Custom Age 625 Plus is a relatively new age-hardenable alloy with slight differences in the contents of Fe, Cr and Mo, when compared to Inconel 625, but with a higher addition of Ti (1.3% as against 0.4%). The weld metal cracking resistance of this alloy has been found to be better than Inconel 718 and it has been attributed to the lower content of Nb as in Inconel 625 (3.8% as against 5.2%).

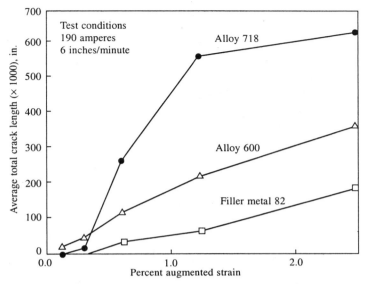

Fig. 4 Fusion zone cracking susceptibility of Inconel alloys 718 and 600 and Inconel filler metal 82 as determined from Varestraint testing

Shielding Gases

The shielding gases normally employed for GTAW are Ar, He or a mixture of Ar + He. The use of N_2 or CO_2 is not recommended in view of the problems such as reduction of service life of the tungsten electrode and weld metal porosity. The use of Ar + 5% H_2 is not recommended in multipass welding though it can be used for single-passes. The addition of 15-20% He is beneficial when welding Ni alloys with short circuiting arc or pulsed arc transfer mode.

Welding Practice

Among the arc welding proceses, GTAW is the most widely employed process for joining Ni-base alloys. DCEN mode is recommended in view of its ability to increase depth of penetration. Good mechanical properties can be achieved in the joints using this process. High degree of automation is possible and the width of HAZ and extent of distortion can be minimized with proper control. When welding thin sections, where heat input is to be controlled to minimize distortion, the pulsed-current mode may be employed and sections up to 3 mm thick can be welded without filler metal. For sections greater than 3 mm, GMAW is preferred as higher deposition rates with deeper penetration are possible with this process but GTAW is used for making root pass. In out-of position welding, pulsed GMAW is preferred. SMAW and SAW are usually not recommended in several applications as they lead to problems of porosity due to atmospheric contamination which are more severe than by inert-gas shielded processes. The use of SMAW is normally restricted to overlaying, repairing and dissimilar joining.

The first and foremost requirement, in any of these welding processes, is to ensure weld-zone cleanliness. The joints and adjoining regions located at distances of at least 25 mm on either side, should be cleaned thoroughly and made free from even traces of ingredients such as grease, oil, paint, marking crayons, temperature indicating crayons, etc. Even trace amounts of these ingredients are known to cause severe embrittlement in the HAZ due to pick-up of sulfur and other low-melting impurities. Alloys, subjected to high temperature service, should be scrupulously cleaned using grinding, abrasive blasting or pickling procedures as oxides of nickel, which form at high temperatures are quite adherent and they do not melt during welding (melting temperature is about 2090°C as against 1350–1450°C for the Ni-base alloys) leading to incomplete fusion and defects.

Secondly, the molten nickel alloy metal does not flow as well as steel leading to problems such as lack of penetration and fusion. Attempts to increase the heat input are futile and can only lead to problems of porosity due to loss of deoxidizers and poor mechanical properties. Hence, joint designs should be made with a wider included angle to improve ease of weaving (which should not exceed three times the wire diameter) and to allow exact placement of weld metal during SMAW (Fig. 5). Root faces of the joints should also be made thinner than that are required for steel to take care of the inherent lack of penetration of nickel alloy melt.

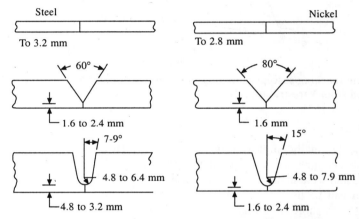

Fig. 5   Comparison of joint designs used for steel and nickel alloys (after Kiser 1988)

Welding is preferably carried out in the solution-treated condition (925–950°C/1 h followed by water quenching) both in the cold worked solid-solution strengthened alloys and precipitation-hardened alloys, without any pre-heat. Also, the interpass temperature should be kept below 125°C, especially in case of precipitation-hardenable alloys.

Post weld heat treatment

PWHT may not be needed in most of the applications except in cases where precipitation-hardening is required and stress relieved joints are needed to combat problems such as SCC. For example, the effect of PWHT on tensile properties of Inconel 718 weld metal is shown in Fig. 6. The data for the parent metal at the same temperature is also provided in the figure for comparison. As it can be seen, in the as-welded condition, the properties of the weld are quite inferior to that of the base metal. A direct age-hardening treatment (normally done for 2 h between 600-650°C), though improves the tensile strength, significantly reduces the ductility. On the other hand, with a full heat tratment cycle, where the age-hardening is preceded by a homogenization treatment (1065°C/1 h), the properties of the welded joints can be made to virtually match those of the parent metal. Such a difference is attributed to the presence of Laves phase in the as-welded condition, which greatly impairs the

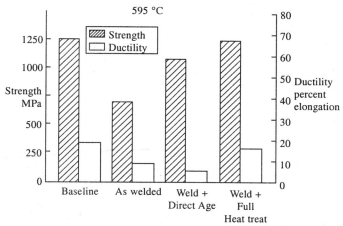

Fig. 6   Effect of PWHT on tensile properties of Inconel 718 weld deposits; data for aged parent metal is also shown (after Owczarski 1980)

ductility and prevents effective γ' precipitation from occurring when welds are subjected to a direct age-hardening treatment. When homogenization is employed prior to the age-hardening treatment, Laves phase is solutionised, leading to a complete recovery of properties in the welds. The presence of Laves phase is also detrimental to impact properties.

WELDABILITY OF COPPER-BASE ALLOYS

Copper and its alloys, by virtue of their unique blend of properties such as strength and ductility, high thermal and electrical conductivity and corrosion resistance continue to find applications in fields as diverse as electric power generation, chemical processing, oil production, electronics, marine and desalination equipment. It is needless to mention here that welding plays a crucial role in relizing the true worth of copper and copper-base alloys in these applications. Hence an understanding of the factors that influence their weldability is very essential. This paper points out the problems faced during their welding and suggests measures to overcome them. As the major emphasis will be given to the welding metallurgy of these materials, the discussions are restricted regarding applicable welding processes and confine only to arc welding processes. It may be mentioned here that brazing is frequently used to join copper alloys where applicable in view of the problems associated with the fusion welding processes and is not covered in this paper.

Copper and its alloys may be broadly classified as under:

1. Copper
2. Silicon bronze
3. Aluminium bronze
4. Phosphor (tin) bronze and gunmetal
5. Brass and nickel Silver
6. Copper-nickel
7. Age-hardenable alloys (Cu-Be etc.)

The compositions of these alloys are provided in Table 3 and both cast and wrought types are available in each of these categories. The physical properties such as their melting range and thermal conductivity are indicated in Table 4. Barring a few exceptions, these alloys are metallurgically

Table 3   Nominal compositions and welding characteristics of some copper and copper alloys

UNS No.	Alloy Name	Nominal Composition, %	Liquidus °C	Relative[1] Thermal Conductivity	Weldability[2] by GTAW	GMAW	SMAW
OFC & ETP Coppers							
C10200	Oxygen-free copper (OFC)	99.95 Cu	1083	100	G	G	NR
C11000	Electrolytic tough pitch copper (ETP)	99.90 Cu, 0.04 O_2	1083	100	F	F	NR
Deoxidised Coppers							
C12000	Phosphorus-deoxidised copper, low-P	99.9Cu, 0.008 P	1083	99	E	E	NR
C12200	Phosphorus-deoxidised copper, high-P	99.9Cu, 0.02 P	1083	87	E	E	NR
Beryllium Coppers							
C17000	High strength beryllium copper	98.3 Cu, 1.7Be	982	27–33	G	G	G
C17200	High strength beryllium copper	98.1Cu, 1.9Be	982	27–33	G	G	G
C17500	High conductivity beryllium copper	96.9Cu, 0.6Be, 2.5Co	1068	53–66	F	F	F
Low-Zinc Brasses							
C21000	Gilding	95Cu, 5Zn	1065	60	G	G	NR
C22000	Commercial bronze	90Cu, 10Zn	1043	48	G	G	NR
C23000	Red brass	85Cu, 15Zn	1026	41	G	G	NR
C24000	Low brass	80Cu, 20Zn	999	36	G	G	NR
High-Zinc Brasses							
C26000	Cartridge brass	70Cu, 30 Zn	954	31	F	F	NR
C26800	Yellow brass	65Cu, 35 Zn	932	30	F	F	NR
C28000	Muntz metal	60Cu, 40 Zn	904	31	F	F	NR
Tin Brasses[4]							
C44300	Admiralty brass	71Cu, 28Zn, 1Sn	937	28	F	F	NR
C46400	Naval brass	60Cu, 39.25Zn, 0.75 Sn	899	30	F	F	NR
Special Brasses							
C67500	Manganese bronze A	58.5Cu, 39Zn, 1.4Fe, 1Sn, 0.1 Mn	888	27	F	F	NR
C68700	Aluminium brass, arsenical	77.5Cu, 20.5Zn, 2Al, (0.06As)	971	26	F	F	NR
Nickel Silvers							
C74500	Nickel silver	65Cu, 25Zn,, 10Ni	1021	12	F	F	NR

Table 3 Nominal compositions and welding characteristics of some copper and copper alloys (Contd.)

UNS No.	Alloy Name	Nominal Composition, %	Liquidus °C	Relative[1] Thermal Conductivity	Weldability[2] by		
					GTAW	GMAW	SMAW
C75200	Nickel silver	65Cu, 17Zn, 18Ni	1110	8	F	F	NR
C75400	Nickel silver	65Cu, 20Zn, 15Ni	1076	9	F	F	NR
C75700	Nickel silver	65Cu, 23Zn, 12Ni	1037	10	F	F	NR
C77000	Nickel silver	55Cu, 27Zn, 18Ni	1054	8	F	F	NR
Phosphor Bronzes							
C50500	Phosphor bronze 1.25% E	98.7Cu, 1.3 Sn, (0.2P)	1076	53	G	G	F
C51000	Phosphor bronze 5% A	95Cu, 5 Sn, (0.2P)	1049	18	G	G	F
C52100	Phosphor bronze 8% C	92Cu, 8 Sn, (0.2P)	1026	16	G	G	F
C52400	Phosphor bronze 10% D	90Cu, 10 Sn, (0.2 P)	999	13	G	G	F
Aluminium Bronzes							
C61300	Aluminium bronze D, Sn. stabil	89Cu, 7Al, 3.5Fe (0.35 Sn)	1046	14	G	E	G
C61400	Aluminium bronze D	91Cu, 6–8Al, 1.5–3. Fe, Mn $\leq$ 1	1046	17	G	E	G
C63000	Aluminium bronze E	82Cu, 10Al, 5Ni, 3Fe	1054	10	G	G	G
Silicon Bronzes							
C65100	Low-silicon bronze B	98.5Cu, 1.5Si	1060	15	E	E	F
C65500	High-silicon bronze A	97Cu, 3Si	1026	9	E	E	F
Cupronickels							
C70600	Cupronickel	88.6Cu, 9-11Ni, 1.4Fe, 1.0 Mn	1149	12	E	E	G
C71500	Cupronickel	70Cu, 30 Ni	1238	8	E	E	E

Notes: 1. Relative thermal conductivity based on that of 10200, 2553.8 kJ/m^2 in meters per hour at 20°C, 2. Weldability: E–excellent, G– good and NR – not recommended, 3. in the precipitation hardened condition, 4. alloys C44300 and C46500 contain nominal 0.06% As; alloys C44400 and C46600 a nominal 0.06% Sb; alloys C44500 and 46700, a nominal 0.06% P

uncomplicated unlike ferrous alloys, where the allotropic transformations lead to a variety of complex microstructures. Certain basic problems that are encountered during welding can be avoided using a combination of inert-gas shielded welding processes and filler metals with deoxidants. Filler metals are available in straight lengths for GTAW, in layer wound reels for GMAW and in the form of covered electrodes for SMAW.

The weldability of Cu-base alloys is principally affected by physical properties such as thermal conductivity and chemical reactions involving oxygen in the form of cuprous oxide (Cu_2O) in the molten metal, which lead to problems such as incomplete -fusion, inadequate joint penetration and porosity. Hence it may be useful. to consider the weldability of copper, to start with, which is more prone to these problems than its alloys.

Copper

The three grades of copper, whose weldability considerably varies, to consider are,

1. Oxygen-bearing (tough-pitch)
2. Oxygen-free
3. Phosphorus-deoxidized

The first and foremost problem encountered during the welding of copper, irrespective of its grade, is its high thermal conductivity which makes welding with a minimal heat input extremely difficult to (1) avoid excessive internal and external oxidation, (2) achieve satisfactory root penetration and (3) minimize distortion. While these deficiencies can be overcome using measures such as Ar+He gas mixtures, preheat and suitable jigs to achieve satisfactory weld deposits, metallurgical defects such as porosity and cracking can be best controlled by only using base and filler materials with a lower crack forming chemistry.

Among the three grades of copper, the tough-pitch type is the most difficult to weld as it is very much prone to the formation of porosity due to the presence of Cu_2O. The formation of porosity has ben attributed to a 'steam reaction' which occurs extensively in such oxygen containing copper grades when welding is attempted either using oxyacetylene process or with filler metals without any deoxidant. The hydrogen, generated by the combustion of acetylene leads to steam reaction in weld metal and HAZ, by reacting with Cu_2O as described in the following equation:

$$Cu_2O + H_2 = 2\ Cu + H_2O$$

This steam reaction calls for effective deoxidation of copper and it should not contain hydrogen at all as it has been found that even as little as 1 ppm of H results in a gas evolution equivalent to 44% of the volume of the metal. The roughness of the butt edges and the contamination of the joining surfaces also significantly contribute to the formation of porosity in copper welds.

Not all porosity is attributable to the steam reaction as nitrogen can also cause porosity and the problem is found to be more severe in the tough pitch grade. The porosity due to N_2 has been found to be more acute in GTA welding than in GMA welding; the threshold levels of N_2 to produce appreciable porosity have been measured and are very low in GTAW, about 0.1% and can be less than 1.0% in GMAW. Thus the porosity can easily occur by entrainment of the atmosphere into the arc during welding of copper even during inert-gas shielded processes. Such porosity from N_2 and steam reaction can be reduced by the use of increased welding speeds and filler metals with Al or Ti, which are more powerful denitriding elements than Si or Mn, which happen to be good deoxidizers as well.

The problem of porosity occurs in phosphorus-deoxidized grades also but to lesser extent than oxygen-bearing grade and filler metals with either Si and Mn or Ti and Al should be used to achieve satisfactory weld deposits.

Porosity in oxygen-free grades of copper (oxygen free high conductivity copper, obtained by either electrolytically refining commercially pure copper or melting and casting copper in the presence of carbonaceous gases) can also be avoided only by using similar filler metals. Embrittlement of the weld metal occurs due to the formation of Cu_2O if deoxidized filler metals are not used. hence such welded joints are often characterized by lower electrical conductivity. Silver bearing phosphorus-deoxidized filler rods can be used if high electrical conductivity is required in such joints. If conductivity is not a requirement, Sn bearing Si deoxidized filler metals can be used.

Phosphorus-deoxidized grades (oxygen has been removed with the addition of 0.01 to 0.04% P) are generally resistant to the formation of porosity. However, they are prone to hot cracking during solidification especially when P content is above 0.015%. While such contents have been found to result in welds less susceptible to the formation of pores, they promote weld metal cracking very much. Low-melting additives such as Pb, Te and S, which are added to improve machinability, also increase the susceptibility of all the grades of copper to hot cracking, especially when their content is about 0.05%.

Silicon bronze

Silicon bronzes (alloys of copper with 3% Si in combination with Mn, Fe, Zn and Sn), among all of the Cu-base alloys, exhibit the best weldability, requiring no preheat and special gas mixtures to increase heat input, as they have a thermal conductivity comparable to steel. They are also not subject to porosity, unlike copper, as Si is readily oxidized to provide inherent oxidation resistance. But this feature may induce weld porosity or lack of penetration that must be overcome by maintaining smooth, non-turbulent arcing to prevent "mixing-in" of the silica slag. In addition to this possibility of entrapment of silica, these alloys are prone to hot cracking in the fusion zone under conditions of restraint as they exhibit hot-shortness at temperatures between 800–900°C. In order to avoid such cracking, a very small weld puddle should be carried, excessive welding currents should be avoided, a low interpass temperature is to be maintained and accelerated cooling is recommended in the hot-shortness range by using, for example, cooled packing pieces.

In welding, use may be made of a filler metal of the same composition or of silicon bronze. In case of coversed electrodes (ECuSi), the core wire contains about 3% Si and has small amounts of Sn and Mn. Bare electrodes are also available with similar composition for GMAW. The Cu-Si (ERCuSi-A) welding rods, used in GTAW, contain 2.8 – 4.0% Si with about 1.5% Mn, 1.5% Sn and 1.5% Zn.

Aluminium bronze

Aluminium bronze alloys (Cu-Al), exhibit welding characteristics similar to silicon bronze. Resistance to porosity due to the presence of Al, no preheat and heat input problems are some of the advantages which improve weldability. They may be welded with filler metals that do not contain any deoxidants. Al is the primary alloying element in these alloys and may be present up to 15%. Normally they also contain Fe, Ni, Si, Mn and Sn in various combinations to achieve a wide range of properties.

Alloys containing up to 7% Al are single-phase (α) and are difficult to weld due to their high hot cracking susceptibility as they experience a fall in ductility at sub-solidus temperatures during the thermal cycle. The use of matching filler metal for welding this type of alloy is thus never recommended. The alloys containing Ni are less susceptible to this problem. However, the alloys with higher amounts of Al (8–15%) are two-phase, with improved hot cracking resistance. These two-phase alloys undergo a martensitic type of transformation and thus they can be hardened by quenching from the temperature range 850–1020°C, followed by tempering as in the case of steels. These alloys have an adequate plasticity retaining their hot cracking resistance even in the hardened state. Hence for welding single-phase aluminium bronze alloys, a duplex filler metal (10% Al, 2.5% Fe and 5.5% Ni) is always recommended.

Among the welding consumables, the most widely used are ECuAl-A2 electrodes which are available in covered form for SMAW as well as in the form of bare wire supplied on spools for GMAW. These electrodes contain 9–11% Al and about 1.5% Fe and are used for joining aluminium bronze, silicon bronze, copper-nickel and many combinations of dissimilar metals. Filler metal selection has to be done carefully keeping in view the service requirements. For example, while joining the single phase aluminium bronze alloys, a duplex filler metal like ECuAl-A2 is used to prevent hot cracking. However, to match the corrosion resistance of the base metal, the weld joint is often capped with a final pass using filler metals of matching composition and this is accomplished with iron-free Cu-Al filler metal, ECuAl-A1. ECuAl-B filler metals are also alloys of Cu-Al-Fe like ECuAl-A2, but with a higher Fe content in the range, 3-4.25% and yield weld deposits with relatively higher mechanical properties. ERCuAl, ERCuAl-A2 and ERCuAl-B rods are similar in composition to their covered electrode counterparts. Apart from Cu-Al-Fe alloys rods, Cu-Al-Ni and Cu-Al-Fe-Ni-Mn rods are also available.

Phosphor (tin) Bronze and Gunmetals

The phosphor bronze alloys are based on the composition Cu-Sn with Sn content up to 10%. The name phosphor bronze is more of a misnomer as neither is phosphorus present in high amounts (only about 0.5%) nor does it play a significant part in the performance and properties of these alloys as the name suggests. Gunmetals are casting alloys with similar Sn content, in combination with Zn, Pb and Ni. Alloys with Sn content < 2% are single phase if they are rapidly cooled from the solution temperature. These alloys exhibit poor weldability and their welding must be approached with caution.

The phosphor bronze alloys are prone to the formation of weld metal porosity as they are not inherently capable of providing completely effective deoxidation unlike silicon and aluminium bronzes during solidification. Hence CuSi or CuAl filler metals are often recommended to weld these alloys although matching filler metals do exist.

The wider solidification range of phosphor bronze alloys promotes the tendency to hot cracking especially under conditions of restraint. Alloys containing higher amounts of Sn (5% or more) are also susceptible to embrittlement due to the formation of a second Sn rich, $\gamma(Cu_3Sn)$ phase. Pb-containing alloys are seldom welded using fusion processes due to their high degree of hot-shortness.

Filler metals such as ECuSn-A and ECuSn-C are available as covered electrodes and bare wire reels. The contents of Sn are higher in the 'C' composition, about 8%, compared to 'A', which is about 5%. Both the electrodes are deoxidized with P (0.3%). The electrode can be used to weld phosphor bronze, brass and also copper if the presence of Sn is allowed. The 'C' class is preferred to weld high strength bronzes, as the deposits made by this electrode have better mechanical properties than those with 'A' class electrode. For GTAW also, filler metals with similar composition to the ones as mentioned above, like, ERCuSn-A and ERCuSn-C are available.

Brass and Nickel Silver

Brasses are alloys of Cu and Zn (Zn contents may vary from 5 to 40%) and nickel silvers are alloys of Cu, Zn and Ni (Zn – 15 to 25%, Ni - 10 to 20%); Ni addition helps to gain additional strength and corrosion resistance. No preheat is usually required during welding of these alloys though their thermal conductivities are much higher than steels but which are still significantly lower than copper. However, both the alloys are difficult to weld on account of volatilization of Zn. While such volatilization leads to porous weld deposits, the fumes are very toxic and impair vision during welding. Only a marginal improvement is achieved when small additions of Al or Si are contained in these alloys which form stable oxide films in the weld pool suppressing fuming of Zn. Use of filler metals such as aluminium bronze or silicon bronze is often sought to control porosity. These alloys are seldom fusion welded when Pb is present which causes hot shortness cracking.

Most of the filler metals, which are used in GTAW of brass, are primarily meant for oxyacetylene welding and braze welding. In oxyacetylene welding, the use of an oxidizing flame and a filler metal deoxidized with Si, Mn or P significantly minimises porosity. The filler metals employed to weld brasses are mostly produced in rod form and can be used in GTAW. The types available are ERCuZn-A (naval brass), ERCuZn-B (low fuming bronze with nickel), ERCuZn-C (low fuming bronze) and ERCuZn-D (nickel bronze). Naval brass rods contain 1% Sn to improve corrosion resistance and are not recommended for GTAW due to their high Zn content. The low fuming bronze, ERCuZn-B is similar to naval brass but contains Si to inhibit excessive Zn fuming. Mn, Fe and Ni are also present in these rods to improve mechanical properties. The nickel bronze rods are lighter in colour than the brass alloy rods of ERCuZn group and they are used to join nickel silvers. They contain 9–11% Ni, 40–50% Zn and small amounts of P and Si to control Zn fuming. It is good practice during welding to lead the arc over the filler metal and not over the base metal to prevent excessive Zn fuming from the base metal.

Copper-Nickel

Copper-nickel alloys are available with Ni contents from 5 to 30% with relatively minor additions of Fe and Mn. These alloys have a low thermal conductivity and hence no preheat is required. However, they are prone to the same problem of porosity as copper itself and require filler metals with strong deoxidants during welding. They are also inherently susceptible to hot cracking as they have a relatively wider solidification range, The susceptibility to such cracking is further promoted if higher amounts of Pb, S or P are present. Especially in the presence of Ni, these elements drastically reduce the weldability of copper alloys. Sn and Zn, which may be present to improve corrosion resistance, also reduce weldability.

The copper-nickel electrodes (ECuNi) have a nominal composition of 70% Cu and 30% Ni. These electrodes are produced in both covered form for SMAW and as spooled wire for GMAW. They are used to weld all the three major types of cupronickel alloys (70/30, 80/20 and 90/10). The bare rods (ERCuNi), used in GTAW, are used to weld Cu-Ni sheets, plates, tubes, and pipes. They also contain 30% Ni along with small additions of Zn, Sn, Mn, Fe and Ti. Ti helps to minimize porosity and refines weld metal structure thereby improving hot-short cracking resistance. Fe also acts as grain refiner and improves the flow properties. Mn plays the role of a desulphuriser. Si provides a fluxing action that floats silicates to the surface.

Age-Hardenable Alloys

Some of the age-hardenable alloys belong to the systems of Cu-Be, Cu-Cr and Cu-Cd. Beryllium bronzes, which can be age-hardened, contain 2% Be. Such alloys have much lower thermal conductivity and can be welded without any preheat unlike the ones with 0.5Be. They also exhibit better weldability compared to the high-conductivity beryllium bronzes as the addition of Be in higher amounts lowers the melting point of the alloy resulting in good penetration. However, such high contents of Be may give rise to problems like lack of fusion due to the priority oxidation of Be. Mention should be made here about the BeO_2 fumes, which are highly toxic. These alloys are also susceptible to hot cracking, particularly in the age hardened state. Hence it becomes necessary to weld these alloys in the non-hardened state to alleviate hot cracking. The welded joints can be subsequently heat treated to achieve age hardening. Over-aged alloys can also be welded satisfactorily. Similar comments apply to Cu-Cr and Cu-Cd alloys also. Cu-Cd alloys, with Cd contents more than 1.25% are difficult to weld due to the evaporation of Cd, thereby creating a potential health hazard. Filler metals with matching composition are available and with suitable PWHT, properties of welded joints can be made to match the parent metal.

Shielding Gases

The use of diatomic gases such as H_2 and N_2, in order to increase the heat input per unit ampere, can result in porous welds, especially in case of oxygen-bearing copper and copper-base alloys which do not contain Al or Si to prevent steam reaction from occurring. However, while employing filler metals with deoxidants and denitriders, a 5 vol.% H_2-Ar gas mixture is recommended which has been found to permit the use of faster welding speeds and achieve good radiographic standards by reducing the extent of porosity. Use of He, is particularly beneficial in the welding of Cu as it enables preheat to be reduced or eliminated. Ar + He mixtures are normally recommended for welding copper and its alloys which combine in some part the advantages of He with some gain in economy. It is better to restrict the amounts of He or N_2 to less than 30 vol.% during GMAW to retain the desirable spray transfer mode.

Welding Practice

Deoxidized copper may be autogenously welded in thin gauges (<3 mm) provided complete inert gas shielding is provided to both the sides of the joint For joining thickness above 3 mm, preheat is required in all the grades of copper. With N_2 shielding, 5 mm thick copper may be joined without any preheat as against 3 mm thick copper using Ar. In GMAW, two welding guns can also be used side by side to increase heat input. Preheat temperatures, as high as 600°C, are often required for welding thick copper plates. However, if the weld area is maintained at such temperatures for a long time, the deoxidants may get consumed in the process, thereby increasing the risk of porosity. GTAW is recommended for root runs and optimum fusion is achieved using He shielding in DCEN mode of operation. GMAW is effective in subsequent fill up runs, especially in thick sections. Joint designs should be made with adequate root gaps with due allowance to counteract the effect of high thermal expansion coefficient of copper which may cause closure of root gaps as welding proceeds. Such gaps also prevent the base metal from conducting heat away and thus allow the molten metal to remain fluid for a longer time to fill the gap. The recommended edge preparations for copper alloy weldments are shown in Fig. 7. The relatively wider root opening in copper and its alloys should be securely backed up with strips (made up of copper, carbon, graphite or ceramic) to prevent the loss of molten metal, which is very fluid.

Mention should also be made here about thermit welding process which is widely practiced to join tough pitch and oxygen-free high conductivity copper for electrical transmission applications. In this process, a mixture of Al and copper oxide powders is held in a graphite crucible provided with an exit hole at the bottom, which is covered with a steel disc. The crucible is heated and Al reacts with Cu_2O to cause a strong exothermic reaction. The molten copper melts the covering disc, flows out into a

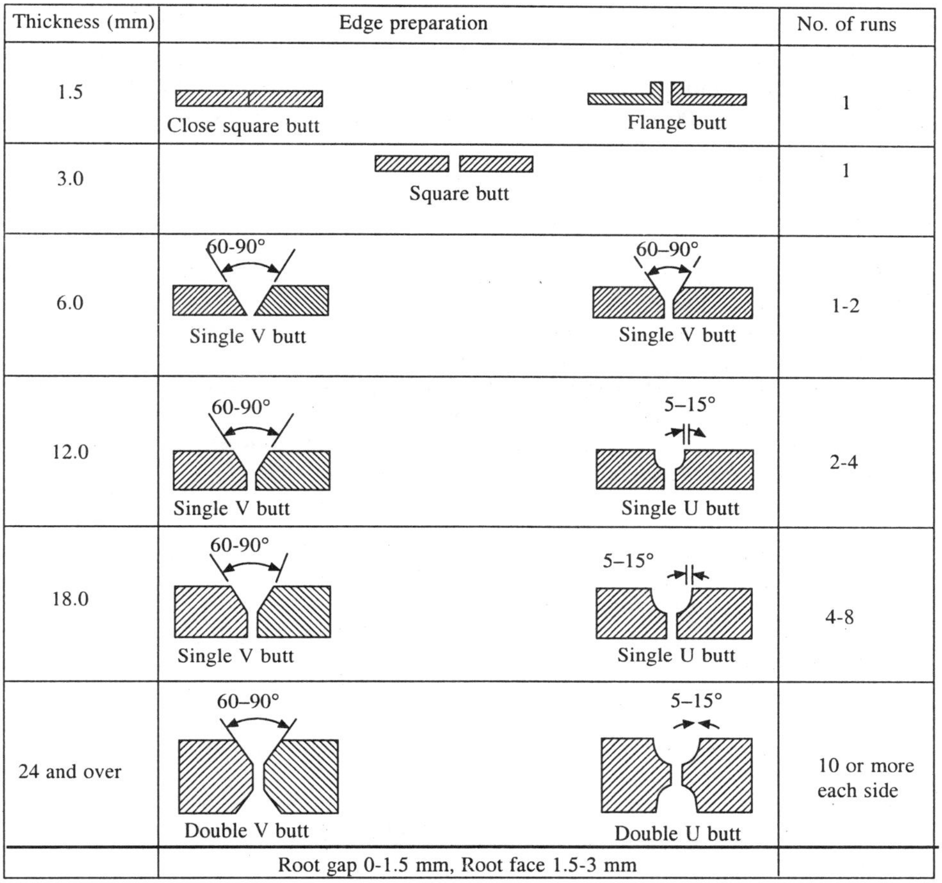

Thickness (mm)	Edge preparation		No. of runs
1.5	Close square butt	Flange butt	1
3.0	Square butt		1
6.0	60–90° Single V butt	60–90° Single V butt	1-2
12.0	60–90° Single V butt	5–15° Single U butt	2-4
18.0	60–90° Single V butt	5–15° Single U butt	4-8
24 and over	60–90° Double V butt	5–15° Double U butt	10 or more each side
	Root gap 0-1.5 mm, Root face 1.5-3 mm		

Fig. 7 Recommended joint designs for welding copper alloys

mould surrounding the joint and retains sufficient superheat to melt and join the joint faces. Such welds are sound and possess high electrical conductivity.

Copper alloys containing substantial amounts of Al or Si such as silicon and aluminium bronzes are often welded using AC GTAW process as the refractory oxides, which are present on the surface of these alloys can be effectively dispersed. Preheat is not required in these alloys as they have a low thermal conductivity and to prevent hot cracking it should be avoided. The interpass temperatures should also be kept below 150-200°C to avoid such cracking.

He-shielded GTAW using DCEN is recommended to weld the alloys brass, tin bronze and cupronickel which are prone to porosity as higher welding speeds are possible using this process which reduces the extent of porosity. No preheat and low interpass temperatures are recommended to minimize the risk of hot cracking.

Post Weld Heat Treatment

PWHT is usually required to achieve age-hardening in alloys such as Cu-Be and improve stress corrosion cracking resistance in alloys like brass. The temperatures employed for stress-relief annealing are lower than the recrystallisation temperature. For Cu-Be, 780-810°C is used and brasses are stress-relieved between 250-300°C. The soaking time is kept at 1 h. In case of aluminium bronze, a high temperature soaking (925–950°C) is first employed to homogenize the structure followed by a low temperature treatment (600–700°C) to develop full mechanical properties and corrosion resistance.

REFERENCES

1. A.W. Dix and W.F. Savage, 'Short time aging characteristics of Inconel X-750', Welding Journal, 52(3)' 1973, p 135-s to 139s, 144-s.
2. W.F. Savage, E.P. Nippes and G.M. Goodwin, 'Effect of minor elements on hot cracking tendencies of Alloy 600', Welding Journal, 56 (8), 1977, p245 –s to 253-s.
3. W.A. Owczarski, 'Process and Metallurgical factors in joining superalloys and other high service temperature materials', in Physical Metallurgy of Metal Joining, Proceedings of a Symposium Sponsored by the TMS-AIME Physical Metallurgy Committee, St. Louis, Edited by R. Kossowsky and M.E. Glicksman, 1980 (published by the Metallurgical Society of AIME), p 167–189.
4. R. Thamburaj, W. Wallace and J.A. Goldak, 'Post weld heat treatment cracking in superalloys', International Metals Reviews, 28 (1), 1983.
5. J.F. Lancaster, 'Metallurgy of welding', 4th edition, 1987, Allen &, Unwin Ltd., U.K, p289-303.
6. M.J. Cieslak, T.J. Headley and A.D. Romig, Jr., 'The welding metallurgy of Hastelloy alloys', Metallurgical Transactions A, 17(11), 1986, P2035–2047.
7. M.J. Cieslak, 'The welding and solidification metallurgy of Alloy 625', Welding Journal, 71 (2), p 49-s to 56-s.
8. M.J. Cieslak, T.J. Headley and R.B Frank, 'The welding metallurgy of Custom age 625 plus alloy', 69(12), 1989, p 473-s to 482-s.
9. S.D. Kaiser, 'Welding high nickel alloys different but not difficult', Welding Journal, 68(10), 1988, p55–57.
10. T.J. Kelly, 'Elemental effects on cast 718 weldability', Welding Journal, 69(2). 1989, p 44-s to 5 1-s.
11. J. Limeton, J. Lammas and M.F. Jordan, 'Nitrogen porosity in gas-shielded arc welding of Copper', Welding Journal, 53(12), 1974, p 561 -s to 565 -s.
12. E.W. Hartsell, Jr., 'Joining Copper and Copper alloys', Welding Journal, 52(2), 1973, p88–100.
13. R.J.C. Dawson, 'Welding of Copper and Copper-base alloys', WRC Bulletin -287, 1983.
14. S.H. Gutierrez, 'Understanding GTA welding of 90/10 CopperNickel', Welding Journal, 71(5), 1991, p 76–78.
15. R.G. thompson and S. Genculu, Welding Journal 63(12), 1983, p337-s to 345-s.
16. R.G. Thompson, J.J. Cassimus, D.E. Mayo and J.R. Dobbs, Welding Journal 65(4) 1985, p. 93-s to 96-s.

7. Dissimilar Metal Welding and Cladding

A.K. Bhaduri

Materials Joining Section, Materials Technology Division, Indira Gandhi Centre for Atomic Research
Kalpakkam 603 102

1 DISSIMILAR METAL WELDING

As various portions of a process system operate at different service conditions, different structural alloys are used in design, and hence, dissimilar-metal welded joints may be required. Many factors must be considered when welding dissimilar metals, and the development and qualification of adequate procedures for the various metals and sizes of interest for a specific application must be undertaken [1].

Most combinations of dissimilar metals can be joined by solid-state welding (diffusion welding, explosion welding, friction welding, or ultrasonic welding), brazing, or soldering where alloying between the metals is normally insignificant. In these cases, only the differences in the physical and mechanical properties of the base metals and their influence on the serviceability of the joint should be considered. When dissimilar metals are joined by fusion welding processes, alloying between the base metals and a filler metal, when used, becomes a major consideration. The resulting weld metal can behave much differently from one or both base metals during subsequent processing or in service.

In this section, the principal factors that are responsible for failure (cracking) of dissimilar metal arc welds are described. These include:

- General alloying problems (brittle phase formation and mutual solubility) of two metals
- Widely differing melting points.
- Differences in coefficients of thermal expansion
- Differences in thermal conductivity

In addition, service considerations that can result in dissimilar-metal weld failure by carbon migration or by corrosion/oxidation are discussed, along with a brief review of specific dissimilar metal combinations and filler metal selection guidelines.

1.1 Factors Influencing Joint Integrity

1.1.1 Weld Metal

In the fusion welding of dissimilar-metal joints, the most important consideration is the weld metal composition and its properties [2]. Its composition depends upon the compositions of the base metals, the filler metal, if used; and the relative dilutions of these. The weld metal composition is usually not uniform, particularly with multipass welds, and a composition gradient is likely to exist in the weld metal adjacent to each base metal. These solidification characteristics of the weld metal are also influenced by the relative dilutions and the composition gradients near each base metal. These characteristics are important with respect to hot cracking of the weld metal during solidification.

The basic concepts of alloying, the metallurgical characteristics of the resultant alloy, and its mechanical and physical properties must be considered when designing a dissimilar-metal joint. For fusion welding processes, it is important to investigate the phase diagram of the two metals involved. If there is mutual solubility between the two metals, the joint can usually be made successfully. If there is little or no solubility between the two metals, the joint will not be successful. The intermetallic compounds that form between the dissimilar metals must be investigated to determine their crack sensitivity, ductility, corrosion susceptibility, etc. The microstructure of the intermetallic compound is extremely important. In some cases, it is necessary to use a third metal that is soluble in each metal in order to obtain a successful joint.

1.1.2 Dilution

In dissimilar-metal welding, the filler metal must alloy readily with the base metals to produce a weld metal that has a continuous, ductile matrix phase. Specifically, the filler metal must be able to accept dilution (alloying) by the base metals without producing a crack-sensitive microstructure. The weld metal microstructure must also be stable under the expected service conditions. A successful weld between dissimilar metals is one that is as strong as the weaker of the two metals being joined, i.e. possessing sufficient tensile strength and ductility so that the joint will not fail.

In multipass welding, the composition of each weld bead should be relatively uniform. However, definite compositional differences are likely in succeeding weld beads, especially between a root bead, the beads adjacent to the base metals, and the remaining fill beads. The average composition of the whole weld metal can be calculated when: (i) the ratio of the volumes of base metals melted to the entire weld metal volume can be determined; and (ii) the compositions of the base and filler metals are known. The dilution can be based on area measurements on a transverse cross section. Figure 1 illustrates how to determine the dilution by two base metals, A and B, when welding with filler metal F.

The average percentage of a specific alloying element in the diluted weld metal can be calculated using the following equation developed by AWS [2]:

$$X_W = (D_A)(X_A) + (D_B)(X_B) + (1 - D_T)(X_F)$$

where X_W is the average percentage of the element X in the weld metal; X_A is the percentage of the element X in the base metal A; X_B is the percentage of the element X in the base metal B; X_F is the percentage of the element X in the filler metal F; D_A is the percent dilution by base metal A, expressed as a decimal; D_B is the percent dilution by base metal B, expressed as a decimal; and D_T is the percent total dilution by the base metals A and B, expressed as a decimal.

To illustrate the calculation of weld metal composition, assume that type 316 stainless steel

(SS) is welded to a 2.25Cr- 1Mo low-alloy ferritic pressure vessel steel with a Ni-Cr alloy filler metal ERNiCr-3. The nominal chemical compositions of the three alloys are:

Alloy	Composition (wt.%)			
	Cr	Ni	Mo	Fe
2.25Cr-1Mo	2.5	–	1.0	95.5
316 SS	17.0	12.0	2.5	63.0
ERNiCr-3	20.0	72.0	–	3.0

Assuming that the total dilution is 35%, 15% by the Cr-Mo alloy steel and 20% from the type 316 SS, the average percentages of Cr, Ni and Mo in the weld metal are calculated as follows:

$$Cr, \% = 0.15(2.5) + 0.20(17.0) + 0.65\ (20.0) = 16.8$$

$$Ni, \% = 0.20\ (12.0) + 0.65\ (72.0) \qquad = 49.2$$

$$Mo, \% = 0.15\ (1.0) + 0.20\ (2.5) \qquad = 6.65$$

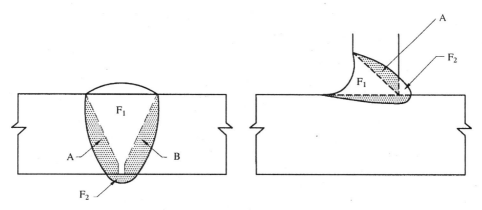

Fig. 1   Schematic for determining dilution by two base metals, A and B, when welding with filler metal F

1.1.3   Melting Temperatures

The difference in melting temperatures of the two metals that are to be joined must also be considered. This is of primary interest when a fusion welding process utilising considerable heat is involved, since one metal may be molten long before the other when subjected to the same heat source. Significant difference between the melting temperatures of the two base metals or between those of the weld metal and a base metal can result in rupture of the metal having the lower melting temperature. Solidification and contraction of the metal, may be with the higher melting temperature, will induce stresses in the other metal while it is in a weak partially solidified condition. This problem may be solved by depositing one or more layers of a filler metal of intermediate melting temperature on the face of the base metal with the higher melting temperature. This procedure is known as buttering. The weld is then made between the buttered face and the other base metal. The buttering layer should serve to reduce the differential in melting temperature. Buttering may also be used to provide transition between materials with substantially different coefficients of thermal expansion but which must endure cycling temperatures in service. Similarly, buttering may be used to provide a barrier layer that will slow the undesirable migration of elements from the base metal to the weld metal during postweld heat treatment or in service at elevated temperatures.

1.1.4 Thermal Conductivity

Most metals and alloys are relatively good conductors of heat, but some are much better than others. Rapid conduction of heat from the molten weld pool by an adjacent base metal may affect the energy input required to locally melt the base metal. When two dissimilar metals of significantly different thermal conductivities are welded together (e.g. plain carbon steel and Cu-base alloys), the welding procedure must provide for this difference. Often the welding heat source must be directed at the metal having the higher thermal conductivity to obtain the proper heat balance.

When welding dissimilar metals, heat loss to the base metals can be balanced somewhat by selectively preheating the metal having the higher thermal conductivity. Dilution is more uniform with balanced heat. Preheating the base metal of higher thermal conductivity also reduces the cooling rate of the weld metal and the HAZ. The net effect of preheating is to reduce the heat needed to melt that base metal.

1.1.5 Coefficient of Thermal Expansion

The coefficient of thermal expansion (CTE) of the two dissimilar base metals is another important factor. Large differences in CTE of adjacent metals during cooling will induce tensile stress in one metal and compressive stress in the other. The metal subject to tensile stress may hot crack during welding, or it may cold crack in service unless the stresses are relieved thermally or mechanically. This factor is particularly important in joints that will operate at elevated temperature in a cyclic temperature mode. A common example of this is austenitic SS/ferritic steel pipe butt joints used in energy conversion plants.

Ideally, the CTE of the weld metal should be intermediate between those of the base metals, especially if the difference between those of the two base metals is large. If the difference is small, the weld metal may have a CTE equivalent to that of one of the base metals.

1.2 Welding Considerations

1.2.1 Welding Process

The three most popular arc welding processes utilised for joining dissimilar metals are SMAW, GMAW and GTAW. Selecting the welding process to make a given dissimilar-metal joint is almost as important as selecting the proper filler metal, as the depth of fusion into the base metals and the resulting dilution may vary with different welding processes and techniques.

It is not uncommon with SMAW for the filler metal to be diluted up to 30% with base metal. The dilution rate can be kept below 25% with this technique. If dilution from one base metal is less detrimental than from the other, the arc should be directed towards that metal. This technique is also applicable to GTAW. Other means to control dilution are described in the subsequent section on "Weld Cladding".

Dilution rates with GMAW can range from 10 to 50%, depending upon the type of metal transfer and the welding gun manipulation. Spray transfer gives the greatest dilution; short-circuit transfer, the least dilution. Penetration with SAW can be greater, depending on polarity, and can result in more dilution.

Regardless of the process, dilution is also affected by other factors, including joint design and fit-up. It is always best to have a minimum uniform dilution along the joint. Variations in dilution may produce inconsistent joint properties.

1.2.2 Selection of Filler Metal

Selection of a suitable filler metal is an important factor in producing a dissimilar-metal joint that will perform well in service. One objective of dissimilar-metal welding is to minimise undesirable interactions between the metals. The filler metal should be compatible with both base metals and be capable of being deposited with a minimum of dilution.

Two important criteria that should govern the selection of proper filler metal for welding two dissimilar metals are as follows:

- The candidate filler metal must provide the joint design requirements, such as mechanical properties or corrosion resistance.
- The candidate filler metal must fulfil the weldability criteria with respect to dilution, melting temperature, and other physical property requirements of the weldment.

The Schaeffler diagram is commonly used to predict weld metal microstructure and subsequent filler metal selection when joining a SS to a carbon or low alloy steel. Figure 2 illustrates the procedure with an example of a single-pass weld joining mild steel to type 304 SS with ER 309

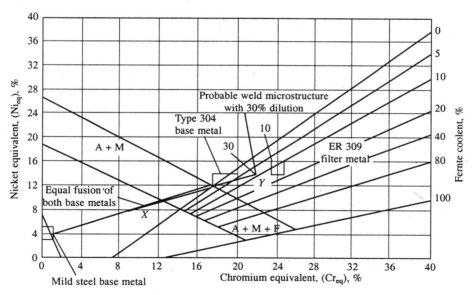

Fig. 2 **Prediction of weld metal composition from the Schaeffler Diagram; A – austenite, F – ferrite, M – martensite [2]**

SS filler metal. First, a connecting point is drawn between the two points representing the base metal compositions, based on their Cr and Ni equivalents. Point X, representing the relative dilutions contributed by each base metal, is then located on this line.

If the relative dilutions are equal, point X is at the midpoint of the line. A second line is drawn between point X and the point representing ER 309 filler metal composition. The composition of the weld pass lies somewhere on this line, the exact location depending upon the total dilution. With 30% dilution, the composition would be at point Y and would be considered acceptable. If a succeeding pass joins the first pass to mild steel, the dilution with the mild steel should be kept to a minimum to avoid martensite formation in the weld metal. For improved accuracy in predicting the microstructure of dissimilar-metal welds, the WRC-1992 diagram [3] should be used.

1.2.3   Buttering

If dilution of austenitic SS filler metal is a problem, it may be controlled by first buttering the joint face of the carbon or low-alloy steel with one or two layers of type 309 or 310 SS filler metal as shown in Figs. 3(a) and 3(b). After machining and inspecting the buttered layer (Fig. 3c), the joint between the SS component and the buttered steel part can be made using conventional welding procedures and the appropriate filler metal for welding the SS base metal (Figs. 3d and 3e). A low-alloy steel component can be heat treated after the buttering operation, then joined to the SS part. This avoids a postweld heat treatment that might sensitise the austenitic SS to intergranular corrosion.

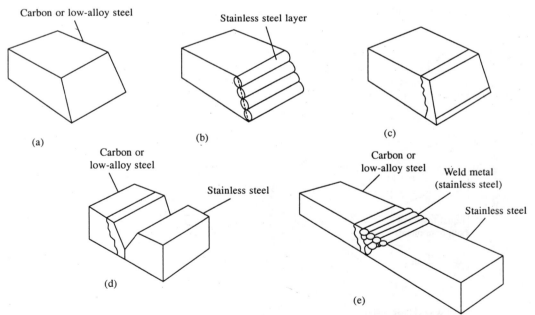

Fig. 3   Buttering technique used to assist in welding stainless steel to carbon or low alloy steel: (a) edge prepared for buttering; (b) face buttered with filler metal; (c) buttered face prepared for welding; (d) joint aligned for welding; (e) joint welded with stainless steel filler metal [2]

1.2.4 Joint Design

When designing butt joints between dissimilar metals, consideration must be given to the melting characteristics of each base metal and the filler metal, as well as to dilution effect. Large grooves decrease dilution permit better control of viscous weld metal, and provide room for better manipulation of the arc for good fusion. The joint design should provide for appropriate dilution in the first few passes placed in the joint when welding from one side. Improper dilution could result in a layer of weld metal possessing mechanical properties that are inappropriate for the intended service, particularly when the joint will be exposed to cyclic stresses. When welding from both sides, back gouging of the first weld can provide better control of dilution in the first few passes of the second weld.

Dissimilar-metal joints are often made with groove geometries similar to those in conventional similar-metal welds and are left in the as-welded condition. However, removing the excess penetration of the weld root eliminates possible defects that may be present, and it eliminates notches and crevices associated with backing rings. Removing the weld root also improves the capabilities of non-destructive tests (radiography, liquid penetrant, and ultrasonic). Provision can also be made for removing the exterior reinforcement to eliminate stress concentrations associated with undercutting and with the change in section thickness across the as welded joint. Again, inspection capabilities are improved.

1.2.5 Preheat and Postweld Heat Treatments

Selection of an appropriate preheat and postweld heat treatment (PWHT) for a welded joint can present a problem with some dissimilar-metal combinations. The appropriate heat treatment of one component of the weldment may be deleterious to the other component for the intended service conditions. For example, if an age-hardenable Ni-Cr alloy is welded to a nonstabilised austenitic SS, exposure of the weldment to ageing treatment for the Ni-Cr alloy would sensitise the SS and decrease its resistance to intergranular corrosion (weld decay). One solution is to use a stabilised austenitic SS if that is acceptable. Another solution might be to butter the face of the age-hardenable Ni-Cr alloy component with a similar alloy that is not age-hardenable. This component is then heat treated to obtain the desired properties. Finally, the buttered surface is welded to the SS component.

1.3 Service Considerations

1.3.1 Property Considerations

A dissimilar metal joint normally contains weld metal having a composition different from that of one or both base metals. The properties of the weld metal depend on the filler metal composition, the welding procedures, and the relative dilution with each base metal. There are two different HAZs, one in each base metal adjacent to the weld metal. The mechanical and physical properties of the weld metal as well as those of the two HAZs, must be considered for the intended service.

Special considerations are given to dissimilar-metal joints intended for elevated temperature service. A favourable condition exists when the joint operates at constant temperatures. During elevated temperature service, internal stresses can decrease by relaxation and reach an equilibrium. However, it is best to reduce the effect of large differences in CTE when temperature fluctuations cannot be avoided in service. The problem can be avoided by selecting base metals with similar thermal expansion characteristics.

Figure 4 gives the mean linear CTE as a function of temperature for several alloys commonly associated with transition butt joints for steam plant applications. The CTE of 2.25 Cr-1Mo steel is about 25% less than that of types 304 and 316 austenitic SS. In certain applications, transition joints between austenitic SS and low-alloy steel may experience numerous temperature changes during operation. For a given change in temperature, the stress imposed at the weld joint is proportional to the difference in their CTE. Stress analyses of welded joints between these two types of steel indicate that the stresses introduced by thermal change are nearly an order of magnitude greater than those produced by the operating pressures and thermal gradients across the joint.

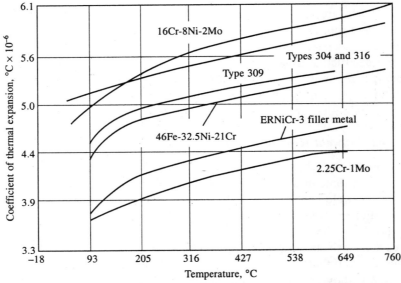

Fig. 4   Mean coefficients of thermal expansion as a function of transition butt joint materials [2]

Experience with dissimilar-metal transition joints has shown a significant number of failures in less than the expected service life. The majority of the transition joint failures in austenitic SS/ferritic steel joints occur in the ferritic steel HAZ adjacent to the weld interface. These failures are generally attributed to one or more of the following causes:

- High stresses and the resulting creep at the interface as a result of the difference in CTE of the weld and base metals.
- Carbon migration from the ferritic steel into the SS, which weakens the HAZ in the ferritic steel.
- Preferential oxidation at the interface, accelerated by the presence of stress.

1.3.2 Carbon Migration

There is the likelihood of significant chemical composition gradients in the weld metal, particularly in the regions adjacent to the base metals. In addition, operation at elevated temperatures can cause interdiffusion between the weld metal and the base metal that, in turn, results in microstructural changes. A dissimilar-metal weld made between low-alloy steel and austenitic SS, with an austenitic SS filler metal, illustrates the problem. Chromium in steel has, a greater affinity for carbon than iron. When a carbon or low-alloy steel is welded with a SS filler metal containing significant amount of Cr, carbon can diffuse from the base metal into the weld metal at temperatures above about 425°C. The diffusion rate is a function of temperature and exposure time, and it increases rapidly at 595°C and above. Carbon migration can take place during PWHT or service at elevated temperatures.

Austenitic steel has greater solubility for carbon than ferritic steel. Therefore, carbon depletion in carbon or low-alloy steel is greater when austenitic SS filler metal is used in preference to ferritic steel filler metal. On the other hand, carbon migration is not as serious a problem when Ni-Cr-Fe filler metal is used.

If carbon migration is extensive, it will be indicated by a lightly etching, low-carbon band in the carbon steel HAZ and a dark, high-carbon zone in the SS weld metal, as seen in a transverse metallographic section. The extent of carbon migration during PWHT or elevated temperature service should be determined during welding procedure qualification. It is known to influence long-time stress-rupture strength during elevated-temperature service.

During cyclic temperature service, the HAZ will be subjected to varying shear stresses because of the differences in CTE of the base and weld metals. These stresses may produce fatigue failure in the decarburised band next to the weld interface.

1.3.3 Corrosion and Oxidation Resistance

The weld metal and both base metals have specific corrosion behaviours that must be considered by the designer in the initial selection of materials. For example, with dissimilar metal weldments, the formation of galvanic cells can cause corrosion of the most anodic metal or phase in the joint. Also, the weld metal is usually composed of several microstructural phases, and very localised cells between phases can result in galvanic corrosion at the microstructural level. To minimise galvanic corrosion, the composition of the weld metal can be adjusted to provide cathodic protection to the base metal that is most susceptible to galvanic attack. However, other design requirements should not be seriously compromised to do this. Instead, some other form of protection should be used.

A galvanic cell associated with high-strength steel may promote hydrogen embrittlement in the HAZ of that steel if it is the cathode of the cell. Hydrogen embrittlement must be considered if the service temperature of the weldment will be in the range of -40 to 95°C, and the weld will be in a highly stressed area of the assembly. Residual stresses developed in the weld zone are often sufficient to promote hydrogen embrittlement and stress-corrosion cracking.

Chemical compositional differences in a dissimilar-metal weld can also cause high-temperature corrosion problems. Compositional variations at the interfaces between the different metals can result in selective oxidation when operating at high temperatures in air and formation of notches at these locations. Such notches are potential stress-raisers in the joint and can cause oxidation failure along the weld interface under cyclic thermal conditions.

1.4 Specific Dissimilar Metal Combinations with Stainless Steels

The emphasis in the following sections will be on joining carbon and low-alloy steels to various dissimilar materials (both ferrous and non-ferrous) by arc welding [2].

1.4.1 Stainless Steels to Carbon or Low-Alloy Steels

Austenitic, ferritic and matensitic SS can be readily welded to carbon and low-alloy steels using a filler metal that can tolerate dilution by both base metals without formation of flaws in the joint. An austenitic SS or Ni-alloy filler metal is commonly used; its choice depends on the application and service conditions.

Generally, carbon or low-alloy steel are joined to 300-type SS using austenitic filler metals, such as types E/ER 308, 309, 316 and 347. Such filler metals are used for service applications below 425°C. For higher temperatures or when high-temperature cyclic service is a concern, high-Ni filler metals such as ERNiCr-3 and ENiCrFe-3 are used. The CTE of high-Ni alloys approximate those of ferritic steels, and during cyclic-temperature service, the major differential expansion stresses are located primarily at the tough SS/weld metal interface. Another advantage of a Ni-base weld metal is that it markedly reduces carbon migration from the ferritic steels to the weld metal. Extensive carbon migration into SS weld metal weakens the HAZ of the carbon or low-alloy steel.

The problem of cracking of joints between ferritic steels, such as 2.25Cr-1Mo steel, and austenitic SS is a recurring problem in such operations as the petrochemical industry and electric utility generating plants. Cracking has been repeatedly observed in HAZs of the ferritic portions of dissimilar-metal welds, particularly those that have been subjected to a large number of thermal cycles and extended time at elevated temperatures around 565°C.

One of the approaches for circumventing the problems associated with these dissimilar-metal welds is to use a trimetallic joint configuration, with the "transition" piece having CTE between those of ferritic steels and austenitic SS, and the weld metals having a CTE intermediate to those of the base metals they join. This would result in a more gradual change in the CTE, and a consequent decrease in the magnitude of stresses from thermal cycling. In addition to thermal expansion characteristics, the weldability, metallurgical compatibility and stability during long-term service must also be considered in the choice of the transition piece and welding consumables, especially because the trimetallic joint configuration will involve two dissimilar weld joints. The mean CTE in the temperature range 0 to 600°C for the ferritic steels 2.25Cr-1 Mo and 9Cr-1Mo are 14.0 and 12.6 μm m^{-1}K^{-1}, respectively, while those for austenitic SS of types 304 and 316 are 18.5 and 18.8 μm m^{-1}K^{-1}, respectively. Among the materials that have CTE intermediate to those of ferritic steels and austenitic SS, Incoloy 800 with a CTE of 17.1 μm m^{-1}K^{-1} is the most attractive choice for the transition piece. Additionally, Incoloy 800 offers advantages in terms of excellent resistance to oxidation and creep at elevated temperatures. Further, detailed stress analysis has shown that the hoop stress values in the 2.25Cr-1Mo steel close to the root region decreases by 37% when Incoloy 800 is used as the transition material. This clearly establishes the superiority of trimetallic joint over the (direct) bimetallic joint. ERNiCr-3 and ENiCrFe-3, which have a CTE of 15.5 μm m^{-1}K^{-1} can be retained for welding the 2.25Cr-1Mo steel/Incoloy 800 joint. For welding the Incoloy 800/austenitic SS joint, austenitic SS welding consumable ER 16-8-2 (16%Cr, 8%Ni and 2%Mo) with a CTE of 17.3 μm m^{-1}K^{-1} is the natural choice. Detailed metallurgical studies have been carried out for the development, characterisation and evaluation of this improved trimetallic joint configuration of austenitic SS/Incoloy 800/Cr-Mo ferritic steel, for use in the steam generator circuits of the 500 MWe prototype fast breeder reactor (Fig. 5). These studies have showed that a marked improvement in performance can be obtained by using the trimetallic joint configuration, with at least a four-fold improvement in its service life over that of direct (bimetallic) joint configuration with austenitic SS weld metals [4].

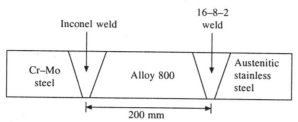

Fig. 5   Schematic configuration of the trimetallic transition joint to be adopted for the Prototype Fast Breeder Reactor

Buttering is also used to improve the weldability between ferritic and austenitic SS joints. A thick overlay (13 mm or greater) of a highly austenitic weld metal, such as type 309 SS, can be deposited on carbon or low-alloy steel components so that the SS/SS welds can be subsequently made on the field. This technique has limited reliability for high-temperature cyclic service and has not been used extensively for material combinations other than ferritic steels, SS, and some high-Ni alloys.

A filler metal for joining a 4xx-series SS to carbon or low-alloy steel can be selected using the following general rules:

- For welding one hardenable Cr-steel to another with a higher Cr content, filler metal containing Cr equal to that of either steel may be used. Furthermore any filler metal whose Cr content lies between these limits is equally satisfactory, provided the weldment is properly heat treated.
- A general rule for welding any Cr-steel to any low-alloy steel is to use a filler metal that has the same composition as the low-alloy steel, provided that it meets the service requirements of the application. With any low-alloy steel filler metal, the Cr that is picked up by dilution with the Cr-steel base metal must be considered.
- For welding any Cr-steel to a carbon steel, carbon steel filler metal can be used. A Cr-steel filler metal can alternatively be used, but it is preferable to use a less hardenable filler metal.

When the properties of the HAZ in the Cr-SS are important, both the SS and the other steel can be buttered with type 309 or 310 austenitic SS weld metal. An appropriate preheat or PWHT can be used to obtain desired properties in the buttered components. The SS surfaces can be welded together without preheat using a suitable austenitic SS filler metal, such as type 308.

1.4.2   Nickel-Base Alloys to Steels

Ni-alloys can be easily welded to steels using a suitable filler metal and proper control of dilution. Ni-base filler metals are generally used because of their good ductility and tolerance to dilution by Fe. Suggested Ni-base filler metals for welding Ni-alloys to steels or SS are listed in Table 1.

Table 1 Suggested filler metals for welding nickel-base alloys to carbon, low-alloy and stainless steels

Nickel Alloy (common designation)	Filler metal from	Filler metal for welding to	
		Carbon or low alloy steel	Stainless steel
Commercially pure Ni	Covered electrode	ENi-1, ENiCrFe-2	ENi-1, ENiCrFe-2, ENiCrFe-3
	Bare wire	ERNi-1, ERNiCr-3	ERNi-1, ERNiCr-3, ERNiCrFe-6
Monel 400	Covered electrode	ENiCu-7, ENi-1	ENiCrFe-2, ENiCrFe-3
Monel K-500 Monel 502	Bare wire	ERNi-1	ERNiCr-3, ERNiCrFe-6
Inconel 600	Covered electrode	ENiCrFe-2, ENiCrFe-3	ENiCrFe-2, ENiCrFe-3
Incoloy 800	Bare wire	ERNiCr-3, ERNiCrFe-6	ERNiCr-3, ERNiCrFe-6
Incoloy 825	Covered electrode	ENiCrMo-3	ENiCrMo-3
	Bare wire	ERNiCrMo-3	ERNiCrMo-3
Hastelloy B-2	Covered electrode	ENiMo-7	ENiMo-7
	Bare wire	ERNiMo-7	ERNiMo-7
Hastelloy C-276	Covered electrode	ENiCrMo-4	ENiCrMo-4
	Bare wire	ERNiCrMo-4	ERNiCrMo-4
Hastelloy C-4	Covered electrode	ENiCrMo-4	ENiCrMo-4
	Bare wire	ERNiCrMo-7	ERNiCrMo-7
Hastelloy G	Covered electrode	ENiCrMo-9	ENiCrMo-9
	Bare wire	ERNiCrMo-1	ERNiCrMo-1

Sulphur and phosphorus in nickel and Ni-alloys cause hot cracking. The melting techniques used to produce Ni and its alloys are designed to keep these elements to low levels. By contrast, S and P contents in some steels are typically higher. Consequently, dilution should be carefully controlled when joining a steel to a Ni-alloy with a Ni-alloy filler metal, to avoid hot cracking in the weld metal.

Most Ni-base weld metals can accept a substantial amount of Fe dilution, but the dilution limit generally varies with the welding process. Weld metal deposited with Ni or Ni-Cr covered electrodes can tolerate up to approximately 40% Fe dilution. With bare Ni or Ni-Cr filler metals, however, dilution should be kept to about 25%.

Acceptable limits of Fe dilution for Ni-Cu weld metal vary, depending on the welding process. With SMAW, Fe dilution of up to about 30% can be tolerated. Submerged arc weld metal should not be diluted by more than 25%.

With gas-shielding processes, Ni-Cu weld metal is less tolerant to Fe dilution, especially if the weld is to be thermally stress relieved. The maximum limit for Fe dilution in a welded joint are 10% when it will be used as-welded and 5% when it will be stress-relieved. A buttering layer of Ni or Ni-Cu weld metal should be applied to the steel face in order to avoid exceeding these limits. Ni-Cu weld metal has a maximum dilution tolerance for Cr of about 8%. Consequently, Ni-Cu filler metal should not be used to join Ni-Cu alloys to SS.

1.4.3   Cobalt-Base Alloys to Steels

Metallurgically, Co-base alloys behave similarly to the high-temperature Ni-Cr alloys with respect to welding. When joining a Co-alloy to a SS, a filler metal with a composition similar to that of the Co-alloy is recommended. A Ni-alloy filler metal may also be suitable for some applications. In any case, the filler metal selection, welding process, and welding procedure for the application should be established by suitable tests.

1.4.4   Copper-Base Alloys to Steels

Copper and many Cu-base alloys can be joined to carbon, low-alloy and stainless steels by GTAW, GMAW, and SMAW. Fe dilution can be minimised by use of appropriate welding procedures or by placement of a buttering layer of Ni on the steel. Tables 2 and 3 show combinations of dissimilar metals by GTAW and GMAW, respectively, with the aid of Cu-base or Ni-base filler metals

Table 2   Filler metals, preheat and interpass temperatures used in gas-tungsten arc welding of coppers and copper-base alloys to steels

Metal	Filler metal (preheat and interpass temperatures) recommended				
	Low carbon steel	Medium-carbon steel	High carbon steel	Low alloy steel	Stainless steel
Coppers	ERCuAl-A2, ERCu, ERNi-3 (540°C)	ERCuAl-A2, ERCu, ERNi-3 (540°C)	ERCuAl-A2, ERCu, ERNi-3 (540°C)	ERCuAl-A2, ERCu, ERNi-3 (540°C)	ERCuAl-A2, ERCu, ERNi-3 (540°C)
Phosphor bronzes	ERCuSn-A (205°C)	ERCuSn-A (260°C)	ERCuSn-A (260°C)	ERCuSn-A (260°C)	ERCuSn-A (205°C)
Aluminium bronzes	ERCuAl-A2 (150°C)	ERCuAl-A2 (205°C)	ERCuAl-A2 (260°C)	ERCuAl-A2 (260°C)	ERCuAl-A2 (65°C max.)
Silicon bronzes	ERCuAl-A2 (65°C max.)	ERCuAl-A2 (65°C max.)	ERCuAl-A2 (205°C)	ERCuAl-A2 (205°C)	ERCuAl-A2 (65°C max.)
Cupro-nickels	ERCuAl-A2 ERNi-3 (65°C max.)	ERCuAl-A2 ERNi-3 (65°C max.)	ERCuAl-A2 ERNi-3 (65°C max.)	ERCuAl-A2 ERNi-3 (65°C max.)	ERCuAl-A2 ERNi-3 (65°C max.)

Note: Filler metal selections in table are based on weldability, except where mechanical properties are usually more important. Preheating is usually used only when at least one member is thicker than about 3.2 mm or is highly conductive. Preheat and interpass temperatures are subject to adjustment based on size and shape of weldment

1.4.5   Aluminium-Base Alloys to Steels

With respect to fusion welding, Fe and Al are not compatible metals. Their melting points differ greatly: 660°C for Al versus 1538°C for Fe. Both metals have almost no solubility for the other

Table 3   **Filler metals, preheat and interpass temperatures used in gas meal arc welding of coppers and copper base alloys to steels**

Metal	Filler metal (preheat and interpass temperatures) recommended				
	Low carbon steel	Medium-carbon steel	High-carbon steel	Low alloy steel	Stainless steel
Coppers	ERCuAl-A2, ERCu, ERNi-3 (540°C)	ERCuAl-A2, ERCu, ERNi-3 (540°C)	ERCuAl-A2, ERCu, ERNi-3 (540°C)	ERCuAl-A2, ERCu, ERNi-3 (540°C)	ERCuAl-A2, ERCu, ERNi-3 (540°C)
Low-zinc brasses	ERCuSn-A (315°C)	ERCuAl-A2 (315°C)	ERCuAl-A2 (315°C)	ERCuAl-A2 (315°C)	ERCuAl-A2 ERCuSn-A (315°C)
High-zinc brasses, tin brasses, special brasses	ERCuAl-A2 (260°C)	ERCuAl-A2 (260°C)	ERCuAl-A2 (260°C)	ERCuAl-A2 (315°C)	ERCuAl-A2 (315°C)
Phosphor bronzes	ERCuSn-A (205°C)	ERCuSn-A (205°C)	ERCuSn-A (260°C)	ERCuSn-A (260°C)	ERCuSn-A (205°C)
Aluminium bronzes	ERCuAl-A2 (150°C)	ERCuAl-A2 (205°C)	ERCuAl-A2 (260°C)	ERCuAl-A2 (260°C)	ERCuAl-A2 (65°C max.)
Silcon bronzes	ERCuAl-A2 (65°C max.)	ERCuAl-A2 (65°C max.)	ERCuAl-A2 (205°C)	ERCuAl-A2 (205°C)	ERCuAl-A2 (65°C max.)
Cupro-nickels	ERCuAl-A2 ERNi-3 (65°C max.)	ERCuAl-A2 ERNi-3 (65°C max.)	ERCuAl-A2 ERNi-3 (65°C max.)	ERCuAl-A2 ERNi-3 (65°C max.)	ERCuAl-A2 ERNi-3 (65°C max.)

Note: Filler metal selections in table are based on weldability, except where mechanical properties are usually more important. Preheating is usually used only when at least one member is thicker than about 3.2 mm or is highly conductive. Preheat and interpass temperatures are subject to adjustment based on size and shape of weldment

in the solid state, especially Fe in Al, and several brittle intermetallic phases can form ($FeAl_2$, Fe_2Al_5, or $FeAl_3$). Consequently, fusion welds joining Fe and Al are brittle. In addition, high welding stresses would be expected because of the significant differences in the CTE, thermal conductivities, and specific heats of Fe and Al. Al can be joined to carbon or stainless steels by brazing, solid-state welding or by high-energy processes such as electron beam welding.

2   WELD CLADDING

The term weld cladding usually denotes the application of a relatively thick layer ($\geq$ 3 mm) of weld metal for the purpose of providing a corrosion resistant surface [1]. Typical base metal components that are weld cladded include the internal surfaces of carbon and low-alloy steel pressure vessels, paper digesters, urea reactors, tube sheets, nuclear reactor containment vessels, and hydro crackers. The cladding material is usually an austenitic SS or a Ni-base alloy, although certain Cu-base alloys are also sometimes used. Some specialised cladding is also carried out using silver filler metal. Weld cladding is usually performed using the submerged arc welding process (SAW). However, flux-cored (either self-shielded or gas-shielded), plasma arc, and electroslag welding methods can also produce weld claddings. Filler metals are available as covered electrodes, coiled electrode wire, and strip electrodes. Table 4 lists some of the filler metals for SS weld cladding.

Table 4 Stainless steel filler metals for weld cladding applications

SS weld overlay type	First layer		Subsequent layers	
	Covered electrode	Bare rod or electrode	Covered electrode	Bare rod or electrode
304	E309	ER309	E308	ER308
304L	E309, E309Nb	ER309L	E308L	ER308L
321	E309Nb	ER309Nb	E347	ER347
347	E309Nb	ER309Nb	E347	ER347
309	E309	EWR309	E309	ER309
310	E310	ER310	E310	ER310
316	E309Mo	ER309Mo	E316	ER316
316L	E309MoL, E317L	ER309MoL, ER317L	E316L	ER316L
317	E309Mo, E317	ER309Mo, ER317	E317	ER317
317L	E309MoL, E317L	ER309MoL, ER317L	E317L	ER317L
320Nb	E320	ER320	E320	ER320

2.1 Application Considerations

The technique of weld cladding is an excellent method to impart properties to the surface of a substrate that are not available from that base metal, or to conserve expensive or difficult-to-obtain materials by using only a relatively thin surface layer on a less expensive or abundant base material [5]. This technique has several inherent limitations or possible problems that must be considered when planning for weld cladding. The thickness of the required surface must be less than the maximum thickness of the overlay that can be obtained with the particular process and filler metal selected.

Welding position also must be considered when selecting an overlay material and process. Certain processes are limited in their available welding positions; e.g. SAW can be used only in the flat position. In addition, when using a high-deposition-rate process that exhibits a large liquid pool, welding vertically or overhead may be difficult or impossible. Some alloys exhibit eutectic solidification, which leads to large molten pools that solidify instantly rather than with a "mushy" (liquid plus solid) transition. Such materials are also difficult to weld except in the flat position.

2.2 Composition Control of Stainless Steel Weld Overlays

The economics of SS weld cladding are dependent on achieving the specific chemistry at the highest practical deposition rate in a minimum number of layers [5]. The fabricator selects the filler wire and welding process, whereas the purchaser specifies the surface chemistry and thickness, along with the base metal. The most outstanding difference between welding a joint and depositing an overlay is in the area of dilution. The percentage of dilution equals the amount of base metal melted (x) divided by the sum of base metal melted and filler metal added ($x + y$), the quotient of which is multiplied by 100.

$$\% \text{ dilution} = \frac{x}{x + y} \times 100$$

For SS cladding, a fabricator must understand how the dilution of the filler metal with the base metal affects the composition and metallurgical balance, such as proper ferrite level to minimise hot cracking, absence of martensite on the interface for bond integrity, and carbon at a low level to ensure corrosion resistance. The prediction of the microstructures and properties (such as hot cracking and corrosion resistance) for the austenitic SS has been the topic of many studies [6]. During the last two decades, three microstructure prediction diagrams have found the widest application. These include the Schaeffler diagram [7], the DeLong diagram [8], and the WRC-1992 [3] diagrams.

2.2.1   *Control of Dilution*

Control of dilution plays an important role in the economics of the weld cladding process. Although each process has an expected dilution factor, experimenting with welding parameters can minimise dilution. A value between 10 and 15% is generally considered optimum. Less than 10% raises the question of bond integrity, and greater than 15% increases the cost of the filler metal. Unfortunately, most welding processes have considerably greater dilution.

Because of the importance of dilution in weld cladding, each welding parameter must be carefully evaluated and recorded. Many of the parameters that affect dilution in weld cladding applications are not so closely controlled when arc welding a joint. These parameters include:

- *Amperage*: Increased amperage (current density) increases dilution. The arc becomes hotter, it penetrates more deeply, and more base metal melting occurs.
- *Polarity*: DCEN gives less penetration and resulting lower dilution than DCEP. AC results in dilution that lies between DCEN and DCEP.
- *Electrode size*: The smaller the electrode, the lower the amperage, which results in lower dilution.
- *Electrode extension*: A long electrode extension for consumable electrode processes decreases dilution. A short electrode extension increases dilution.
- *Travel speed*: A decrease in travel speed decreases the amount of base metal melted and increases proportionally the amount of filler metal melted, thus decreasing dilution.
- *Oscillation*: Greater width of electrode oscillation reduces dilution. The frequency of oscillation also affects dilution—the higher the frequency of oscillation, the lower the dilution.
- *Welding position*: Depending on the welding position or work inclination, gravity causes the weld pool to run ahead of, remain under, or run behind the arc. If weld pool stays ahead of or under the arc, less base metal penetration and resulting dilution will occur. If the pool is too far ahead of the arc, there will be insufficient melting of the surface of the base metal, and coalescence will not occur.

- *Arc shielding*: The shielding medium, gas or flux, also affects dilution. The following list ranks various shielding mediums in order of decreasing dilution: granular flux without alloy addition (highest), He, CO_2, Ar, self-shielded FCAW, and granular flux with alloy addition (lowest).
- *Additional filler metal*: Extra metal (not including the electrode), added to the weld pool as powder, wire, strip, or with flux, reduces dilution by increasing the total amount of filler metal and reducing the amount of base metal that is melted.

2.3   Procedures for Stainless Steel Weld Cladding

2.3.1   Submerged Arc Welding

SAW is by far the most commonly used process for weld cladding. The process is adaptable for use with single wires as the electrode filler metal, multiple wires, or strip. AC is often used, but DC, with either reverse or straight polarity, has been found preferable in numerous instances. Oscillation of the filler metal is frequently found desirable.

The fluxes for submerged arc overlays should have low bulk density, especially for wide weld beads produced with multiple wire or strip electrodes. Standard fused fluxes, therefore, are usually unsuitable. Agglomerated fluxes, which have much lower bulk density, are commonly used for this purpose. Low bulk-density fused fluxes have been successfully produced by a manufacturing process known as foaming. Such foamed fluxes have even lower bulk density than agglomerated fluxes.

Agglomerated fluxes (or bonded fluxes) have a distinct advantage over fused fluxes in that it is possible to introduce alloying elements by means of the flux. When this is done, they are known as reinforced, or alloyed, fluxes. For SS weld claddings, Cr is commonly added to the fluxes to overcome oxidation of Cr, which is characteristic of SAW of SS alloys, and to compensate for the dilution with the non-Cr or low-Cr base metal. Other alloying elements often added to reinforced fluxes are Mn, Ni, Mo and Nb. With reinforced fluxes, it is possible to produce various modified SS weld overlays using a single filler metal as an electrode, e.g. a type 347 overlay with a 308 or 309 filler metal using a Nb-alloyed flux. Another method of providing the desired SS cladding composition is to introduce a layer of powdered metal under the submerged arc flux. This procedure is sometimes known as bulk welding. The powdered metal not only provides the alloying elements needed in the overlay, but it also greatly reduces the dilution. The method of adding alloying elements by using powdered alloys, either as an ingredient of the flux, or separately, is subject to variability of deposit composition. Thus, it is unwise to rely on these methods of alloy adjustment of the weld overlay composition for more than 3%.

Still another method of providing the desired composition for the cladding is to use tubular wire for the filler metal. Whereas the solid wire producer is limited in the compositions that can be produced and still provide hot workability and cold drawing capability, the producer of tubular wire is virtually unlimited as to the compositions that can be produced. For example, the strip can be Cr-or Cr-Ni steel, to which the core ingredients are added to give a weld deposit of austenitic SS, rich enough in the essential alloys to compensate for both oxidation and dilution losses.

2.3.2 Self-Shielded Flux-Cored Wire

Tubular wires are produced that contain not only the alloying ingredients, but also the fluxing and gas-shielding ingredients. This permits the deposition of weld claddings, without the need of an external flux, as is needed with SAW, or an external gas, as is needed with gas-shielded solid wire welding. Weld claddings are produced by manually directed welding guns for limited areas using a single tubular wire. High productivity procedures also have developed using multiple wires in a manner similar to SAW.

Metallurgically, flux-cored wires offer potentially higher alloyed claddings, permitting a considerable cost saving to produce the desired composition in a single layer. Also, dilution is minimised with this process. Furthermore, carbon content can be kept to much lower levels than is possible with solid wires, partly due to the ability to have very low-carbon ingredients in the flux-cored wire and partly due to the low dilution.

2.3.3 Plasma Arc Hot Wire Process

The plasma arc hot wire process is used for depositing SS claddings on pressure vessels subjected to corrosive, high-temperature, and high-pressure hydrogen environments. Advantages of the hot wire process include:

- Accurate control of dilution and thus composition of the overlay
- Little or no changes due to oxidation of the elements in the process
- Parameters that can be independently and accurately controlled
- Single-layer overlays that can be produced in thickness ranging from 4.0 to 8.0 mm
- Applicability to many corrosion-resistant alloys, such as Monel, Inconel, and Hastelloy alloys.

2.3.4 Electroslag Overlays

The electroslag welding process has been adapted to produce SS weld claddings. This process offers the ability to use wider strip (up to 300 mm) than the SAW process and more uniform penetration into, and lower dilution with, the base metal. Its principal disadvantages are operator exposure to radiant heat from the molten slag and a sharper compositional change at the fusion line, which may give unsatisfactory service in some high-temperature pressure vessels (e.g. disbanding in hydrocrack or hydrosulphuriser service). Because of problems with weld claddings on pressure vessels in a hydrogen environment, electroslag weld claddings are not for preferred single-layer overlays; but where two-layer overlays are specified, the electroslag process being used for the second layer. Higher productivity, and a smoother surface are thus obtained, the first layer having been deposited by SAW.

Extremely low carbon levels are possible because of low dilution with the base metal and removal of carbon through oxidation in the process. For example, using a 0.18%C base metal and a 0.01%C strip, weld-metal carbon levels of 0.02% in the first layer and 0.01% in the second layer have been produced [5]. The electrosiag weld cladding process can also be applied for weld overlays of Ni-Cr (Inconel) alloys in the same manner as for SS.

2.4 Weld Overlays Other Than Stainless Steels

Many of the procedures described for SS weld cladding are applicable to other alloys [5] Generally, Ni-base alloys can be produced successfully using essentially the same procedures as for SS. Some of the common alloy filler metals used are given in Table 5.

Table 5 Nonferrous filler metals used for weld cladding of steels

Weld overlay type	Covered electrode	Bare rod or electrode
Al-bronze	ECuAl-A2	ERCuAl-Al
Si-bronze	ECuSi	ERCuSi
Cu-Ni	ECuNi (a)	ERCuNi (a)
Nickel	ENi-1	ERNi-1
Monel	ENiCu-7	ERNiCu-7
Inconel	ENiCrFe-3	ERNiCr-3
Inconel 625	ENiCrMo-3	ERNiCrMo-3
Hastelloy B	ENiMo-7	ERNiMo-7
Hastelloy C	ENICrMo-4	ERNiCrMo-4

(a) first layer must be nickel or Monel

Metals and alloys that do not tolerate significant amounts of Fe cannot be used in weld overlays on steels. Ti, Zr, Mg and Al are examples of incompatible metals for cladding steel. Pure Cu is also unsatisfactory, but some Cu-alloys, such as Al-bronze and Si-bronze, can be applied to steels. The incompatible metals are usually bonded by explosion cladding or roll bonding techniques.

REFERENCES

1. J.R. Davis, Hardfacing, Weld Cladding, and Dissimilar Metal Joining, ASM Handbook, Vol. 6 (Welding, Brazing, and Soldering), ASM International, Ohio, USA, 1993, pp. 789–829.
2. Dissimilar Metals, Welding Handbook, 7th Edn., Vol. 4, American Welding Society, Miami, USA, 1982, pp. 514–547.
3. D.J. Kotecki and T.A. Siewert, WRC-1992 constitution Diagram for Stainless Steel Weld Metal: A Modification of the WRC-1988 Diagram, Welding Journal, 71(5), 1992, pp. 171 s- I78s.
4. A.K. Bhaduri, S. Venkadesan, R Rodriguez and PG. Mukunda, Transition Metal Joint for Steam Generators—An Overview, International Journal of Pressure Vessel and Piping, 58, 1994, pp. 251–265.
5. R.D. Thomas et al., Weld Overlays, Metals Handbook, 9th Edn., Vol. 6 (Welding, Brazing, and Soldering), American Society for Metals, Ohio, USA, 1983, pp. 804–819.
6. D.L. Olson, Prediction of Austenitic Weld Metal Microstructure and Properties, Welding Journal, 64(10), 1985, pp. 281 s-295s.
7. A.L. Schaeffler, Constitution Diagram for Stainless Steel Weld Metal, Metal Progress, 56(11), 1949, pp. 680–680B.
8. W.T. DeLong, Ferrite in Austenitic Stainless Steel Weld Metal, Welding Journal, 53(7), 1974, pp. 273s–286s.
9. T.A. Siewert, C.N. McCowan and D.L. Olson, Ferrite Number Prediction to 100 FN in Stainless Steel Weld Metal, Welding Journal, 67(12), 1988, pp. 289s 178s.

8. Arc Welding Processes

S. Manoharan

Deputy General Manager, Welding Research Institute, BHEL, Tiruchi 620 041

I GAS METAL ARC WELDING

1 PRINCIPLE OF OPERATION

Gas metal arc welding (GMAW) is an arc welding process in which an electric arc is formed and maintained between a continuously fed filler metal electrode wire and the weld pool. In the arc heat, the electrode wire is melted and the molten metal (droplets) is transferred across the arc into the weldpool. The arc and the weld pool is shielded from the atmospheric contamination by an externally supplied shield gas. The process is illustrated in Figure 1. The shield gas can be argon, CO_2 or Ar + CO_2 gas mixture depending on the type of base metal being welded. Generally for welding of nonferrous metals argon is used as the shield gas and for welding of ferrous metals, CO_2 or Ar + CO_2 gas mixture is used. The process is found to provide a stable arc and good process control when a direct current (DC) power source is employed with electrode positive (DCEP) polarity. The DCEP provides stable arc, greater heat input to the cathodic base metal for good penetration and a fluid weld pool.

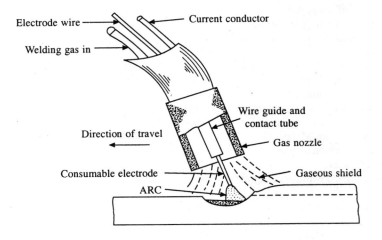

Fig. 1 Gas shielded metal arc welding process

Equipment required for GMAW is shown in Figure 2. The system comprises *of* a DC power source with flat characteristics, wire feed unit, welding gun, cable assembly and gas cylinder. The wire electrode is fed continuously into the arc by the wire feed unit at a speed preset by the operator. The wire feed rate can be varied generally from 1 m/min. to 20 m/min. For a given wire material and diameter, the arc current is determined by the wire feed rate. The required voltage is selected by adjusting the voltage control knobs provided at the power source.

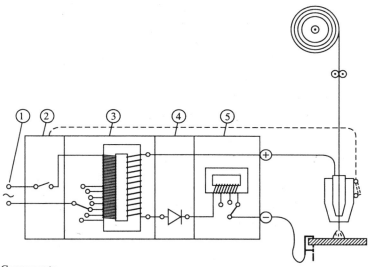

Components
1. Mains supply line
2. On/Off switch for welding current
3. Transformer with current switch
   Function: reduce mains voltage to welding voltage increase mains
           current to welding current
4. Rectifier
   Function: convert alternating or three-phase current to direct current
5. Welding regulator
   Function: smooth out current surges in the welding circuit

Fig. 2   Schematic diagram of the metal gas shielded arc welding current source

2   WIRE MELTING CHARACTERISTICS

A non-linear relationship exists between the rate at which the wire is fed into the arc and the current required to burn it off to maintain a constant arc length. This is known as the burn-off characteristic and differs for each filler wire composition and diameter. The curves shown in Figure 3 illustrate the burn-off characteristics of steel in $Ar+O_2$ mixture. It will be seen that to alter the welding current a proportionate increase in the wire feed rate is required. The smaller the diameter of the wire, the faster is the wire feed speed required to reach the same current.

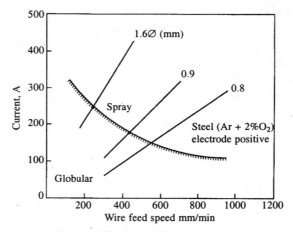

Fig. 3   Wire burn-off characteristics

3   POWER SOURCE COMPARISON

A power source with a flat characteristic is almost universally used for GMAW process as it offers several advantages e.g., latitude in setting the welding conditions, and self-regulated arc. Besides it also meets the special requirements of dip transfer welding.

The static volt-ampere characteristics of two power sources are shown in Figure 4. The curves labeled (d) are those of a "drooping arc characteristic" power source and the one labeled (f) the "flat characteristic". The lower graph (b) represents the typical burn-off characteristics of a wire and depicts the increase in current that results from an increase in wire feed rate. With the wire feed rate set at W1 m/min. the lower graph shows that A1 amps is required to burn off this

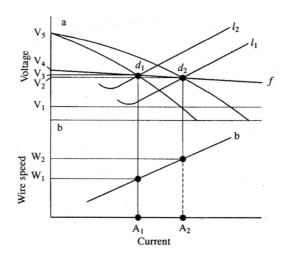

Fig. 4   Latitude in setting the welding conditions

particular wire diameter at this speed. Projecting up to the source curves shows that this current can be supplied at V3 Volts on both power sources f and d. If the wire speed is now increased to W2 m/min. the burn off characteristic curve (b) indicates that A2 amperes is required to burn off this amount of wire. Projecting up to the source curves shows that the constant voltage power source can supply this higher current at practically the same voltage as V2 is nearly equal to V3 but the drooping characteristic source can supply A2 amperes only at V1 vol. This is an impractical low arc voltage and the arc would be extinguished. A new curve d2 must be selected on the drooping characteristic power source so that the desired current A2 can be supplied at the right voltage V2. Because of this latitude in setting the welding conditions and the independent control of current by wire feed speed, constant voltage power sources are by far the most popular for GMA welding. The control of current with this type of power source merely involves selecting a wire speed from the burn off characteristic. The current will rise automatically to the required value at a voltage not greatly below the selected open circuit voltage.

Another important advantage provided by the flat characteristic power source is its ability to produce self-regulated arc. Self regulated arc means maintaining the arc length constant. The principle of self-regulation of the arc length in GMAW is illustrated in Figure 5. With a constant potential power source, changes in arc voltage will have marked effects on current. Thus if the arc length is reduced from the set value, there will be an increase in current resulting in a faster burn off rate and the arc length will be adjusted back to its originalvalue.. On the other hand, an increase in arc length from the set value would increase the arc voltage resulting in less current—a lower burn off rate. The arc length would be restored to the original length. Self-adjustment will only operate successfully when the change in current produced by voltage fluctuations is sufficiently large to produce a large alteration in burn off, and rapid response rate and correction that the disturbance cannot beat.

4   METAL TRANSFER

The continuously fed electrode wire is melted in the arc heat and the droplets thus formed at the wire tip are transferred to the weld pool. The three basic modes by which metal is transferred

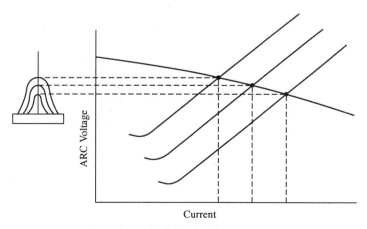

Fig. 5   Principle of self regulation

from the electrode to the weld pool are short-circuiting transfer, globular transfer and spray transfer. These basic modes of metal transfers are controlled by the various forces that are acting on the droplet. The electromagnetic pinch force and the surface tension force are considered as the primary forces responsible for the various modes of metal transfer in GMAW process.

4.1 Short Circuiting Transfer

Short-circuiting transfer occurs when the welding current and arc voltage are low. Metal is transferred from the electrode to the work only when the electrode is in contact with the weld pool. No metal is transferred across the arc gap. The short circuiting frequency varies from 20 to 200 Hz. The sequence of events in the transfer of metal and the corresponding current and voltage waveform are shown in Figure 6. As the droplet on the wire tip makes short circuit with the weld pool, the current increases until the arc is reignited again. The rate of current rise during short-circuiting must be properly controlled. It must be high enough to maintain a molten electrode tip until filler metal is transferred. Yet, it should not be a sudden surge that causes

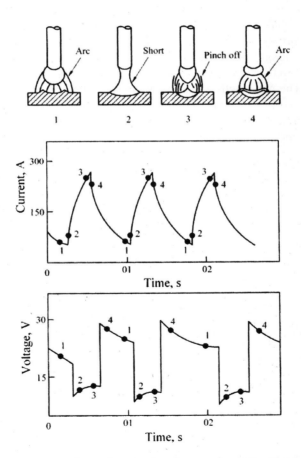

Fig. 6 Gas metal arc welding using the shorting-arc from the electrode to the work

spatter by disintegration of the transferring drop of the filler metal. The current increase is controlled by adjusting the inductance in the power source. The influence of low and high inductance setting on spattering during short-circuiting transfer welding is illustrated in Figure 7. The current setting of the inductance will depend on the type of shield gas and the welding parameters used. For short circuit transfer welding the open circuit voltage should be low enough so that arc cannot continue under the existing welding conditions. A portion of the energy for arc maintenance is provided by the inductive storage of energy during the period of short-circuiting. Short circuiting transfer offers a number of operating advantages. The small fast-freezing weld pool produced is well suited to joining thin sheets, for out of position welding and for bridging large root openings.

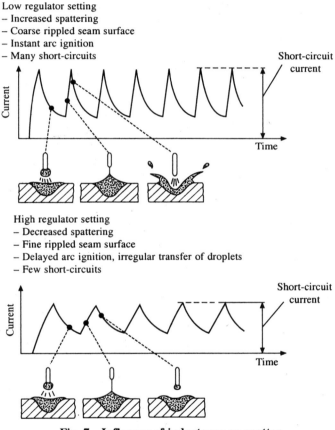

Fig. 7 Influence of inductance on spatter

4.2 Globular Transfer

Globular transfer as shown in Figure 8 is characterized by a drop size of greater diameter than that of the electrode wire. The large drop is easily acted on by gravity, generally limiting successful transfer to the flat position. Globular transfer occurs in the current range higher than

Long Arc
Description
– Electrode material transferred in large globules: not free from
   short-circuits
– Weld pool of low viscosity
– About 100 droplets transferred per second

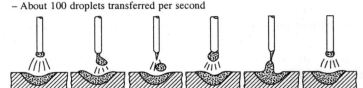

Setting range
High voltage (above 20 V)
Example for: Wire electrode of 1.0 mm diameter
           Protective gas in accordance with DIN
           32526-C1 (carbon dioxide)

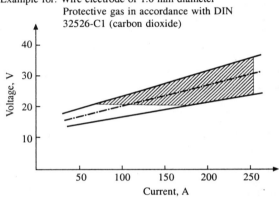

Fig. 8   Globular transfer

that of short circuiting transfer. The arc length must be long enough to assure detachment of the drop before it contacts the molten metal. CO_2 shielding results in randomly directed globular transfer. The non-axial transfer is due to electromagnetic repulsive force acting upon the bottom of the molten drop.

4.3 Spray Transfer

In a gas shield of argon or argon-rich mixture (i.e., Ar+CO_2 gas mixture containing more than 80% Ar) the metal transfer changes from globular to spray type as welding current is increased beyond the transition current. The current value at which the metal transfer mode changes from globular to spray is known as "transition current". Spray type transfer as shown in Figure 9 has a typical fine arc column and pointed wire tip associated with it. Molten filler metal transfers across the arc as fine droplets. The reduction in droplet size is also accompanied by an increase in the rate of droplet detachment. One important characteristic of spray mode of transfer is the "finger" penetration that it produces. The spray transfer mode can be used to weld any metal. However, applying the process to thin sheets may be difficult because of the high currents

Spray arc

Description

– No short-circuit on droplet transfer
– Weld pool of low viscosity
– About 100 to 300 droplets transferred per second

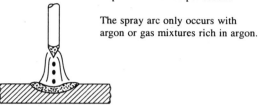

The spray arc only occurs with argon or gas mixtures rich in argon.

Setting range

High voltage (above 25 V)

Example for: Wire electrode of 1.0 mm diameter
Protective gas in accordance with DIN 32526-M2 (gas mixture)

Fig. 9   Spray transfer

needed to produce the spray arc. Also the large weld pool produced due to the high deposition rate makes it difficult to use it in vertical or overhead positions.

When CO_2 is used for shielding, a globular to spray transition does not occur. Drops become smaller as the current increases, but they are not at all axially directed. The spatter is more than that with argon or argon-rich mixed gas shield. The spatter is minimized if "buried arc" technique is used. Buried arc technique involves using a low voltage for any given current, forcing the arc to locate within the cavity created by the arc force. Under this condition, most of the non-axially directed droplets are trapped in the weld pool.

5   PROCESS VARIABLES

The process variables that affect fusion characteristics and weld bead geometry in GMAW are welding current, arc voltage, welding speed, electrode extension, electrode diameter and shielding gas.

5.1   Welding Current

The welding current is directly related to the electrode feed rate as mentioned previously.

Welding current has a strong influence on the bead characteristics. With all other variables held constant, an increase in welding current will result in increase in depth and width of penetration, increase in deposition rate, and increase in the size of the weld bead.

5.2   Arc Voltage

In a flat characteristic power source, the required arc voltage is selected at the power source by adjusting the knobs provided. Arc voltage is dependent upon the position of welding, electrode size, shielding gas composition and the type of metal transfer. From any specific value of arc voltage, voltage increases tends to flatten the bead and increase the fusion zone width. Reduction in voltage results in a narrower weld bead with a high crown. Excessively high voltage may cause porosity, spatter and undercutting while excessively low voltage may cause stubbing of the electrode.

5.3   Welding Speed

With all other parameters held constant, maximum penetration occurs only at a particular welding speed. When the welding speed is decreased below this, there will be a drastic decrease in the penetration. The reason for this behavior is that the filler metal deposited per unit length is more at very low welding speed. The arc will be acting directly on the molten pool rather than on the plate surface. When the welding speed is increased above the critical value, the penetration decreases slowly but almost in a linear manner. The reason for this behavior is that as the welding speed is increased, the thermal energy transferred to the base metal from the arc decreases. But if the welding speed is increased further, there is a tendency towards undercutting.

5.4   Electrode Extension

The electrode extension is the distance between the contact tube and the end of the electrode. As this distance increases, the electrical resistance also increases. Therefore, due to resistance heating the electrode temperature rises. Then, only less welding current is required to melt the electrode at a given feed rate. The electrode extension length has to be controlled because too long an extension results in excess weld metal being deposited with low arc heat. This may cause cold lapping and poor bead shape. Also, as the electrode extension increases the arc becomes less stable and shielding will not be effective. Proper electrode extension would be 6 to 12 mm for short circuiting transfer welding and 12 to 20 mm for globular and spray type of metal transfer.

Each electrode diameter of a given composition has a usable range of currents. The welding amperage range is limited by undesirable effects, such as the absence of proper wetting at very low currents, and spatter, porosity and poor bead appearance with excessively high currents. The wire melting rate is a function of current density. If two wires of different diameters are operated at the same amperage the smaller will have the higher melting rate. Penetration is also a function of current density. Smaller diameter wire will produce deeper penetration than the larger diameter wire when they are used at the same current. However, the weld bead profile will be wider with the larger diameter electrode.

5.5 Shielding Gas

The primary function of the shielding gas is to exclude the atmospheric air from the arc zone. However, the shielding gas has significant influence on the arc characteristics, mode of metal transfer, speed of welding, cleaning action and bead geometry. Pure argon is used only for welding of non-ferrous metals. However, pure argon shielding on ferrous alloys causes an erratic arc and a tendency for undercuts to occur. Hence, for welding of ferrous alloys, either CO_2 or Ar + CO_2 gas mixture is used. Addition of 1 to 5% O_2 or 3 to 25% CO_2 produces a noticeable improvement in arc stability and freedom from undercut. Argon-rich gas mixtures produce a finger shape penetration whereas CO_2 shielding gas produces wide and deep penetration.

6 ADVANTAGES

Some of the advantages of GMAW process as compared to other processes are as follows:

- It is a continuous welding process and can be mechanised
- Welding can be done in all positions
- Higher welding speed
- Deeper penetration is possible, which permits the use of smaller size fillet welds for equivalent strength
- Open arc nature of the process aids monitoring and control of the arc during welding
- Higher metal deposition rate
- Less distortion due to higher welding speed
- Avoids the chore of cleaning a solidified slag from the surface of each weld pass

II Coated Electrodes and their Classification

1 INTRODUCTION

Welding technology has changed tremendously over the past few decades. Its application is found in all sectors of industries smal or large and welding is instrumental in industrial development. In manual welding several coated electrodes have been developed to cope up with the greater need of reliability and better control of physical and metallurgical properties of welds.

2 DEVELOPMENT OF COATED ELECTRODES:

It was in 1801 that electric arc was first discovered by Sir Humphry Davy while conducting experiments in electricity. In the year 1889 Slavianoff made an attempt to weld with bare wires. But, welding with bare wires gave rise to many difficulties like instability of arc, lack of shielding of molten metal, which resulted in poor mechanical properties. In 1920 for the first time coated electrodes were developed. It was found that with a mixture of minerals covering the wire, virtually every aspect of the process could be controlled and improved. The first coated electrodes contained iron oxide and natural silicates in the coating.

The coating was further improved upon by adding deoxidisers and denitriders in addition to iron oxide and silicates. These electrodes were known as acid coated electrodes. But weld deposits by these electrodes also had a substantial quantity of gases and most of the useful elements like carbon and manganese were lost in transfer. The coatings employed in those early years of development were thin and their function was more of an arc stabiliser. They did very little by way of purifying or strengthening the weld. The weld was not better than the weld deposits obtained with bare wire electrodes.

Further research in improving coatings gave rise to rutile coated electrodes which had better control in positional welding. In these electrodes the oxygen and hydrogen entrapped impaired the physical properties of the weld metal. The rutile coated electrodes had limited use (up to 15 mm thickness of mild steel). The increased use of higher thickness and steels of high tensile properties limited the use of rutile electrades. The main source of hydrogen in the weld metal the water-forming compounds and organic chemicals in the coating. Hence efforts were made to develop low hydrogen electrodes.

The oxygen, nitrogen and hydrogen content of the weld metal and iron oxide content of the slag decreases as move down from iron oxide to basic coated types (Table 1). Also the fillet weld profile changes from a concave profile in case of oxide coated electrodes to convex profile in case of basic coated electrodes.

Table 1   Gaseous impurity levels in steel weld metal deposited using electrodes coated with different types of flux

Electrode Type	Oxygen %	Nitrogen %	Hydrogen %
Bare wire	0.25	0.15	–
Iron oxide	0.22	0.06	–
Acid	0.12	0.035	0.0150
Rutile	0.06	0.025	0.0220
Basic	0.03	0.010	0.0004

3 ˙ TYPES OF COATING

To impart certain properties in the flux coating, various organic and inorganic materials in appropriate mesh sizes and proportions are mixed together, a paste being formed by adding suitable liquids. Thereafter binders are added taking care to see that the final paste possesses adequate slippage, amenability to high extrusion pressures and good green strength. Functions of some of the materials used in the flux coating are given below.

(a) **Cellulosic Material:** This material is used in the flux coating under various brand names. It is produced by digesting hard or soft wood or similar substances such as coconut shells, bleaching the pulp so formed and finally washing, dying and grading it to the required mesh size. Cellulose imparts a high arc force resulting in deep penetration welds. This is a major constituent in deep penetration electrodes belonging to class AWS XX10 and XX11. Apart from providing a high arc force, cellulose emits a large volume of gases, mostly hydrogen, that protect the weld metal from atmospheric contamination. Cellulose is also used in relatively small percentages in electrodes of other classes such as AWS E6012 and E6013 for the purpose of giving good slag control.

(b) **Rutile:** Rutile is a crystalline form of titanium dioxide that occurs in certain rocks. However, in India it is found mainly in beach sands, where it is concentrated with other heavy minerals as a result of weathering of the rutile bearing rocks. Large deposits of rutile are present in beaches of Kerala. They are firstly separated from sand and other foreign materials, dried in rotary kilns and then passed through electrostatic and magnetic separators to obtain a concentrate containing 87% titanium dioxide. Rutile is then ground to appropriate mesh size in ball mills and when so treated varies in colour from gray to brown; this is one of the factors causing changes in the colour of the flux coating of rutile electrodes but it must be understood that such colour changes do not reflect any change in quality. Rutile is one of the most widely used minerals in electrode coatings. It is an efficient arc stabiliser, generally confers good running properties on the electrodes and is also a slag former. Rutile is the major ingredient in class E6012 and class E6013 coatings and its properties contribute notably to the popularity enjoyed by such electrodes.

(c) **Ball Clay:** Ball clay is a compound of silica and alumina and is commonly known as aluminosilicate. The variety used for electrode manufacture has a buff colour and it must be highly consistent in composition. Clay particles are produced as a result of weathering of granite and are washed down by rain and settle in the form of a bed. Clay is cut out in about 10 inch cubes from the quarries or mines and hence the name "ball clay". In order to develop adequate plasticity the balls are weathered in wind and rain and then shredded and pulverised until all particles pass through a 200 mesh sieve. Although ball clay is used in electrode coverings as general fluxing ingredient and slag-former, its most important attribute is the plasticity it confers on the wet paste facilitating extrusion. It gives the paste good plastic flow with a high "green" strength to resist markings on the electrode during manufacture and possesses the desirable property of liquid retention under high extrusion pressures. It is widely used in flux coatings of all electrodes that will tolerate the inclusion of materials containing "combined" water. This covers most electrodes except hydrogen controlled types.

(d) **Iron Powder:** Iron powder is sometimes added to the flux coating. It imparts some desirable operating characteristics to the electrodes. The presence of iron powder appears to improve arc stability perhaps by providing Fe^{2+} and Fe^{3+} ions; the powder added to the coating makes it electrically conducting and the electrode can be operated as a 'contact electrode'. The powder must be of high purity.

(e) **Ferro-Alloys:** Ferro-alloys like ferro-manganese, ferro-silicon, ferro-chromium, ferromolybdenum, ferro-niobium etc. are used in the flux coating as deoxidisers and to provide alloying elements in the deposited material.

(f) **Limestone (calcium carbonate):** In hydrogen-controlled electrodes, instead of cellulose, limestone is used, which decompases to generate large quantities of CO_2. It also serves as a good slag former. The CO_2 generated from its decomposition affords effective shielding to the weld.

(g) **Potassium and Sodium Silicates:** These serve as binding agents and give the flux paste good green strength. Potassium, in addition, is an arc former and helps stabilisation of the arc.

4   FUNCTIONS OF THE FLUX COATING

The electrode coating performs very important functions that are essential for obtaining a weld of required quality; in terms of chemical composition, mechanical properties and weld metal cleanliness.

(a) The primary function of the coating is to initiate and maintain the arc column between the electrode and the work. This requires a continuous supply of ionized gas or continuous ionization of the medium between the two terminals. Arc initiation requires a higher voltage than that to sustain it. The ionizing elements help the easy initiation and further maintenance of a column of ionized gas.

(b) Having established a stablized arc, the coating carries out its second function of protecting the molten metal that is transferred from the electrode to the weld below. The gas forming materials in the coating produce arc a gas shield by burning or decomposing in arc heat. The shielding is by active gases like carbon-di-oxide, hydrogen and oxygen. These isolate the weld area from the surrounding atmosphere.

(c) The slag that forms as a result of the reaction between the flux and the oxides, further protects the weld pool by covering it completely. This prevents any possible absorption 'of gas by the molten weld metal. In addition the slag slows down the freezing rate of molten metal. Also it slows down the cooling rate of solidified weld metal.

(d) To compensate for the loss of alloying elements additional quantity of these elements are introduced into the weld metal through the electrode coating.

(e) Deoxidisers which remove dissolved oxygen from the weld metal are brought to the reaction zone through the coating.

(f) Because of the cup that is formed at the tip of the electrode during welding, the arc stream is concentrated and is directed towards the weld pool. The concentrated arc agitates the weld pool. This allows the dissolved gases to be released and also helps to achieve uniform weld structure.

(g) Flux acts as scavenger of impurity elements.

(h) Finally the electrode coating, except in the case of iron powder electrodes, is a poor conductor of electricity. This property is very much useful when welding has to be carried out in a deep narrow groove.

5   TYPES OF COATED ELECTRODES

Following are the types of coated electrodes manufactured in India:

1. Mild steel core wire electrodes:

   (a) Cellulosic electrodes
   (b) Rutile electrodes
   (c) Iron powder electrodes
   (d) Low hydrogen electrodes
   (e) Low alloy high tensile steel electrodes
   (f) Low alloy creep resisting electrodes
   (g) Hardfacing

2. Stainless steel core wire electrodes:
3. Cast iron electrodes;
4. Inconel electrodes:

1(a) Cellulosic Electrodes: In the AWS E6010 and E-6011 series of electrodes, the protective covering is composed of cellulose ($C_6H_{10}O_5$) and silicate binders. The cellulose decomposes in the arc according to the following equation:

$$C_6H_{10}O_5 + 1/2\ O_2 = 6\ CO + 5\ H_2$$

Cellulose + Oxygen = Carbon Monoxide + Hydrogen
The products of this reaction, carbon monoxide and Hydrogen represent a 350 to 400 times increase in the volume of gas generated over the volumes of the unburnt coating. These gases rush outward from the arc and push the atmosphere away from the puddle. The gases so produced raise the arc voltage and thereby increase the amount of heat produced from the electricity in the arc. The cellulosic electrode has, therefore, a very hot arc even at lower current value and this together with the gases evolved from the coating at high pressure give rise to a "digging" arc and deep penetration. Naturally there is very little slag formed, and this makes welding possible in all positions.

This electrode is extremely good for pipe welding. The weld metal "is of good quality and generally meets with high pressure tests and x-ray tests" very easily. This electrode requires a slightly longer arc for complete burning of the cellulose in the flux coating.

1(b) Rutile Electrode: This type has thicker coating than cellulosic coated and the flux is mainly composed of rutile (titanium di-oxide) and silicates, with a negligible amount of cellulose, but a higher proportion of ferroalloys than in the cellulosic electrode. These is hardly any gas shielding in the arc, but the slag takes care, of refining of the weld puddle and strengthening of the weld metal.

The slag covers the weld completely and peels off very easily on cooling. The penetration is just sufficient. The electrode can therefore be used for bridging wide gaps in the joint. The electrode also causes very little undercut, if any. The electrode is easy to use in all positions.

1(c) Iron Powder Electrodes: Iron powder is a widely used covering ingredient. It is incorporated in certain coverings to the extent of one half the total weight. Iron powder imparts a number of desirable operating characteristics to the electrode. Large amounts will make the covering an electrical conductor and allow the electrode to be operated as a "contact electrode". The presence of iron powder appears to add metal ions to the arc and thus improves arc stability. Iron powder also will join the weld pool and increase the amount of metal deposited.

On account of the deep cup, touch welding can be done with the electrode. Other important advantages of the contact electrodes are the large quantity of metal deposited per unit time and the deep penetration. Contact electrodes can be provided with an acid, rutile or a basic coating.

Fundamentally the welding properties of the "ordinary" electrodes and the respective contact electrodes are the same. The main advantage of the contact electrodes is the large deposition rate, where heavy welds have to be made, as an example when a single V groove in thick plate is filled. The acid contact electrode is very slow setting and can be used for horizontal closed grooves, (mainly Vee and double Vee grooves) and for large weld lengths in standing fillet welds.

A zircon-basic contact electrode also has been developed. This electrode has a deposition rate that is not inferior to that of any other kind. The appearance of the weld is likewise extremely good and the mechanical properties are adequate.

1(d) Low Hydrogen Electrodes: Low hydrogen electrodes are so called because their covering is low in hydrogen-bearing compounds and only traces of hydrogen or moisture are present in the arc atmosphere.

The low-hydrogen electrodes were developed for welding hardenable high tensile, high carbon alloy steels to eliminate underbead cracking, which occurs when heavy sections of high tensile steel are welded with conventional high cellulose, rutile or iron-oxide type electrodes. These underbead cracks occur in the base metal just under the weld metal and are caused by the absorption of hydrogen into the weld metal from the arc atmosphere. This absorbed hydrogen then migrates into the base metal and collects in the highly restrained and fast cooled martensitic area causing cracking. Underbead cracking results only when hydrogen is present in the arc atmosphere and martensite forms during cooling of the heat-affected zone. Although these cracks do not normally occur in mild (low carbon) steels, they may occur whenever an ordinary electrode is used on high tensile steels. The elimination of hydrogen permits the welding of "difficult-to-weld" steels with less preheat than that necessary with other types of electrodes.

The arc of the low hydrogen electrode is not as harsh or as deeply gouging as the arc of some other electrodes, such as E6010, but penetration is sufficient for most welding jobs. Some welders may have difficulty when first using these electrodes because of porosity and slag inclusions. However, high quality radiographically sound welds can be made with proper welding technique. The currents used with these electrodes generally are higher than those recommended for other types of electrode of the same diameter.

As short an arc as possible should be used in all welding positions for best results. A long arc and "whipping" will generally result in porosity and trapped slag. Porosity may also be produced by moisture pick-up and too long an exposure to high humidity air. Porosity may also result unless the arc is struck ahead of the puddle each time a weld is started.

The deposited metal has a high resistance to hot and cold cracking; accordingly these electrodes are particularly suitable for the welding of heavy work pieces and very rigid mild steel constructions. They are also recommended for welding low-alloy steel as well as high carbon high sulphur steel. The mechanical properties of the deposited metal are excellent; the notch toughness value at temperatures below 0°C is high as well. Owing to the high solidification rate of the pool, which permits use of high welding currents for welding in difficult positions the low-hydrogen electrode is the fastest type for these positions.

The weld metal of the low-hydrogen electrodes sets rapidly. The slag, on the other hand, does not solidify quickly. The slag is not shut in by the weld metal. When welding is done, attention must be paid to the necessity of having a very short arc and to the somewhat different technique for linking beads. The bridging of large openings, the penetration possibilities, the small number of layers and as a result the smaller deformations are factors highly appreciated in practice. They are attributable to the fore mentioned solidification rates of the pool and the slag. For vertical position welding the welder prefers an electrode by which the slag flows out of the weld pool. The low hydrogen electrode has this property to a large extent. The zircon basic type electrodes produce smooth weld bead finish.

1(e) Low Alloy Tensile Steel Electrodes: The flux coating of this class of electrodes contains small amounts of alloying elements like Cr, Ni, Mo, V, Co to impart necessary mechanical properties to the weld metal. These are used in fabrication of reactors, pipelines, tanks, ship building, bridge construction, fabrication of penstocks etc. These steels have a minimum YS of 35 kg/mm^2. The structure of these steels is ferritic and often contains small quantity of pearlite, carbide, nitrides or carbonitrides.

1(f) LowAlloy Creep Resisting Electrodes and Electrodes For Cryogenic Applications: The flux coating contains small amounts of alloying elements like Cr, Mo and sometimes V for creep resistance. By these alloy additions these steels become air-hardening and therefore preheating and stress relieving after welding are mandatory. The electrodes in this category are known as 5 Cr-1/2 Mo. For cryogenic applications the addition of Ni is very useful. Nickel steels can be used down to −50 to −60°C with 2.5% Ni and down to −100°C with 3.5% Ni.

1(g) Hardfacing Electrodes: There are many types of hardfacing electrodes. These electrodes are mainly useful in the maintenance and repair of machinery parts and equipments subjected to wear and tear. By rebuilding these parts there is enormous cost saving. Abrasion and impact resistant electrodes may be based on ferritic, austenitic and martensitic hardenable alloys.

2 STAINLESS STEEL ELECTRODES

A variety of stainless steel electrodes are manufactured to produce weld metal similar in composition to most base metals. However, the composition of the core wire may differ from that of the base metal in order to improve corrosion resistance of the weld deposit, eliminate underbead cracking and minimise carbide precipitation. In the transfer of metal through the arc very little nickel is lost from nickel bearing stainless steel electrodes. There is a slight loss of chromium and a greater loss of some of the other elements but this loss may be compensated by alloy additions to the coating.

Manganese and silicon are included in the stainless steel electrode coverings to reduce oxidation. Titanium is added to promote weldability, to produce an easily removable slag and to prevent carbide precipitation. In most designs, niobium is used to prevent carbide precipitation. Lime is an extremely important ingredient in the covering since it tends to eliminate hydrogen.

Any material that is high in carbon is excluded because of the affinity of chromium for carbon especially at welding temperatures. The covering used on stainless steel electrodes is similar to that employed on the low-hydrogen type carbon steel welding electrodes.

3 CAST IRON ELECTRODES

There are three types of electrodes for welding of cast irons.

  (a) Monel cored electrodes (30% Ni 70% Cu)
  (b) Fe-Ni (40% Ni)
  (c) Ni-electrodes (97 E)

These electrodes can be used for welding of machinable castings whereas for non-machinable parts of cast iron, any low-hydrogen electrode can be used with proper preheating of the job.

4   INCONEL ELECTRODES

These electrodes are used in petrochemical, fertilizer and other chemical industries. The weld composition contains small percentages of alloying elements like V, Mo, Co, Cu, Mn, and Cr with Ni as remainder.

5   STORAGE AND HANDLING OF ELECTRODES

It is recommended that electrodes should be stored in a warm and dry place. Generally conditions of storage in the shop are not very conductive to desirable performance of the electrode. At this juncture, knowledge of the factors leading to deterioration of the electrode can be helpful. The coating of the welding electrode is produced from powdered materials bound together with binders, usually including sodium or potassium silicate. Such a coating is not impervious to water vapour, which is absorbed from the atmosphere and held by the binders, in the capillary spaces between the powder grains. This action takes place until equilibrium is reached between the coating and the atmosphere surrounding it and may proceed in either direction.

When the relative humidity is high, baking the electrode reduces the moisture content in the arc. If the coating is impervious to moisturing the steam produced during baking cannot escape and this will result in bursting of the coating. Some electrodes have moisture content as low as 1/2% or less while some with as high as 6% moisture content perform well. The diversity in their performance can be attributed to the degree of porosity of the electrode coatings. Electrode coatings containing a high proportion of cellulose must contain adequate moisture if they are to give the best results. Excessive moisture leads to porosity in the weld, but unsatisfactory results are also obtained if the electrodes are baked at higher than recommended temperature because of decomposition of the ingredients.

Electrodes with coatings of predominantly mineral composition appear to be more tolerant of moisture. They may be redried at temperatures not exceeding 100°C and held at this temperature for some hours without serious harm, Some at least will give satisfactory welding performance with moisture contents in excess of 5% "low hydrogen" or "hydrogen controlled" electrodes are intolerant even of traces of moisture and drying immediately before use at temperatures of the order of 400°C is recommended for some types. The exact baking temperature will depend on the actual ingredients in the coating and the electrode manufacturer's recommendation should be followed.

A second from of deterioration is the formation of white fur on the electrodes. This is produced as a result of the irreversible chemical reaction between the carbon dioxide of the atmosphere and the sodium silicate binder. When formed in excessive quantities this fur disrupts the coating to the rusting of the core wire. The appearance of this may be taken to indicate the unsatisfactory storage conditions.

For classification of coated electrodes, the following standards may be referred to:

IS 814-1991 Classification of Carbon and Carbon-Manganese Steel Electrodes.
IS 13043: Covered Electrodes—Determination of Efficiency, Metal Recovery and Deposition Coefficient.
IS-13851: 1993 Storage and Redrying of Covered Electrodes Before Use—Recommendations.

IS-11802: 1986: Methods for Determination of Deposited Weld Metal from Covered Electrodes in Welding Mild Steel and Low Alloy Steels.

IS-815: 1974: Classification Coding for Covered Electrodes for Metal Arc Welding of Structural Steel.

ASME Section-II, Part C classifies electrodes as mentioned below:

AWS 5.1 SFA 5.1 Carbon Steel Electrodes

AWS 5.4 SFA 5.4 Stainless Steel Electrodes

AWS 5.5 Low Alloy Steel Electrodes

AWS 5.11 Nickel Alloy Electrodes

AWS 5.13 Hardfacing Rods and Electrodes

AWS 5.15 Cast Iron Rods and Electrodes

6 LOW HYDROGEN ELECTRODES (BASIC ELECTRODES)

6.1 Coating Composition

Low hydrogen electrodes are designed to deposit welds with hydrogen content below a specified value. Coating constituents such as clays, mica and cellulose are therefore not included in the formulation as they retain some combined water even after baking at 450°C. Limestone is the major constituent of the coating formulation (up to 40%). This material ionises easily and breaks down to form a carbon-di-oxide/carbon monoxide shield. The high melting point of limestone is lowered by addition of up to 25% fluorspar. The fluorspar also decreases the oxidising effect of the limestone and increases slag fluidity. Efficient deoxidation of the weld pool is attained by additions of ferro manganese, ferro silicon and ferrotitanium.

A small amount of rutile is normally present to aid arc stabilization. Certain types of low hydrogen electrodes also contain a substantial amount of iron powder. Other materials normally present are extrusion aids and a sodium or potassium silicate binder.

6.2 Running Properties

The gas shield of low hydrogen electrodes consists almost entirely of carbon-di-oxide. The relatively low rate of gas evolution and the less reducing nature of this type of mixture renders it less protective than the rutile or cellulosic types. It is therefore essential to maintain a constant short arc length for the gas shield to be fully effective.

The penetration characteristics of low hydrogen electrodes are similar to those of rutile electrodes. The slag is heavy but fluid and so is easily controlled when welding positionally. The wetting action is excellent and incidences of undercut rarely occur. Slag release although not as good as rutile types is not difficult to remove. As the slag of a basic electrode has a lower melting point than other electrode types, the chances of slag entrapment are very low. The weld metal profile tends to be convex and is not as good as for rutile type. Invariably the current carrying capacity of basic electrodes is higher than rutile or cellulosic electrodes of the same diameter. This enables faster deposition in a variety of positions, especially vertically upwards.

6.3 Mechanical Properties

Low-hydrogen electrodes do not contain materials that retain moisture above the manufacturer's baking temperature of 450°C. The moisture levels are therefore, extremely low, normally less than 0.20%. This results in hydrogen levels of less than 5 ml/100 g of weld metal. Typical analysis of weld metal deposited using a low hydrogen electrode is:

C.05% Mn 1.2% Si 0.40% S. 02% P 0.02%

Low hydrogen electrodes are used for three major applications:

A To prevent cold cracking this is major reason for the use of low-hydrogen electrodes. The presence of hydrogen in conventional rutile and cellulosic welds can cause cracking during the welding of higher strength, high carbon and low alloy steels under certain conditions. The elimination of hydrogen enables the welding of these "difficult-to-weld" steels with less preheat than that necessary with conventional products.

B To prevent hot cracking (solidification cracking)—the use of rutile electrodes on high sulphur steels (~0.1%5) results in hot cracking. This is caused by a semi-continuous film of iron sulphide that forms in the final stages of solidification. The basic slag and higher manganese deposit of low-hydrogen electrodes are more capable of absorbing sulphur, and this passes into the slag. The formation of the weak low melting point film does not therefore take place.

C To give good toughness-the weld metal form basic electrodes is radiographically clear of all defects. Control of welding procedure results in good toughness at very low temperatures. This type of product is therefore used for high technology applications such as pressure vessels and offshore structures.

6.4 REBAKING OF LOW HYDROGEN ELECTRODES

Low hydrogen electrodes pick up moisture very quickly from the atmosphere. Irrespective of storage conditions, it is, however, always advisable to re-dry low hydrogen electrodes before use. The re-drying temperature depends on the level of hydrogen considered permissible in the weld metal. For maximum X-ray clarity and the lowest possible hydrogen content, re-drying for 1 hour at 450°C (excluding heating time) is recommended immediately before use. It is not sufficient to set the oven at 450°C and place the electrodes in it for the duration of one hour.

IV GAS TUNGSTEN ARC WELDING

Gas tungsten arc welding (GTAW) process uses an arc between a tungsten electrode (non consumable) and the workpiece. An inert gas sustains the arc and protects the molten metal from atmospheric contamination. The inert gas is normally argon, helium or a mixture of argon and helium. The process may be used with or without the addition of a filler metal. This process was developed in the late 1930s to provide a joining method for aluminium and magnesium components of aircraft, replacing riveting. This process was then called heliarc process as helium was used for shielding.

GTAW is widely used as a fabrication tool in many industries because of high quality welds produced. The fundamentals of the process; the equipment, the procedures and variables, applications and safety considerations are discussed.

1   THE PROCESS

GTAW process is illustrated in Fig. 10. The process uses a nonconsumable tungsten (or tungsten alloy) electrode held in the torch. Shielding gas is fed through the torch to protect the electrode, molten weld pool, and solidifying weld metal from contamination by the atmosphere. The electric arc is produced by the passage of current through the conductive ionized shielding gas.

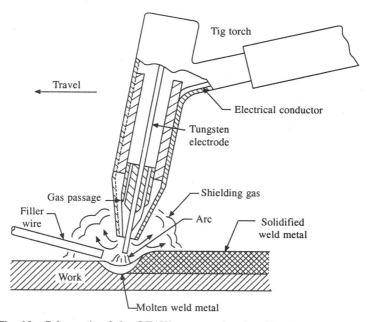

Fig. 10   Schematic of the GTAW process showing filler metal addition

The arc is established between the tip of the electrode and the work. Heat generated by the arc melts the base metal. Once the arc and weld pool are established, the torch is moved along the joint and the arc progressively melts the faying surfaces. Filler wire is added to the leading edge of the weld pool to fill the joint. Four basic components are common to all GTA welding setups, as illustrated in Fig. 11.

1.1   Advantages

- Produces high-quality, low-distortion welds
- Free from spatter
- Can be used with or without filler wire
- Can be used with a range of premier supplies
- Welds almost all metals

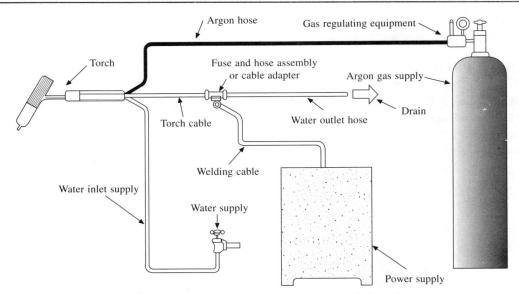

Fig. 11 GTA welding unit with a water-cooled torch

- Gives precise control of welding heat
- Allows excellent control of root pass weld penetration

The GTAW process is applicable when highest weld quality is required. It can be used to weld almost all types of metals. The operator has excellent control of heat input and vision is not limited by fumes or slag from the process.

1.2 Limitations

- Produces lower deposition rates than consumable electrode arc welding processes
- Requires slightly more skill as compared to GMAW or shielded metal arc welding (SMAW).
- Less economical for section thickness greater than 9.5 mm.
- Problematic in drafty environments because of difficulty in shielding the weld zone properly
- Tungsten inclusions if the electrode is allowed to contact the weld pool
- Contamination of the weld metal, if proper shielding of the filler metal by the gas stream is not maintained
- Low tolerance for contaminants on filler or base metals
- Arc blow or arc deflection, as with other processes

2 WELDING TORCHES

GTA welding torches hold the tungsten electrode, which conducts welding current to the arc, and provide a means for conveying shielding gas to the arc zone. Torches are rated in accordance with the maximum welding current that can be used without overheating. A range of electrode sizes and various types and sizes of nozzles can normally be used in the same torch.

The heat generated in the torch during welding is removed either by gas cooling or water cooling. Gas cooled torches provide cooling by the flow of the relatively cool shielding as through the torch. Gas cooled torches are used for maximum welding current of about 100 amperes.

In water-cooled torches cooling water enters the torch through the inlet hose, circulates through the torch, and exits through an outlet hose. The power cable from the power supply to the torch is enclosed within the cooling water outlet hose (Fig. 12). Water-cooled torches are designed for use at higher welding currents in the range of 200 to 500 amperes. Most machines for automatic welding applications use water-cooled torches.

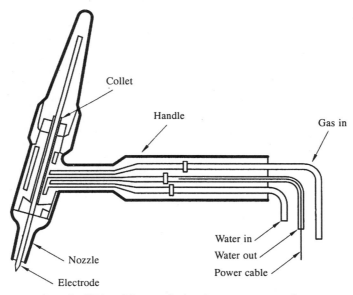

Fig. 12   Schematic cross section of a GTA welding torch showing arrangements for water cooling and gas flow

Tap water can be used to cool water-cooled torches. In this case water flows through the torch and then down a drain, or a closed system involving a reservoir, pump, and radiator or water chiller to disperse heat from the system can be used.

2.1   Collets

Collets are used to grip the tungsten electrodes of various diameters in the electrode holder. Good contact between the electrode and the inside diameter of the collet is essential for proper current transfer and electrode cooling. Tungsten electrode of any particular diameter will require a collet of matching size.

2.2   Nozzles

Shielding gas is directed to the weld zone by gas nozzles or cups fitted onto the head of the torch. Gas nozzles are made of various heat-resistant materials like ceramic, metal, metal-jacketed ceramic, fused, quartz, or other materials. They are made in different shape, diameters and lengths. The gas nozzle or cup must be large enough to provide shieldings gas coverage of the weld pool area and surrounding hot base metal and the stiffness needed to sustain coverage in drafts. A delicate balance exists between the nozzle diameter and the flow rate. If the flow rate for a given diameter is excessive, the effectiveness of the shield is destroyed because of turbulence. High flow rates without turbulence require large diameters, which are used at high currents. Size selection depends on electrode size, type of weld joint, weld area to be effectively shielded, and access to the weld joint.

Gas Lenses: Gas lenses are used to provide a laminar flow of shielding gas. These attachments contain a porous barrier diffuser and are fitted around the electrode or collet and remain inside the nozzles. With the gas lenses, it is possible to keep longer gap between the nozzle and the work piece and to weld joints with limited accessibility providing adequate shielding.

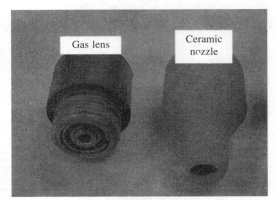

Fig. 13   Gas lens used in GTA welding

3   ELECTRODES

Tungsten electrodes are non-consumable because they do not melt or transfer to the weld. The function of a tungsten electrode is to serve as one of the electrical terminals of the arc that supplies the heat required for welding. Its melting point is 3410°C. Approaching this high temperature, tungsten becomes thermionic; it is a ready source of electrons. It reaches this temperature by resistance heating and, were it not for the significant cooling effect of electrons boiling from its tip, resistance heating would cause the tip to melt. In fact, the electrode tip is much cooler than that part of the electrode between the tip and the externally cooled collet.

3.1   Classification of Electrodes

Tungsten electrodes are classified on the basis of their chemical compositions, as specified in Table 2a as per AWS and in Table 2b as DIN specifications. Tungsten electrode sizes and current ranges are listed in Table 2 along with shielding gas cup diameters recommended for use with different types of welding power.

Electrode Classifications: (as per AWS) Pure tungsten electrodes (EWP) contain a minimum of 99.5 percent tungsten, with no intentional alloying elements. The current-carrying capacity of pure tungsten electrodes is lower than that of the alloyed electrodes. Pure tungsten electrodes are used mainly with AC for welding aluminium and magnesium alloys.

Thoriated Tungsten (EWTh): The thermionic emission of tungsten can be improved by alloying it with metal oxides that have very low work function. As a result, the electrodes are able to handle higher welding currents without failing. Thorium oxide is one such additive. Two types or thoriated tungsten electrodes are available. The EWTh-1 and EWTh-2 electrodes contain 1

Table 2 Colour codes and alloy element contents of tungsten electrode alloys (source: AWS Welding Handbook, IX Ed., vol. 2, 2004

AWS Classification	Colour	Alloying Element	Alloying Oxide	Nominal Content (wt.%)
EWP	Green	–	–	–
EWCe-2	Orange	Cerium	CeO_2	2
EWLa-1	Black	Lanthanum	La_2O_3	1
EWLa-1.5	Gold	Lanthanum	La_2O_3	1.5
EWLa-2	Blue	lanthanum	La_2O_3	2
ERTh-1	Yellow	Thorium	ThO_2	1
EWTh-2	Red	Thorium	ThO_2	2
EWZr-1	Brown	Zirconium	ZrO_2	0.25

and 2 percent thorium oxide (ThO_2) or thoria, respectively, evenly dispersed through their entire lengths. Thoriated tungsten electrodes are superior to pure tungsten electrodes in several respects. The thoria provides about 20 percent higher current-carrying capacity, generally longer life, and greater resistance to contamination of the weld. With these electrodes, arc starting is easier, and the arc is more stable than with pure tungsten or zirconiated tungsten electrodes.

The EWTh-1 and EWTh-2 electrodes are designed for DCEN applications. They maintain a sharpened tip configuration during welding, which is desirable for welding steel. They are not used with AC because it is difficult to maintain the balled end, which is necessary with AC welding.

Ceriated Tungsten (EWCe): The EWCe-2 electrodes are tungsten electrodes containing 2 percent cerium oxide (CeO_2), or ceria. Compared with pure tungsten, the ceriated electrodes exhibit a reduced rate of vaporization or burn-off. EWCe-2 electrodes will operate successfully with AC or DC.

Lanthanated Tungsten (EWLa): These electrodes contain 1 percent lanthanum oxide (LaO_3), or lanthana. The advantages and operating characteristics of these electrodes are very similar to the ceriated tungsten electrodes.

Zirconiated Tungsten (EWZr): Zirconiated tungsten electrodes (EWZr) contain a small amount of zirconium oxide (ZrO_2), as listed in Table 2. They are used for AC welding because they combine the desirable arc stability characteristics and balled end typical of pure tungsten with the current capacity and starting characteristics of thoriated tungsten. They have higher resistance to contamination than pure tungsten, and are preferred for radiographic quality welding applications where tungsten contamination of the weld is not desirable.

Electrode Tip Configuration: The shape of the tungsten electrode tip is an important process variable in TIG welding. Tungsten electrodes may be used with a variety of tip preparations. With AC welding, pure or ziconiated tungsten electrodes form a hemispherical balled end. The size of the hemisphere should not exceed 1-1/2 times the electrode diameter, otherwise it may fall off while it is molten, Fig. 14. For DC welding with thoriated, ceriated, or lanthanated tungsten electrodes, the end is typically ground to a specific included angle, often with a truncated end. In general, as the included angle increases, the weld penetration increases and the width of the weld bead decreases.

Electrode Contamination: Contamination of the tungsten electrode is most likely to occur when a welder accidentally dips the tungsten into the molten weld pool or touches the tungsten with the filler metal. The tungsten electrode may also become oxidized by an improper shielding gas or insufficient gas flow, during welding or after the arc has been extinguished. The contaminated end of the tungsten electrode will adversely affect the arc characteristics and may cause tungsten inclusions in the weld metal. If this occurs, the contaminated portion of the electrode is removed.

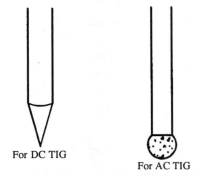

For DC TIG

For AC TIG

Fig. 14   Electrode tips

4   POWER SOURCES

TIG power sources typically have either drooping or nearly true constant-current static output characteristics, such as those shown in Fig. 15. The static output characteristic is a function of the type of welding current control used in the power source design. A drooping volt-ampere characteristic is typical of magnetically controlled power source designs including the moving coil, moving shunt, moving core reactor, satiable reactor, or magnetic amplifier designs and also rotating power source designs. With a drooping characteristic, the welder may vary the current level slightly by changing the arc length. The advantages of magnetically controlled power sources are that they are simple to operate, require little maintenance and are relatively inexpensive. The disadvantages are that they are large in size and weight and have a lower efficiency compared to electronically controlled power sources. Also, most magnetic-control techniques are open loop, which limits repeatability, accuracy, and response.

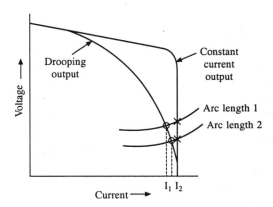

Fig. 15   Static volt-ampere characteristics for drooping and constant current power supplies

An essentially constant-current volt-ampere characteristic can be provided by electronically controlled power sources, such as the series linear regulator, silicon controlled rectifier, secondary switches, and inverter designs. Inverter power sources are the most versatile, offering multi-process capabilities and variable welding current waveform output. Inverters are also lighter and more compact than other power source designs of equivalent current rating.

The advantages of electronically controlled power sources are that they offer rapid dynamic response, provide variable current waveform output. Most truly constant current power sources are closedloop controlled, in which the actual current is measured and compared to the desired current setting. Adjustments are made electronically within the power source to maintain the desired current as welding conditions change. The disadvantages are that they are more complex to operate and maintain and are relatively expensive. It is important to select a TIG power source based on the type of welding current required for a particular application. The types of welding current include AC sine wave, AC square wave, DC, and pulsed DC.

4.1 Direct Current

Using direct current, the tungsten electrode may be connected to either the negative or the positive terminal of the power supply. In almost all cases, electrode negative (cathode) is chosen. With that polarity, electrons flow from the electrode to the work and positive ions are transferred from the work to the electrode and the connection is known as DCEN or (straight polarity) connection. When the electrode is positive (anode), the directions of electron and positive ion flow are reversed, the connection is known as DCEP (reverse polarity) connection.

With DCEN and a thermionic electrode such as tungsten, approximately 70 percent of the heat is generated at the anode and 30 percent at the cathode. Since DCEN produces the greatest amount of heat at the workpiece, for a given welding current DCEN will provide deeper weld penetration than DCEP, (Fig. 16). DCEN is the most common configuration used in TIG welding and is used with argon, helium, or a mixture of the two to weld most metals.

When the tungsten electrode is connected to the positive terminal (DCEP), a cathodic cleaning action is created at the surface of the workpiece. This action occurs with most metals but is most important when welding aluminum and magnesium because it removes the refractory oxide surface that inhibits arc stability and wetting by the weld metal.

Unlike DCEN, in which the electrode tip is cooled by the evaporation of electrons, when the electrode is used as the positive pole, its tip is heated by the bombardment of electrons as well as by its resistance to their passage through the electrode. Therefore, to reduce resistance heating and increase thermal conduction into the electrode collet, a large diameter electrode is required for a given welding current when reverse polarity is used. The current-carrying capacity of an electrode connected to the positive terminal is approximately one-tenth that of an electrode connected to the negative terminal. DCEP is generally limited to welding thin sheet metal.

4.2 Pulsed DC Welding

Pulsed DC involves the repetitive variation in arc current from a background (low) value to a peak (high) value. Adjustments of the pulse current time, background current time, peak current level, and background current level can be made to provide a current output waveform fitted to

Current type	DCEN	DCEP	AC (balanced)
Electrode polarity	Negative	Positive	
Electron and ion flow			
Penetration characteristics			
Oxide cleaning Action	No	Yes	Yes-once every Half Cycle
Heat balance in the arc (approx.)	70% at work end 30% at Electrode End	30% at work end 70% at Electrode End	50% at work end 50% at electrode end
Penetration	Deep, Narrow	Shallow: wide	Medium
Electrode Capacity	Excellent e.g. 3.2 mm 400 A	Poor e.g 6.4 mm 120 A	Good e.g., 3.2 mm 225 A

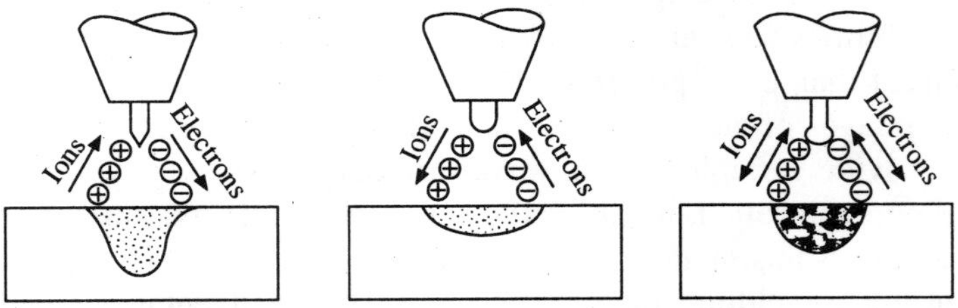

Fig. 16   Welding characteristics of DCEN, DCEP and AC arcs

a particular application (Fig. 17). Generally, pulse frequencies are adjustable from 0.5 to 20 pulses per second. Pulsed DC is usually applied with the electrode negative (DCEN).

In pulsed DC welding, the pulse current level is typically set at 2 to 10 times the background current level. This combines the driving, forceful arc characteristics of high current with the low-heat input of low current. The pulse current achieves good fusion and penetration, while the background current maintains the arc and allows the weld area to cool.

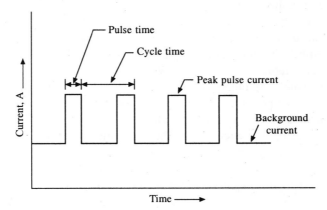

Fig. 17   Pulsed DC waveform characteristics

There are several advantages of pulsed current. For a given average current level, greater penetration can be obtained than with steady current, which is useful on metals sensitive to heat input and minimizes distortion. Very thin metals can be joined with pulsed DC. In addition, one set of welding variables can be used on a joint in all positions, such as a circumferential weld in a horizontal pipe. Pulsed DC is also useful for bridging gaps in open root joints.

4.3 Alternating Current

Alternating current undergoes periodic reversal in polarity from electrode positive to electrode negative. Thus, AC can combine the work cleaning action of electrode positive (reverse polarity) with the deep penetration characteristic of electrode negative (straight polarity). AC welding is compared with DCEN and DCEP welding in Fig. 16.

Conventional AC welding power sources produce a sinusoidal open circuit voltage output. The frequency of voltage reversal is typically fixed at the standard 50/60 Hz frequency of the primary power. When the current decays to zero, different effects will occur, depending on the polarity. When the thermionic tungsten electrode becomes negative, it supplies electrons immediately to reignite the arc. However, when the weld pool becomes negative, it cannot supply electrons until the voltage is raised sufficiently to initiate cold-cathode emission. Without the voltage, the arc becomes unstable.

Some means of stabilizing the arc during voltage reversal is required with conventional sinusoidal welding power sources. This has been done by using high voltage high-frequency sparks in parallel with the arc; and by using power supplies with a square wave output. Square wave AC welding power sources can change the direction of the welding current in a short period of time. The presence of high voltage, coupled with high electrode and base metal temperature at current reversal, allows the arc to be reignted without the need for an arc stabilizer. Also, the lower "peak" current of the square-wave form tends to increase the usable current range of the electrode. Since it is easier to provide electrons needed to sustain an arc when the electrode is negative, the voltage required also is less. The result is a higher welding current during the DCEN interval than during DCEP. In effect, the power supply produces both direct current and alternating current. Such rectification can cause damage to the power supply due to overheating or, with some machines, decay in the output. Rectification is eliminated by wave balancing AC waveforms as shown in Fig. 18.

Early balanced-current power supplies involved either series-connected capacitors or a DC voltage source (such as a battery) in the welding circuit. Modern power supply circuits use electronic wave balancing. Balanced current flow is not essential for most manual welding operations. It is, however, desirable for high-speed machine for automatic welding. The advantages of balanced current flow are the following:

- Better oxide removal
- Smoother, better welding
- No requirement for reduction in output rating of a given size of conventional welding transformer (the unbalanced core magnetization that is produced by the DC component of an unbalanced current flow is minimized).

The following are disadvantages of balanced current flow:

Larger tungsten electrodes are needed. Higher open-circuit voltages generally associated with some wave balancing means may constitute a safety hazard. Balanced wave welding power sources are more costly.

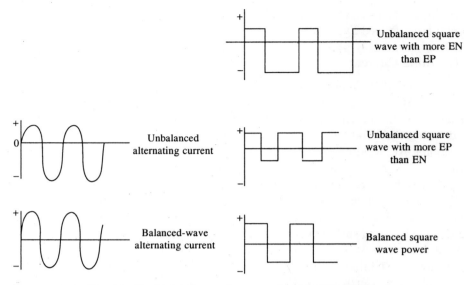

Fig. 18 Typical AC waveforms used with GTA welding

Some square wave AC power sources adjust the current level during the electrode positive and electrode negative cycles at standard 50/60 Hz frequency. More expensive power sources adjust the time of each polarity half cycle as well as the current level during that half cycle. Such variable waveforms will adjust the welding current to suit a particular application Fig. 19.

Shielding Gas: Shielding gas is directed by the torch to the arc and weld pool to protect the electrode and the molten weld metal from atmospheric contamination.

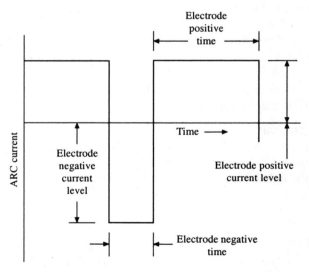

Fig. 19 Characteristics of variable square wave AC

5 TYPES OF SHIELDING GASES

Argon and helium or mixtures of the two are the most common types of inert gas used for shielding. Argon-hydrogen mixtures are used for special applications.

5.1 Argon

Argon is approximately one and one-third times as heavy as air and ten times heavier than helium. Argon, after leaving the torch nozzle, forms a blanket over the weld area. Welding grade argon is refilled to a minimum purity of 99.95 percent. This is acceptable for GTA welding of most metals except the reactive and refractory metals, for which a minimum purity of 99.997 percent is required.

The advantages of argon as a shielding gas are,

> smoother, quieter arc action
> reduced penetration
> cleaning action when welding materials such as aluminium and magnesium
> lower cost and greater availability
> lower flow rates for good shielding
> better cross-draft resistance
> easier arc starting due to low ionization potential of 2.52×10^{-18} J (15 JeV)

The reduced penetration of an argon shielded arc is particularly helpful in vertical or overhead welding since the tendency for the base metal to sag or run is decreased.

5.2 Helium

Helium (He) is an inert, very light monatomic gas, having atomic weight of four. It is obtained by separation from natural gas. Welding grade helium is refined to a purity of at least 99.99 percent. As helium is lighter, it tends to rise around the nozzle and hence to produce equivalent shielding effectiveness, the flow of helium must be two to three times that of argon. The same general relationship is true for mixtures of argon and helium, particularly those high in helium content.

For given values of welding current and arc length, helium transfers more heat into the work than argon. The greater heating power of the helium arc can be advantageous for joining metals of high thermal conductivity and for high-speed mechanized applications. Also, helium is used more often than argon for welding heavy plate. Mixtures of argon and helium are useful when some balance between the characteristics of both is desired.

5.3 Argon-Hydrogen Mixtures

Argon-hydrogen mixtures are employed in special cases, such as mechanized welding of light gage stainless steel tubing, where the hydrogen does not cause adverse metallurgical effects such as porosity and hydrogen-induced cracking. Increased welding speeds can be achieved in almost direct proportion to the amount of hydrogen added to argon because of the increased arc voltage. However, the amount of hydrogen that can be added varies with the metal thickness and type of joint for each particular application. Excessive hydrogen will cause porosity. Argon-hydrogen mixtures are limited to use on stainless steel, nickel-copper, and nickel-base alloys.

The most commonly used argon-hydrogen mixture contains 15 percent hydrogen that is used for mechanized welding of tight butt joints in stainless steel up to 1.6 mm thick. For manual welding, hydrogen content of five percent is sometimes preferred to obtain cleaner welds.

6   GAS FLOW RATES

Shielding gas flow requirements are based on cup or nozzle size, weld pool size, and air movement. In general, the flow rate increases in proportion to the cross-sectional area at the nozzle.

Back Purge: Back purge gas can also be used to protect the underside of the weld and its adjacent base metal surfaces from oxidation during welding. Uniformity of root bead contour, freedom from undercutting, and the desired amount of root bead reinforcement are more likely to be achieved when using gas backup under controlled conditions. In some materials, gas backup reduces root cracking and porosity in the weld.

Argon and helium are satisfactory for the back purge when welding all materials. Nitrogen may be used satisfactorily of backing welds in austenitic stainless steel, copper, and copper alloys. As a rule of thumb, a relatively inert atmosphere will be obtained by flushing with four times the volume to be purged. After purging is completed, the flow of backing gas during welding should be reduced until only a slight positive pressure exists in the purged area. After the root and first filler passes are completed, the back purge may be discontinued. When using argon or nitrogen, the backing gas should preferably enter the system at a low point, to displace the atmosphere upwards and be vented at a point beyond the joint to be welded.

7   ARC INITIATION

With the power supply energized, and the shielding gas flowing from the cup, the torch is lowered toward the workpiece until the tungsten electrode makes contact with the workpiece. The torch is quickly withdrawn a short distance to establish the arc. The advantage of this method of arc initiation is its simplicity of operation. The disadvantage of touch starting is the tendency for the electrode to stick to the workpiece, causing electrode contamination and transfer of tungsten to the workpiece.

High-Frequency Start: High-frequency starting can be used with DC or AC power sources for both manual and automatic applications. High-frequency generators usually have a spark-gap oscillator that superimposes a high-voltage AC output at radio frequencies in series with the welding circuit. The circuit is shown in Fig. 20. The high voltage ionizes the gas between the electrode and the work, and the ionized gas will then conduct welding current that initiates the welding arc.

8   PROCESS VARIABLES

The main process variables in GTA welding are arc voltage (arc length), welding current, travel speed and shielding gas. The amount of energy produced by the arc is proportional to the current

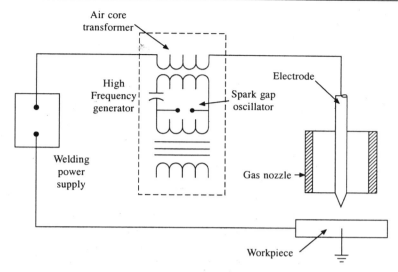

Fig. 20   High frequency arc starting

and voltage. The amount transferred per unit length of weld is inversely proportional to the travel speed. The arc in helium is more penetrating than that in argon. However, because all of these variables interact strongly, it is impossible to treat them as truly independent when establishing welding procedures for fabricating specific joints.

8.1   Arc Current

In general, arc current controls the weld penetration, the effect being directly proportional, if not somewhat exponential. The process can be used with either direct or alternating current, the choice depending largely on the metal to be welded. Direct current with the electrode negative offers the advantages of deep penetration and fast welding speeds. Alternating current provides a cathodic cleaning (sputtering) which removes refractory oxides from the joint surfaces of aluminum and magnesium, allowing superior welds to be made.

8.2   Arc Voltage

The voltage measured between the tungsten electrode and the work is commonly referred to as the arc voltage. Arc voltage is a strongly dependent variable, affected by the following

- Arc current
- Shape of the tungsten electrode tip
- Distance between the tungsten electrode and the work
- Type of shielding gas

When the other variables such as the shield gas, electrode, and current have been predetermined, arc voltage becomes a way to control the arc length. Arc length is important with this process because pool width is proportional to arc length. Therefore, in most applications other than those involving sheet, the desired arc length is as short as possible. Care should be taken to avoid the possibility of short circuiting the electrode to the pool or filler wire if the arc is too short.

8.3   Travel Speed

Travel speed affects both the width and penetration of a TIG weld, the effect being more pronounced on width than on penetration. In mechanised welding travel speed is normally given priority and other variables like current or voltage are adjusted accordingly. In other cases, travel may be a dependent variable along with other variables selected to obtain the required weld quality and uniformity.

8.4   Wire Feed

In manual welding, the way filler metal is added to the pool influences the number of passes required and the appearance of the finished weld. In machine and automatic welding, wire feed speed determines the amount of filler deposited per unit length of weld. Decreasing wire feed speed will increase penetration and flatten the bead contour. Feeding the wire too slowly can lead to undercut, centerline cracking, and lack of joint fill. Increasing wire feed speed decreases weld penetration and produce a more convex weld bead.

9   WELDING TECHNIQUES

The GTAW process is used for manual as well as machine and automatic welding. Each mode has its own advantages and limitations and the selection is made depending upon the quality and quantity requirements and the available facility at the workshop and economy of production.

9.1   Manual Welding

In manual welding, the process functions like manipulation of the torch, control of filler metal additions, welding current, travel speed and arc length are controlled by the welder, Fig. 20. Manual GTA welding is extensively employed for positional welding.

9.2   Machine Welding

Machine welding is done with equipment that performs the welding operation under the constant observation and control of a welding operator. Machine welding provides greater control over travel speed and heat input to the workpiece. The higher cost of equipment to provide these benefits must be justified by production and quality requirements.

Machine welding equipment ranges from simple weld program sequencer and mechanical manipulators to orbital tube and pipe welding systems. The sequence automatically starts and completes the weld, stepping from one variable setting to another at predetermined times or locations along the weld joint. Part tolerances must be controlled closely and fixturing must be strong, since the sequencers cannot compensate for unwanted movement of the parts during welding. High precision parts and sturdy fixturing increase production costs, but welding sequencers usually cost less than more sophisticated automatic controllers.

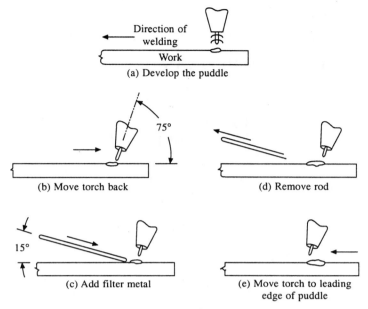

Fig. 21 Mode of manually feeding filler metal into the weld puddle when GTA welding

9.3 Automatic Welding

In automatic welding the equipment performs the welding operation without adjustment of the controls by a welding operator. Some modern automatic welding systems (frequently called adaptive or feedback control) make corrections to welding variables based on information gathered during welding. The objective is to maintain weld quality at a constant level in the presence of changing weld conditions.

10 WELD PREPARATION

10.1 Joint Tolerance

The allowable tolerance of joint dimensions depends upon whether the welding is to be done manually or by mechanized means. Manual welding applications can tolerate greater irregularities in joint fit-up than mechanized welding. The particular tolerance for a given application can be determined only by actual testing, and this tolerance should be specified for future work.

10.2 Cleaning

Cleanliness of both the weld joint areas and the filler metal is an important consideration when welding with the gas tungsten arc process. Oil, grease, shop dirt, paint, marking crayon, and rust or corrosion deposits all must be removed from the joint edges and metal surfaces, to a distance beyond the heat-affected zone. Their presence during welding may lead to arc instability and contaminated welds containing pores, cracks, and inclusions. Cleaning may be accomplished by mechanical means, by the use of vapor or liquid cleaners, or by a combination of these. Chlorinated organic solvents like carbon tetrachloride should not be used as any trace of chlorine coming under the arc may lead to formation of phosgene, a toxic gas. Acetone may be used.

11 DISCONTINUITIES AND DEFECTS

11.1 Tungsten Inclusion

Tungsten inclusion is a discontinuity found only in GTA welding. Particles of tungsten from the electrode can be embedded in a weld when improper welding procedures are used. Typical causes are the following:

- Contact of electrode tip with the molten weld pool
- Contact of filler metal with hot tip of electrode
- Contamination of the electrode tip by spatter from the weld pool
- Exceeding the current limit for a given electrode size or type
- Extension of electrodes beyond their normal distances from the collet (as with long nozzles) resulting in overheating of the electrode.
- Inadequate tightening of the holding collet or electrode chuck
- Inadequate shielding gas flow rates or excessive wind drafts resulting in oxidation of the electrode tip.
- Defects such as splits or cracks in the electrode.
- Use of improper shielding gases such as argon-oxygen or argon-CO_2 mixtures that are used for gas metal are welding.

11.2 Lack of Shielding

Discontinuities related to the loss of inert gas shielding are the tungsten inclusions, porosity, oxide films and inclusion, incomplete fusion, and cracking. In addition, the mechanical properties of titanium, aluminum, nickel, and high-strength steel alloys can be seriously impaired with loss of inert gas shielding.

12 APPLICATION

GTAW process can be used to weld almost all metals. It is especially useful for joining aluminium and magnesium, which form refractory oxides, and also for joining reactive metals titanium and zirconium. This process is extensively used to join stainless steels, copper, alloy steel and carbon steels. In carbon steels, it is primarily used for root pass welding with the application of consumable inserts or open root techniques on pipes. This process finds applications where quality and reliability of welded joint is more important than only cost considerations. GTAW is widely used to produce high quality joints required in the aerospace and nuclear industries.

13 SAFETY IN GTAW

13.1 Gaseous and Metal Fume Hazards

The major toxic gases associated in GTAW welding are ozone, nitrogen dioxide and phosgene

re also produced during welding due to the vaporization of alloying elements.
required about those elements producing toxic fumes. The ultraviolet rays
lding arc act on the oxygen of the surrounding atmosphere to produce ozone.
ed in GTAW, though not toxic in nature, can cause suffocation if accumulated
one of the welding personnel.

hosgene could be produced if chlorinated hydrocarbon cleaning agents, such
ne, perchloroethylne and carbon tetrachloride are present near the welding arc.
ning agents should not be used to clean the workpiece or filler rod. Good
welding area is required so that the concentration of these gases and fumes in
e of the welder remains well within the safe limit. If natural ventilation is not
velding area is a confined space or if toxic metal fumes are produced artificial
is such as fume extractors should be provided.

13.2   Radiation Energy Hazard

Radiant energy may cause injury to the welder in two areas—eye and the skin. Any personnel, whether welder, inspection personnel or helper, present within the immediate vicinity of a welding operation, should be adequately protected from the radiation, particularly ultraviolet (UV) radiation produced by the welding arc. Generally the highest ultraviolet radiant energy intensities are produced when argon shielding gas is used and when aluminium or stainless steel is welded. For eye protection, filter glasses of proper shade depending on the welding current should be used. The recommended shades for different welding current as prescribed in national and international safety standards and codes should be selected.

V SUBMERGED ARC WELDING

1   INTRODUCTION

The optimum performance of welded vessels and structures in service has led to the full exploitation of automatic welding processes. Submerged arc welding is an automatic welding process and plays a prominent role in fabricating a variety of components ranging from pressure vessels, structures, machine building elements, hard facing of components exposed to wear, etc. In submerged arc welding process, the heat energy for welding is supplied by an arc developed between a consumable electrode and the work piece, under a blanket of granulated welding flux.

1.1   Principle of Operation

In submerged arc welding, the arc zone is submerged beneath the molten flux and hence there is no visible sign of the arc. Welding current flows through the arc and the heat energy released from the arc melts the electrode, flux and some base metal to form a weld puddle that fills the joint. Sufficient depth of flux present in this process completely shields the arc column and protects the weld pool from atmospheric contamination. As a result of this unique protection, the weld beads are exceptionally smooth. The flux around the arc column melts, undergoes thermo-chemical transformations and finally solidifies on the surface of weld metal as slag.

1.2 Welding Set Up

Submerged arc welding system consists of the following basic modules:
1. Welding head, 2. Power source, 3. Flux feeding and recovery units
A schematic diagram of submerged arc welding is shown in Fig. 22 illustrating the arc cavity, weld metal and molten slag locations in cross section. General arrangement of power source and wire feed in submerged arc welding is given in Fig. 23. Continuous wire feeding, flux delivery and power source connections are shown in this diagram.

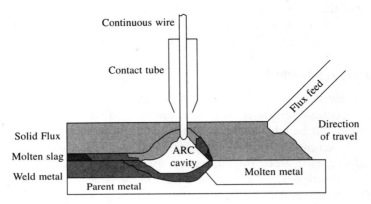

Fig. 22   Schematic diagram of submerged arc welding

1.3 Welding Head

Submerged arc welding head (Fig. 23) consists of the wire spool, wire feed system, flux delivery hopper and electrical contact nozzle. The electrode wire is unwound from the spool by power driven rolls, straightened by a set of pressure rolls and fed through the contact nozzle into the weld pool. The drive for wire feed is from a motor with speed control provided either by means of a gearbox or by means of thyristor controls.

1.4 Wire Feed System

In submerged arc welding machine the wire feed control may be of the following types:

1. Voltage-sensitive system 2. Constant wire feed

The voltage-sensitive system operates on the principle of feedback control. The wire feed is driven by a variable speed DC motor. The arc voltage is monitored by a sensing element, amplified and fed to the armature of the wire feed motor. Thus, the wire feed rate increases when the arc voltage rises up and vice versa. The arc voltage remains constant during the process. The constant wire feed system operates through a constant speed motor, usually an induction motor. No feedback control is used in this system, other than a constant voltage or constant potential characteristic power source. The arc voltage is held constant due to the self-adjusting nature of the constant voltage power source.

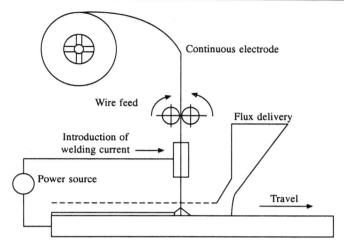

Fig. 23   General arrangement of submerged arc welding

1.5   Mounting Systems for the Welding Head

Submerged arc welding head may be mounted by any one of the following three methods.

(a) Fixed type (b) Carriage mounted type (c) Boom mounted type

(a) **Fixed type:** In this set-up, the welding head is kept fixed and the movement required during welding is provided through the jobs to be welded. A typical application of this arrangement is in the welding of circumferential joints in cylindrical vessels. The job is mounted on powered roller positioners and the welding speed is maintained by controlling the speed of rotation of the job.

(b) **Carriage mounted type:** In this setup, the welding head is mounted on a movable carriage. The carriage is mounted on rails and powered by a variable speed electric motor. The main controls such as carriage speed, current, voltage, etc., are provided on the carriage itself for facilitating ease of operation. Carriage mounted welding heads are most suitable for butt and fillet welding of plates. Depending on weld length, the rail length will be extended to complete the welding.

(c) **Boom mounted type:** These are the most versatile type of welding systems. Normally the boom is supported by means of a column. The welding head along with carriage is mounted on to the boom and longitudinal movement is provided on the carriage. The boom itself is provided with a drive, to move in the transverse direction. Because of the X and Y movements available to this set-up, they find extensive applications in longitudinal welding of internal and external surfaces of cylinders and in the manufacture of plate-formed pipes and shells.

2.0   Power Sources

Submerged arc welding is carried out using both direct current (DC) and alternating current (AC) power sources. Hence a DC generator, a transformer-rectifier or a transformer can be used as the power supply unit. The main requirement of the submerged arc welding power source is that it should be capable of supplying heavy current at hundred percent duty cycle.

Direct current power source, with flat characteristics, provides more versatile control over the bead shape, penetration and welding speed. Difficult contours can be welded at high speeds using this type of power source. Control of bead shape is found to be best with direct current DCEP while high deposition rates are obtained with direct current straight polarity—DCEN—with less penetration. However, direct current welding at high currents creates the phenomenon of magnetic arc blow.

Alternating current is usually preferred for high current levels or when the diameter of the wire is 4 mm or more. Multiple arc welding is possible using AC power source. The bead shape and penetration with AC arc are intermediate between DCEP and DCEN.

3   Flux Feeding & Recovery System

The flux is fed by gravity from the flux delivery hopper mounted on the welding head through a tube into the welding zone. Flux feeding is normally effected through gravity and in some cases by pneumatic feeding systems in automatic machines. The conveyor flux feed tube is also provided with a stop valve to control the flow of the flux. This tube is always kept ahead of the contact tube to ensure adequate supply of flux ahead of the arc.

A vacuum system is used for the recovery of flux. This system sucks the unmelted flux from the weld puddle for reuse. It is important that the flux recovery be carried out after the weld pool has completely solidified.

4   Welding Variables

The following major process variables play an important role in shaping the weld bead and the resultant weld metal in submerged arc welding:

   (a) Welding current
   (b) Welding voltage
   (c) Welding speed
   (d) Electrode stick-out or wire extension
   (e) Height of the flux layer
   (f) Joint design
   (g) Electrode polarity

   (a) Welding current: Welding current is the most influential process variable. It controls the rate at which the electrode is melted, the depth of fusion and the amount of base metal melted. Excessively high current produces a digging arc and the weld joint may melt through the backing, causing burn-through. Other side effects are high current undercuts, highly narrow weld seam and large heat affected zone (HAZ). Too low a welding current produces an unstable arc in the cavity. The optimum ranges of current for various wire diameters are given below (applicable for solid wires only):

Wire dia (mm)	Current Range (A)
1.6	150–300
2.0	200–400
2.4	250–500
3.15	300–650
4.0	450–750
5.0	600–1000
6.3	700–1200

(b) Welding voltage: The welding voltage is a function of arc gap. This primarily determines the shape of the fusion zone and reinforcement. High welding voltage produces a wider, flatter, less deeply penetrating weld. The wider bead increases the flux consumption and decreases the resistance to porosity caused by rust or scale. However, a wide bead can accommodate poor joint fit up. Excessively high voltage produces a hat shaped bead that is prone to cracking. Low arc voltage produces a stiffer arc and improves the penetration in a deep groove joint. However, slag removal is poor in such cases. Excessively low voltages produce a high, narrow bead with poor bead shape resulting in very difficult slag removal.

(c) Welding speed: The welding speed has an important influence on the weld bead size and penetration. Very high travel speeds decrease the wetting action and increase the possibility of undercuts, arc blow, porosity and uneven bead shapes. Since welding speed, i.e. travel speed determines the amount of weld metal deposited per unit length of the weld, the bead shape is essentially controlled by the welding speed. Too low travel speed increases the heat input into the weld, produces a heavy reinforcement and causes slag inclusion. However, porosity is advantageously reduced since sufficient time is permitted for the gases to escape into the atmosphere during slag-metal reactions.

(d) Electrode Stick-out: Stick-out or electrode extension plays an important role for current densities higher than 12800 A/cm^2. The electrode stickout is the length of the wire extending beyond the tip of the contact tube up to the surface of the work piece. Higher stick-out imparts resistance heating to the wire before it enters the arc, hence deposition rate is increased. Too high a stick-out would soften the wire and stiffness of the wire would be lost at higher temperatures resulting in improper bead formation.

(e) Height of flux layer: The height of the flux layer affects the shape and penetration of the weld. If the flux layer is too shallow, the arc is exposed, resulting in a porous weld. If the layer is too deep, the weld is rough and uneven. This may result in porosity and blow holes as the gases generated during slag metal reaction can not escape to the atmosphere.

(f) Joint design: Major joint designs used in submerged arc welding are the single-V, single U and double-V or U joints. Square butt, fillet and plug welds can also be used in submerged arc welding. Because of the high currents used in submerged arc process, wherever possible a backing is necessary to avoid burn through. Depending on the application, backing can be temporary or permanent. Temporary backing of ceramic, synthetic tape, flux and copper are widely used.

(g) Electrode polarity For welding applications usually DCEN is employed in order to ensure higher penetration. However, DCEP results in higher dilution which is not desirable in surfacing applications. Hence, for surfacing applications, DCEN is employed. In tandem submerged arc welding, lead wire alone is DCEP to ensure full penetration and AC is used with the second wire to prevent arc blow.

5   WELD DEFECTS

Common defects encountered in submerged arc welding are slag inclusions, porosity and cracking.

(a) Slag inclusion: Slag inclusions are the result of incomplete deslagging of each layer during multipass welding. By proper cleaning of each pass, this defect can be avoided. Improper wire positioning creates undercuts resulting in slag inclusion in those areas.

(b) Porosity: Porosity in submerged arc welding occurs mainly due to the presence of contaminants in the metal surface or electrode and due to moisture pick up by the flux. In addition, the gases generated during welding may get entrapped in the weld due to improper selection of process parameters such as excessive current, too high a welding speed or excessive height of the flux layer.

(c) Cracking: The main factor in promoting cracking in the weld is the chemical composition of the steel itself. If the steel is hardenable, cracking can be avoided by proper selection of preheat and by controlling the hydrogen level during welding. Cracking may also occur due to susceptibility of the material to hot shortness.

This defect is mainly associated with the sulfur content in the weld and can be controlled by the adjustment of manganese content in the flux. The other major cause of cracking could be the external restraints forced on to the joint during cooling. In general, weld metal cracking can be avoided by proper selection of current, voltage and travel speed to yield a weld deposit with a bead formation factor, i.e. bead width to depth ratio around 3:2 or more.

9. Resistance and Solid State Welding Processes

K.G.K. Murthy

Professor, GRIET, Bachupally, Nizampet Road, Hyderabad 500 050

1   INTRODUCTION

Welding involves joining of two or more piece of metal by the application of heat and sometimes pressure. SMAW, GMAW, GTAW and SAW are examples of "fusion welding", where pressure is not used. Resistance Welding is a process where both heat and pressure are used.

2   RESISTANCE WELDING – PRINCIPLES

In this process, heat is generated in the parts to be welded, by the resistance offered by these parts to the passage of an electric current. Heated parts are forged together by application of pressure,

Heat generated in any electrical circuit is $H = I^2RT$

Where, H – Heat, I – Current, R – Contact Resistance, T – Time duration

Controlling resistance welding processes accordingly involve means of adjustment for:

(a) Welding force – to establish contact resistance and provide forging.
(b) Welding Current (I)
(c) Welding time (T)

Resistance welding machines typically involve

(a) Step down transformer
(b) Pair of electrodes-connected to transformer secondary
(c) Pressure head assembly
(d) Electronic control – for current and time

3   RESISTANCE WELDING MACHINES

Resistance welding machines can be classified in following different types

(A) Spot Welding
(I) Stationary
   (a) Bench type – 5 to 25 KVA
   (b) Pedestal type – 25 to 200 KVA
(II) Portable
   (a) Overhead transformer – 75 to 200 KVA
   (b) Integral transformer – 15 to 75 KVA

(B) **Projection welding** – 50 to 300 KVA
(C) **Seam welding** – 75 to 300 KVA
(D) **Flash butt welding** – 50 to 600 KVA

4   MACHINE SELECTION

Selection of machine capacity and model depends upon welding capacity i,e.:

  (i) Sheet thickness or cross section of jobs to be welded
  (ii) Throat depth and throat gap of machine
  (iii) Maximum short circuit current requirement
  (iv) Duty cycle
  (v) Production capacity

In terms of electrical classification, resistance welding machines can be classified under:

  (i) AC
  (a) Single Phase
  (b) Three Phase
  (ii) DC
  (a) Single Phase
  (b) Three Phase

Single phase AC machines are most widely used in Indian Industry. Its main advantages over other configurations are:

  (a) Low equipment cost and
  (b) Low maintenance

However, single-phase AC machines have several disadvantages

  (a) Unbalanced load on power supply,
  (b) High current surge and
  (c) Low powerfactor

Above limitations are overcome in 3-phase DC resistance welding machines, which offer following benefits.

  (a) Low electrical installation cost
  (b) Better power factor
  (c) Balanced load
  (d) Reduced line current surges
  (e) Better quality welds
  (f) Higher quality life

(g) Welding current not affected by magnetic material in the throat

(h) Higher speeds in seam welding

(i) Lower welding costs

However, 3 Phase DC machines are expensive and may require additional investments in water cooling system for machine as well as involve more careful maintenance of machine by skilled technicians.

Applications

Typical industrial applications of different types of resistance welding machines are as follows:

M/c type	Applications
Spot	
(i) Stationary	
(a) Bench	TV picture tube, electronic components, electrical switchgear
(b) Pedestal	Scooter, motorcycle, electronic switchgear, home appliances
(ii) Portable	Car and truck body
Projection	Engine valves, shock absorbers, auto electricals
Seam	Cycle and motorcycle rims, transformer radiators, fuel tanks, drums and barrels, sheet rolling and processing lines
Flash	Cycle, motor cycle, car and truck wheel rims, chains and shackles, window frames, tools and ring gears

RESISTANCE WELDING PROCESSES FOR SHEET METAL FABRICATION
Industrial Quality Control Methods for Mass Production

1 INTRODUCTION

Sheet metal fabrication is essential in many industrial sectors such as transportation, power, construction and domestic utilities. Many products involving sheet metal are manufactured using resistance welding processes: spot, seam, projection, upset butt and flash butt welding. In resistance welding the heat for joining is provided by the resistance to electric current at the contact surfaces between the pieces. The method of heat generation differs from process to process. The two main configurations used for resistance welding are "lap" (one kept over the other) and "butt" (end to end). Lap type joints are used for spot, seam and projection welding processes. Butt type joints are used for upset butt, flash butt, high frequency butt seam and foil butt seam processes.

In spot welding, electrode tips are used to make individual spots at the desired locations between two sheets to be welded. Single spot welding, multispot welding and portable spot welding machines are widely employed for mass production applications.

Projection welding machines have flat platens unlike spot welding electrode tips and the process is highly flexible. By incorporating a suitable projection (defined geometry) on one of the members to be welded joints can be made for manufacture of various industrial components. Simultaneous welding is possible at two or more locations. Annular projections facilitate welding of nut to plate, bush to plate etc. Projection geometry and reproducibility are essential for maintaining consistent quality. Seam welding uses circular electrodes and the process is ideally suited for liquid- leak-tight joints; radiator panels, car petrol tanks, food containers, cans etc.

Butt welding of strips to build up length find wider use in many industries: wheel rims, strips for tube miles require upset butt of flash butt for mass production.

Automation of resistance welding processes (and robotics) facilitated increased production rate for sheet metal parts especially for cars, domestic appliances, etc.

In the field of resistance welding control, there are rapid advances due to the availability of industrial type integrated circuit devices and high power thyristor switches.

Synchronous controls are available now for weld times of less than 5 cycles. A more sophisticated range of IC synchronous digital timer controls intended primarily for welding of aerospace components and exotic material are developed. These facilitate pre squeeze, squeeze, and weld cool, hold, off, which together with options of spot (single or repeat), pulsation seam (modulated and continuous) and upslope control as well as the usual phase-shift heat control and delayed firing. This type of control can be used for spot, seam, and projection or roll spot machines.

Though weld sequences timers control the duration of current flow, the total heat input depends on the supply voltage. The fluctuations in voltage, affect the quality. Constant current and voltage control system is most advantageous for consistent quality.

It is most important to measure the RMS value of weld current and the exact duration of current flow. A suitable instrumentation system should be used during mass production operations. This will help in process control as well as quality monitoring.

The non-destructive testing methods are needed for sheet fabrication industries to ensure reliable joints for many industrial sectors. The principal aim of any such technique is to provide an "in process" indication of the quality of the weld so that no separate inspection at a later stage is necessary.

Destructive tests such as peel test, tension-shear, cruciform tensile, macro-etch test can be carried out for procedure qualification as well as for production quality control (sampling). The limitation of these tests is that no corrective action can be carried out. Reported literature shows that the patterns of variation exhibited by voltage, current and resistance can be related to good weld characteristics in mild steel.

2 SPOT WELDING OF SHEETS

Sheet metal products required for many industries are generally welded by spot welding process. The steels used are of low carbon variety (C 0.068 to 0.125%) and thickness of the sheets generally ranges from 0.8 to 2.0 mm. The equipments like single spot, multi spot and portable guns with controls need to be selected depending on the job configuration, quality requirements and production rate. Low cost automation or full automation may be required for some jobs in transportation sectors. One of the very interesting contribution to high production resistance welding is a dial indexing table which can be mounted on standard or special machines to load, position, weld and eject parts at a high rate. For relatively small components, hopper feed mechanisms can be used to increase productivity. These mechanisms sort, stack and transfer the parts to the welding fixture.

2.1 Spot Welded Industrial Products

Energy meter mainframe requires spot welding at many locations. The material is of low carbon steel (SAE 1010). This is a mass production item and normally 4 or 5 machines are used to weld all the spots required in the assembly. In this application electrode shape selection is of importance apart from selection of suitable electrode material. Though this application may mot call for too much strength for the joint, improper weld may cause rejection of the entire assembly in the final stages. Hence, quality of joints should be assured during production.

A similar application of spot welding is in control panel assembly work where a number of spots at various locations have to be done. The importance in this application is to guarantee distortion free assembly. Proper sequencing as well as selection of proper nugget size is of vital importance to control the distortion. The job has to be done first time correctly as correction in final assembly is not possible and leads to delay in entire operations. Appearance is also of importance in applications of this nature. Too much indentation if not acceptable and gives shabby appearance even after painting. While welding dissimilar thickness proper electrode tip size and reproducibility of parameters need special attention.

Some of the other industrial applications for spot welding are

   (i)   weather resistant steels for railway coaches.
  (ii)   motor vent spacers
 (iii)   transformer radiator flute
  (iv)   automobile vee pulley assembly
   (v)   communications equipment assembly involving aluminium alloys
  (vi)   corrugated elements.
 (vii)   cross bearer assembly for heavy duty vehicles

2.2 Testing of Spot Welds

Production quality control requires destructive and non destructive testing. The destructive test methods such as peel test, tension-shear, U-tensile and cruciform tensile are required for production quality control based on defined norms. Different practices are followed in industries viz., start and end of shift testing, percentage testing, testing after fixed number of joints etc. In the absence of any non destructive testing method applicable for the product.

Non-destructive testing methods such as LPI, MPI, ultrasonic and radiography are not applicable to spot welding for revealing the quality of the joints. Hence, the present day trend is to go in for in process quality monitoring.

This involves using of a built in programmer cum controller, which will assist in sequencing of operation as well as simple production as well as simple production quality control. A typical unit of this nature has the following features.

A. Sequence control: up to 99 programs, each of 34 parameters for selection.

B. Quality control: compensation for the mains voltage fluctuation, current rise in case of electrode wear, secondary constant current regulation due to change in impedance caused by job.

C. Weld parameter monitoring: secondary welding current (effective and peak value), weld time and charge (voltage × current × time). Optimum quality ocurrence with possibility of documentation on built in or external printer.

This type of control unit will be highly useful for normal machines as well for portable guns.

At the Welding Research Institute, BHEL, Tiruchirapalli, a simple GO-NO GO monitor has been developed with the following features:

1. Monitoring upper/lower limit of welding current/time
2. Display of secondary current (peak or RMS) and weld time
3. Display of electrode load prior to weld time

This simple system can be connected to any type of spot or projection welding machines. The advantage of such a system is that when connected to a production machine the welds falling beyond tolerance limits can be detected and also it will be a useful tool for finding the behaviour of the machines.

3 PROJECTION WELDING OF SHEET METAL PRODUCTS

Projection welding is a highly flexible process and can be employed for a variety of products involving sheet metal. In this process it is essential to have standard projection geometry for achieving good welds. Projections can be machined, formed or sometimes, natural projections on the member can best be used. The machines employed for this process are provided with flat electrodes with "*T*" slots. These flat platens (top and bottom) can be used for clamping any type of fixture designed for specific application. The sequence programmer controls various timings required for the process.

3.1 Projection Welded Industrial Products

Automobile parts require use of projection welding. Some of the examples are joining mild steel pins, bolts, bosses and nuts to mild steel pressings for automobile brake members, chassis subassembly parts, brackets to parts, bracket to car instrument lay-outs, door lock assemblies as well as bosses and brackets to agricultural implement subassembly parts. There are also many applications for domestic and electrical appliances. Some of the applications may require multi-projection welding. This is possible only with high electrical and mechanical capacity machines.

3.2 Testing of Projection Welds

When light assemblies are welded it is important to avoid premature projection collapse. The machine should have provision for gradual increase of pressure during weld time. Good strength welds can be obtained by close control of welding current and time.

Destructive tests like tension shear and U-tension give the quantification of the weld strength percentage testing during production quality control helps in identifying process consistency to some extent. Some of the critical applications may require proof testing. To be done by loading the component to 85% of yield stress. This way every joint can be assured of the quality.

Dynamic resistance and thermal expansion based monitors can also be used on specially built projection welding machines to monitor the quality of the joints during mass production.

4 SEAM WELDING APPLICATIONS

Seam welding machines are often used for manufacturing oil and chemical drums, petrol tanks, motor pressings, pressed steel radiator assemblies, washing machine casings and interiors, car silencers and similar applications. A large number of machines are also employed for aircraft such as tail pipe sections, exhaust casings, flame tubes, and guided missile assemblies.

The types of joints generally are longitudinal or circumferential. Variable heat control or phase shift control for secondary current adjustment is required for welding a variety of materials. In order to maintain consistency in weld quality electrodes should be dressed for every 10 meters length of seam completed.

4.1   Testing of seam welds

Test pieces from seam-welded joints are subjected to tension, torsion, peel tests and metallographic examination. The non-destructive tests are external inspection and radiography. Leak tight joints are tested by pillow test. This test reveals quality of the joint for the intended service.

Monitoring of the weld parameters is necessary for production quality control. This involves measurement and display of secondary current (peak/RMS), weld time, (on time) and welding speed.

5   FOIL BUTT SEAM WELDING FOR SHEET METAL PRODUCTS

Foil Butt Seam Welding is ideally suited for the production of large area sheets required for railway coaches and bus bodies, This is accomplished by joining several single sheets of commercially available standard dimensions. Other applications of this process are pipelines for transporting agricultural products, air conditioning and boiler chimneys, silencers and mesh filters for cars.

The quality of the joints can be tested by "Erichsen test" to reveal the ductility. For continuous quality control a current metering and checking device is recommended with an electronic signal output, in case pre selected upper and lower tolerance limits are exceeded. With this device either the r.m.s value or the peak value of the largest half-wave within each current pulse (pulse current measurement) or the total amount of energy transmitted during each current pulse (charge measurement) may be recorded.

6   FLASH BUTT WELDING OF SHEET METAL STRIPS

Sheet metal strips have to be butt welded for a variety applications. Automobile wheel rims and tube mills require welding of sheet metal strips and the mass production necessitates consistent quality. The flash welder should have features for proper weld sequence, fast, accurate repeatable movements. The flash welder should have features for proper weld sequence, fast, accurate repeatable movements.

The destructive tests such as tensile and bend, give the joint strength and ductility of the joints. Material quality is very important for reproducible joints. The initial condition of the material has got relevance in selection of weld cycle and proper parameter levels.

Production quality control has to be carried out by destructive tests and non-destructive tests. Two test welds at the beginning of each welding period and at the end shift have to be carried out for subjecting to mechanical tests. In case the machine is not in operation for more than I hour during a welding period, two test welds on recommencement of welding are required. In case there is change of settings or procedure, two test welds have to be done. Monitoring device has to be fitted on the machine for display/recording of critical parameters for every weld. The variables to be monitored and recorded are (a) current (b) upset force (c) displacement (d) time. Monitoring records shall be attached to the procedure approval test record.

FRICTION WELDING – PRINCIPLES AND APPLICATIONS

1 INTRODUCTION

Friction welding process was introduced in industries in 1960s and only few machines were in operation in Soviet Union, Czechoslovakia and China. Today the process is fully exploited by industries all over the world due to its special advantages; efficient energy utilization, consistent weld quality, high production rates, welding of many types of similar and dissimilar metal combinations as well as plastics.

Friction welding technology is established at WRI for carbon steel to carbon steel automobile components, stainless steel to carbon steel pump shafts, high speed steel to medium carbon steel tools, stellite to martensitic stainless steel valve discs. Also technology for copper to stainless steel, tungsten copper to copper, aluminium to stainless steel for electrical and other critical products is established. Friction welding in its simplest form has one circular component rotated an other component is advanced into contact under preselected axial pressure. Rotation continues for a specific time for the frictional heat to achieve an interfacial temperature at which the metal is in a plastic state near and away from the interface to a particular depth. After this the rotation is stopped while the pressure is maintained or increased to consolidate the joint. This simple mechanism has facilitated design of many types of friction welding machines, continuous drive, inertia drive, radial, orbital, micro friction, friction stud, friction surfacing and under water friction welding machines.

Friction welding process facilitates controlled heat generation and hence overheated microstructures are avoided in carbon steels, low alloy steels and stainless steels. Since the process is a solid phase bonding technique dissimilar metal combinations like high speed steel to medium carbon steel, stainless steel to carbon steel, stellite to martensitic stainless steel, aluminium to stainless steel and copper to stainless steel can be successfully welded without difficulty. Fusion welding techniques require elaborate procedures and sometimes it is impossible to achieve the required mechanical properties due to the formation of intermetallic compounds.

2 APPLICATION OF FRICTION WELDING AND ITS EFFECTS

Friction welded components will be economical and reliable and exhibit performance depending on the condition of application. Past experience by many industries on high accuracy parts, dissimilar materials and large sized parts, proves excellent dependability (1).

A complicated forging can be simplified by the judicious introduction of friction-welded joint in between simpler forging and standard wrought product. Wherever it is difficult to achieve reproducible quality on complicated castings, the designers can have flexibility by adopting friction welding suitably on simplified cast members. Many components are manufactured by machining involving enormous wastage of material and machining time. These components can best be economically mass-produced by frication welding and with minimum machining.

Many components are designed with dissimilar metal combinations in order to obtain the maximum benefit from the respective metals. These dissimilar metal components are very difficult to fabricate by fusion welding methods. The problems like difference in coefficient of thermal expansion, difference in physical and mechanical properties, and intermetallic compound formation cause considerable difficulties while doing fusion welding. Since friction welding is a solid phase bonding method, these problems are not causing major difficulties for getting good quality joints. Environmentally, friction welding is better than conventional welding as there are no fumes, spatter, unlike many are welding processes and flash butt welding. Tooling costs can be low and if tooling is simple the change over time is low, making friction welding process well suited to even batch production of assemblies.

3   FABRICATION OF PRODUCTS

Many industries in India require friction welding process for fabrication either for mass production or for batch production. Since friction welding facilitates high production rate with consistent quality many automobile components can be switched over to friction welding from conventional methods like machining, casting and forging. Welding Research Institute at Tiruchirapalli, is engaged in the development of technology for various industrial products using friction welding process. The machine used for various welding products mentioned in Table I has the following features.

Type   : Continuous drive friction welding machine
Capacity : 12 MT maximum upset force
Speeds   : 1125, 2250, 1500, 3000 rpm

3.1   Joining Products of Similar Metals

There are many automobile components where friction welding is ideally suited for joining of similar metals. Front wheel axle, main shaft and rocker arm shaft are the three products required for 2-wheelers manufacture. These are mass production items and also undergo dynamic loading during service. The quality of the products need to be of very high standard. Hence, the process of manufacture selected should give reliable products in mass production. As friction welding process is amenable for mass production and assures the quality of every joint produced on the machine, it is ideally suited for these components. It is heartening to note that in India friction welding process is being implemented for these components after establishing the technology at the Welding Research Institute, The benefits accrued are indicted in Table 1, compared to the previous methods of manufacture: (1) Machining from single bar stock (2) Complicated forging and machining. It may be worth noting that per piece cost can be considerably reduced by adopting friction welding. In these products by switching over to friction welding the savings can be as high as 50% per piece. The production rate of 500 pieces/shift can easily be achieved which gives overall cost reduction.

Table I   Applications and Benefits of Friction Welding

Product	Industry & Previous Method	Benefits by Friction Welding
Front wheel axle (EN19B to EN 19B)	Automobiles 1. Machining from bar stock 2. Forging and machining	1. Improved quality 2. Higher productivity 3. Simplified production method 4. Better dimensional control 5. Minimum rejections
Main shaft (EN 354 to EN 354)	Automobiles 1. Machining from single bar stock 2. Forging	1. Saving in material and machining time 2. Improved quality and productivity
Rocker arm shaft (SAE 8620 to SAE 8620)	Automobiles Forging and machining	1. Saving in forging cost 2. Improved forging quality 3. Standardised forging 4. Reduction in bar stock inventory 5. Reduction in cycle time
Bimetal drill tools (high speed steel to medium carbon)	1. Brazing 2. Flash butt welding	1. Saving in HSS 2. Dimensional accuracy 3. Less power consumption 4. Clean process 5. Improved productivity, quality 6. Cost per piece reduced 7. Elimination of preweld heat treatment
Machine tap tools (HSS to carbon steel)	Brazing	1. Tool life increased 2. Minimum rejections 3. Higher Productivity 4. Improved quality 5. No filler material
Vertical milling tools (HSS to carbon steel	Brazing	1. Higher Joint efficiency 2. Improved productivity and dimensional accuracy 3. Tool life increased 4. No filler material
Pump shaft (SS 316 to EN8)	Pumps Fully stainless steel shaft	1. Saving of stainless steel material 2. Reduced machining time 3. Reduced of cost per piece
Valve disc assembly	Valves Gas stelliting	1. Higher productivity 2. Reduced consumption of stellite 3. No rework 4. Elimination of skill requirement 5. Ease of machining 6. Elimination of perheating

(Contd.)

Product	Industry & Previous Method	Benefits by Friction Welding
Air nozzle (316 stainless steel – EN 8)	Power generation Fully stainless steel	1. Saving of stainless steel 2. Reduced machining time, cost/piece
Contact Rod Assembly (Tungsten copper to copper)	Electrical power transmission Brazing	1. Improved service performance 2. Minimised rejections 3. increased life
Transition Joint (stainless steel-aluminium)	Nuclear and cryogenics Fusion Welding	1. Improved quality 2. Efficient method of fabrication 3. Ease of operation 4. No intermediate layer required
Component Detector Assembly (316 SS to AL)	Instrumentation 1. Fusion welding 2. Brazing	1. Better and easy method of manufacture 2. No filter or better layer required 3. Good quality joint

3.2 Joining Products of Dissimilar Metals

Dissimilar metal joints are essential for some products required for electrical, chemical and tools industries. Considerable cost saving can be achieved by selecting sizes of costly material and judiciously placing the friction welded joint in the product.

3.2.1 *Hard to Hard Dissimilar Metal Joints*

Tool industry uses high speed steel extensively for making twist drills, taps, milling cutters, reamers and chisels. As high speed steel is very costly the method of manufacture selected should give maximum savings on high speed material.

Bimetallic drills are ideally suited for friction welding as joining of high speed steel to medium carbon steel poses no problem as melting is absent in friction welding. Compared to flash butt welding the loss of high speed steel in friction welding is less. The other savings resulted are less power consumption, no fume extraction equipment, pre-weld heat treatment necessary for good electric contact was eliminated [2].

Machine taps and vertical milling cutters can be manufactured with ease compared to complicated brazing method. Rejection rates are very much minimised and more accurate finished parts are obtained. In a 2-shift mass production situation it is possible to recover the initial cost of the machine in a year or two by high speed steel material saving alone [3].

Pump shafts are required for special pumps for use in a corrosive atmosphere. Typically carbon steel is the shaft of an electric motor and the stainless steel is an extension required for corrosive medium. Friction welding offers savings in costly stainless steel and better quality joints are produced. Air nozzle is another product where austenitic stainless steel is used for hot air zone and carbon steel in low temperature zone. In this case also considerable stainless steel material saving is obtained by using friction welding.

Valve disc assembly involves stellite disc for wear resistance which requires to be joined to carbon steel or martensitic stainless steel. The method of gas stelliting involves pre and post weld heat treatment and excess deposition of costly stellite material. The machining of stellite leads to wastage of costly material. The rejections are more due to metallurgical problems (cracking). Gas stelliting requires trained operators and also since welding has to be done after heating the job to 650°C causes operator fatigue. This leads to lesser productivity and more rejections. Friction welding for this product improves productivity and eliminates rejections.

3.2.2   *Hard to Soft Dissimilar Metal Joints*

Many industrial products are now designed keeping in view the technoeconomics. This calls for not only selection of appropriate materials but also suitable methods of joining. Most of the metal combinations of the products will have metals of widely differing physical and mechanical properties. The joining of such metal combinations poses considerable difficulties while fusion welding. Friction welding being a solid phase bonding method is highly amenable for joining many dissimilar metal combinations required for critical components.

Transition joints of aluminium to stainless steel are needed for chemical, electrical, nuclear and cryogenic applications [4]. This dissimilar metal combination is difficult to weld on account of the formation of brittle intermetallic phases and due to the wide difference in physical and mechanical properties. Table I indicates the transition joints and detector assembly used for instrumentation. Friction welding for these applications is ideal and replaces fusion welding and brazing processes.

3.3   Other Engineering Applications

There is increasing use of friction welding and the products already discussed are only a few typical among many. On some occasions it is worthwhile to implement friction welding though quantum may not be very high like that of shaft for rotating anode tube required for electronics industry, where quality is a major consideration. Crankshaft is conventionally produced by forging but can easily be replaced by simple forging and friction welding bar stock. Foundation bolts are made by shielded metal are welding which is a slow process. The joints between plate and rod can done by friction welding, which can achieve considerable cost reduction (Table I).

4   SIGNIFICANCE OF FRICTION WELDING FOR PRODUCTION

Designing products suitable for friction welding process can curtail production costs considerably. Typical designs are rod-to-rod, rod-to-plate, tube-to-plate and disc-to-shaft. On some occasions flash trap joint design can be adopted where there are difficulties for removing internal flash. Every product calls for proper tooling for mass production. It is worth considering this aspect while purchasing the machine itself. Considering the fact that ultrasonic testing and radiography are not very well suited for quality monitoring it is better to go for in process quality monitors. These monitors assure the quality of every joint that is made on the machine [5].

5 TRENDS AND PROSPECTS FOR FRICTION WELDING

There are many developments in the areas of friction welding. Orbital welding for non circular components, positional arrest friction welding for non-circular members, friction stud welding, under water friction welding and friction surfacing are some of the processes available for full exploitation by industries. In India, there are only about 30 machines as compared to Japan where thousands of machines are in operation. There is lot of potential for exploiting friction welding for automobile parts, construction machinery parts, agricultural machinery parts, printing machine parts, oil hydraulic machine parts, pneumatic machine parts, electrical machinery parts, cutting tools, manual tools etc. Many times, maintenance of machines calls for reclamation and repair of damaged or worn out components like shafts of pinions, gears, motors. Friction welding facilitates joining of suitable shaped part with undamaged portion of the component. The attached part can be machined to the original shape of the components thereby enabling the component to be put into service quickly with consequent commercial benefits.

ULTRASONIC METAL WELDING PRINCIPLES APPLICATIONS

PRINCIPLE OF ULTRASONIC WELDING

Metallurgicaly, the US metal welding process comes under the heading of cold welding. Intense frictional contact at the weld joints breaks up the oxide skin and the two parts are pressed together under pressure. This causes the two materials to come so closely together, that the atomic bonding forces come into play. The relatively small temperature increase remains well below melting temperature and makes no material contribution to the welding process. Since there is no fusion of the base metal there are also no changes in the structure with their attendant detrimental effects.

APPLICATION

The process is of particular interest for those applications where other welding methods fail or prove uneconomical. In contrast to other welding methods it allows different materials to be joined, provided the difference in their hardness is not excessive. Excellent results can be achieved with pure aluminium. Aluminium can be joined not only to itself but also to many other metals, such as gold, silver, silicon, copper, nickel, etc. In general, the parts cannot be too thick or too heavy, otherwise no relative movement is possible. For aluminium sheet one component should not be more than ~ 2 mm thick but for the other part there is no limit.

DIFFUSION WELDING-PRINCIPLES-APPLICATIONS

In diffusion welding, welding materials are heated to high temperature and pressed to effect welding with diffusion of atoms across the interface. Thus, welding temperature, welding time, pressure, pressing time, joint surface conditions, welding atmosphere, and the use if any, of inserted metal, are important factors that affect weld properties.

Temperature, time and pressure

Let us consider welding temperature and time. The diffusion welding process can be treated zero more or less as a zero velocity process. The diffusion depth is increased with increased welding temperature and time.

Next, let us consider pressure and pressing time. These factors, which contribute to contact between the welding surfaces, must be sufficient to cause any irregularities of the welding surfaces to yield through creep deformation, and thus make good contact at welding temperature. The temperature necessary for welding is higher than recrystallizing temperatures of both materials, and required pressure is greater than the yield point of the weaker material at welding temperature. Welding time, although effective in increasing diffusion depth, may cause formation of brittle intermetallic phases in some cases. Joining time should therefore be kept to a minimum.

Surface roughness

Roughness of joint surfaces affects considerably the contact between them. Greater roughness requires higher temperature and pressure for welding.

Atmosphere

The welding atmosphere relates to oxidation of welding surfaces. As oxide film, if formed on a welding surface, hampers diffusion of atoms and adversely affects welding quality. This requires the use of vacuum or Ar atmosphere (after evacuation Ar is sealed in).

Inserted Metal

To provide a good joint, it is essential to ensure sufficient diffusion of atoms by applying appropriate temperature, time and pressure. With some dissimilar combinations, joint strength is lowered due to formation of brittle layers and material deterioration. These can be remedied with inserted metal layer compatible with the metals being joined.

Practical Application

Diffusion welding enables production of multi layer clad materials and complicated parts that can not be achieved by alternative methods in addition to producing high quality dissimilar metal joints and high accuracy welding. Many kinds of clad steels for chemical plants such as Cu alloy clad steel, stainless clad steel, three layer clad steel of copper steel-stainless-steel, copper stainless steel clad electrodes for marine equipment and chemical plant, and copper alloy steel wear resistant material, clad machine parts in steel manufacturing etc., have been widely put to use.

SUMMARY

A good joint can be provided under the following basic welding conditions.
Higher welding temperature than recrystallizing temperature, higher welding pressure than yield point of welded material at welding temperature, a few micron roughness of weld surface (vacuum of about $5 \times 10-4$ Torr for material forming dense oxide films such as stainless steel, etc.) are applied.

For joints that will form a brittle layer, it is necessary to use the correct inserted metal. For example, inserted metal of Mo or Ni for Ti-stainless steel and of Mo or Ni for Ti-carbon steel are used to provide good joint strength and corrosion resistance.

Joints produced under the above conditions exhibit the same mechanical properties and corrosion resistance as those of the base metals. Clad steels for example, meet the specifications such as JIS and ASTM. Diffusion welding in addition to providing high quality welding of various dissimilar metals, enables precise and high quality welding for complicated parts and hollow parts. Many kinds of clad steel and clad parts manufactured with this welding procedure have been put to practical use and these features are being applied enthusiastically aiming at further development.

REFERENCES

1. Welding in Japan '86, Sanpo publications Inc. Journal of the Japan Welding Engineering Society (Welding Technique extra issue).
2. A.F. Vavilov and V.P. Voinov, Friction welding, Translated by J.H. Dixon, National Lending Library for Science and Technology, England, 1968.
3. C.R.G. Ellis, A survey of friction welding application in the UK, DVS-Berichte 29, International Institute of Welding Annual Assembly 1973.
4. S. Sundaresan and KGK Murti, Friction Welding of Aluminium to Austenitic Stainless Steel. The International Journal of Joining of Materials 5(2): 66–70, 1993.
5. K Asok kumar et al, in, process quality control monitors for resistanc and friction welding processes, WRI Key words, 57–61 Sept-Dec 1988.

10. Residual Stresses in Weldments

S. Suresh

Dy. Gen. Manager, Welding Research Institute, BHEL, Tiruchi 620 014

1 INTRODUCTION

Residual stresses are self balancing internal system of stresses arising from non-uniform mechanical or thermal straining with some measure of plastic flow. These stresses exist in a body when all external forces are removed.

During welding a weldment experiences complex temperature changes that cause transient thermal stresses and non-uniform distribution of elastic strains that are produced in the weld and in the regions near it. Due to this, both distortion and residual stresses result in the welded part. These stresses are elastic in nature and exist in a body without any external force. Hence, they are self-equilibrating type (i.e), the summation of the forces and moments about any point in the cross section of the body is equal to zero.

The most obvious manifestation of the mechanism producing residual stress is distortion, which cannot be considered in isolation from residual stress. In simple terms high conditions of restraint during welding limit distortion but impose large local strains at the welded joint giving rise to higher residual stress, which greatly increases the risk of failure. Conversely, low restraint does not inhibit the local contractions which result in larger displacements or distortion and lower levels of residual stress.

2 BASIC MECHANISM

Residual stresses in welded components arise directly from the localised shrinkage associated with the cooling down of the hot weld metal which is restrained, either internally or externally, by the cold sections of the fabrication surrounding the weldment. But, this does not accurately describe the true mechanism, which in reality is a highly transient condition, being modified continually, depending on the nature of the joint, the number of passes involved, and to some extent the welding parameters themselves. At any moment any one of the influencing parameters could be different making study of the mechanism an extremely complex exercise.

A better understanding of the process each incremental element of material experiences can be obtained from Fig. 1, which illustrates a typical thermal stress cycle for an element of material with yield strengths in tension and compression decreasing with temperature. The cycle starts at room temperature, 0, the initial thermal expansion is restrained by the surrounding cold material, thus generating plastic compressive stresses until the yield strength is reached at position A. With further increase in temperature plastic strains occur following the material's

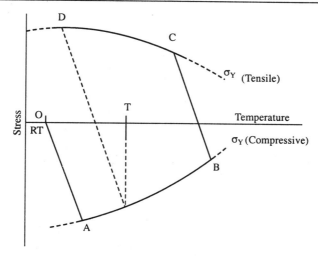

Fig. 1 **Schematic illustration of the origin of residual stresses during heating and cooling of welds**

characteristic compressive yielding curve, AB. On cooling the response is once again elastic, but opposite in sense to the heating cycle, until the tensile yield strength is achieved at position C. Cooling back to room temperature then follows the material's characteristic tensile yield strength curve, thus generating yield magnitude residual stresses at room temperature, position D. In addition Fig. 1 illustrates clearly that the magnitude of residual stress is also a function of the temperature difference experienced. In the case considered any temperature rise exceeding T on Fig. 1 will always generate yield magnitude elastic residual stresses, whereas at lower temperatures the shrinkage strains are not sufficient to reach the tensile yield limit and will result in less than yield magnitude elastic residual stress. The critical temperature difference is a function of material yield strength, which for typical mild steel is of the order of 175°C, with reference to room temperature. Fig. 2 illustrates the commonly observed classical distribution of residual stresses arising from this simple contraction and reaction mechanism that are produced in three directions viz. longitudinal, transverse and in the thickness directions during welding of thick low carbon ferritic steel plates. The peak magnitude of the longitudinal residual stress is usually of the order of yield stress level. The magnitude of the transverse residual stress is much lower than the magnitude of the longitudinal stress component. Often a ratio of 1:4 to 1:3 is reported for the magnitude of both residual stress components.

3   TYPES OF RESIDUAL STRESSES

Residual stresses are commonly classified into two groups as either macro or micro. Macro residual stresses, or residual stresses of the first kind, are those of engineering nature and which are measured over a gauge length that encompasses several grains. Micro residual stresses, or residual stresses of the second kind, relate to stress systems set up by microstructural inhomogeneities which can either be confined within a single grain or a particular set of grains of the same preferred orientation.

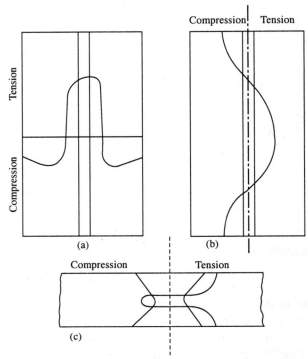

Fig. 2 Typical 'traditional' residual stress distributions in plates without fixed ends (a) longitudainal, (b) transverse and (c) through thickness

Though doubts do exist, over which of these mechanisms is to be considered important to stress corrosion cracking-brittle fracture or fatigue initiation-it is likely that both types can contribute depending on the situation. However, it is suggested that for all mechanisms it is the first kind that is of fundamental interest. The two measurement techniques used in this study namely strain relaxation technique and X-ray diffraction technique measure macro residual stresses.

4   FACTORS INFLUENCING RESIDUAL STRESSES

Among the various factors influencing residual stress magnitude and distribution, the material properties, specimen dimension, heat input, welding process and welding sequence are considered to be the most important ones.

4.1   Material Properties

The magnitude of residual stresses is affected by,

1. The temperature distribution in the weldment characterised by thermal conductivity and diffusivity.
2. The thermal expansion characteristics of the material, and
3. The mechanical properties of the material at elevated temperature.

Residual stresses as high as the yield stress of the weld metal and the base metal are produced on carbon steel weldments. Residual stresses near the weld zone in aluminium joints are as high as the yield stress of the metal. In the case of high strength steels the residual stresses in the welds are often considerably lower than the yield stress values of the parent material.

4.2   Specimen Dimension

Reports indicate that the specimen length in the case of low carbon steel butt welds should be at least longer than 457 mm to produce high tensile stresses in the longitudinal direction. Longitudinal residual stresses become uniform in the central region for welds longer than 457 mm. Specimen length seem to have little effect on the transverse residual stresses. The effect of specimen width is negligible as long as it is several times the width of the residual stress zone.

As far as the effect of the plate thickness is concerned, it is found that when weldments are made in plates thicker than 25 mm, residual stresses in the thickness direction can become significant. However, lack of a simple and reliable measuring technique appears to limit the studies conducted so far.

4.3   Welding Processes

It is generally believed that similar residual stresses are produced in welds made by various arc processes including the shielded metal arc, submerged arc, gas metal arc and gas tungsten arc processes.

4.4   Welding Sequence

As far as residual stresses along the weld are concerned, the effect of welding sequence is minor. High tensile longitudinal stresses are found in all welds tested. Block welding sequences generally produce less shrinkage, less strain energy, and less reaction than multilayer sequences.

4.5   Different Sources of Residual Stresses

Welding residual stresses arise not only because of the variation in shrinkage of differently heated areas but also as a result of a surface quenching effect and transformation of austenite.

4.5.1   *Residual Stresses Owing to the Shrinkage Process of the Seam and HAZ*

An important source of residual stress is the difference in shrinkage of differently heated and cooled arm of a welded joint. The weld metal subjected to the highest temperature tends to contract more than all other areas, but this contraction is hindered by the cooler parts of the joint. Thus the weld metal is subjected to tensile stresses in the longitudinal direction, and it increases with increase in yield strength of the material as a result of decrease in temperature. Due to the shrinkage effect stresses also arise in a direction perpendicular to the seam. The final stresses, remaining after cooling are called as residual stresses due to the shrinkage process. The magnitude to the transverse stress component at the centre line of the seam ($Y = 0$) is much lower than the longitudinal stress component (Fig. 3). Comparing different materials, higher residual stresses brought about by welding should be found in materials with a larger product of Young's modulus and coefficient of linear thermal expansion.

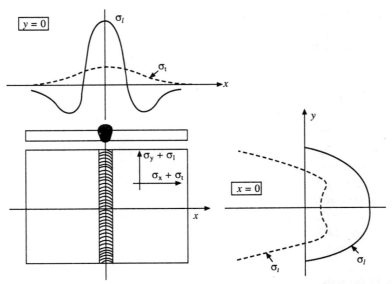

Fig. 3 Longitudinal (s_1) and transverse (s_t) residual treasses showing shrinkage along lines parallel (Y axis) and perpendicular (X axis) to seam

4.5.2 Residual Stresses Owing to the More Rapid Cooling of the Surface

During the cooling process, the surface layers of the weld and the highly heated areas close to it may cool more rapidly—even with air cooling—than the interior of the weld. Due to this reason temperature differences are present not only over the width of the joint but also across the thickness. As time progresses an increasing temperature difference develops between the surface and the interior. Thus, thermal stresses arise over the cross-section which can lead to inhomogeneous plastic deformation and eventually to residual stresses. The more rapid cooling of the surface is called a quenching effect, and the residual stresses resulting from this process are quenching residual stresses.

Plastic deformation at elevated temperatures is necessary for the formation of quenching residual stress. If the surface quenching effect were to be the only source of residual stresses, compressive residual stresses would be obtained at the surface of the highly heated areas, especially the seam, and would be in equilibrium with the tensile residual stresses in the inner part of the seam.

4.5.3 Residual Stresses Owing to a Phase Transformation

During cooling of welded steel plate phase transformation from austenite to ferrite, bainite or martensite will occur, either at a certain temperature or over a temperature range. Due to transformation there is an increase in specific volume and so the material in the seam and the HAZ which is being transformed tends to expand. But the expansion is hindered by the cooler material not being transformed. Thus the area being transformed is subject to compression, if the transformation temperature is sufficiently low, so that the material has a marked yield strength after transformation. Therefore compressive residual stresses parallel to the seam should be expected in this area and for reasons of equilibrium, tensile residual stresses should exist in the region not being transformed. However the transformation will occur with different heating temperature at different times. Therefore only a narrow strip of the weld material being transformed would be subjected to compressive residual stresses. In all areas being transformed earlier, for instance at the top—tensile residual stresses will increase if this transformation occurs mainly at low temperature after the weldment has attained strength. Transformation residual stresses will appear, especially if bainite or martensite is formed. These transformation stresses diminish as the area being transformed becomes wider.

4.5.4 *Superimposition of Residual Stresses Owing to Shrinkage, Quenching and Transformation*

In reality the various stress sources are not independent from one another. At least two or even three different kinds of stress in a cooling welded joint are superimposed, leading to a complicated total state of stress. Therefore, statements concerning the finally resulting residual stress state can be made only on distinct assumptions. The most simple is that a linear superimposition of residual stresses owing to different sources can describe the total residual stress state. Figure 4. schematically illustrates the linear superimposition of residual stresses owing to shrinkage, quenching and transformation. All diagrams show the transverse stress components as a function of the distance from the centre line of the weld. In all instances maximum tensile residual stresses are not present at the centre line of the seam but at the top. These tensile stress maxima

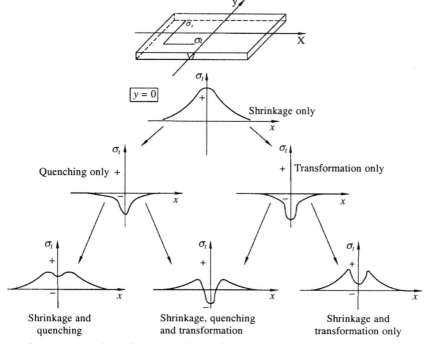

Fig. 4 **Schematic representation of superposition of transverse residual stresses owing to shrinkage, quenching and transformation**

represent the residual stresses owing to shrinkage. The difference between the maximum tensile stress and the stress value at the centre line represents either the surface quenching type of residual stress, the transformation type or both together.

4.6   Effects of Residual Stresses on Performance

4.6.1   Effect of Residual Stress on Fatigue Strength and Structural Behaviour

Residual stresses have a serious and usually deleterious effect on fatigue failure, brittle fracture and structural behaviour. Fatigue strength (the number of cycles at fracture under a given load) increases when a specimen has compressive residual stresses, especially on the specimen surface. Many investigators have reported that the fatigue strength increased when specimens had compressive residual stresses, whereas tensile residual stresses increased fatigue crack propagation rate.

Residual compressive stresses can cause premature buckling of structural members loaded in compression such as struts, columns and stiffened diaphragms. More recently they have also been thought to interfere with the detection of subsurface flaws, using ultrasonic methods, by holding the flaw together and making it transparent to the ultrasound.

4.6.2   Fracture Under Tensile Loading

Figure 5 shows the residual stress distribution in the longitudinal direction in a butt weld in the as-welded condition and also the stress distribution when an external tensile load is applied. The figure also shows the resulting residual stress distribution after the release of the externally applied tensile load. It can be seen from the figure that as a result of tensile loading the peak stress has become more even and has also decreased.

The following basic effects of residual stresses have been revealed by investigations:

1. The effect of residual welding stresses on the performance of welded structures is significant only on phenomena which occur under low applied stress, such as brittle fracture and stress corrosion cracking.

2. As the level of applied stress increases, the effect of residual stress decreases.

3. The effect of residual stress is negligible on the performance of welded structures under applied stresses beyond yielding.

4. The effect of residual stress tends to decrease after repeated loading.

4.6.3   Effects of Environment

Cracking can occur in weldments, even without external loading, when the material is embrittled by exposure to certain environments and residual stresses are present. Stress corrosion cracking is a brittle type fracture and has been observed in a number of ferrous and non-ferrous alloys exposed to certain sensitive environments containing nitrates, chlorides, hydroxides, hydrogen sulphide, etc.

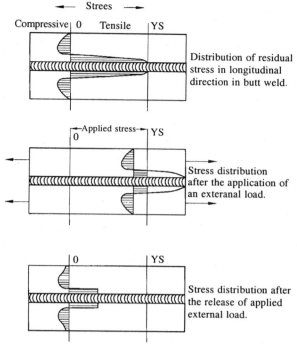

Distribution of residual stress in longitudinal direction in butt weld.

Stress distribution after the application of an exteranal load.

Stress distribution after the release of applied external load.

Fig. 5   Effect of proof stressing on residual stresses in a weldment

4.7   Methods of Reducing Residual Stresses

Residual stresses have their origin in complex thermal and/or mechanical interactions. Consequently their reduction or removal demands the use of mechanical or thermal treatments. The various mechanical and thermal treatments performed on weldments to reduce residual stresses include proof stressing, peening, vibratory conditioning, preheating, post weld thermal treatments and so forth.

Thermal and mechanical treatments are necessary to maintain or restore the properties of the base metal affected by the heat of welding. Among the many properties controlled or improved by suitable treatments are,

1. Distortion during welding
2. Reduction of stresses that could seriously affect the service performance of a weldment.
3. Weldability (which may be improved considerably by preheat treatment, for example).
4. Improvement of dimensional stability and machinability.

Of the mechanical and thermal treatments, vibratory conditioning and post weld thermal treatments are dealt with here in great detail because of their wide usage.

4.7.1   Mechanical Methods

Mechanical methods of stress relief can be divided essentially into two basic kinds, monotonic overload and vibratory conditioning. The former consists of continuously increasing load to the maximum level required, prior to unloading; the latter utilises an oscillating load, which, by hysteresis causes changes to occur that cannot be achieved by monotonic loading.

4.7.2 Monotonic Overload

The two methods of relieving stresses by monotonic overload are proof stressing and peening.

Proof Stressing: Investigations indicate that uniform heavy loading of weldments decrease longitudinal residual stresses by the amount of overload.

Cylindrical and spherical pressures vessels can be proof stressed readily by hydrostatic loading. Most critical fabrications are subjected to such an overload treatment in a proof test prior to being put into service. The reduction of residual elastic stress is effected by the conversion of stored elastic strain to plastic strain.

Peening: Peening is a local form of overload. Peening produces a local compressively stressed surface layer so that the magnitude and uniformity of stress, and the depth of layer, can be held constant over the whole, of the component and between individual components.

4.7.3 Vibratory Conditioning

Vibratory conditioning commonly known as vibratory stress relief (VSR) uses mechanical energy in the form of low and high frequency vibrations to relieve residual stresses in weldments.

VSR consists, in essence, of a vibrating device to induce vibration at the natural resonant frequencies of the structure treated. The induced frequency is varied until it coincides with one of the natural frequencies of the structure when resonance occurs, and the amplitude of vibration increased until it is limited by the natural damping characteristics of the vibrating mass. The frequency is then raised and resonance ceases gradually, until another resonant frequency is found, when the process is repeated.

The effect of the high amplitude resonant vibration is to induce an overall elastic distortion into the structure, similar to that which might be achieved by mechanical loading. Because the position of the vibrator must correspond to an antinode, several points of application have to be made to get the maximum number of modes of vibration and applied load in a variety of directions. Due to the gradual application of the load in a cyclic manner, the material will follow its cyclic stress/strain curve, which is lower than its monotonic stress/strain curve.

ADVANTAGES OF VSR

1. The stress reduction caused by VSR is greater for a given applied strain than that achieved by a single overload.

2. VSR is most effective in enabling shape stability of internally stressed items to be achieved for machining purposes.

3. In circumstances where for good metallurgical reasons heat treatment is not desirable, a mechanical treatment such as VSR is the only alternative.

4. Also, where it provides a technically viable alternative, VSR tends to be much cheaper, quicker and more convenient than thermal methods.

5. A variety of loading patterns can be obtained in complex structures which would be very difficult or impossible using a direct mechanical loading device.

DISADVANTAGES OF VSR

1. VSR is capable of causing fatigue or sudden fracture if it is applied to structures which contain severe welding defects or brittle regions, eg., HAZ areas, which are not capable of withstanding mechanical strain.

2. VSR by its very nature is most unlikely to give any significant metallurgical benefits, and may in some circumstances cause mechanical and/or metallurgical damage.

4.7.4 Thermal Methods

Thermal methods of stress relieving commonly known as 'thermal stress relief' (TSR) is defined as the uniform heating of a structure to a temperature below the critical range, holding it at this temperatue for a predetermined period of time, followed by uniform cooling. Stresses are reduced to a level just below the yield point of the material at the temperaure of the stress relief treatment. The residual stress remaining in a material after thermal stress relief will depend on the rate of cooling. Uneven cooling from stress relief to ambient temperatures may undo much of the value of the heat treatment and result in additional stresses within the weldment.

The percentage of relief of internal stresses is dependent on steel type, composition, or yield strength. The effects of varying time and temperature are shown in figure 6. The temperature reached during the stress relief heat treatment has a far greater effect in relieving stresses than the length of time the specimen is held at that temperature. The closer the temperature is to the critical or recrystallisation temperature, the more effective it is in the removal of residual stresses, provided proper heating and cooling cycles are employed.

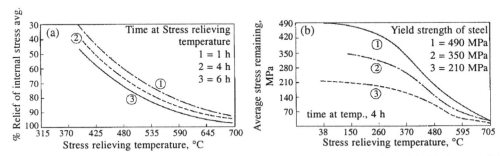

Fig. 6 **Effect of temperature and time on stress relief of steel structures, effect of hold time and (right) effect of material yield strength**

Advantages

1. Thermal stress relief improves mechanical properties of HAZ.

2. There is a reduction of 'metallurgical notch' effect resulting from abrupt changes in hardness or other microstructural discontinuities around holes.

3. The resistance of the components to the propagation of cracks improves, especially in the HAZ adjacent to the weld.

4. The corrosion resistance of the weld is greatly improved.

Disadvantages

1. In thick structures there is reduction in yield strength if treatments are extended.

2. Uneven heating can lead to distortion and warpage in the component while an uneven cooling rate may result in additional stresses within the weldment.

4.8 TECHNIQUES OF RESIDUAL STRESS MEASUREMENT

The methods of residual stress measurement available at present fall into two main categories, physical and mechanical. The physical methods are used to measure the existing total stress directly without destroying the specimen under test whereas the mechanical techniques require the stress to be relieved by removal of material and are therefore destructive or at best, semi-destructive in nature.

Mechanical methods of stress measurement require comparing the stressed state of a body with the relaxed state. Physical methods, however, are capable of stress measurement without relaxation and are therefore nondestructive. To date, the most powerful and widely used physical method of stress measurement in engineering components is x-ray diffraction. It is the only means presently available for the measurement of residual stress in ball bearings, in gear teeth, and in material surfaces after machining or grinding. The mechanical methods include stress-relaxation techniques, cracking techniques etc.

11. Corrosion of Steel and Stainless Steel Weldments

Hasan Shaikh

Corrosion Science and Technology Division, Indira Gandhi Centre for Atomic Research
Kalpakkam-603 102, Tamil Nadu, India
Email: hasan@igcar.ernet.in

1 INTRODUCTION TO CORROSION

The word "CORROSION" comes from the Latin word "CORRODERE", which means 'gnaw away'. Corrosion can be defined as the *physio-chemical interaction between a metal and its environment* which results in *changes in properties of the metal* which may often lead to *impairment of the function of the material, the environment or the technical system* of which these form a part. A metal will not corrode when it is exposed to an environment in which a chemical reaction is thermodynamically impossible. Thermodynamically, corrosion can never be prevented because almost all the metals and alloys are in their lowest free energy state when in the form of a compound. Corrosion is an enemy of mankind. It causes destruction of components and structures, production and monetary losses, unplanned shutdowns, health hazard etc. However, understanding of the basic principles of corrosion have led to the development of (a) concept of cathodic protection and sacrificial anodes and (b) newer materials and processes.

1.1 The Electrochemical Nature of Corrosion

Many corrosion processes are, in the widest sense of the expression, electrochemical in nature and the basic conditions for corrosion by electrolytes are shown in Fig. 1. They involve an oxidation reaction, which occurs at a location called the 'anode', as:

$$M \rightarrow M^{n+} + ne^-$$

The electron released during this reaction is consumed at a different location called the 'cathode'. Examples of reactions at the cathode are:

$$M^+ + e^- \rightarrow M$$

$$H^+ + e^- \rightarrow H$$

$$2H_2O + O_2 + 4e^- \rightarrow 4(OH)^-$$

Thus, the anode is the area at which corrosion occurs and in which the current leaves the metal. The cathode is the area at which practically no corrosion occurs and through which the

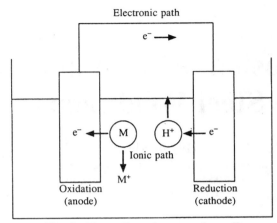

Fig. 1   Formation of a corrosion cell

current enters the metal. Anodes and cathodes can form on a single piece of metal due to physical or chemical heterogenetities on the metal surface, such as presence of impurities, oxides, grain boundaries, grain orientation, differences in the composition of the various phases in a multi-phase alloy, localised stresses, scratches and nicks. Areas subjected to deformation, such as bending, stamping, drilling, threading, rolling and welding, are more anodic to rest of the metal.

1.2   Factors Affecting Corrosion

Metallurgical and environmental factors affect corrosion of a metal. Some of the metallurgical *factors* that affect corrosion are grain size and orientation, stacking fault energy (SFE), cold work, secondary phases, residual stresses, segregation, Irradiation, sensitisation and chemical composition. *Environmental factors* that influence corrosion are pH (acidity), concentration (solution constituents), velocity of fluid, temperature (heat transfer), microbial features etc.

1.3   Manifestations of Corrosion

The various forms of corrosion are briefly discussed below. They are classified based on the various forms in which corrosion manifests itself on the basis of appearance of the corroded metal. Each of these forms can be merely identified by visual examination. There are eight basic forms of corrosion, which are unique. These are: uniform or general corrosion, galvanic or two-metal corrosion, crevice corrosion, pitting corrosion, intergranular corrosion (IGC), selective leaching, erosion corrosion and environment sensitive cracking. Other forms of corrosion such as cavitation corrosion, filliform corrosion, fretting corrosion are minor variants of some of these basic forms.

1.3.1   Uniform Corrosion

This is the most common form of corrosion seen. It accounts for nearly 40% of industrial corrosion failures. It is normally characterised by a chemical or electrochemical reaction that proceeds uniformaly over the entire exposed surface or over a large area. The metal becomes thinner and eventually fails. This form of corrosion results in greatest destruction of metal in tonnage basis. However, technically this does not pose an unexpected threat since necessary allowances can be made in thickness to account for metal loss during service. A structure or component immersed in a solution is far safer than which is partially immersed or undergoing alternate wet and dry conditions. The usual solutions to general corrosion involve the choice of more suitable materials, addition of inhibitors, application of protective coatings, suitable cathodic protection either by application of current or by sacrificial anode or a combination of them. The frequently used tests for assessing uniform corrosion are immersion tests and electrochemical tests. Corrosion rates are usually measured as thickness loss or penetration in metal or as weight loss in different units such as mils/year, mpy, inches/year, ipy, millimeters/\year, mm/y, milligrams per square decimeter per day, mdd. Corrosion rate is given by the equation

$$\text{Corrosion Rate} = 534 * \Delta W/D * A * t$$

Where ΔW is weight loss in milligrams, D is density of metal in gms/cc, A is area in square millimeters and t is time in hours. The mdd values can be converted to ipy as 1 ipy = 0.00144* mdd or 1 mdd = 696 * ipy. In electrochemical method, corrosion rate can be estimated by determining critical current density from the polarisation curves using the Tafel extrapolation method. AC impedance and linear polarisation methods can give information on polarisation resistance, $\Delta E/\Delta I$, from which the corrosion rates can be calculated. The conversions of various units of corrosion rates are listed in Table 1.

Table 1 Corrosion current, mass loss and penetration rates for all *metals* and for *steel*

	mA cm^{-2}	mm y^{-1}	mpy	gm^{-2} day^{-1}
mA cm^{-2}	1	3.28 M/nd	129 M/nd	8.95 M/n
mm y^{-1}	0.306 nd/M	1	39.4	2.74 d
mpy	0.00777 nd/M	0.0254	1	0.0694 d
g m^{-2} day^{-1}	0.112 n/M	0.365/d	14.4/d	1

where: mpy = milli-inch per year, n = number of electrons freed by the corrosion reaction, M = atomic mass, d = density. For example, if the metal is *steel* or *iron* (Fe), $n = 2$, $M = 55.85$ g and $d = 7.88$ g cm^{-3} and the Table of conversion becomes:

	mA cm^{-2}	mm y^{-1}	mpy	gm^{-2} day^{-1}
mA cm^{-2}	1	11.6	456	249
mm y^{-1}	0.0863	1	39.4	21.6
mpy	0.00219	0.0254	1	0.547
g m^{-2} day^{-1}	0.00401	0.0463	1.83	1

1.3.2 *Galvanic or Two-Metal Corrosion:*

A potential difference usually exists between two dissimilar metals when they are immersed in a corrosive or conductive solution. When these metals are placed in contact (or otherwise electrically connected), this potential difference produce electron flow between them. The less resistant metal becomes *anodic* and the more resistant metal *cathodic*. As electric current and dissimilar metals are involved, this form of corrosion is called galvanic, or two-metal corrosion. The driving force for the corrosion is the potential developed between the two metals. The relative reactivity of one metal to another is listed with respect to the hydrogen eletrode in an EMF series. EMF series gives an idea of the thermodynamic possibility of galvanic corrosion. However, it is not very reliable since the reported potentials are very sensitive to composition of electrode and electrolyte, temperature, velocity, pH etc. Besides these, the EMF series lists only pure metals while alloys are used in industrial service. Hence, galvanic series were developed for metals and alloys in various environments (Table 2). Galvanic corrosion is usually greatest at the galvanic junction. It is very dependent on the ratio of areas of anode and cathode. An unfavorable area ratio consists of a large cathode and a small anode. Factors that affect the occurrence of galvanic corrosion are environment, distance between the dissimilar metals and area of cathodic and anodic metal Harmful effects apart, galvanic corrosion has several beneficial applications like electric power generation using dry cell and cathodic protection.

Table 2   Galvanic series in seawater

Cathodic (noble)
↑
Platinum
Gold
Graphite
Titanium
Silver
Zirconium
AISI types 316L, 317 stainless steels (passive)
AISI type 304 stainless steel (Passive)
AISI type 430 stainless steel (Passive)
Nickel (passive)
Copper–Nickel (70-30)
Bronzes
Copper
Brasses
Nickel (active)
Naval Brass
Tin
Lead
AISI types 316L, 317 Stainless Steels (active)
AISI type 304 stainless steel (Active)
Cast Iron
Steel or Iron
Aluminum alloy 2024
Cadmium
Aluminum alloy 1100
Zinc
Magnesium and its alloys
↓
Anodic (active)

1.3.3 *Pitting Corrosion*

Pitting refers to the formation of small cavities/holes on the surface of the material that is otherwise protected by an adhesive, tenacious and self-healing thin film. The formation of pits is attributed to the interaction of the aggressive ions with the film at the locations where it is defective or weak in nature. The pits may be visible to the naked eyes in some cases but in general they are invisible, and dangerous to the extent they can allow the formation of SCC or fatigue cracks, which can catastrophically fail the component in service. Depending on the metallurgy of the alloy and chemistry of the environment, pits may be shallow, elliptical, deep undercut of sub surface and may follow metallurgical features. Pitting can occur in a number of metals and alloys, and, as a rough guide, the more expensive the alloy, the lower its propensity for pitting. Thus Fe-17Cr stainless steel is more susceptible to pitting in chloride solutions than Fe-18Cr-8Ni, which in turn is more susceptible than the Fe-18Cr-8Ni-3Mo steel, and titanium is superior to all of them. It is important to consider each alloy system independently, as they will behave separately under different chemical environments. Thus the pitting of stainless steels will occur in halide ions like F, Cl, B and I, HOCl and HCN, but pitting will tend to be suppressed by the presence of oxyanions such as NO^{3-} and SO^{4-}. On the other hand, copper pits in natural fresh waters containing a very small concentration of chloride ion, and at significantly higher concentration of SO^{4-}; in waters with a higher Cl-ion concentration, the attack is far less localised. Practical importance of pitting depends on the thickness of the metal and on the penetration rate. The rate usually decreases with time. Thus on thin sections pitting may be serious when compared to thick sections. In general, the rate of penetration decreases if the number of pits increases. This is because the adjacent pits have to share the available adjacent cathode area, which controls the corrosion current that can flow. Stagnant liquids often aid in formation of pits when compared to moving liquid. A pit may go through four separate stages (1) initiation (2) propagation (3) termination (4) re-initiation. Since pitting is an electrochemical process, it can be stopped by cathodic protection. It can also be prevented by using inhibitors, which alter the electrode reactions of the local cell and remove their driving force.

1.3.4 *Crevice Corrosion*

Crevice corrosion refers to the formation of selective corrosion attack at local or shielded regions of metal-to-metal or metal to non-metal joint, where stagnation of electrolyte is possible. It can occur also under scale and surface deposits that do not prevent the entry of liquid between them and the metal surface exposed to air or immersed in an environment. To function as a corrosion site, a crevice must be wide enough to permit liquid entry but sufficiently narrow to maintain a stagnant zone. The differences in the concentration of coroding species and of oxygen between the local region and the bulk causes the selective attack at this local region called the "crevice" which is defined by its size, gap and area. A crevice is called so when it is capable of generating such concentration cells inducing corrosion attcak. The formation of crevice corrosion generally proceeds as pitting corrosion or filiform corrosion, which is known as self-propagating crevice. In crevice corrosion also, the state and the stability of the passive film formed at the crevice and the remaining region plays a vital role in affecting the severity of the attack. Crevice corrosion can be prevented by adopting designs and fabrication procedures that eliminate crevices e.g. elimination of rivet or threaded joints or avoid undercuts during welding etc. In case crevices cannot be avoided, cathodic protection and inhibitors could provide adequate corrosion control.

1.3.5   Selective Leaching or Dealloying

In certain environments, one element of an alloy may dissolve with respect to the others, because of the differences in the corrosion rate of the various elements in the specific environment. Dezincification of high zinc brasses is a classic example of this type of corrosion. In these alloys both Zn and Cu corrode, but Cu immediately plates back on the metal because it is much more noble than Zn. Selective leaching also occurs in gray cast iron embedded in soil. Iron corrodes leaving the graphite flakes in place.

1.3.6   Erosion Corrosion

Thinning or removal of material by flowing environment is called erosion corrosion or impingement attack. Rapidly flowing environments can often disrupt adherent surface films that would otherwise offer protection against corrosion. It often occurs at locations in the plant where there are sudden changes in flow conditions, such as flow direction or flow velocity, in the plant. For example, nozzles or locations, where tube constrictions exist, can be the most susceptible areas in the plant where erosion corrosion could occur. Suspended solids aggravate the problem of erosion corrosion because surface films could be easily removed. Erosion corrosion takes the form of grooves, waves, gullies, teardrop shaped pits and horse-shoe shaped depressions on the surface. Erosion corrosion can be controlled by designing to reduce surface velocity and turbulence, and by careful material selection. In general, stainless steels and Ti and Ni-base alloys are resistant to erosion corrosion because of their tenacious surface film. Hard and strong metals, though resistant to wear, are not resistant to erosion corrosion if their corroion resistance is low or if they have a weak passive film.

Cavitation is a special form of erosive attack, which results from collapsing bubbles created by pressure changes across surfaces exposed to high velocity liquid flow. Flow across a curved surface produces a pressure drop that causes local boiling when pressure is reduced below the vapour-pressure of the liquid. When the bubbles land on the surface and collapse, the repeated pressure impacts are sufficient to erode or cavitate the surface. Once the surface has been roughened at a point, this serves as a nucleus for the new cavitation bubbles to form. A protective film on the metal surface is not necessary for cavitation damage to occur. Cavitation damage is a well-known cause of trouble in ships underwater fittings, especially propellers and rudders and in pumps and pipe work circulating water. The fundamental remedy of cavitation damage is change in design, which stops the cavitation. Pressures may be raised, abrupt changes in section removed to eliminate severe turbulence and vibration reduced. Cathodic protection is some times beneficial, not because of reduced corrosion rate but because of the cushioning effect of hydrogen evolved on the surface. Removal of dissolved air is often beneficial because dissolved gases more easily nucleate cavitating bubbles.

1.3.7   Environment Sensitive Cracking

Environment sensitive cracking or corrosion cracking processes i.e. stress corrosion cracking (SCC), hydrogen embrittlement (HE) and corrosion fatigue (CF) account for almost half of the corrosion related failures in industries. This is to be expected because most of the components have some amount of residual stresses present in them due to fabrication processes involved. In many cases, these stresses cannot be relieved and they get added on the service stresses leading to premature failure of the components. Thus, corrosion-cracking processes assume significant importance with respect to mitigation of corrosion problems in industries. Table 3 lists the materials that fail by SCC in industrial environment [1].

Table 3 Statistics of SCC failures of materials with respect to environment

Environment	Mild steel	Low alloy steel	Cu alloy	Al alloy	Austenitic SS	Martensitic-precipitation hardened SS	Ferritic SS
H,H_2	4	3	—	—	1	1	—
H (plating)	3	2	—	—	—	—	—
Cl^-	—	—	4	3	85	2	—
S^{2-}	2	6	—	—	17	1	—
OH^-	7	—	1	—	7	—	—
NH_3	2	—	6	—	1	—	—
NO^{3-}	2	—	1	—	—	—	—
H_2O,H_2O vapour	2	2	3	—	20	3	2
Organic substance	1	—	—	—	2	—	—
N compound	1	1	—	—	—	—	—
Atmosphere	—	—	1	—	—	2	—
Miscellaneous	3	—	3	—	8	1	—

Stress Corrosion Cracking: Stress corrosion cracking is the degradation of the material under the combined action of a load and a corrosive medium, neither of which when acting alone would cause considerable damage. The degradation in the material property includes loss in ductility and tensile strength. Stress corrosion cracking occurs only in a specific medium, in which a critical balance between mechanical factors, passivation and corrosion exists. SCC is a brittle failure that occurs even in ductile materials. It can also occur below yield stress. SCC occurs in a definite range of strain rates. Strain rates lower than this range cause general corrosion or no failure will occur. Above this range of strain rates, the material will fail by pure mechanical failure.

SCC is a complex phenomenon and involves five important factors: stress, environment, temperature, alloy structure and composition. The stress has to be necessarily tensile in nature for SCC to occur. The stresses could be either residual or service induced. These could also act together and induce a very premature failure. Environmental factors that contribute to SCC failure include (i) concentration of aggressive species, (ii) temperature, (iii) pH and (iv) dissolved oxygen. Increasing temperature enhances SCC susceptibility of the material. SCC is known to occur at ambient temperatures in sensitised stainless steels during storage. Increase in concentration of aggressive species decreases the SCC resistance and determines crack morphology. It is difficult to determine a minimum chloride concentration below which SCC will not occur because of the possible concentration processes such as wetting and drying or local boiling. The pH of the environment plays a sensitive role in SCC. Low pH in the acidic range promotes SCC. But very low pH could cause general corrosion. As the pH value increases to the alkaline end of the pH scale, cracking tendencies decrease. However, austenitic stainless steels of AISI 300 series undego caustic cracking at high temperatures. Metallurgical factors such as cold working, welding, sensitisation, grain size, stacking fault energy, segregation have a significant influence on SCC. Increase in amount of cold work, degree of sensitisation, and segregation, deteriorate SCC resistance. Materials with low stacking fault energy and coarse grain size are susceptible to SCC.

A threshold stress, below which SCC would occur, is not a concept in vogue today. Instead, threshold stress intensity factors (K_{ISCC} & J_{ISCC}), which define the stress disribution ahead of the crack-tip, and crack growth rates are used as design concepts. Fracture mechanics approach is used to determine these parameters. Figure 2 gives a typical da/dt vs K_1 curve [2]. Fracture mechanics approach also helps in defining the maximum flaw size that can be tolerated in the material without incipient crack growth by SCC.

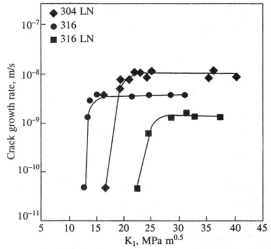

Fig. 2   A typical SCC crack growth rate (da/dt) curve for type 304 SS in annealed and sensitized conditions

Hydrogen embrittlement: Hydrogen embrittlement (HE) is a form of environment-assisted failure caused by the combined action of hydrogen and tensile residual or applied stress, which results in the reduction of the load-bearing capacity and tensile ductility of the material. Hydrogen must be present in the metal lattice in its nascent form to have an effect on the overall embitterment process. It may be made available to a metal surface from various sources including cathodic reduction of hydrogen of water during corrosion, cathodic protection, pickling and electroplating. Dissolved poisons, such as P, As, Sb, S, Se, Te and cyanides, which retard the formation of molecular hydrogen and increase the residence time of nascent hydrogen on the surface enhance hydrogne entry and increase hydrogne damage. H_2S is especially aggressive in promoting HE because it supplies not only the hydrogen recombination poison but also the H^+ ion. Hydrogen may also enter the material from hydrogen bearing atmospheres during heat teatment, welding and other manufacturing processes. Hydrogen dissolved in liquid metal gets trapped in the metal as it cools down and gives rise to porosity. When mechanically worked, such casting may undergo blistering or flaking.

Hydrogen damage could occur in a number of ways viz. (i) creation of internal flaws (ii) hydride formation and (iii) hydrogen embrittlement. Hydrogen accumulation could result in high internal pressure to cause either blisters or intergranular fissures. This is called hydrogen attack. If temperature is high enough, dissolved carbon diffuses to the surface to combine with hydrogen gas causing overall decarburisation and thus loss in strength. A number of transition, rare earth and alkaline earth metals and their alloys form brittle hydrides and are prone to hydride embrittlement. The susceptibility is dependent on numerous variables like hydrogen content, hydride orientation, distribution, morphology, and temperature and strain rate. Hydrogen can also get adsorbed on the free surface adjacent to the crack-tip and decrease the surface energy required for crack growth.

Hydrogen interaction with material is multifold. Hence, the solutions to prevent HE are also multifold. Selection of material to resist HE is very important, though difficult. If an alloy is primarily of a transition metal, it is susceptible to HE unless proved otherwise. Hydride formers should not be used in hydrogen atmospheres. In many applications, a lower strength material will function better than high strength material and use of such material will eliminate HE. Essentially, alloys with low hydrogen-dislocation binding energy, high stacking fault energy and lower hydrogen solubility appear to be desirable. Anything that will hinder the hydrogen transport process will reduce susceptibility to HE. Alloying the steel with Cu, for use in H_2S environment, will considerably decrease the HE susceptibility due to formation of Cu_2S surface film, which reduces hydrogen absorption. Reducing sulphur content and other trace impurities will improve resistance to HE. A fine distribution of sulphides in the steel can reduce the susceptibility of the steel to high temperature hydrogen attack. Addition of rare earth elements such as La and Ce reduces HE susceptibility because they act as innocuous trap sites for hydrogen. Avoiding pickling, cathodic cleaning and activation treatments can prevent HE. Lowering the applied load to values below the threshold value for HE, increasing the cross-section of the components, decreasing the residual stresses can prevent HE.

Corrosion fatigue: Corrosion fatigue is defined as a deleterious effect of corrosive environment on one or more of the progressive stages of damage acumulation during cyclic loading, such as cyclic plastic deformation, microcrack initiation, small crack growth to link up and coalesce into a single short crack, and crack propagation, as compared to behavior in inert surroundings. Damage results from synergistic interaction of cyclic plastic deformatin and local chemical and electrochemical reactions. In addition to the material parameters (chemical composition, microstructure, yield strength) and solution parameters (pH, temperature, potential), loading parameters viz. ΔK range, stress ratio, K_{max}, frequency and wave form can have a large influence on the crack growth behavior. The fatigue propagation rates in metals and alloys depend on alternating stress intensity factor, ΔK and vary over a wide range of crack growth rates from 10^{-8} to 10^{-2} mm/cycle. The corrosion fatigue crack growth rates increase with an increase in mean stress, (R ratio). There is no effect of mean stress on crack growth per cycle, in vacuum. However, in an aggressive environment, the crack growth rates are found to increase with increasing mean stress. Frequency too has a strong influence on the corrosion fatigue behavior of a material. The maximum effect is felt at low frequencies. However, very low frequencies do not influence. This behavior is understandable in terms of the time of interaction between the environment and the crack-tip, and metal dissolution characteristics. At high frequencies, sufficient time is not available for metal-environment interaction; while at low frequencies generation of fresh bare metal is so slow that the environmental effects are negligible.

1.4.8 Intergranular Corrosion

Under certain condition, grain interface are very reactive due to which intergranular corrosion results. Localized attack at and adjacent to grain boundaries with relatively little corrosion of the grain is known as intergranular corrosion. Factors affecting the occurrence of IGC are accumulation of impurities at the grain boundaries, enrichment of alloying element or depletion of one of the elements in the grain boundary areas.

2   CORROSION OF WELDMENTS

A welded joint is required to perform either equal to or better than the base metal it joins. However, in practice, this objective is never achieved since the welding process itself introduces features, which degrade the mechanical and corrosion properties of the welded joints as compared to the wrought base metal. Despite shielding by a gas or by slag, the weld metal can get contaminated by slag inclusions, tungsten inclusions etc. The fast cooling rates associated with the weld metal causes the formation of a dendritic structure besides straining of the weld metal. Also, several metallurgical transformations can take place in the weld metal during this cooling. Apart from weld contamination and metallurgical changes, improper welding procedures can leave behind a host of defects, such as porosities, undercuts, microfissures, in the weld metal. All these detrimental features do not augur well from the mechanical and corrosion properties point of view. In fact, a majority of the corrosion failures in components could be directly or indirectly related to the corrosion of the weld metal or the heat-affected zone (HAZ). Both the uniform and localised corrosion attacks can take place in the base metal as well as the weldments. Weldments, because of their microstructural and compositional heterogeneties, are inherently more prone to corrosion than the unaffected base metal, though the basic corrosion mechanisms are the same.

The various regions of a weldment are schematically illustrated in Fig. 3. The composite zone, also known as mixed zone or fusion zone, is the conventional fused region in the weldment where the filler material has been diluted with material from the base metal. The composition of this zone depends on the compositions of filler and base material. The extent of dilution is a function of heat input, joint geometry, position and the welding process. In an autogeneous weld metal, where no filler metal is employed, the solidified material composition is very close to that of the base metal. However, in case of welding using a 'matching' consumable, the composition of the weld metal tends to be different from the base metal. Many a times, it is mandatory to weld a joint with a consumable with composition entirely different from the base metal it joins, thereby resulting in additional problems of galvanic corrosion. Next to the mixed zone is the narrow region of unmixed zone where the base metal is melted but not fused with the filler metal and its composition is close to the base metal. In fact, mixed zone can be considered to be the equivalent of an autogeneous weld. The occurrence of an unmixed zone depends on a number of

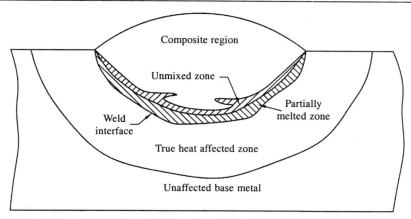

Fig. 3   A schematic illustrating the various regions of a weldment

factors such as welding process, welding parameters, composition of filler metal and its physical properties. The extent of unmixed zone in a GTAW weld is less than in SMAW, GMAW and SAW weld, thus indicating that metal transfer from the filler rod, and the weld pool motion play a very significant role in the formation of unmixed zones. The width of the unmixed zone varies with distance from the surface to the root of the weld, as shown in Fig. 4 for the C-22 and Inconel 625 filler metals used for welding AL6XN alloy [3]. The difference in the width and extent of unmixed zone with location is because the surface of the weld pool is more turbulent as compared

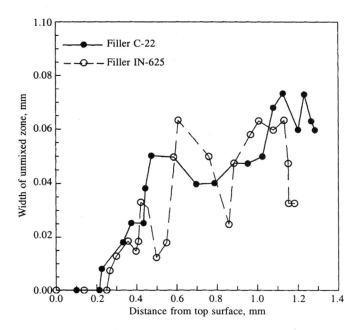

Fig. 4   Change in the width of the unmixed zone as function of distance from root to the surface of weld

to that at the root thus causing differences in mixing of filler and base materials. The HAZ in a weldment is situated in the base metal adjacent to the fusion line. It experiences different thermal cycles depending on the distance from the fusion line. Each thermal cycle is characterised by a heating and cooling cycle and a peak temperature. The subsequent sections deal with the corrosion of the varius regions of the weld joint and suggest remedies to counter them.

2.1 Corrosion of Weld Metal

A number of factors influence the corrosion properties of a steel weld metal. These include the solidification process, micro-segregation, alloying element partitioning, formation of multi-phase microstructure, heat input, high temperature aging, welding defects etc. These aspects are discussed in detail below.

2.1.1 Effect of Welding Defects on Weld Metal Corrosion

Welding defects such as slag and other entrapments, cracks, microfissures, porosities, inclusions, lack of penetration and fusion etc., oxide and other scales etc. deteriorate the corrosion properties of a weld metal. All of these defects contribute to reduce the localised corrosion resistance of the weld metal. These defects normally cause early pitting and crevice attacks in the weld metal [4]. A number of investigators have shown that sulphide inclusions are most susceptible sites for pitting and crevice attack; however, others suggest that other non-metallic inclusions are also capable of causing pit nucleation. Also, these defects act as regions of stress concentration which aid in faster initiation of SCC. Non-metallic inclusions, such as sulphides, are undesirable from SCC point of view. Influence of non-metallic inclusions in reducing the SCC life is directly related to the easy initiation of pitting corrosion at inclusion sites [5]. In acid solutions, and hence in occluded cells, sulphide inclusions dissolve to form H_2S, which has an accelerating effect on corrosion of steel [6]. H_2S is reported to accelerate both the anodic and cathodic processes [5]. In many service applications, SCC initiated from pits which act as stress raisers [7, 8]. In these cases, the induction times for SCC were longer than those for pitting [7]. Apparently, the non-metallic inclusions do not participate directly in crack nucleation, but their presence is undesirable, as they give rise to pitting. However, Clarke and Gordon reported a strong effect of secondary phases and inclusions on crack nucleation [9]. They reported that cracking nucleated from the crevice corrosion attack around the included particle. Non-metallic inclusions also play a role in hydrogen embrittlement of stainless steel welds. Surface inclusions facilitate entry of hydrogen into the weld and thus induce cracking [5]. Bulk inclusions may act as trap sites for hydrogen and thus assist in nucleation and development of internal crevices and cracks [5]. The shape of the sulphide inclusion influences the crack initiation time. Elongated sulphide particles may six-fold increase hydrogen entry into the metal as compared to spherical inclusions [5]. Non-metallic inclusions also cause stress concentration in the material. The extent of stress concentration would depend on the shape of the inclusion [5]. Sharp edged inclusions act as more effective notches than spherical or elliptically shaped inclusions. Apart from the shape, the ratio of thermal expansion coefficients and modulus of elasticity of the inclusion to that of the matrix also contributes to a lesser extent in determining the magnitude of stress concentration [5]. Apart from sulphide inclusions, weld metals can contain other inclusions resulting from the oxidation and deoxidation reactions in the molten weld metal. They may also contain slag inclusions, which could result from slag entrapment in the solidified weld bead. The extent of slag entrapment is dictated by the flux coating on the welding consumable. Rutile coatings give ease of slag detachment and good bead shape. Out-of-position welding can also cause slag entrapment.

In designing of welding consumables, it is a common practice to adjust weld metal composition by adding alloying elements in the flux. During welding, these elements may not get mixed well in the molten pool thus leaving regions rich in these elements which may act as nucleation sites for localised corrosion attacks. For example, in offshore applications, the electrode coating contains ferro-manganese particles, which if not homogeneously mixed in the weld metal leaves areas harder than the adjoining matrix [10]. These hard areas provide sites for initiation of SCC in sour service (Fig. 5). Certain measures during welding, such as increase in welding current, reducing travel speed or the width of weaving, may help in mitigating the problem.

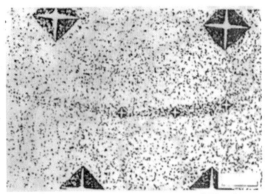

Fig. 5 **Site of partially dissolved Mn or Fe-Mn particles in weld metal marked by high microhardness value (after D.J. Kotecki and D.G. Howden, WRC Bulletin 184, 1973)**

Porosities can lead to faster initiation of pitting attack or SCC since they act as sites for stress concentration [11]. Appropriate choice of heat input could reduce the amount of porosities in the weld metal. Cracks and microfissures also contribute to reduction in localised corrosion resistance of weld metal. The weldment may undergo cracking during welding, or immediately after welding, or during service or during post weld heat treatment (PWHT) in the solidified weld metal, HAZ of base metal or HAZ of weld metal. These cracks may act as sites for crack initiation or as crevices. In stainless steels and Ni-base alloys, microfissuring and hot cracking are a major problem. C-Mn steels and low allow steels normally undergo cold cracking and reheat cracking. Undercuts, lack of fusion and lack of penetration are preferential sites for corrosion attacks. Judicious selection of the weld joint design, welding parameters, consumables and welding process may avoid corrosion problems associated with such faulty joints. Certain joint designs, like lap and stake joints may result in crevice corrosion attack and should be avoided and instead full penetration butt joints should be preferred [12]. In some applications, it is a common practice to use welding inserts, which may not get properly fused in the weld metal and leave regions, which may become prone to crevice attack. In addition to crevice corrosion problems, the crevices thus formed will act as stress raisers and cause SCC. In welding of steels, if the electrodes are overbaked, the amount of hydrogen, which increases bead penetration, is reduced thus leading to lack of penetration defects in the weld metal. Some of the alloys, like Ni base alloys, show poor fluidity, which is a common cause for lack of fusion and associated corrosion problems.

2.1.2   *Effect of Solidification and Microsegregation*

Several important changes that take place during cooling of the molten weld metal dictate the corrosion properties of the solidified weld metal. The welding of austenitic stainless steel (SS) has two major problems viz. hot cracking of weld metal and sensitisation of the HAZ. The understanding of the corrosion problems associated with austenitic SS could be best understood by understanding the solidification of a SS weld metal. To overcome the problem of hot cracking the following methods could be resorted to (i) reduction of the S+P content of the weld to less than 0.01% and (ii) addition of Mn to form high melting MnS instead of low melting FeS. However, the most common method adopted is retention of some amount of high temperature δ-ferrite to room temperature. δ-ferrite can be retained by appropriate choice of the filler metal composition which could be done in consultation with the 70% iron isopleth (Fig. 6) [13]. This diagram determines the position of the alloy composition with respect to the liquidus minimum. Alloys with compositions located on the Ni-rich side solidify as primary austenite, while those located on the Cr rich side solidify as primary ferrite. In both the solidification modes, the δ-ferrite is enriched in ferritisers like Cr, Mo, Si, while the austenite is enriched in austenitisers,

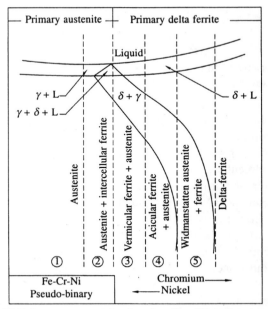

Fig. 6   **A schematic of the 70% iron cross-sectoin showing the effect of composition on the austenite and δ-ferrite morphology in austenitic SS weld metal**

such as Ni, Mn, C, N etc (Fig. 7) [14]. The extent of partitioning of alloying elements would also depend on heat input [15]. Apart from partitioning of alloying elements, impurites such as S and

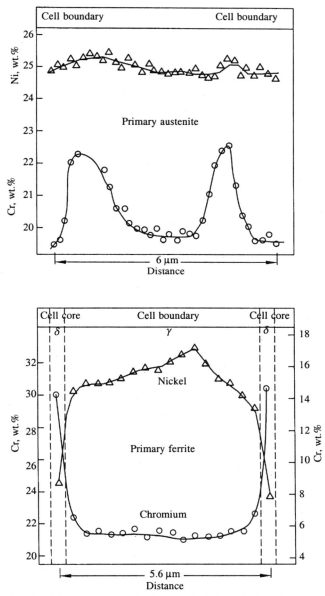

Fig. 7 **Effect of heat input on partitioning of Cr, Mo and Ni in type 316 L weld metal**

P segregate to the δ-ferrite/austenite (DF/A) interface. The extent of segregation depends on the solidification mode and heat input [14, 15]. These micro-segregations cause preferential corrosion attacks of the weld.

The beneficial effect of δ-ferrite in controlling hot cracking is offset by the fact that in some corrosive media, it can cause severely localised corrosion attacks. However, δ-ferrite is not harmful under all conditions of environmental corrosivity. The attack on δ-ferrite is controlled by material composition and does not solely depend on its mere presence in the austenite matrix. Also, preferential weld metal corrosion involving δ-ferrite takes two principal forms: attack on the ferrite or attack along the DF/A interface. Both these types of attack can occur in Mo-containing and Mo-free austenitic SS weld metals. But attack along the interface is more common in the former while attack on the δ-ferrite is often encountered in the latter. This behaviour can be rationalised by considering the polarisation characteristics of δ-ferrite. The polarisation behaviour of austenite and ferrite are schematically shown in Fig. 8 (a) [16]. The open circuit potential and the flade potentials of δ-ferrite are more cathodic to those of the austenite phase. It is seen that the potential range most immediately apparent as causing attack on δ-ferrite is that corresponding to the marginally oxidising conditions at around points AA', since the corrosion current corresponding to δ-ferrite is much higher than that of austenite. Whether or not the attack occurs on or around δ-ferrite depends on the location of cathodic curves as shown in Fig. 8 (b). If the cathodic curve corresponds to:

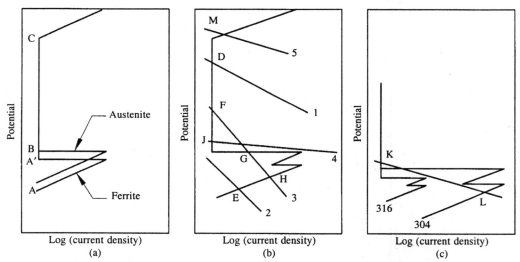

Fig. 8 (a) Schematic anodic polarisation curves for δ-ferrite and austenite, (b) effect of cathodic reaction in the determination of the corrosion behaviour, and (c) effect of anodic curves for type 316 and 304 SS in the determination of focus of attack

   (a) curve 1—service potential, point D, is in the passive range and there is no corrosion of the weld metal.

   (b) curve 2—under these marginally oxidising conditions, point E, the weld metal will be active and corrode generally, although ferrite will corrode at a higher rate than austenite.

   (c) curve 3—In the environment corresponding to this curve, the potentials can be at points F, G or H. If attained, F is a stable point. However, the cathodic curve is likely to shift slightly during plant warm-up of shut down, for example, when the potential falls to G. This is an unstable condition as both anodic and cathodic reactions are favoured by fall in potential. As a result the system will adopt potential H, which would again result in attack on δ-ferrite in the weld metal.

(d) curve 4—In the cathodic reaction corresponds to curve 4, potential J will be stable and attack on DF/A interface will occur.

(e) curve 5—under this highly oxidising condition corresponding to point M, the attack occurs both in the austenite and ferrite.

The difference in corrosion behaviour of weld metals of types 304 and 316 SS is most pronounced in moderately oxidising media corresponding to curves 3 and 4. Figure 8 (c) shows the anodic curves for both these SS with one anodic curve superimposed. The potential K is stable for type 316 SS, but not for type 304 SS. The attack in this environment will occur at DF/A interface for type 316 SS, but will occur on the ferrite for type 304 SS at point L.

Studies on the polarisation behaviour of 9Cr-1Mo ferritic steel [17], indicated a far superior corrosion resistance for base metal as compared to weld metal (Fig. 9). The current densities for

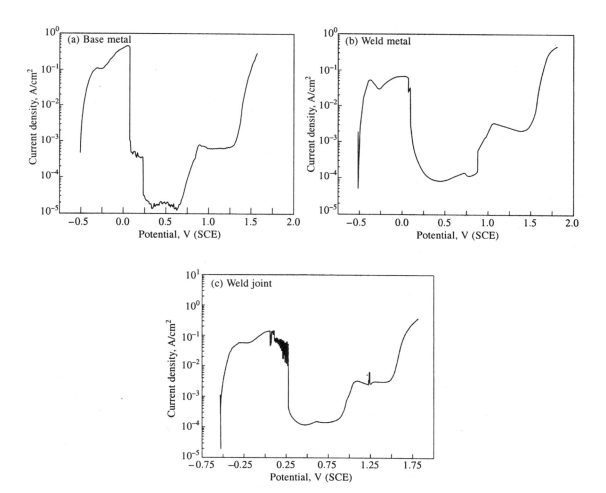

Fig. 9   Electrochemical polarisation diagrams in 0.5 M H$_2$SO$_4$ solution at room temperature for (a) base metal, (b) weld metal, and (c) weld joint

both the active peaks and current densities for primary and secondary passivities were much higher for weld metal. However, the weld joint showed far inferior corrosion properties vis-à-vis the base and weld metals.

Rao et al. reported that the chemical composition of the austenitic SS weld metal did not affect the critical current density (CCD) [18]. Instead, increase in δ-ferrite content increased the CCD besides lowering the values of equilibrium corrosion potential and increasing the range of passive potentials of the weld metal. However, variations in the amount of δ-ferrite did not alter the passive current density (PCD). Marshall and Gooch reported lower pitting corrosion resistance (PCR) for weld metal vis-à-vis base metal with same chemical composition (Fig. 10) [19]. This was attributed to the detrimental effect of δ-ferrite on the PCR of the austenitic SS [20]. Increasing the Mo content increased the PCR of welded 18Cr-12Ni SS [21]. In the case of type 304 SS weld metal, the most susceptible sites for pitting corrosion were the DF/A interfaces, where extensive segregation of S and P caused difficulty in passivation [22]. In type 316 SS weld metal, the preferential sites for pit initiation were found to be the interior of the austenite cells where depletion of Mo occurred [23].

The difference in SCC behaviour of base and weld metals has been a subject of much

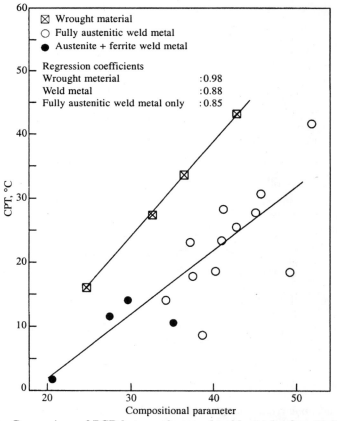

Fig. 10 Comparison of PCR between base and weld metals of austenitic SS

disagreement in literature. The differences in SCC behaviour between the base and weld metals depend on the chemical composition, environment and testing techniques. Weld metal of austenitic SS possessed equal or better SCC resistance than the base metal of similar composition when tested by slow strain rate technique (SSRT) in boiling 45% $MgCl_2$ solution [24–26]. The better SCC resistance of the weld metal was attributed to the cathodic protection offered to the austenite by the corroding DF/A interface [27]. Tests on type 304 SS in $MgCl_2$ boiling at 408 K and in 1 N HCl showed a much higher SCC resistance for the base metal [28]. Raja et al. reported that the base metal of type 316 stainless steel had better SCC resistance than its autogeneous weld in a 5 N H_2SO_4 + 0.5 N NaCl solution at room temperature [29]. Shaikh et al. reported lower K_{ISCC} and higher plateau crack growth rates for type 316 LN SS weld metal vis-à-vis its base metal (Fig. 11) [30]. Shaikh et al. [31] reported that a sensitised HAZ was the weakest link in a weld joint from SCC point of view. In case of a non-sensitised weldment, they reported failure in the weld metal [31].

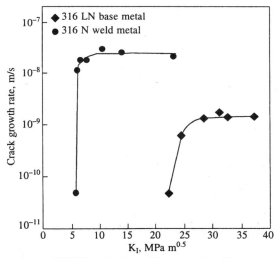

Fig. 11   Comparison of SCC resistance of base and weld metals of austenitic SS

The presence of δ-ferrite can appreciably alter both the SCC resistance and the crack morphology of the weld metal. The SCC resistance of the weld metal depends on the δ-ferrite content, its distribution and the solidification mode. Duplex weld metal, which solidifies in the primary ferritic or primary austenitic solidification mode, has SCC resistance similar to that of the base metal [32]. Fully austenitic weld metal has the most degraded SCC property and fails by IGSCC due to extensive segregation of S and P at the grain boundaries [32]. In NaCl and HCl solutions, both at ambient and high temperatures, the weld metal failed by stress-assisted dissolution (SAD) (Fig. 12) of δ-ferrite and SCC of austenite [31]. In boiling 45% $MgCl_2$ solution, the failure occurred due to cracking of the DF/A interface (Fig. 13) and SCC of austenite [25, 26, 28]. The amount, morphology and continuity of the δ-ferrite network influences the SCC resistance of the weld metal. A continuous network of δ-ferrite was most harmful for SCC of weld metal as it provided a continuous path for crack propagation (Fig. 14) [28]. Shaikh *et al.* reported that on polarising the weldments anodic to the critical cracking potential (CCP), a decrease in SCC

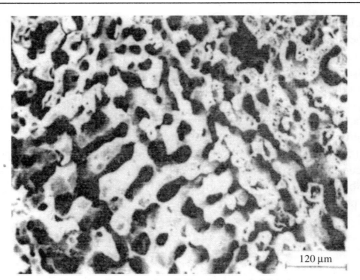

120 μm

Fig. 12   Stress-assisted dissolution of *d*-ferrite

Fig. 13   Cracking of *d*-ferrite/austenite interface

resistance was observed, while slight cathodic polarisation prevented failure (Fig. 15) [31]. This suggested that dissolution-mechanism was operative during SCC of type 316 SS weldments.

Corrosion problems related to partitioning of alloying elements and segregation in the weld metal can be overcome by a high temperature annealing treatment; or by choosing a filler metal with Mo content higher than base metal; or by cathodic or anodic protection techniques.

The significance of the unmixed zone in corrosion service is evidenced when austenitic SS are required to be welded with high Ni filler metal to give a fully austenitic structure. However, the microstructure in the unmixed zone would be duplex which will offset the beneficial efffect of austenitic base and weld metals. The recently developed high Mo and N SS, such as AL6XN and

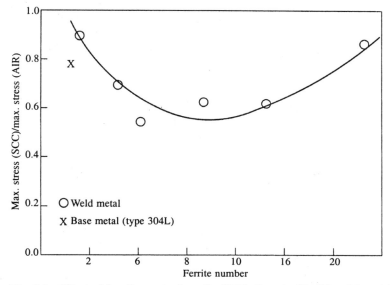

Fig. 14   Effect of ferrite content on the SCC of austenitic SS weld metal

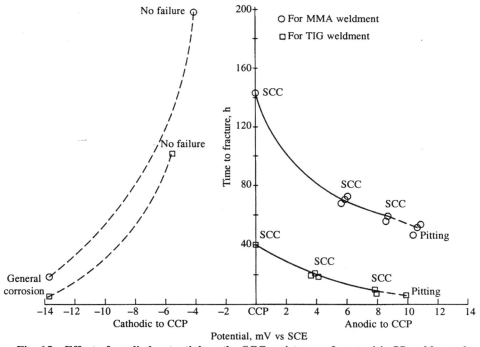

Fig. 15   Effect of applied potential on the SCC resistance of austenitic SS weld metal

254SMo are designed for certain specific corrosion applications. However, autogeneous welds of these steels corrode preferentially because of extensive Mo segregation thus necessitating a post weld annealing. The high temperature treatment is not always possible. Therefore, special filler materials with higher Mo content (C-22 and Incoloy 625) have been designd for welding. Lundin had reported preferential pitting attack in the unmixed zone of the weld metal [3].

2.1.3 Heat Input

Heat input affects the microstructure and hence the microstructure-sensitive properties of the weld metal. Increasing the heat input decreases the cooling rate of the weld metal, which increases the partitioning of the alloying elements and segregation of S and P, coarsens the δ-ferrite dendrites and increases the mean spacing between its secondary arms [15]. This is because decrease in the cooling rate of the weld metal increases solid-state diffusion and aids the redistributing the solute between the austenite and ferrite phases. Figure 16 shows that the critical pitting potential decreased with heat input for weld metal of type 316 LN SS due to increased partitioning of ferrite-formers, such as Mo, to δ-ferrite [15]. This deterioration in PCR, on increasing heat input, was attributed to the coarser microstructure, which is accompanied by increased segregation

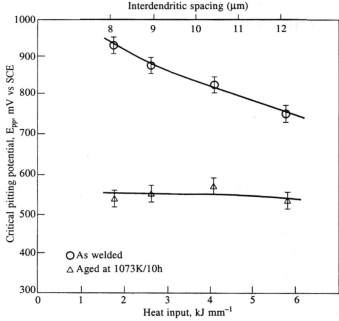

Fig. 16 **Variation of critical pitting potential with heat input for as-welded and heat treated type 316 L SS weld metal**

of S and P to the DF/A interface [33]. Nitrogen addition improved the PCR of weld metals of types 304 and 316 SS [34]. The PCR of weld metal decreased with increasing heat input, but the deleterious effect of heat input was readily offset by nitrogen additions (Fig. 17) [35]. Very little work has been done on the influence of heat input on the SCC susceptibility of welds of austenitic SS. Sensitivity to intergranular corrosion (IGC) is increased with increasing heat input and it would seem the risk of intergranular SCC (IGSCC) is also promoted at higher heat inputs

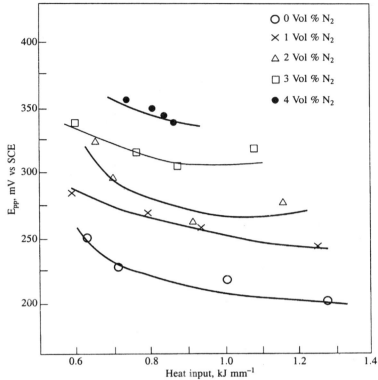

Fig. 17 **Effect of heat input and nitrogen content on pitting corrosion resistance of weld metal of type 304 austenitic SS**

[27]. To a lesser extent, a similar adverse effect of high heat input has been found also for transgranular SCC (TGSCC) [27]. However, Franco et al. reported an increase in SCC resistance of weld metal of AISI type 304 SS with increasing heat input in boiling 45% $MgCl_2$ solution [36] while Anita et al. reported improvement in SCC resistance with increasing heat input of a multipass weld of AISI type 316LN SS in boiling acidified NaCl solution (Fig. 18) [37].

2.1.4 *Secondary Phases*

The use of welded components of austenitic SS would result in its degradation with time on exposure to elevated temperature during service or during post-weld heat treatment (PWHT), when the δ-ferrite component of the duplex weld metal microstructure tends to transform to intermetallic phases, small quantities of which lead to large variations in the material's mechanical and corrosion properties. Hence, the knowledge of the type, the amount and the physical parameters of all phases is vital in designing the optimum operational parameters for achieving the desired life time for austenitic SS components. The various phases which transform from δ-ferrite include carbides, σ, η, χ, μ, R-phase etc. The transformation kinetics of δ-ferrite is dependent on various factors like chemical composition of the weld metal, size and shape of δ-ferrite, diffusion of chromium in ferrite etc. σ is known to nucleate and grow easily in SS containing low concentration

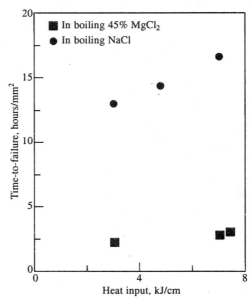

Fig. 18   Effect of heat input on the SCC behaviour of type 316 LN SS weld metal

of carbon [38, 39] while χ phase is preferentially precipitated in medium to high-carbon containing weldment of austenitic SS. Elements like chromium and molybdenum, apart from the carbon content, influence the formation of σ phase and determine the kinetics of the ferrite transformation. SS welds with higher chromium and molybdenum contents transform faster, as shown in the TTT diagram in Fig. 19 [40]. Increasing temperature increases the rate of transformation of ferrite (Fig. 20) [40].

Shirley and Garner reported that formation of σ phase impoverishes the surrounding matrix of Cr and Mo, thus making the alloy susceptible to corrosion attack [11, 42]. σ phase precipitation leads to increase in CCD; while the corrosion behaviour in the passive conditions remained unaffected as evidenced by no variation in PCD (Fig. 21) [18, 43]. Pujar et al. reported that aging type 316 SS weld metal, with two different carbon concentrations, between 773 K and 1073 K, did not affect the corrosion rates at open circuit potentials (OCP) while the CCD increased steeply with aging time [44]. At 1073 K, the increase in CCD was slow and steady because of self-healing of the Cr depleted regions as a result of faster diffusion of Cr from the bulk at this temperature. The weld metal with higher carbon content showed higher CCD on aging.

Warren showed that for types 316 SS, pit initiation times decreased and weight loss due to pitting increased when σ phase was introduced to the microstructure [45]. Shaikh et al reported lower pitting resistance and narrower range of passive potentials with increasing amount of σ phase in weld metal of aged type 316 LN austenitic SS (Fig. 22) [43]. The reduction in PCR was directly attributed to the dominating effect of depletion of Cr and Mo vis-à-vis the competing process of self healing in the austenite matrix. Spherodisation of σ phase did not have a direct influence on the improvement in PCR of aged weld metal. Improvement in PCR of type 316 LN weld metal aged for long durations of time at 1023 K was attributed to the dominance of the process of self-healing rather than spherodisation of σ phase [43]. Since σ contains higher Cr

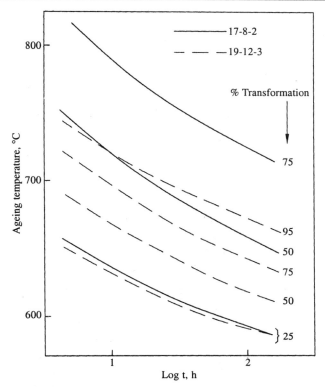

Fig. 19   TTT diagram for δ-ferrite transformation in 17Cr–8Ni–2Mo and 19Cr–12 Ni–3Mo weld metals

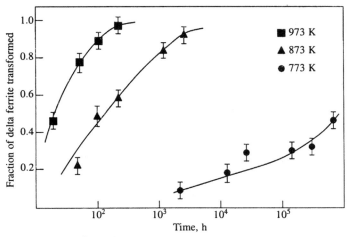

Fig. 20   Fraction of δ ferrite transformed during aging at various temperatures

and Mo than the austenite and exhibits more noble potentials in chloride solution, it is unlikely that the lower PCR is associated with direct attack on σ phase. Instead, Cr and Mo depletion occuring within austenite matrix just adjacent to the σ phase could cause the lowering of PCR

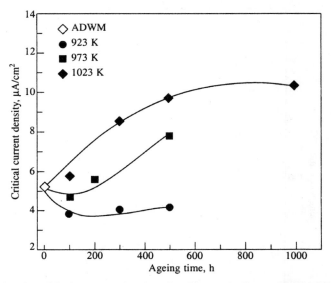

Fig. 21   Variation in critical current density of weld metal of type 316LN SS with aging time

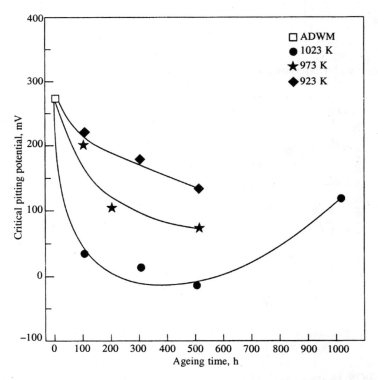

Fig. 22   Dependence of critical pitting potential of type 316LN SS weld metal on aging time

[46]. Gill et al. showed a sharp decrease in pitting potential of weld metal of type 316 SS when the Cr+Mo content decreased from 20 to 19 weight percent in the austenite matrix (Fig. 23) [23].

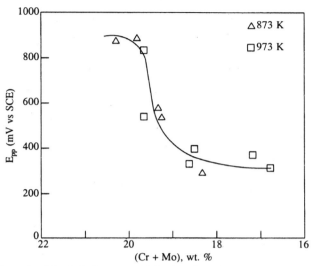

Fig. 23 **Variation of critical pitting potential with Cr + Mo content of the austenite matrix**

SCC studies on aged weld metal of type 316L SS showed that, on aging at 873 K, the SCC resistance of the weld metal was governed by the occurrence of two complementary processes of matrix hardening and softening [47]. Maximum SCC resistance was observed for weld metal aged for 200 hours (Fig. 24) because effects of matrix softening, caused by processes such as dissolution of ferrite network, overwhelmingly dominated the effects of matrix hardening, caused by factors like σ phase precipitation. Deterioration of SCC resistance was observed beyond 200 hours aging because the effects of matrix hardening dominated. PWHT of weld metal of Nb stabilised austenitic SS, at 873 to 1073 K, resulted in decreased SCC resistance due to σ phase precipitation while improvement in SCC resistance was observed on aging at 1073 K [48].

To overcome the corrosion problems associated with secondary phases precipitation in weld metal, it is recommended that a judicious choice of filler metal be made. In austenitic SS, where δ-ferrite is expected to be attacked preferentially during service, its amount and morphology should be controlled. If the SS weldment is to undergo PWHT to reduce the residual stresses, PWHT temperature should be selected so as to minimise formation of secondary phases.

2.1.5 Residual Stresses

During welding, residual stresses are retained in the component due to faster cooling rates associated with the weld metal. These stresses increase the dissolution rate of the material, thus deteriorating its corrosion properties. The major impact of residual stresses is felt on the SCC properties of the material. Many SCC failures have been reported on welded components during storage [49]. During service, residual stresses add on to the service load and accelerate SCC failures. Hence, the control and management of residual stresses assumes significance.

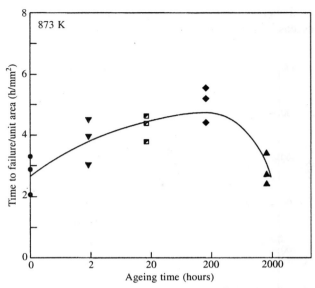

Fig. 24 Effect of high temperature aging on the SCC resistance of type 316L SS weld metal

PWHT is most commonly employed to rid welded components of their residual stresses. In austenitic SS components, PWHT can be of substantial benefit in avoiding IGSCC. In this regard, a stabilising anneal at 1143 to 1223 K is frequently applied to welded components in petrochemical industry to guard against polythionic acid attack. For chloride-induced SCC, cracking occurs where environment conditions are adverse and threshold stress for this form of failure is low. Service experience shows that when loaded components suffer chloride SCC, cracking occurs where environment conditions are adverse and threshold stress for this form of failure is low. Service experience shows that when loaded components suffer chloride SCC, cracking preferentially occurs in weld areas, strongly implying weld residual stresses to be a significant factor. Hence, PWHT is advisable, at least for critical applications. The high coefficient of thermal expansion and the extremely low limits of elasticity for austenitic SS would mean that residual stresses would readily arise during cooling from peak PWHT temperature, unless the operation is carefully controlled. Heating to over 1203 K is necessary to achieve maximum stress relief, and these high temperatures can pose critical problems such as control of distortion, scaling etc. Slow heating and cooling is preferred, subject to avoidance of sensitisation during cooling part of the cycle. Heat treatment at intermediate temperature, say 823 to 1023 K, represents an easier operation but only about 60% residual stress will be relieved. However, the problems of sensitisation and formation of intermetallic brittle phases, such as σ phase, rule out this heat treatment cycle. Low temperature stress relief at 673 K has been advocated to avoid SCC even though less than 40% stress relief is achieved [50]. Due to the above considerations, it may not be possible to guarantee that PWHT can avoid chloride SCC under the said service condition [51, 52]. Elimination of chloride ions, minimising operating temperature and appropriate design to eliminate crevices could prevent SCC of austenitic SS weld joints in preference to PWHT. This is not to say that PWHT should be overlooked. PWHT is definitely beneficial in countering chloride SCC and should be resorted to when other properties, like creep and fatigue, render them essential.

2.2 Corrosion of Heat Affected Zone

The rapid thermal cycles experienced in the HAZ of a fusion weld promote some metallurgical changes that would significantly affect the corrosion resistance of the weld joint eg. formation of martensite in the coarse grained region of the HAZ of steels. Martensite formation leads to increase in hardness. In sour gas application, the hardened HAZ may undergo sulphide SCC. It is specified that a maximum hardness of HRC 22 is adequate to avoid this problem (Fig. 25) [12]. Electrochemical polarisation studies of HAZ structures of 9Cr-1Mo steel in 0.5M sulphuric acid medium, indicated that the corrosion properties of the coarse and fine grained HAZ regions was as good as that of the normalised and tempered steel while the intercritical region possessed the worst corrosion resistance [17]. In austenitic SS, a degree of grain coarsening could be experienced just adjacent to the fusion line. However, the extent of grain coarsening is not significant enough to impair the SCC properties [27].

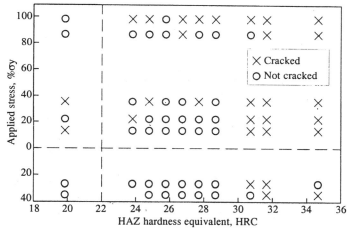

Fig. 25   Effect of hardness and applied stress on sulphide SCC in NACE TM-01-77 solution

The more often encountered phenomenon, which degrades the corrosion resistance of an austenitic SS weld joint is the sensitisation of the HAZ. Sensitisation of austenitic SS occurs in the temperature range of 723 to 1123 K. During this high temperature exposure, depletion of Cr to less than 12% occurs in the region around the grain boundary, due to the precipitation of a continuous network of $M_{23}C_6$ carbides. Sensitisation makes the steel susceptible to intergranular attack The probability of the HAZ being sensitised during welding would depend on the time it spends in the sensitisation temperature range. Figure 26 illustrates the maximum time spent by four different regions of the HAZ in the sensitisation temperature range. The region, which experiences a peak temperature of 1123 K is sensitised maximum. Below 723 K, carbide precipitation is too sluggish to cause any concern. The residence time spent by the HAZ in this temperature range depends on the heat input, which in turn decides the heating and cooling rates. Figure 27 shows that for a butt weld configuration for thicker sections, increasing heat input increases the time spent by the HAZ in the sensitisation temperature range. Also, the use of higher interpass temperatures increases the probability of sensitisation of HAZ [53]. Figure 28 schematically

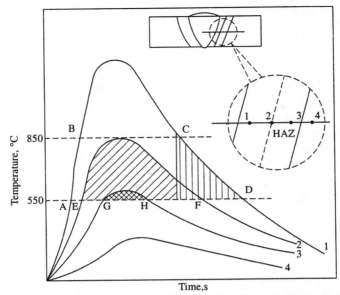

Fig. 26   A schematic diagram indicating the effect of thermal cycling in inducing sensitisation in the HAZ

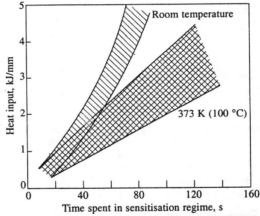

Fig. 27   Relationship between heat input and maximum time spent by HAZ for welds made with interpass temperatures of 373 K and room temperature

illustrates the microstructure of a sensitised austenitic SS after etching in oxalic acid. Optical microscopy reveals any of the three structures viz. step, ditch and dual. Step structure corresponds to clean grain boundaries. Ditch structure means continuous carbide precipitation and dual structure would mean discontinuous carbide precipitation. Normally step and dual structures are screened to be non-sensitised as per ASTM standards. This could be a mistake since dual structure could result in a fully ditched structure during low temperature service due to low temperature sensitisation (LTS), as in boiling water reactors (BWRs) where LTS is known to cause IGSCC of nuclear reactor components. Figure 29 illustrates the relationships between

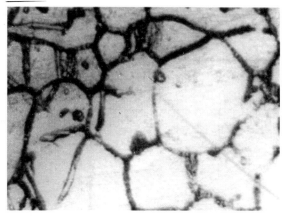

Fig. 28   Microstructure of sensitised austenitic SS

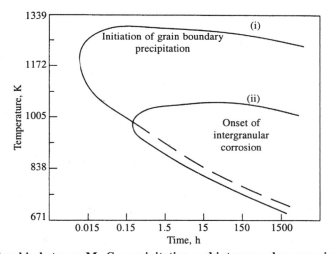

Fig. 29   Relationship between $M_{23}C_6$ precipitation and intergranular corrosion in type 304 SS

$M_{23}C_6$ precipitation and IGC. It is seen that the curve indicating IGC is offset to the right of carbide precipitation curve. This indicates a time lag between onset of carbide precipitation and susceptibility to IGC. This is because though carbide precipitation would occur, the regions adjacent to the carbides at grain boundaries have to be sufficiently depleted of Cr (< 12%) for IGC to occur [54]. The kinetics of the chromium carbide precipitation, and, hence, the resultant sensitisation could be predicted from a time-temperature-sensitisaton diagram (TTS) (Fig. 30) [55]. These curves represent sensitisation during isothermal heat treatments. However, sensitisation during welding can be predicted by means of a continuous cooling sensitisation (CCS) diagram (Fig. 31) [56].

The CCS curves are constructed from the TTS diagrams by superimposing the cooling curves. Dayal and Gnanamoorthy have reported a method to predict the extent of sensitisation during cooling/heating of the material [57]. The principle of this method is described in Fig. 32. The cooling curve is divided into a number small segments (ΔT) from the highest temperature (T_H)

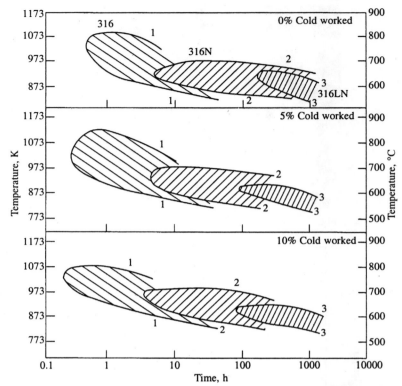

Fig. 30 **Time-temperature-sensitisation (TTS) diagram for types 316 (1–1), 316N (2–2) and 316 LN (3-3) SS**

to the lowest temperature (T_L) of the relevant TTS diagram. The time of transit Δt is determined for each segment of the cooling curve and is divided by the sensitisation time (t_s) at the mean temperature T of this segment from the TTS diagram. The cumulative fraction (α) of the resident time in successive segments from T_H to T_L is calculated and is defined as

$$\alpha = \sum_{T_L}^{T_H} \frac{\Delta t}{t_s}$$

Sensitisation takes place if $\alpha >$ or $= 1$. With this equation a critical cooling rate (R) to cause sensitisation can be calculated and is given as per the equation

$$R = \Delta T \sum_{T_L}^{T_H} \frac{1}{t_s}$$

The value of α is not dependent on magnitude of ΔT. For a given cooling rate slower than the critical cooling rate, a temperature can be found at which $\alpha = 1$. This gives one point on the CCS diagram. For different cooling curves, the loci of such points determine the continuous cooling sensitisation diagram.

Susceptibility to IGC caused by sensitisation in austenitic SS can be determined by systematically

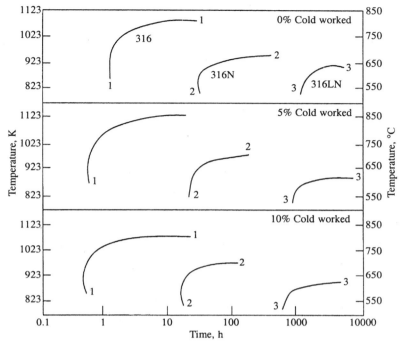

Fig. 31 **Continuous cooling sensitisation (CCS) diagram for types 316 (1–1), 316N (2–2) and 316LN (3–3) SS**

carrying out ASTM standardised tests. The ASTM tests for IGC are either chemical or electrochemical in nature and are applicable for austenitic SS and some Ni-base alloys. ASTM Standard A 262 Practice A to F are the standards for chemical and metallographic tests to determine IGC in austenitic SS [58]. Table 4 gives a comparative analysis of the variosu ASTM A 262 Practices to detect sensitisation. These standard tests are commonly used as qualification/acceptance criteria during purchase/fabrication stage. However, non-inclusion of acceptance limits in these standards leaves the interpretation of results open to users. Besides not quantifying the degree of sensitisation (DOS), these chemical tests are also destructive and slow-a situation that is not welcome at plant site. The oxalic acid etch test (A262 Practice A) is normally used as a screening test. Only if a ditched microstructure is observed in oxalic etch test, the need for confirmatory tests (Practice B to F) is necessary. The most often used chemical technique is the ASTM A262 Practice E test, which is popularly known as the Strauss test. The test recommends a bend test after exposure to Cu-$CuSO_4$-H_2SO_4 test medium to qualify the material. However, the bend test does not give any quantitative value for the DOS. Eectrical resistivity and tensile properties are changed considerably by the intergranular attack in the Strauss test medium. Hence, the changes in these properties can be used to quantify the DOS after exposure to the Strauss test solution [59]. To overcome these limitations of chemical tests, an electrochemical technique, known as electrochemical potentiokinetic reactivation (EPR) technique, was developed by Cihal et al. [60], Novak et al. [61] and Clarke et al. [62]. This technique is a quantitative, non-destructive and rapid method, which is essentially suitable for field use. This technique was standardised by ASTM to quantify the DOS in AISI types 304 and 304L SS [63]. The EPR

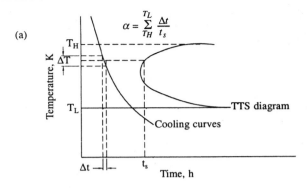

(a)

$$\alpha = \sum_{T_H}^{T_L} \frac{\Delta t}{t_s}$$

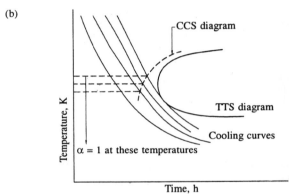

(b)

Fig. 32   Continuous cooling sensitisation diagram obtained from TTS diagram (a) principle of the method, and (b) the procedure

Table 4   ASTM Evaluation Test for Detecting Sensitisation

ASTM practice	Test Environment	Potential range	Alloys	Phases attacked	Evaluation criteria
A	Oxalic Acid Etch	+1.76 V (SCE)	304, 304L, 316, 316 L, 317, 317 L, 321, 347	Carbides	YES
B	$Fe_2(SO_4)$ – 50% H_2SO_4	+0.6 V (SCE)	321, 347	σ in 321 & 347	NO
C	HNO_3	+0.96 V (SCE)	321, 347	Cr-depleted regions, carbides & Mo-bearing σ	NO
D	HNO_3 – HF	+0.3 to –0.1 V (SCE)	316, 317, 317 L	Cr-depleted region	NO
E	Cu—$CuSO_4$/16% H_2SO_4	+0.34 V (SCE)	316, 316 L, 317, 317 L	Cr-depleted region	YES
F	Cu-$CuSO_4$/50% H_2SO_4	—	Low carbon and Mo-bearing SS	Cr-depleted regions	NO

technique has been successfully used to quantify the DOS in other SS and Ni base alloys [64, 65]. Table 5 gives the conditions for the EPR test. Two versions of the EPR technique are

Table 5 EPR Test conditions used by Clarke et al. [62]

Electrolyte	0.5M H_2SO_4 + 0.01M KCNS
Temperature	30°C
Specime surface finish	1 micron (diamond paste)
Reactivation Sweep Rate	6 V/h
Passivation Potential/Time	+200 mv for 2 minutes
Deaeration	Nitrogen

practiced today, viz. the single loop technique (Fig. 33) and the double loop technique (Fig. 34). Double loop technique has advantage over single loop technique in that it automatically compensates for changes in alloy composition, and in that the surface finish is not very critical, which makes it an automatic choice for on-field applications. Reactivation charge, ratio of reactivation to activation charge, peak reactivation current density, ratio of peak current densities on reactivation to activation are some of the parameters used to quantify degree of sensitisation. However, discrepancies exist between the DOS determined by chemical methods and the EPR method [65]. The threshold EPR charge value above which a SS is susceptible to IGC in ASTM A262E is not a unique number, but depends on temperature at which the material was sensitised. This is because the ratio of the width to depth of the Cr-depleted regions affects the reactivation charge during the EPR test. Also, EPR tests have an inherent disadvantage in that they are very sensitive to changes in Cr-depletion anywhere in the alloy and cannot easily differentiate between matrix and grain boundary depletion.

Sensitisation of austenitic SS requires the precipitation of Cr-rich carbides along grain boundaries, which makes carbon and Cr the predominant compositional variables for sensitisation. By reducing

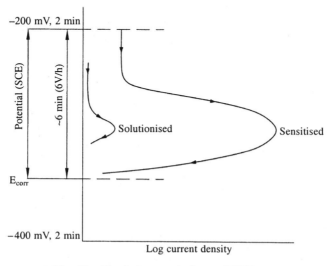

Fig. 33 Single loop technique of EPR test

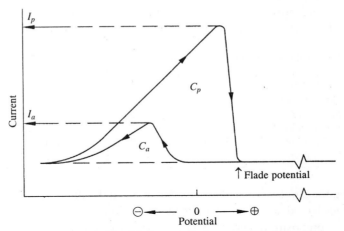

Fig. 34   Double loop technique of EPR test

the carbon content in SS, TTS curve is displaced towards longer times because carbon concentration in austenite becomes insufficient to form Cr-carbide readily (Fig. 35 a) [66]. The limit of C content for which steel is not sensitive to IGC is closely connected with the presence of other alloying elements such as Cr, Mo, Ni, N, Mn, B Si as well as Ti & Nb in stabilised steel. The detrimental effect of C on sensitisation can be reduced by the addition of stabilising elements like Ti and Nb. These elements form TiC and NbC, which results in reduction of Cr available for Cr-carbide precipitation. Cr has a pronounced effect on the passivation characteristics of SS. With higher Cr contents, time to reach resistance limit of Cr depletion at the grain boundaries is shifted to longer times (Fig. 35 b). Higher Cr contents facilitate the diffusion of Cr into depleted grain boundary area [66]. Ni is required in austenitic SS to stabilise the austenite and must be increased with increasing Cr concentration. Increasing the bulk Ni content decreases the solubility and increases the diffusivity of C. This effect is much more pronounced when Ni content is greater than 20%. It is generally recommended that in 25/20 G-Ni steel, C content should be less than 0.02% to guarantee resistance to IGC. Mo reduces the solubility of C in austenite. Carbide precipitation is accelerated at higher temperatures whereas at lower temperatures it is slowed down (Fig. 35 c) [66]. When Mo is present, it is also incorporated in $M_{23}C_6$. Therefore, in addition to Cr depletion, Mo depletion is also revealed. In Mo-containing Cr-Ni austenitic SS, $(Fe, Cr)_{23}C_6$ is precipitated first at 1023 K to 1123 K. With prolonged aging, Mo is also incorporated as $(Fe,Cr)_{21} Mo_2C_6$ which is finally converted to χ phase. With increasing Mo contents, $M_{23}C_6$ precipitation and IGC become increasingly influenced by the precipitation of intermetallic phases. The influence of Mn is of special importance because in fully austenitic welds, this element is added. Mn reduces the carbon activity and increases its solubility. Carbide precipitation is slowed down and hence it appears to inhibit carbide precipitation [67]. Boron retards the precipitation of Cr-carbide but depending upon the heat treatment it promotes IGC [66]. Si promotes IGC of high purity and commercial SS. Steels containing Mo were found to be much more sensitive to Si additions. The increased susceptibility to IGC in highly oxidising solution is due to the segregation of Si to grain boundaries [66]. Figure 35 (d) represents the influence of Si on the kinetics of sensitisation. One of the alloying additions studied extensively in the recent years is

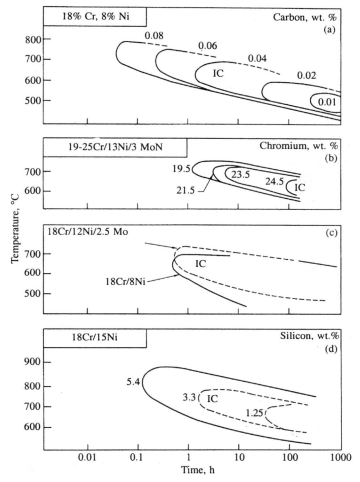

Fig. 35 **Influence of (a) carbon (b) Cr (c) Mo and (d) Si, on the sensitization kinetics of austenitic stainless steel base metals**

nitrogen. Its effect is quite complex and is dependent on the presence of other alloying additions. N content up to 0.16 weight % is reported to improve sensitisation resistance by retarding the precipitation and growth of $Cr_{23}C_6$ [68]. Parvathavarthini et al. have established that as the nitrogen content increases, time required for sensitisation at the nose temperature increases from 0.5 hours (316 SS) to as much as 80 hours (316 LN SS) indicating the beneficial effect of N [69].

Cr-carbides precipitate at grain boundaries because they are high energy areas. As the grain size decreases, the grain boundary area available for Cr-carbide precipitation increases. This would cause the effective depletion of Cr per unit grain boundary area to reduce. Also, Cr has to diffuse smaller distances to heal the Cr-depleted regions to desensitise the material. Cold work is reported to increase the sensitisation kinetics of austenitic SS at moderate cold works and decrease the kinetics at higher cold works. Parvathavarthini et al. [56] reported that TTS diagrams of cold worked materials are shifted to the left (shorter times) with increasing cold work, and below that of the as-received material. The nose temperature corresponding to maximum rate of sensitisation is also shifted to lower temperature with increasing cold work. Desensitisation is faster at higher levels of cold work especially at high aging temperatures.

A sensitised HAZ could fail by TGSCC or IGSCC. The most commonly encountered environments that cause failure in austenitic SS are those containing chlorides. It is very difficult to specify chloride levels below which SCC will not occur since other environmental factors such as oxygen content and pH of environment play a role in the failure. The combined role of oxygen and chloride ions in causing IGSCC of BWR piping (Fig. 36), which has been a major problem in the safe and economical operation of BWRs. IGSCC has been observed mainly in small diameter pipes where the stresses are expected to be very high. The cracks were mostly circumferential due to axial stresses.

The problem of IGSCC in BWRs can be overcome by resorting to modifications in welding processes, or by altering the material or by modifying the environment. Modifications in welding process include:

Last pass heat sink welding: A TIG welding arc is used as the heat source to heat the outer surface while simultaneously melting the filler metal. During the process, the inner surface is flushed with water, thus cooling it. A temperature difference is thus established between the outer and inner surfaces. The resulting thermal stresses produce localised plasticity inducing compressive stresses on the inner surface of the pipe [70].

Induction heat stress improvement: In this process, the weld area in the pipe is inductively heated from outside. The pipe is simultaneously cooled from inside with water. Just as in the above process, compressive stresses are induced on the inner surface of the pipe [70].

Mechanical stress improvement: In this process, the pipe is radially compressed a slight amount on one side of the weld by means of hydraulic jaws to produce a permanent deformation. The deformation involved is less than 2%. The resulting curvature reduces the tensile stresses, produced by welding, on the root side of the weld area and produces compressive stresses in both the axial and radial directions [70].

Solution annealing treatment: Helps in dissolving the grain boundary carbide network and evens out the material composition.

Corrosion resistant cladding: The weld joint is deposited with weld overlays which have a duplex microstructure. In the BWR environment, the weld overlay may crack but complete resistance to IGSCC is ensured for the pipe.

Alternate pipe material: Choose better materials for the application, such as types 304 LN SS, which is resistant to sensitisation and hence to IGC.

3 SUMMARY

This paper deals with the corrosion behaviour of weld joints of austenitic SS. The major problems faced during welding of austenitic SS include hot cracking of weld metal and sensitisation of

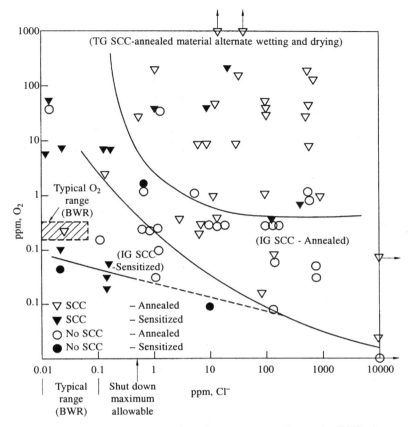

Fig. 36   Effect of chloride and oxygen ions in aqueous media on the SCC of austenitic SS

HAZ. Hot cracking is usually overcome by retaining some amount of high temperaure δ-ferrite in the weld metal. Presence of δ-ferrite deteriorates the pitting and stress corrosion properties of weld metal vis-à-vis the base metal. Increasing amounts of δ-ferrite in the weld metal increases critical current density and decreases pitting corrosion resistance. The SCC resistance of the weld metal depends on the δ-ferrite content, its distribution and the solidification mode Higher heat input into the weld metal causes deterioration in its localised corrosion properties. High temperatue aging causes preipitation of a number of deleterious phases, of which σ phase is the most encountered one. Increasing amounts of σ phase cause an increase in critical current density, and deterioration in pitting and stress corrosion cracking resistance. Residual stresses are also detrimental from weld metal corrosion point of view since their presence increases the dissolution rate. Residual stresses add on to the service stresses and accelerate the stress corrosion failure. Sensitisation of heat affected zone leads to a decrease in all localised corrosion properties. The maximum impact of a sensitised HAZ is felt on the intergranular SCC of the austenitic SS weld joint. The paper also discusses remedies to the various problems of corrosion of weld joints of austenitic SS.

4   REFERENCES

1. K. Komai, Proceedings of the International Conference on Case Histories on Integrity and Failures in Industry, Italy, (1999) 31.
2. T.V. Vinoy, H. Shaikh, H.S. Khatak, N. Sivaibharasi and J.B. Gnanamoorthy, Journal of Nuclear Materials, 238 (1996) 278.
3. C.D. Lundin, WRC Progress Report, (1994) 64.
4. T. Rogne, J.M. Drugli and S. Valen, Corrosion, 48 (1992) 864.
5. S. Szklarska-Smialowska and E. Lunarska, Werkstoffe und Korrosion, 32 (1981) 478.
6. H. Holtan and H. Sigurdsson, Werkstoffe und Korrosion, 32 (1981) 478.
7. S. Szklarska-Smialowska and J. Gust, Corrosion Science, 19 (1979) 753.
8. R.L. Shamakian, A.R. Troiano and R.F. Hehemann, Corrosion, 36 (1980) 279.
9. W.L. Clarke and G.M. Gordon, Corrosion, 29 (1973) 1.
10. Kotecki and D.G. Howden, WRC Bulletin No. 184, (1973).
11. H.T. Shirley, Journal of Iron and Steel Institute, 174 (1954) 242.
12. Noble, Welding and Metal Fabrication, 59 (1991) 295.
13. J.C. Lippold and W.F. Savage, Welding Journal, 59 (1980) 362-s.
14. J.A. Brooks and A.W. Thompson, International Metals Review, 36 (1991) 16.
15. T.P.S. Gill, V. Seetharaman and J.B. Gnanamoorthy, Corrosion, 44 (1988) 511.
16. T.G. Gooch, The Welding Institute Research Bulletin, 13 (1974) 83.
17. G. George, H. Shaikh, N. Parvathavarthini, R.P. George and H.S. Khatak, Journal of Materials Engineering and Performance, 10 (2001) 460.
18. B.R. Rao, K.P. Rao and K.J.L. Iyer, Proceedings of the International Conference on Stainless Steel, Indian Institute of metals, New Delhi, (1992) 427.
19. P.I. Marshall and T.G. Gooch, Corrosion, 49 (1993) 514.
20. H.J. Dundas and A.P. Bond, NACE Corrosion/75, (1975) preprint No. 159.
21. A. Garner, Pulp and Paper Industry Corrosion Problems, NACE, Vol. 2, (1977).
22. P.E. Manning, C.E. Lyrnan and D.J. Duquette, Corrosion, 36 (1980) 246.
23. T.P.S. Gill, J.B. Gnanamoorthy and K.A. Padmanabhan, Corrosion, 43 (1987) 208.
24. D.H. Sherman, D.J. Duquette and W.F. Savage, Corrosion, 31 (1975) 376.
25. F. Stalder and D.J. Duquette, Corrosion, 33 (1977) 67.
26. W.A. Baeslack III, W.F. Savage and D.J. Duquette, Metallurgical Transactions A, 10A (1979) 1429.
27. T.G. Gooch, Welding in the World, 22 (1984) 64.
28. W.A. Baeslack III, D.J. Duquette and W.F. Savage, Corrosion, 35 (1979) 45.
29. K.S. Raja and K.P. Rao, Corrosion, 48 (1992) 634.
30. H. Shaikh, G. George, F. Schneider, K. Mummert and H.S. Khatak, Werkstoffe und Korrosion, 51 (2000) 791.
31. H. Shaikh, H.S. Khatak and J.B. Gnanamoorthy, Werkstoffe und Korrosion, 38 (1987) 183.
32. W.A. Baeslack III, W.F. Savage and D.J. Duquette, Welding Journal, 58 (1979) 83-s.
33. A. Garner, Materials Performance, 21 (1982) 9.
34. U.K. Mudali, R.K. Dayal, T.P.S. Gill and J.B. Gnanamoorthy, Werkstoffe und Korrosion, 37 (1986) 637.
35. U.K. Mudali, R.K. Dayal, T.P.S. Gill and J.B. Gnanamoorthy, Corrosion, 46 (1990) 454.
36. C.V. Franco, R.P. Barbosa, A.E. Martinelli and A.J.A. Buschinelli, Werkstoffe und Korrosion, 49 (1998) 496.
37. T. Anita, H. Shaikh and H.S. Khatak, Corrosion 60 (2004) 873.
38. V.S. Raghunathan, V. Seetharaman, S. Venkadesan and P. Rodriguez, Metallurgical Transactions A, 10A (1979) 1683.
39. G.F. Slattery, S.R. Keown and M.E. Lambert, Metal Technology, 10 (1983) 373.
40. R.G. Thomas and S.R. Keown, Proceedings of the International Conference on Mechanical Behaviour and Nuclear Applications of Stainless Steels at Elevated Tempertaures, Varese, Italy, May (1981), The Metals Society, (1981) 30.

41. T.P.S. Gill, M. Vijayalakshmi, P. Rodriguez and K.A. Padmanabhan, Metallurgical Transactions A, 20A (1989) 1115.

42. A. Garner, Metal Progress, 127 (1985) 31.

43. H. Shaikh, G. George, F. Schneider, K. Mummert and H.S. Khatak, Transactions of the Indian Institute of Metals, 54 (2001) 27.

44. M.G. Pujar, R.K. Dayal, T.P.S. Gill and J.B. Gnanamoorthy, Proceedings of the International Conference on Welding Technology, University of Roorkee, Roorkee, (1988), II-33.

45. Warren, Microstructural and Corrosion Resistance of Austenitic Stainless Steel, Sixth Annual Liberty Bell Corrosion Course, NACE, Philadelphia, PA, September 1968.

46. U.K. Mudali, T.P.S. Gill, V. Seetharaman and J.B. Gnanamoorthy, Proceedings of the National Welding Seminar, Madras, (1986) 265.

47. H. Shaikh, H.S. Khatak, S.K. Seshadri, J.B. Gnanamoorthy and P. Rodriguez, Metallurgical and Materials Transactions A, 26A (1995) 1859.

48. K.N. Krishnan and K.P. Rao, Proceedings of the International Conference on Stainless Steel, Indian Institute of Metals, New Delhi, (1992) 419.

49. H.S. Khatak, V. Seetharaman and J.B. Gnanamoorthy, Practical Metallography, 20 (1983) 570.

50. C.L. Cole and J.D. Jones, Proceedings of Conference on Stainless Steels, ISI Publication 117, (1969) 71.

51. C. Edeleanu, Corrosion Technologyh, 4 (1957) 49.

52. T.G. Gooch, Proceedings of the Conference on The Influence of Welding and Welds on Corrosion Behaviour of Constructions, IIW Annual Assembly, Tel Aviv, (1975) 1.52.

53. T.P.S. Gill, Proceedings of the Corrosion Management Course, The Indian Institute of Metals, Kalpakkam, October 1995, Paper No. L-6.

54. C.J. Novak, Handbook of Stainless Steels, 1977.

55. S.K. Mannan, R.K. Dayal, M. Vijayalakshmi and N. Parvathavarthini, Journal of Nuclear Materials, 126 (1984) 1.

56. N. Parvathavarthini, R.K. Dayal, J.B. Gnanamoorthy and S.K. Seshadri, Journal of Nuclear Materials, 168 (1989) 83.

57. R.K. Dayal and J.B. Gnanamoorthy, Corrosion, 36 (1980) 104.

58. ASTM Standard A262-93a, ASTM Book of Standards, American Society for Testing of Metals, Philadelphia PA, (1993) 42.

59. P. Muraleedharan, Corrosion and Maintenance, (1984) 47.

60. V. Cihal, Corrosion Science, 20 (1980) 737.

61. P. Novak, R. Stefec and F. Franz, Corrosion, 31 (1975) 344.

62. W.L. Clarke, W.M. Romero and J.C. Danko, Report GEAP-21382, GEC, California, (1976).

63. ASTM Standard G. 108-94, ASTM Book of Standards, American Society for Testing of metals, Philadelphia PA, (1994) 444.

64. W.L. Clarke, J.R. Kearns, J.Y. Park and D. van Rooyen, ASTM Research Report, Subcommittee G01.08, 1989.

65. P. Muraleedharan, J.B. Gnanamoorthy and K. Prasad Rao, Corrosion, 45 (1989) 142.

66. E. Folkhard, Welding Metallurgy of Stainless Steels, Springer-Verlag, Vienna (1988).

67. C.L. Briant, R.A. Mulford and E.E. Hall, Corrosion,38 (1982) 468.

68. T.A. Mozhi, W.A.T. Clarke, K. Nishimoto, W.B. John and D.D. McDonald, Corrosion, 41 (1985) 555.

69. N. Parvathavarthini, R.K. Dayal and J.B. Gnanamoorthy, Corrosion, 208 (1994) 251.

70. J. Schmidt, D. Pellkofer and E. Weiss, Nuclear Engineering and Design, 174 (1997). 301.

12. Non-Destructive Testing of Welded Components

C.V. Subramanian
NDT Consultant, Chennai

INTRODUCTION

Present day engineering industry relies heavily on the integrity of welds for adequate and reliable performance of components, structures and plants. Weld integrity is dependent on the base material, specifications and welding processes. Reliability of weld performance is evaluated by measurement and control of weld properties. It is accepted widely that testing, measurement and control of welds should be optimized based on fitness-for-purpose approach taking into account the welding processes and economical aspects of ensuring the desired levels of reliability. Recent advances in test techniques for ensuring the desired quality have met high technological demands.

WELD IMPERFECTIONS AND IMPORTANCE OF THEIR EVALUATION

Historically welding has replaced riveted construction in engineering structures. It is now scarcely possible to design an industrial structure without a welded joint. No weld is completely perfect. Welds may be compared to small castings except that weld metal cools much more rapidly mainly due to heat sinks provided by the base metals. This results in thermal stresses that may lead to cracking and also due to the entrapment of gases or foreign materials within the weld. These and other defects may cause premature failure of the weld in service.

Defects in Welded Joints

Defects can be of three types:

1. Physical discontinuities
2. Microstructural defects
3. Defects related to residual stress and distortion

The relevance and importance of defects are best understood through fracture mechanics concepts, wherein the following parameters are important:

(a) defect size, (b) defect shape, (c) defect location and (d) loading, including both externally imposed and arising out of the presence of residual stresses. The objective of a good and effective testing programme is to detect defects as specified by the design based on fitness-for-purpose.

Choice of NDE techniques to evaluate Fitness for Purpose (FFP)

For many highly stressed components, failure occurs in an elastic manner involving fast fracture. The capability to detect planar defects is the first criterion that decides the relative merits of various NDT techniques, since fracture mechanics concepts indicate the prime importance of detecting and measuring planar defects. Hence the NDT techniques that are most appropriate for use in conjunction with a FFP approach are those that are:

(a) sensitive to planar defects, whatever their orientation and position
(b) sensitive to surface breaking defects
(c) capable of discriminating planar from non-planar defects

NON-DESTRUCTIVE TESTS

Non-destructive testing (NDT) is an integral and the most important constituent of the quality assurance (QA) programme of any industry. The objectives of the QA programmes are safety, reliability and economy. Non-destructive evaluation (NDE) places due emphasis on characterisation of materials including quantitative determination of the size, shape and location of a defect or abnormalcy thus enabling evaluation of structural integrity of a component, particularly in the context of 'fitness-for-purpose'. NDT along with material properties and operational history is vital for successful prediction of damage and residual life.

VISUAL INSPECTION

Visual inspection is probably the most widely used among the non-destructive tests. It is simple, easy to apply, quickly carried out and usually low in cost. Even though a component is to be inspected using other NDT methods, a good visual inspection should be carried out first. A simple visual test can reveal gross surface defects thus leading to an immediate rejection of the component and consequently saving much time and money, which would otherwise be spent on more complicated means of testing. It is often necessary to examine the weld joint for the presence of finer defects. For this purpose, visual methods have been developed to a very high degree of precision. With the advent of CCD cameras, microprocessors and computers, visual examination can be carried out very reliably and with minimum cost. Image processing, pattern recognition and automatic accept/reject choice are used when large numbers of components are to be assessed.

Visual inspection (VI) has wide applications for inspection of wrought, cast and welded materials. However, for welds, this is all the more important as at various stages of welding, visual inspection gives useful information. Many characteristics of a weld can be evaluated by visually examining a completed weld, but much can be learnt by observing the weld as it is being made. For many non-critical welds, integrity is verified principally by visual inspection. Even when other non-destructive methods are used, visual inspection still constitutes an important part of quality control. Visual inspection should be done before, during and after welding. Visual inspection is useful for assessing the following: (a) dimensional accuracy, (b) conformity of welds to size, fit up and control requirements, (c) acceptability of weld appearance with regard to surface roughness, weld spatter, undercuts and overlaps and (d) imperfections and cracks on the observed surfaces. Although visual inspection is a very valuable method, it is unreliable for detecting subsurface flaws. Therefore, judgement of weld quality must be based on information from bulk material in addition to that from surface indications. Capabilities of VI can be enhanced considerably by using simple gadgets and instruments for viewing, dimensional measurements etc. In spite of the developments in the field of visual aids, as yet there is no decision-making electronic computer that can emulate the human brain. The experienced eye is invaluable for an intelligent first inspection. Many visual aids are available to enhance the inspection ranging from a pocket magnifier to microscope and monochromatic illlumination to CCD-camera colour video presentation. Intra scopes are available to permit entry and inspection of internal surfaces through access openings and the human inspector is equipped to supply a wealth of primary NDT results.

Optical Aids used for Visual Inspection

The use of optical instruments in visual inspection is beneficial and is recommended to (a) magnify defects that can not be detected by the unaided eye and (b) permit visual checks of areas not accessible to the unaided eye. In performing visual/optical checks, it is of utmost importance to know the type of defects that may develop and to recognize the areas where such failures may occur. Magnifying devices and lighting aids should be used wherever appropriate. The general area should be checked for cleanliness, presence of foreign objects, and corrosion damage. In many cases, the area to be inspected should be cleaned before the visual examination.

Microscope

An optical microscope is a combination of lenses used to magnify the image of a small object. Minute defects and details of fine structure on a surface can be detected more easily with the help of a microscope. The practical upper limit of the magnifying power of a simple microscope is in the region of 10 X. Optical microscopes are used to evaluate cracks with respect to their shape and orientation. Low power microscopes are used at a magnification of 2 to 20 X to examine external cracks on unprepared surfaces. Observation of microstrutural details alongside the crack location usually requires a magnification of 100 – 500 X after metallographic preparation.

Borescope

As the name implies, a borescope is an instrument designed to enable an observe to inspect the inside of a narrow tube, bore or chamber. Borescope consists of precision built-in illumination system having a complex arrangement of prisms and plain lenses through which light is passed to the observer with maximum efficiency. The light source located in front or ahead of the objective lens provides illumination for the part being examined. Borescopes are available in numerous models from 2.5 to 19 mm in diameter and a few metres in length. Optical systems are generally designed to provide direct, right-angle, retrospective and oblique vision. The choice of the inspection angle is determined by flaw type and location. In most borescopes, the observed visual area is approximately 25 mm in diameter and 25 mm from the object. The size of the visual field usually varies with the diameter, for a given magnification system.

Endoscope

The endoscope is much like a borescope except that it has a superior optical system and a high-intensity light source. Various viewing angles, as discussed in the case of borescope, can be used. A unique feature of the endoscope is that objects are constantly in focus from about 4 mm to infinity. Endoscopes are available in diameters down to 1.7 mm and in lengths from 100 to 1500 mm.

Flexible Fibre-Optic Borescope (Flexiscope)

Flexible fibre-optic borescopes permit manipulation of the instrument around corners and through passages with several directional changes. Woven stainless steel sheathing protects the image-relaying fibre optic bundle during repeated flexing and maneuvering. These devices are designed to provide sharp and clear images of parts and interior surfaces that are normally impossible to inspect. Remote end-tip deflection allows the viewer to thread the fibroscope through a complex series of bends. High resolution CCD camera-based fibroscopes are available for examination of the inner surface of the tubes.

LIQUID PENETRANT INSPECTION

Liquid penetrant inspection (LPI) is another NDT method to detect surface defects and also sub-surface defects open to surface in welded materials. This method is used in root pass and subsequent passes to detect surface defects so that repair work can be undertaken to remove the defects in the weld. In this method, a liquid penetrant is applied to the surface of the product for a certain predetermined time during which the penetrant seeps through the surface opening defects by capillary action. The excess penetrant is removed from the surface. The surface is then wiped with solvent, dried and a developer applied to it. The penetrant which remains in the discontinuity is absorbed by the developer to indicate the presence as well as the location, size and nature of discontinuity. The procedural sequence adopted for liquid penetrant inspection is shown in Fig. 1. Care should be taken so that chemical contents in the liquid penetrant do not affect the material. This method is best adopted for inspection of all types of suface cracks, porosity, laminations and lack of bond at exposed edges or joined materials and leaks in welded tubes and tanks. It has been used with excellent success on ferrous and non-ferrous materials, ceramics, powder metallurgy products, weldments, glass as well as on some plastics and synthetic materials.

Types of Penetrants

Liquids having good penetrating ability and potent coloured dyes are required to achieve the desired sensitivity. These are clearly visible either under white light or ultraviolet light. The amount of penetrant that can enter extremely fine surface discontinuities is quite minute. The visibility of the penetrant brought out of the flaw must be extremely high. The contrast between the penetrant and the developer or surface of the part should be as great as possible. Some penetrants are water-washable and can be removed from the surface by washing with ordinary tap water. Other penetrants are removed with special solvents.

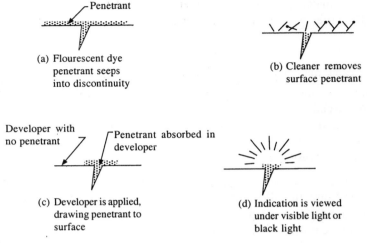

(a) Flourescent dye penetrant seeps into discontinuity

(b) Cleaner removes surface penetrant

(c) Developer is applied, drawing penetrant to surface

(d) Indication is viewed under visible light or black light

Fig. 1   Sequence of liquid penetrant testing

Types of developers: Two types of developers are employed:

(1) A dry developer consists of a dry light-coloured powdery material. Dry developer is applied to the surface of the parts after removal of the excess penetrant and drying of the part.
(2) A wet developer which consists of a powdered material suspended in suitable liquid such as water or a volatile solvent.

Penetration Time: The penetration time varies considerably depending upon, (1) The type of penetrant used, (2) type of materials to be inspected (3) the sensitivity desired and (4) the type of defects to be found. The time may vary from as little as one minute to one hour.

Inspection: Inspection is carried out by viewing the part for colour contrast between the penetrant drawn out from a defect and the background surface. In the case of fluorescent dyes, viewing is done under ultraviolet or black light. The important thing is to look for very small amounts of penetrant that indicate discontinuities.

Post-Emulsifiable Fluorescent Penetrant System

This is the most sensitive of all penetrant systems; this procedure will locate wide and shallow flaws as well as tight cracks. It requires only a short penetration time and thus is ideal for high-speed production work. On the other hand, emulsification requires an extra operation, which increases the cost. Also, it requires a water supply and facilities for inspection under black light.

Solvent-Removable Fluorescent Penetrant System

This employs a procedure similar to that used for the post-emulsifiable fluorescent system, except that excess penetrant is removed with a solvent. This system is especially recommended for spot inspection or where water cannot be conveniently used. It is more sensitive than the water-washable system but extreme caution is needed and the additional time required for application of the solvent often precludes its use.

Water Washable Fluorescent System

It is the fastest of the fluorescent procedures. It is also reliable and reasonably economical. It can be used for both small and large work pieces and is good on rough surfaces. However, it cannot reliably reveal open shallow flaws and in some cases, will not locate the very tight cracks because it is less sensitive than the two fluorescent systems described above. Other limitations are that the inspection must be carried out where there is adequate water supply and where a black light can be used.

MAGNETIC PARTICLE TESTING (MPT)

For detection of surface and sub-surface defects in welded components, liquid penetrant testing or magnetic particle testing are being widely used. In the case of ferromagnetic materials, magnetic particle technique has been preferred since this will also detect subsurface flaws that are not open to the surface. Because of this advantage over liquid penetrant, it has become customary to specify magnetic particle testing for all ferromagnetic materials.

This method is based on the principle that when a ferromagnetic materials under test is magnetised, discontinuities that lie in a direction generally transverse to the field will cause a leakage field around the discontinuity. The procedure adopted for magnetic particle testing is shown in Fig. 2. When finely divided ferromagnetic powder is sprinkled over the surface, some of these particles will be gathered and held by the leakage field. This magnetically held collection of particles forms an outline of the discontinuity and indicates its location, shape and extent. To get the highest sensitivity, fluorescent magnetic particles suspended in oil using full wave DC continuous technique is employed.

The test method consists of magnetisation of the component, applying magnetic powder,

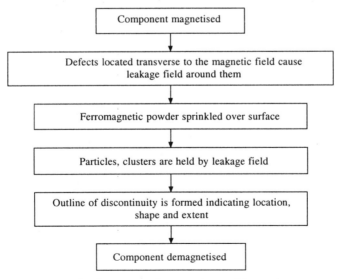

Fig. 2 Sequence of magnetic particle testing

examination of powder patterns and demagnetisation of the component. Magnetic particle testing is a sensitive means of locating small and shallow surface cracks in ferromagnetic materials. Indications may be produced at cracks that are large enough to be seen by the naked eye. Wide cracks will not produce a particle pattern if the surface opening is too wide for the particles to bridge. If a discontinuity is fine and sharp and close to the surface, such as a long stringer of nonmetallic inclusions, a sharp indication will be produced. If the discontinuity lies deeper, the indication is less distinct. Magnetic particle indications are produced directly on the surface of the part, and constitute magnetic pictures of actual discontinuities. There is little or no limitation on the size or shape of the part being inspected. Ordinarily no elaborate pre-cleaning is necessary and cracks filled with foreign materials can be detected.

Magnetisation Methods

In magnetic particle testing, the magnetic particles may be applied to the part while the magnetising current is flowing or after the current has ceased to flow, depending largely on the retentivity of the part. The first technique is known as the continuous method and the second one is known as the residual method. The residual method can be used only on materials having sufficient retentivity. Usually, the harder the material, the higher the retentivity. The continuous method is the only method used on low-carbon steels or iorn having little or no retentivity.

Magnetising Current

Each direct current and alternating current are suitable for magnetising parts. The strength, direction and distribution of magnetic fields are greatly affected by the type of current that is used for magnetisation. Fields produced by direct current generally penetrate the cross section of the part, whereas the fields produced by alternating current are confined to the metal at or near the surface of the part which commonly known as the skin effect. Therefore, alternating current should not be used in detecting sub surface discontinuities. Most satisfactory source of direct current is the rectification of alternating current. configuretions of magnetic arts omitable for inspection of pipe and rod geometrics are shown in Fig. 3 and 4, respectively.

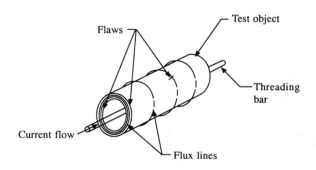

Fig. 3   Circular magnetization using single turn of coil

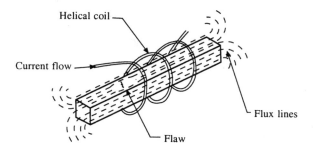

Fig. 4   Longitudinal magnetization using coil

Inspection of Weldments

Many weld defects are open to the surface and are readily detectable by magnetic particle inspection using prods and yokes (Fig. 5). For detection of sub-surface discontinuities, such as slag inclusions, voids and inadequate joint penetration at the root of the weld, prod magnetisation is the best, using either alternating current, direct current or half-wave current.

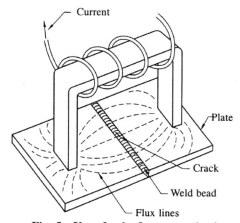

Fig. 5   Use of yoke for magnetisation

Positioning of a yoke with respect to the direction of the discontinuity sought is different from the corresponding positioning of prods. Because the field traverses a path between the poles of the yoke, the poles must be placed on opposite sides of the weld bead to locate cracks parallel to the weld axis and adjacent to the bead to locate transverse cracks. Prods are spaced adjacent to the weld for parallel cracks and on opposite sides for transverse cracks.

For applications in which holding of prod contacts by hand is difficult or tiring, prods incorporating magnetic clamps or faches that hold the prods magnetically to the part to be tested are available. The prods carrying the magnetising current are held firmly to the part by an electromagnet. Both prods may be attached by the magnets, or one of the prods may be held magnetically and the other by hand.

The detectability of sub-surface discontinuities in butt welds made between relatively thin plates often can be improved by positioning a direct current yoke on the side opposite the weld bead. Magnetic particles are applied along the weld bead. Improvement is achieved because of the absence of extraneous leakage flux that normally emanates from the yoke's pole pieces.

Demagnetization after Inspection

All ferromagnetic materials after having been magnetized will retain some magnetic field which is known as residual magnetic field. This field is negligible in magnetically soft materials. However, in magnetically hard materials, it may be comparable to the intense fields associated with the special alloys used for permanent magnets. Demagnetization is easy or difficult depending upon the type of material. Metals having high coercive force are difficult to demagnetize. There are many reasons for demagnetizing a part after magnetic particle inspection. For example, during subsequent machining of a part, chips may adhere to the surface being machined and adversely affect surface finish, dimensions and tool life. During electric arc welding operations, strong residual magnetic fields may deflect the arc away from the point at which it should be applied.

Methods of Demagnetization

Thermal Method: A ferromagnetic component can be demagnetized if it is raised above its curie temperature (for example 1023 K for iron) but often this is not practicable or convenient. This can be employed where post-weld heat treatment to a temperature above curie temperature follows magnetic particle inspection.

AC Circular Field Demagnetization: This is useful for large parts. This is similar to A.C. coil method in that the field reversal is provided by the cyclic nature of the current. In this method, the desired field is obtained by passing current through the part where the current intensity is gradually reduced to zero.

AC or DC Yoke Method

This is suitable for parts having very high coercive force. Some yokes are similar in operation to the A.C. coil method whereby the part is passed between pole faces and then withdrawn. A modified version of this uses a solenoid type electromagnet.

EDDY CURRENT TESTING

Eddy current inspection is based on the principle of electromagnetic induction. Eddy current test procedure is shown schematically in Fig. 6. It is a technique based on the induction of electrical currents in the material being inspected and observing the interaction between test currents and the material, and is used to identify or differentiate between a wide variety of physical, structural and metallurgical conditions in electrically conductive materials and metal parts. Being based on the principle of electromagnetic induction, the technique does not require direct electrical contact with the part being tested. The eddy current method is adaptable to high speed inspection and because it is non-destructive, it can be used to inspect an entire production if desired. The method is based on indirect measurement and the correlation between the instrument readings and the structural characteristics and the serviceability of the parts being inspected must be carefully and repeatably established. It is used extensively to identify or differentiate between a wide variety of physical, structural and metallurgical conditions in welded stainless steel tubes. It has also been successfully used to locate defects like lack of fusion, incomplete penetration, cracks, oxidation and changes in chemical composition and hardness of welds. One of the difficulties in using electromagnetic testers is that the instruments must be made to measure the desired weld properties without interference from non-critical characteristics. Many improvements in the newest electronic instruments have made electromagnetic testing equipment more suitable for evaluation of production welds.

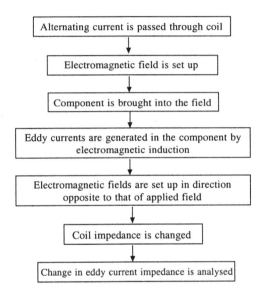

Fig. 6   Sequence of events in eddy current testing

The test coil is the main link between the test instrument and the test object and serves two main functions, the first to establish a varying electromagnetic field, which induces eddy currents within the test objects, and the second is to feed the response due to the electromagnetic field to a signal analysis system. The part to be inspected is placed within or adjacent to an electric coil in which an alternating current is flowing. This alternating current, called exciting current causes eddy currents to flow in the part as a result of electromagnetic induction. These currents flow within closed loops in the part, and their magnitude and timing (or phase) depend upon (1) the original or primary field established by the exciting currents, (2) the electrical properties of the part and (3) the electro magnetic fields established by currents flowing within the part.

The electromagnetic field in the part and surrounding the part depends on both the exciting current from the coil and eddy currents flowing in the part. The change in eddy curent flow pattern in the inspected part with coil configuration is shown in Fig. 7. The flow of eddy currents in the part depends on the electrical characteristics of the part, the presence or absence of flaws

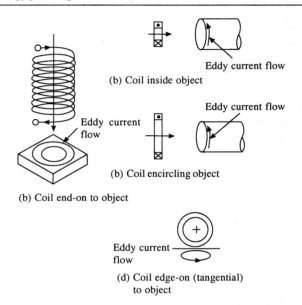

(b) Coil inside object

(b) Coil encircling object

(b) Coil end-on to object

(d) Coil edge-on (tangential)
to object

Fig. 7   Variation of eddy current flow with different coil arrangements

or other discontinuities in the part and the total electromagnetic field within the part. Since eddy currents are induced by a varying magnetic field, the magnetic permeability of the material being inspected strongly influences the eddy current response. Consequently, the techniques and the conditions used for inspecting magnetic materials differ from those used for inspecting non-magnetic materials. However, the same factors that may influence electrical conductivity (composition, hardness, residual stress and flaws) also may influence magnetic permeability. Thus eddy current inspection can be applied to both magnetic and nonmagnetic materials.

Basically, any discontinuity that appreciably alters the normal flow of eddy currents can be detected by eddy current inspection. With encircling-coil inspection of either solid cylinders or tubes, surface discontinuities having a combination of predominantly longitudinal and radial dimensional components are readily detected. When discontinuities of the same size are located beneath the surface of the part being inspected at progressively greater depths they become increasingly difficult to detect and can be detected at depths greater than 12.5 mm only with special equipment designed for this purpose. On the other hand, laminar discontinuities such as those found in welded tubes may not alter the flow of eddy currents enough to be detected unless the discontinuity breaks either outside or inside surfaces or unless it produces a discontinuity in the weld from fibres caused by extrusion during welding. A similar difficulty could arise for the detection of a thin planar discontinuity that is oriented substantially perpendicular to the axis of the cylinder.

Weld Inspection

For complete evaluation of welds, it is essential to verify the alloy composition. There is always a possibility that the wrong welding rod or wire is accidentally used for a critical weld and this may cause a premature failure of the weld. Many types of ECT instruments are currently available for sorting various types of welding consumables and the weld metal, provided their electrical conductivity or magnetic permeability values are sufficiently different.

Longitudinal welds in welded tubing and pipes can be inspected for discontinuities using ECT with an external encircling coil and a probe-type detector coil. The inspection is performed by passing the tube or pipe longitudinally through the primary energising coil causing the probe-type detector coil to traverse the longitudinal weld from end to end. The primary coil is energised with alternating current at a frequency that is suitable for the part being inspected and induces eddy currents in the tube or pipe.

For the inspection of ferromagnetic products, a direct current magnetic coil is located concentrically around the primary energising coil. The direct current coil is energised at high current levels to magnetically saturate the tube or pipe. This improves the penetration of the eddy currents and cancels the effect of magnetic variables. Due to circumferential orientation of the eddy current flow, this type of inspection is effective in detecting most types of longitudinal weld discontinuities such as open welds, weld cracks, penetrators and pinholes.

It is important that the longitudinal weld be carefully positioned under the detector coil before the pipe is passed through the tester. It is essential to provide good scanning equipment so that, as the pipe is propelled longitudinally, the longitudinal weld will always be located under the detector coil.

ULTRASONIC TESTING

Ultrasonic testing is an NDT method in which sound waves of high frequency (in MHZ) are introduced into the material being inspected to detect internal flaws (defects) and to study the properties of the material. The sound waves travel into the material with some loss of energy due to attenuation and are reflected at interfaces. The reflected beam (in most of the applications) is detected and analysed to define the presence and location of defects and for quantitative evaluation.

The degree of reflection depends largely on the physical state of matter on the opposite side of the interface and on specific physical properties. The sound waves are almost completely reflected at metal-gas (air) interfaces, while partial reflection occurs at metal-liquid or metal-solid interfaces. The reflected energy depends mainly on the ratios of certain properties of the matter (e.g., impedance = density × velocity). Defects like cracks, shrinkage cavities, lack of fusion, pores, bonding faults can be easily detected by this method. Inclusions and other inhomogeneities in the metal can also be detected due to partial reflection or scattering of the ultrasonic waves. This widely used NDT method has many applications like defining bond characteristics, measurement of thickness of components, estimation of corrosion and determination of physical properties, structure, grain size and elastic constants.

Ultrasonic inspection is mostly carried out at frequencies between 1 to 25 MHz. The inspection system includes:

(1) An electronic flaw detector having a sweep circuit, pulse generator, clock circuit and a cathode ray tube.
(2) A transducer (probe or search unit) having a piezoelectric crystal that emits a beam of ultrasonic waves when bursts of alternating voltages are applied to it.
(3) A couplant to transfer energy of the ultrasonic waves to the test piece (material).

Ultrasonic inspection is used for quality control and materials inspection in many industries. In-service ultrasonic inspection for preventive maintenance is used for detecting impending failure of rail-road rolling stock axles, mill rolls, earth moving equipment, mining equipment, welded pipe lines in chemical and nuclear plants, boilers, pressure vessels, nozzle welds etc.

For successful application of ultrasonic inspection, the inspection system must be suitable for the type of inspection being done and the operator must be sufficiently trained and experienced. If either of these pre-requisites is not met, there is a possibility of gross error in interpretation of results.

Characteristics of Ultrasonic Waves

In many respects, a beam of ultrasound is similar to a beam of light, both are waves and obey a general wave equation. Each travels at a characteristic velocity in a given homogeneous medium a velocity that depends on the properties of the medium and not on the properties of waves. Like a beam of light, ultrasonic beams are reflected from surfaces, refracted when they cross a boundary between two substances that have different characteristic sound velocities, and diffracted at edges or around obstacles.

Types of ultrasonic waves: Ultrasonic waves are classified on the basis of the mode of vibration of the particles of the medium with respect to the direction of propagation of the waves, namely longitudinal, transverse and surface waves.

Longitudinal Waves: These are called compression waves. In this type of ultrasonic wave, alternate compression and rarefaction zones are produced by vibration of particles parallel to the direction of propagation of the wave. Because of its easy generation and detection, this type of ultrasonic wave is most widely used in ultrasonic testing. Almost all of the ultrasonic energy used for the testing of materials originates in this mode and then is converted to other modes for special test applications. This type of waves can propagate in solids, liquids and gases.

Transverse Waves: This type of ultrasonic wave is called a transverse or shear wave because the direction of particle displacement is at right angles or transverse to the direction of propagation. For all practical purposes, transverse waves can only propagate in solids.

Surface or Rayleigh Waves: Surface waves were first described by Rayleigh and that is why they are called Rayleigh waves. These waves can travel only along the surface bounded on one side by strong elastic forces of the solid and on the other side by nearly non-existent elastic forces between gas molecules. The waves have a velocity of approximately 90% of that of an equivalent shear wave in the same material and these can propagate only in a region no thicker than about one wavelength below the surface of the material.

Types of Transducers, Probes/Sensors: Conventionally, ultrasonic waves are generated by piezoelectric transducers that convert high frequency electrical signals into mechanical vibrations. These mechanical vibrations form a wavefront, which is coupled to the component being inspected through the use of a suitable medium (couplant). Several wave modes can be used for inspection depending upon the orientation and location of discontinuities that exist. The three most common piezoelectric materials used are quartz, lithium sulphate and polarized ceramics. The most common ceramics are barium titanate, lead metaniobate and lead zironate titanate. The most important characteristics of ultrasonic probes are sensitivity, resolution, dead zone and near field effects.

Ultrasonic Flaw Detector: The most common technique employed is the pulse echo technique. The basic equipment comprises of an ultrasound pulse generator, a receiver, and its amplification and display system. Depending on the display of information, pulse echo equipment can be sub-divided into three groups namely A-scan, B-scan and C-scan.

Test Techniques: Techniques of ultrasonic testing are either of the contact type or the immersion type. In the contact type, the probe is placed in direct contact with the test system with a thin liquid film used as couplant for better transmission of ultrasonic waves into the test specimen. In the immersion method, a waterproof probe is used at some distance from the test specimen and the ultrasonic beam is transmitted into the material through a water path or water column. Contact techniques use normal beam techniques, angle beam techniques and surface wave techniques. Immersion testing techniques are mostly used in the laboratory and for large installations doing automatic ultrasonic testing.

Ultrasonic Testing of Weldments

There are two aspects that distinguish ultrasonic testing of welds from UT of other products like forgings, castings, pipes etc. They are (a) area of interest is well defined and limited (weld and heat affected zone) and (b) knowledge of a specific set of defects whose probable location and orientation is known. Most welds fall into one of the following categories: (1) Butt weld (2) Tee-weld and (3) Nozzle weld. Various butt weld configurations are shown in Fig. 8.

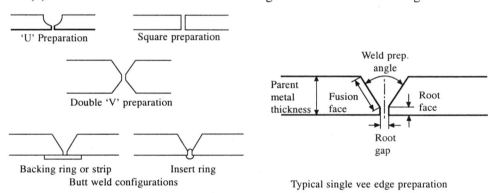

Fig. 8 Various butt weld configurations and terminology

Typical ultrasonic testing procedure for the examination of weld root and weld body is shown in Fig. 9. Typical pattern of indications where a weld defect is encountered is shown in Fig. 10, while Fig. 11 gives the methods for angle beam examination of various locations in a single vee weld joint. Method of examination for other joint configuratins such as double vee, nozzle and tee joints is detailed in Fig. 12.

Welds of certain materials like austenitic stainless steel and nickel based alloys pose serious problems for ultrasonic testing. These problems are primarily due to the acoustic anisotropy of these materials and the cast structure of the weld. Heavy scattering of the ultrasonic beam, false indications and wrong judgment of position and size of the defect can be encountered in these materials. This results from heavy attenuation of the beam as well as "noise" signals reaching the probe. The combined effect of these, results in loss of sensitivity and low signal to noise ratio.

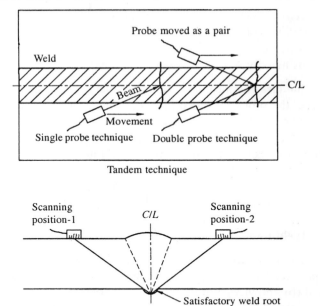

Fig. 9 Ultrasonic test scanning methods for weld inspection

These problems are greatly minimised by the utilisation of longitudinal angle beam probes for such applications.

RADIOGRAPHIC TESTING

Radiography is based on the differential absorption of short wavelength radiations such as X-rays and gamma rays on their passage through matter because of differences in density and variations in thickness or differences in absorption characteristics. The principle of radiographic examination is shown in Fig. 13. A shadow projection is obtained on a detector which is normally a grey level image with varying grey tones depending on the quantum of radiation received at that point. The source of radiation can be X-rays, gamma rays, neutrons, protons or electrons. X and gamma rays are the most commonly used source of radiation. The detector can be photographic films, image intensifiers or scintillator screens/counters. However, double-coated, fine-grain, high-contrast industrial X-ray films are the most widely used means of detecting the transmitted

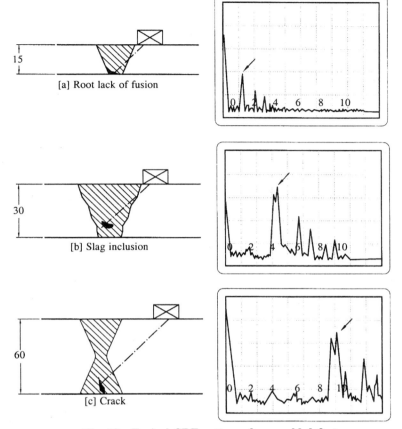

Fig. 10   Typical CRT patterns from weld defects

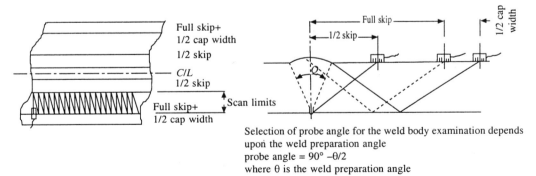

Selection of probe angle for the weld body examination depends upon the weld preparation angle

probe angle = 90° −θ/2

where θ is the weld preparation angle

Fig. 11   Angle beam examination of a single vee joint weld

radiation. Conventional radiography is the most widely used method for the inspection of welds. Radiography is the best method for the detection of volumetric defects such as porosities, slag inclusions and other defects such as crater cracks, lack of penetration and incomplete fusion.

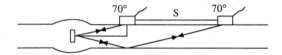

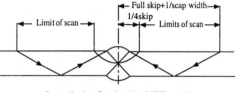

Root scan for double vee welds
$$S = 2(t - d) \tan \theta$$
where θ = probe angle, S = distance between
probe indices, d = depth of aiming point
and t = specimen thickness

Scan limits for double VEE-weld

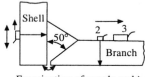

Examination of nozzle weld

Examination of nozzle welds
Scan 1 & 2 to determine
thickness of the shell and branch, lamination
in shell and branch, lack of fusion of shell
wall and weld body defects
scan 3-lack of side wall fusion and weld
body defects

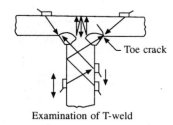

Examination of T-weld

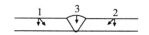

Scanning positions for double 'V' weld

Scanning positions for single 'V' weld

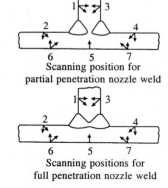

Scanning position for
partial penetration nozzle weld

Scanning positions for
full penetration nozzle weld

Fig. 12   Normal and angle beam examination of various weld configurations

Geometric factors in Radiography

Since a radiograph is a two dimensional representation of a three dimensional object, the radiographic images of most test pieces are somewhat distorted in size and shape as compared to the actual test piece. The severity of distortion depends primarily on source size (focal spot size for X-ray sources), source to object and source-to-film distances and position and orientation of the test piece with respect-to-source and film.

In conventional radiography, the position of a flaw within the volume of a test piece can not be determined exactly with a single radiograph, since depth parallel to the radiation beam is not

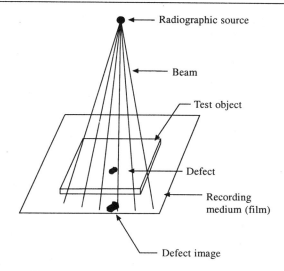

Fig. 13   **Principle of radiographic inspection**

recorded. However, techniques like stereo radiography, tomography and double-exposure parallax methods can be used to locate flaws more exactly within the test-piece volume.

Sources

Radiography has been used for years in evaluating welds and standard radiographic techniques have been well documented. Today we have X-ray machines with a maximum output voltage of 450 kV and 15 mA tube current. Such machines can be used for the examination of steel up to thickness of 120 mm. Apart from X-rays, isotopic sources emitting gamma rays also find extensive application. The main advantage of a gamma ray source is its simplicity of apparatus, compactness and portability. It does not require cooling of the power supply and is thus ideal for field applications. However, the main disadvantage of these sources is that they decay with time and hence require replacement. Commonly used gamma sources are Cobalt-60, Iridium-192, Caesium-137 and Thulium-170.

Gamma ray sources are housed in protective containers made of lead, depleted uranium or other dense materials like tungsten that absorb gamma rays, thus providing protection from exposure to radiation. Two types of containers are generally used. One type incorporates a conical plug that is swung away from the enclosed radioactive source to permit radiation to escape. This type is referred to as a radioisotope camera. The second type incorporates a remote controlled mechanical or pneumatic positioner that moves the encapsulated radioactive source out of the container and into a predetermined position where it remains until exposure is completed, the source is then returned to the container again by remote control. Remote control of the positioner allows the operator to remain at a safe distance from the source while manipulating the capsule out of and into the protective container.

Apart from improved equipment, far more is known today about the art of making good radiographs, the factors which control contrast and sensitivity and the limitations of radiography in what it can detect. Various codes have been evolved for the evaluation of radiographs. Sets of reference radiographs showing the appearance of weld and casting defects of different metal thicknesses are commercially available which are extremely valuable for instructional purposes also. ASTM E 99 deals with reference radiographs for steel welds. The International Institute of Welding has also brought out such reference radiographs for steel weldments up to 125 mm.

Radiographic Sensitivity

The sensitivity and quality of radiographs is normally judged by image quality indicators (IQI). Both wire and plaque type indicators are available today. These IQIs are normally placed on the source side of the weld and should be of the same material as the weld. The quality of the radiographs is always quoted in terms of the amount of detail discernible in the image of the IQI. The sensitivity depends on the radiographic technique, the type of IQI used and the specimen thickness.

ASTM penetrameters of plaque and wire type are widely used, as shown in Fig. 14. In **UK** and other European countries wire type penetrameters are used. The plaque type penetrameters as per **ASTM E-142** have 2T, 1T and 4T diameter holes. In a wire type penetrameter, the wires are arranged by diameter ranging from 0.1 mm to 3.2 mm and all wires are of the same length. The wire material is chosen to match the material to be tested. In normal use, specifications will indicate the minimum the diameter of wire to be seen on a radiograph or a 2T hole, 1T hole or 4T hole depending on the application. Typical radiographic sensitivities to be achieved in various applications range from 0.5% to 4% of wall thickness.

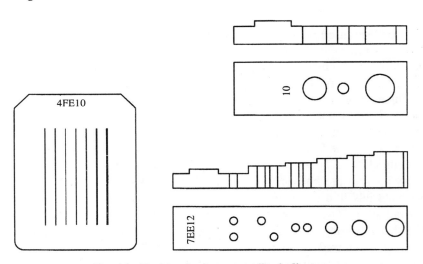

Fig. 14   Designs for image quality indicator

Industrial X-ray Films: In general, the films consist of an emulsion–gelatin containing a radiation-sensitive silver compound and a flexible transparent blue-tinted base. Emulsion on both sides (0.001 inch thick) doubles the amount of radiation-sensitive silver compound and thus increases the speed. Where highest visibility of detail is required, film with emulsion on one side is preferred. When X-rays or gamma rays strike the grains of the sensitive silver compound in the emulsion, a change takes place in the physical structure of the grains. This change is of such a nature that it can not be detected by ordinary physical methods. However, when the exposed film is treated with a chemical solution (called a developer), a reaction takes place, causing the formation of black metallic silver. It is this silver suspended in the gelatin on both sides of the base that constitutes the image of the object. The selection of a film for radiography of any particular part depends on the thickness and material of the specimen and on the voltage range of the available X-ray machine. In addition, the choice is affected by the relative importance of high radiographic quality or short exposure time.

If high quality is the deciding factor, a slower and hence fine-grained film should be used. If short exposure times are essential, a faster film (or film-screen combination) can be used. Direct exposure films can be used with or without lead screens depending upon kV, time and geometry of the object. Fluorescent intensifying screens must be used in radiography requiring the highest possible photographic speed.

Film Viewing: To assess the radiograph and the sensitivity achieved, the radiograph is placed on an illuminated screen of appropriate brightness (luminescence) and the film is suitably masked to eliminate glare emanating from around the film or any part of the film having particularly low density. The diameter of the smallest wire or drilled hole which can be detected with certainty is taken as a measurement of the attained sensitivity. Good film viewing conditions are essential as it is possible to overlook information on the radiograph because of too high a film density of low illuminator luminance. The importance of relating illuminator luminescence to film density has been recognised by IIW Commission V-A (Radiography) which has brought out a recommendation that an illuminated radiograph should not be less than 30 and whenever possible 100 cdm^{-2} or greater. This minimum value requires illuminator luminance of 300 for a film density of 1, 300 cdm^{-2} for a film density of 2 and 30,000 cdm^{-2} for a film density of 3.

Radiographic Defect Evaluation: Generally, by radiography, one can recognise the nature of a defect and also measure its effective length and width parallel to the plane of the film but the through-thickness dimension (height) is less easy to determine. The distance of a defect from the surface can be found by stereometric methods. In principle, it is possible to measure the height of a defect from the density of the image on a radiograph using a microdensitometer. The densities determined from the micro densitometer trace can be converted into thickness either by absolute calculations using the film characteristics and exposure curves, or by having an appropriate step wedge on the radiograph along side the weld.

Halmshaw has found that for general weld defects occupying 10 to 30% of the thickness, this method can be applied with an accuracy of 8%. However, this method has not been found suitable for planar defects such as cracks. While defects such as porosities, lack of fusion, lack of penetration, voids, inclusions etc. in welds and hot tears, shrinkage cavities etc. in castings can be easily detected, the detectability of cracks by radiography is influenced by the position and size of the crack, the incident angle of X-rays, the distance between the film and the crack, size of the focal spot, sensitivity of films, screens and so on. Good amount of work has been done on crack detectability and sensitivity. Conventional radiography is being widely used for the inspection of a variety of weldments, castings and complete assemblies in various industries.

Applications: Radiography is widely used in evaluating different type of weld joints and configurations for their integrity.

Butt Weld: Butt joints on the flat plates are usually made with edge preparation of single "*V*", double "*V*" or square. Inspection techniques for butt welds with **ASTM** penetrameter are shown in Fig. 15.

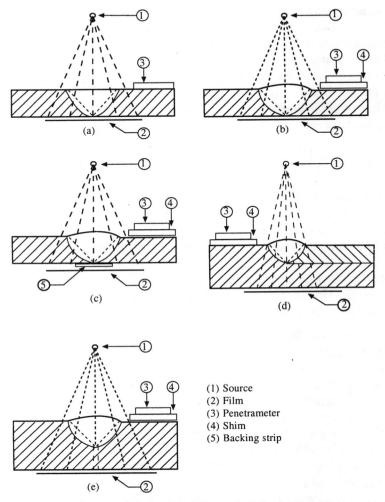

(1) Source
(2) Film
(3) Penetrameter
(4) Shim
(5) Backing strip

Fig. 15   Radiography configurations for butt welds

Fillet Welds: Fillet welds are generally made with square or bevel edge preparation. The exposure set up for different fillet joints are shown in Fig. 16.

Fusion welds on Pipes and Cylindrical objects: Depending upon the size and accessibility on either side of the pipe, the following techniques are recommended.

Single Wall Penetration: Single wall penetration method with source inside and film outside or vice versa is shown in Fig. 17. The ideal position to locate the source is the centre of the pipe which enables coverage of the entire circumferential weld in a single panoramic exposure.

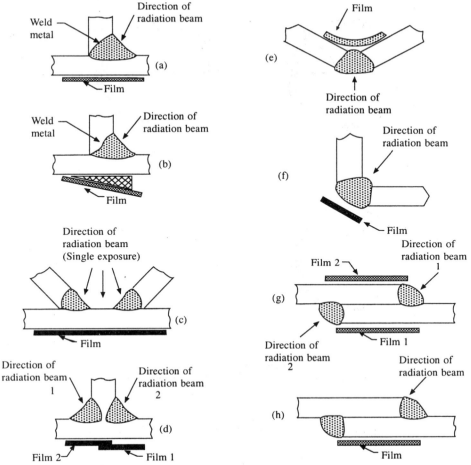

Fig. 16   **Direction of radiographic exposure for various fillet weld configurations, (a) Single-fillet T joint (b) Single-fillet T joint with equalizing wedge (c) Two adjacent single-fillet joints radiographed simultaneously. (d) Double-fillet T joint (e) Corner joint with film positioned at the inside surface. (f) Corner joint with film positioned at the outside surface. (g) & (h) Alternative views for double welded lap joint.**

Butt welds of thick walled pipes are radiographed with source located either in the centre or eccentrically. To facilitate radiographic inspection of thick walled steam pressure pipe welds, usually a hole is provided adjacent to the circumferential weld for insertion of radioisotope inside the pipe. (Fig. 17(d)).

Double wall Penetration: Both film and the source are placed external to the pipe when there is no access to the inside of the pipe. Here the radiation beam passes through both the walls but only the bottom weld image is evaluated. (Fig. 18).

Double wall Single Image: This technique is used for pipes with OD > 89 mm. The source is either placed on the top of the weld (superpositioned) technique or it is slightly offset. Degree

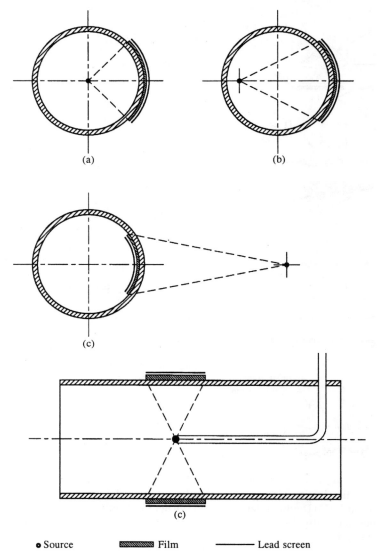

● Source   ▨▨▨▨ Film   ——— Lead screen

Fig. 17   Single wall penetration

of offset depends on the SFD (source-film distance) chosen. The radiation source is placed at a minimum SFD compatible with source size and wall thickness of the pipe. The film is wrapped on the portion further from the radiation source. Overlapping of the images is avoided by placing the source offset by about 10 degrees from the plane of the weld.

Double Wall Double Image: This technique is specially suited for smaller pipes up to 89 mm diameter. The source is placed offset to the weld, the inclination being 10 to 15 degrees to avoid the overlap of top and bottom weld images. A minimum of two exposures are taken, the second one after rotating the weld through 90 degrees. Both the top and bottom images are recorded on film with suitable separation.

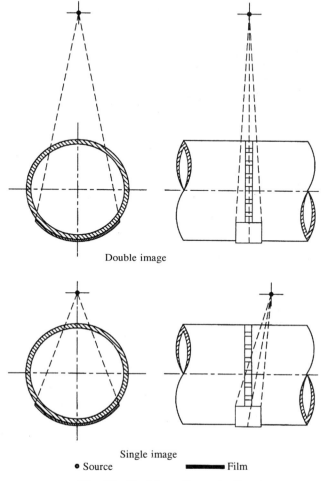

Double image

Single image

● Source   ▬▬▬ Film

Fig. 18   Double wall penetration

Conclusion

Non-destructive testing plays a crucial role in early detection of defects and the subsequent remedial measures during various inspection stages of welded components to assess their structural integrity.

Further Reading:

1. Welding Handbook, Vol. 1, Chapters 11, 12, and 15, American Welding Society, 550, N.W. Lejeune road, Miami, U.S.A.
2. American Society of Metals Handbook, Vol. 6 and Vol. 11, ASM International The Materials Information Society, Materials Park, Ohio, U.S.A.
3. Takeshi Kanazava and Abert Kobayashi. S., Significance of defects in welded structures, Proceedings of the Japan-U.S Seniinar, University of Tokyo press, 1974.
4. Halmshaw. R, Non-destructive Testing, Metallurgy and Materials Science Services, 1987.

13. Quality Assurance and Welding Qualifications

B.S.C. Rao

Quality Assurance Division, IGCAR, Kalpakkam 603 102

QUALITY

The term quality can be defined as conformance of a material or product to drawings and specifications.

This is an outdated definition and does not meet the objectives of the term quality. The product may conform to drawings and specifications but may not serve the purpose satisfactorily. To-day quality means ability of a product to serve the purpose reliably with minimal maintenance. With the advent of quality movement in many countries in the recent past, the most accepted definition world over of the term quality is as given below:

"Quality may be defined as the totality of features and characteristics of a product or service that bears its ability to satisfy a given need".

QUALITY ASSURANCE

Quality Assurance (QA) is a term related to the efforts of manufacturer/supplier in order to create confidence with the clients that the supplied product will perform intended service satisfactorily over the period of design life. The term Quality Asurance can be defined as all those well planned and systematic actions taken by a supplier or service organisation to instill confidence in the minds of buyers that the product or service is made as per a standard and it serves the purpose well.

In pursuance of Quality Assurance in the fabrication of welded structures, the following activities are to be carried out by the manufacturer. This topic explains the specific activities, called "Welding qualifications" in the implementation of a Quality Assurance programme.

1. Approval of detailed drawings by the client.
2. Approval of raw materials and consumables by client.
3. Preparation of Q.A. Plan, manufacturing and N.D.T. procedures
4. Calibration of testing equipment.
5. Qualification of welding consumables, welding procedure and welders.
6. Qualification of NDT Personnel.

7. Quality control during production welding.
8. Non-Destructive Testing (NDT) of welds.
9. Quality Control during Post Weld Heat Treatment PWHT).
10. NDT after PWHT.
11. Hydraulic testing or load testing of welded structures
12. Leak testing of welds.
13. Documentation.

In the above mentioned Q.A. activities, qualification of welding consumables, welding procedures and welders are most important steps which facilitate the quality of production welding.

WELDING CONSUMABLE QUALIFICATION

Material selection for a component is one of the design criteria. The material is selected based on its physical characteristics such as strength, ductility, fatigue, resistance to service temperature, creep resistance etc. and its compatibility and corrosion resistance to the fluids handled in servic;e. Once the parent material is specified for a welded structure, selection of appropriate welding consumable to join the material is done such that the weld produced will be better than or equal to parent material in strength, with specified ductility, impact strength and corrosion resistance to fluids handled in service. Apart from the above factors the weld metal produced should be sound and metallurgically merge with parent material. Factors like chemistry, coefficient of thermal expansion, dilution of elements and metallurgical structure of parent metal and weld metal are considered while selecting the welding consumable.

Once welding consumable is specified to a particular standard, it is to be ensured that the welding consumable manufactured in a factory should conform to that standard.

The manufacturer of the welding electrodes has to qualify each lot of welding electrodes produced with one set of production variables such as flux mix and core wire composition and issue certificate with test results conforming to the standard.

The covered electrode is qualified by depositing from each lot of electrodes weld pads for testing as shown in Fig. 1, which indicates the testing scheme for qualifying steel weld metal as per the 2004 ASME Boiler and Pressure Vessel Code. The tests performed on the deposited weld metal are 1) Chemical Analysis, 2) Radiography to assess the soundness, 3) All weld tensile test and impact test to assess mechanical properties and 4) Fillet weld test to assess usability characteristics.

All the above tests should meet the acceptance criteria specified in the standard. For Chromium, Nickel and Chromium Nickel bare electrodes and solid welding rods the qualification is based on chemical analysis of the as manufactured filler metal.

WELDING PROCEDURE QUALIFICATION

Though it is possible to make welds for the given set of materials and working conditions, in actual production welding there are many factors which influence the weld metal quality. These are:

1. Joint configuration.

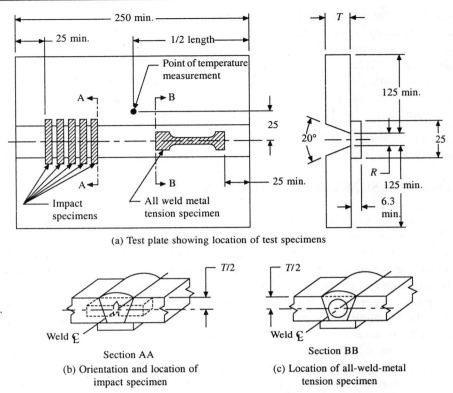

(a) Test plate showing location of test specimens

Weld $\mathcal{L}$

Section AA

(b) Orientation and location of
impact specimen

Weld $\mathcal{L}$

Section BB

(c) Location of all-weld-metal
tension specimen

Fig. 1   Typical details of test assembly for soundness and mechanical tests of welding consumables for steel (Reprinted from ASME BPVC 2004, Section II-Part C, by permission of the American Society of Mechanical Engineers. All rights reserved)

2. Base metal chemistry.
3. Filler metal chemistry.
4. Position of welding.
5. Pre-heating.
6. Post heating.
7. Type of gas used for shielding and purging.
8. Electrical characteristics and
9. Welding Process.

For the given set of conditions of the welding in the shop floor one should "prove that the weld produced under fabricating conditions should at least meet the strength of the base metal and should have specified ductility and impact strength. This proving is done in welding procedure qualification. For the given set of fabricating conditions the manufacturer of welded structures should write down the welding procedure specification before undertaking the procedure qualification. After preparing the welding procedure specification, the manufacturer should qualify the procedure by welding a plate or pipe test coupon. The tests performed on the weld test coupon are:

1. Transverse tensile tests (2nos.) to meet the base metal minimum tensile value.
2. Transverse root bends (2nos.) and transverse face bends (2nos.) to prove the ductility and soundness of the weld and,
3. One set of impact test at specified temperature, where the base metal is specified for notch toughness in service.

The American Society for Mechanical Engineers have specified in ASME Code Section IX, the type and number of tests to be done and the range of thickness qualified for a given size of plate test coupon used for procedure qualification.

Procedure qualification done on plate is valid for pipe of any diameter and the range of thickness qualified is given in the ASME Code. Procedure qualification on pipe is valid for plate welding within the range of thickness qualified. The procedure qualification on a groove weld is valid for fillet weld but not vice versa. Groove weld procedure qualification on plate or pipe qualifies fillet welding of any size on plate or pipe without limitation on thickness or diameter. Fillet weld procedure qualification on plate or pipe qualifies only fillet welding on plate or pipe respectively.

Any procedure qualification is valid for a given set of parameters such as joint configuration, base metalcomposition, filler metal composition, position of welding, preheating, post heating, type of gas used for shielding and purging, process of welding and electrical characteristics.

Variation in the above parametes from the procedure qualified which influence the strength and ductility of the weld are called essential variables.

Variation in the parameters which influence impact properties are called supplementary essential variables. Change in essential variables and supplementary essential variables in the parameters call for requalification of welding procedure.

While essential variables are applicable for all materials, the supplementary essential variables are applicable only for the materials selected for notch toughness requirements in the service.

The variables which do not influence the weld metal strength, ductility and toughness are non-essentail variables which do not call for requalification of a procedure qualified.

When a welding procedure is qualified by a manufacturer he should document the procedure details and test results in the Procedure Qualification Record (PQR). Once a procedure is qualified and documented, the manufacturer need not requalify the same unless otherwise essential or supplementary essential variables call for a different welding procedure.

WELDER PERFORMANCE QUAIFICATION

In welding performance qualification, the welder's ability and skill to make a sound weld, following a qualified procedure is verified. This is done by giving a test to the welder on a pipe or plate as applicable to the job. The soundness of the weld made by him is checked by either radiography of test coupon or by two transverse bend tests, one on root side and the other on face side of the weld. The welder qualified on pipe welding is qualified to do plate welding but not vice versa.

Since varying degrees of the skill is required to make sound welds in different positions of welding, with different types of welding consumables, in different welding processes and techniques, with different electrical characteristics and different material configuration such as plate and pipe, all these variations form the essenial variables which call for requalification of a welder. The ASME - Section IX specifies the range of thickness and diameters qualified by a welder for groove and fillet welds in terms of thickness of the test coupon and diameter of pipe welded.

The welder who makes the successful welding procedure test is thereby qualified for the welding process and procedure. Other welders who are to be employed on the same job are separately performance tested and qualified. A qualified welder's skill will be consistent if only he is continuously employed on the welding process in which he is qualified. Renewal of qualification of a welder or welding operator is required in the following conditions:

1. When he is not employed on the specific process, viz., metal arc, gas, submerged arc etc. for a period of 6 months.
2. When there is a specific reason to question his ability to make welds that meet the specification, the qualification which supports the welding he is doing is revoked.

CONCLUSION

The qualifications of the welding consumable, welding procedure and welder performance are the most important activities to ensure the quality or welds. Once these activities are performed properly by the manufacturer it greatly facilitates the manufacturer to implement Quality Assurance on welded structures.

REFERENCE

ASME BPVC 2004, Section IX, Qualification standards for welding and brazing procedures, welders, brazers and welding and brazing operators.

14. Leak and Pressure Testing of Welds and Field NDT Experience

M. Palaniappan

Quality Assurance Division, IGCAR, Kalpakkam 603 102

1 INTRODUCTION

Leak testing is one of the non-destructive testing methods used for detection and location of leaks in either pressurized or evacuated systems and components as a result of a presure differential between the two regions. The word "leak" refers to the physical hole that exists and does not refer to the quantity of fluid passing through that hole. A leak may be a crack, crevice, fissure, hole or passageway that admits fluids or lets fluid escape. The word "leakage" refers to the flow of fluid through a leak without regard to the physical size of the hole through which flow occurs. "Leakage rate" refers to the rate of fluid flow per unit of time under a given set of conditions, and is expressed in units of mass per unit of time.

Leaks are a special type of flaw that can have tremendous importance where they influence the safety or performance of engineering systems. Leak testing is performed for three basic reasons:

1. To prevent material leakage loss, which interferes with system operation
2. To prevent environmental contamination hazards caused by accidental leakage
3. To detect unreliable components and those whose leakage rates exceed acceptance standards.

The end purpose of leak testing is to ensure reliability and serviceability of components and to prevent premature failure of systems containing fluids under pressure or vacuum.

The term "minimum detectable leak" refers to the smallest hole or discrete passage that can be detected and "minimum detectable leakage rate" refers to the smallest detectable fluidflow rate, generally known as sensitivity of the test system. The sensitivity of the instrument is the amount of leakage required for a leak testing instrument to give a minimum detectable signal. The instrument sensitivity is independent of test conditions, but when an instrument is applied to a test, the sensitivity of the test depends on existing conditions of pressure, temperature and fluid flow.

1.1 Leak Testing Units

The leak is measured by how much leakage it will pass under a given set of conditions, as leakage will vary with conditions. At a given temperature, the product of pressure and volume of a given quantity of gas is proportional to its mass. Therefore, leakage rate is often expressed as the product of some measure of pressure and volume per unit of time. The basic SI units used in leak testing are: pressure—Pascal ($1N/m^2$), volume in m^3 and time in seconds.

The fluid quantity can thus be expressed as Pascal cubic meter (Pa·m^3) and the fluid leakage rate as Pascal cubic meter per sec (Pa. m^3/s) or in terms of std. cc/s (0.1 Pa.m^3/s). SI unit for vacuum is Pa (132 Pa is 1 mm of Hg = 1 torr).

1.2   Types of Leaks

There are two basic types of leaks – real leaks and virtual leaks. A real leak is an essentially localized leak – that is, a discrete passage through which fluid may flow. Such a leak may take the form of a tube, a crack, an orifice etc. The flow can be of permeation type or diffusion type. Virtual leaks are leaks that involve the gradual de-sorption of gases from surfaces or components within a vacuum system.

2   LEAK TESTING METHODS

Leak testing methods can be classified according to the pressure and fluid in the system. The commonly used methods of leak testing of systems at pressure are (i) Pressure change, (ii) Acoustic, (iii) Bubble leak testing, (iv) Flow detection, (v) Specific gas detectors, (vi) Quantity loss determination etc. Leak testing is also performed by creating vacuum inside the component and applying the tracer gas on the other side to indicate the location and quantity of leak. The major factors that determine the choice of the leak testing methods are the physical characteristics of the system, the tracer fluid, the size of the anticipated leak and the reason for the testing. Leak testing can be employed for the variety of components and different ways ranging from a small hermetically sealed component to very large vessels and piping systems. If the volume under test is filled with fluid at a pressure higher than the atmospheric pressure, then the method is called pressure leak testing method. If the volume is evacuated below the atmospheric pressure, then the test involved is called vacuum method. It is convenient under certain circumstances to carry out vacuum tests.

2.1   Pressure Change Method

The component or assembly is either pressurized or evacuated to a known value and then sealed. After a known time of hold, the pressure drop or pressure rise, if any, is measured, while maintaining the volume and temperature constant. The leakage rate can be arrived at from these. Atmospheric air or nitrogen are often used as pressurizing fluids in the leak testing. Their fluid pressure serves to create a pressure differential, which causes the pressurizing gases to flow, by various mechanisms, through leaks. In general, the higher the differential pressure, the greater the rate of leakage.

The leakage rate Q (*Pa.* m^3/s) can be calculated using the relationship

$$Q = (P_1 - P_2) \cdot V/\Delta t$$

at constant volume (V in m^3) and temperature (T in K). ($P_1 - P_2$) is the pressure difference (in absolute) and Δt is the time of hold (sec). Depending upon the leak tightness required and the sensitivity of the differential pressure gauge, the time required for the reading of pressure drop varies. It should also be noted that the sensitivity depends on the volume of the component also.

The above is valid under the conditions that volume and the temperature do not change during the test, as it is a short duration test. When the same is conducted under varying temperature conditions which require measurement of both gauge pressure and temperature, and the barometric pressure is assumed to be one standard atmosphere (101.3 kPa.), the pressure loss per unit of time is then determined from the initial gauge pressure P_1 and temperature T_1 and the final gauge pressure P_2 and final temperature T_2. by the equation:

$$\Delta P/\Delta t = [P_1 - P_2(T_1/T_2)]/\Delta t, \text{ where } P_1, P_2 \text{ and } T_1, T_2 \text{ are absolute.}$$

If they are measured as pressure in *kPa*, temperature in °C, and time in seconds, then the equation will be:

$$\Delta P/\Delta t = [(P_1 + 101) - (P_2 + 101) (T_1 + 273)/(T_2 + 273)/\Delta t - (kPa/s)$$

$$Q = (\Delta P/\Delta t) \cdot V$$

2.1.1 Evacuated Systems

Any pressure less than standard atmospheric pressure (101 kPa) is some form of vacuum. An enclosure is said to be under vacuum if its internal pressure is less than that of the surrounding atmosphere. The vessels and components to be tested under vacuum should be designed for vacuum application. While designing such vessels care has to be taken to provide vacuum compatible weld joints, material of construction to minimize outgassing etc.

The vacuum hold test or pressure rise test is a pressure change leakage measurement test performed on a system evacuated below atmospheric pressure. It is mostly done by evacuating the vessel to an absolute pressure in the range from 10 Pa to 1 mPa (10^{-1} to 10^{-5} mm of Hg or torr). The leakage rate test is performed by isolating the system under test after it has been evacuated to the required absolute pressure (vacuum). Then the pressure and the surface temperature of the system are observed for a specific time to determine the rate of pressure rise per unit of time for the system. Fig. 1 shows the schematic of the test set-up on smaller test systems. The leakage sensitivity increases with the decrease of volume and however, the sensitivity diminishes as the size or volume increases. In addition, the location of the leak cannot be detected by this test. Moreover, the sensitivity of the leakage rate test increases directly with elapsed time during the test.

2.2 Bubble Emission Techniques

When one fluid gets trapped in another fluid, a bubble is formed. Most common examples are air bubbles in water and soap bubbles in air. Even small pressure differences are enough to form bubbles with liquids of low surface tension. This is taken due advantage of in selection of liquid and to increase the sensitivity.

In this type of test, a gas pressure differential is established across a pressure boundary to be tested. A test liquid is then placed in contact with the lower pressure side of the pressure boundary. The gas leakage through the pressure boundary can then be detected by observation of bubbles formed in the detection liquid at the exit points of leakage through the pressure boundary. This method provides immediate indication of the existence and location of large

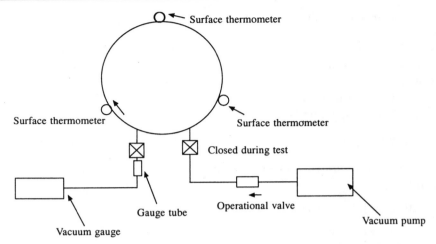

Surface thermometer

Surface thermometer

Surface thermometer

Closed during test

Gauge tube

Operational valve

Vacuum gauge

Vacuum pump

Fig. 1 Arrangement of equipment for pressure rise leakage rate testing of an evacuated system (vacuum retention test)

leaks (10^{-3} to 10^{-5} Pa m^3/s). Somewhat longer inspection time periods may be needed for detection of small leaks (10^{-5} to 10^{-6} Pa m^3/s) where the bubble indication forms slowly. In bubble leak testing, the rate of bubble formation, size of bubbles formed, and rate of growth in size of individual bubbles provide means for estimating the size of leaks. The bubbles are continuously supplied by gas and bubble formation or flow rate is proportional to the square of the pressure.

Bubble detection techniques can be divided into three major classifications:

1. Liquid Immersion Techique – the pressurized test object is submerged in the test liquid. Bubbles then form at the exit point of the leakage and tend to rise towards the surface of the immersion bath.
2. Film Application Technique – a thin layer of test liquid is flowed over the low pressure surface of the test object; best suited for large volume / surface area components. For detection of small leaks, the test liquid should from a thin, continuous, wetted film covering all areas to be examined.
3. Foam Application Technique – used for detection of large leaks in which the applied liquid forms thick suds or foam. When large leaks are encountered, the rapid escape of gas "blows a hole" through the foam blanket, revealing the leak location.

Sub-classifications such as:

1. Controlled heating of sealed objects and small components to cause internal gas expansion. This increases the pressure differential to aid gas flow outward.
2. Applying partial vacuum above the surface of the test liquid also results in increased pressure differential across the system boundaries. Refer Fig. 2 (vacuum chamber technique)

Oils are a more sensitive medium than water. Because of this, it is common to test electrical components in a bath of hot glycerin. When testing by reducing the pressure above the liquid, several precautions must be observed, as the reduced pressure brings the liquid closer to boiling

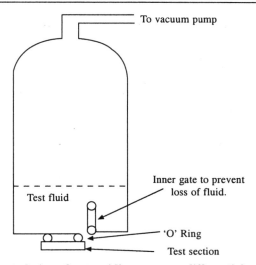

To vacuum pump

Inner gate to prevent
loss of fluid.

Test fluid

'O' Ring

Test section

Fig. 2   Vacuum chamber technique for providing pressure differential across leaks during bubble

point. The test vessel must be thoroughly cleaned to increase surface wetting, to prevent bubbles clinging to its surface and to prevent contamination of the fluid. If water is used, it must be of distilled or de-ionized grade. A small amount of wetting agent normally is added to water to reduce surface tension.

Immersion testing may be used on any internally pressurized component that would not be damaged by the test liquid. Bubble testing methods are quite inexpensive and require little operator skill.

Vacuum box technique is used for detection of leaks via through-thickness discontinuities in welds and pressure boundaries of systems containing air at atmospheric pressure. Different forms of vacuum boxes can be designed and made as per the configurations of the area to be tested to accommodate joints like corner joint, lap joints, circumferential pipe and tank joints etc.

2.3   Ultrasonic Leak Detection

In this method, use is made of the fact that any gas at high pressure leaking out into the atmosphere produces acoustic disturbances in the air in a range of different frequencies. High wave intensities are observed to be produced in the ultrasonic range of 40 kHz. The detector comprises of the probe or a receiving transducer which picks up the ultrasound and converts it into an electrical signal, a pre-amplifier and an amplifier to amplify the low signal, a converter circuit and a display system to indicate the amplified output.

The sensitivity of the system depends on the pressure of the gas used, the distance of the leak from the probe and the sensitivity of the circuit. The system must be calibrated with a standard leak. This method can be applied on (1) pipelines carrying chemicals. (2) air conditioning units, (3) pressurized cables, (4) boilers, (5) gas cylinders etc.

2.4 Halogen and Sulphur Hexa-Fluoride (SF 6) Detectors

2.4.1 Halogen-Diode Leak Detection

In the case of closed loop refrigeration systems there is a need for detection of leakage of freon and other refrigerant gases. Halogen detectors meet this requirement. In halogen-diode testing, a leak detector is used that responds to most of the gases containing chlorine, fluorine, bromine or iodine. Therefore, one of these halogen-compound gases is used as tracer. The most popular halogen tracer gases are the two refrigerant gases R-12 (dichlorodifluoromethane, CCl_2F_2) and R-22 (monochlorodifluoromethane, $CHClF_2$). Some common trade names for these refrigerant gases are Freon, Genetron, Isotron etc. When a vessel is pressurized with such a tracer gas or mixture of a halogen compound and air or nitrogen, the sniffing probe of the leak detector is used to locate the leak. Three types of halogen leak detectors used are: (1) the halide torch, (2) the heated anode halogen detector and (3) the electron capture detector.

The halide torch is used to locate leaks in systems pressurized with air containing halogen tracer gas. The halide torch consists of a burner connected to a tank of halide-free fuel such as acetylene gas or alcohol (Refer Fig. 3). Some of the air for combustion is drawn into the flame through a tube near the bottom of the burner, which heats a copper plate. A flexible extension of this air intake is a snifer tube used as a probe to locate leaks. When the open end of this tube passes near a halogen tracer gas leak, some of the gas is drawn into the flame. The flame is a pale blue if only air is pulled into the burner through the suction hose. If small amounts of vapour containing halogen compounds enter the suction tube, the flame turns green. The sensitivity of the halide torch is approximately 10^{-5} Pa m^3/s.

The heated anode halogen leak detector shown in Fig. 4 makes use of a red-hot platinum and ceramic heater element which emits positive ions. These ions are collected on a negatively charged cylindrical cathode to provide a leak signal current. The presence of small traces of halogen vapours increases the emission of positive ions markedly. It is this increase in positive-ion emission that is measured to indicate the presence of a leak.

The sensitivity of halogen detectors operating at atmospheric pressure is about 10^{-9} Pa.m^3/s, but this will vary depending on the specific gas that is used. All the detectors mentioned above, include a control unit and a probe through which air is drawn. When searching for leaks from an enclosure pressurized with a tracer gas, the probe tip is moved over joints and seams suspected of leaking. When the probe passes over or close to a leak, the tracer gas is drawn into the probe with air and through a sensitive element, where it is detected. The leak signal is either audible or visual.

The major advantage of these detectors are ready applicability to various types of refrigeration systems with adequate sensitivity. Other advantages are the simple construction, ruggedness, portability and low cost. They can be operated by unskilled personnel.

2.4.2 SF6 Detector

SF6 is a highly electronegative gas with a large electron capture cross section. It is also safe to handle, inert chemically and non-toxic in nature. The actual sensitive element is an electron capture detector employing a disc containing tritium as an anode-cum-beta emitter and a stainless

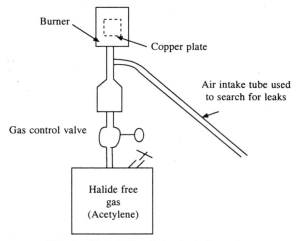

Fig. 3   Halide Torch for leak detection

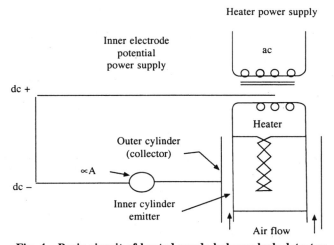

Fig. 4   Basic circuit of heated anode halogen leak detector

steel mesh at a negative potential with respect to the tritium source. The beta particles (electrons) continuously emanating from the tritium disc produce a large amount of ionisation in the region and the standing current is in the order of 10^{-9} A. When the detector cell volume contains some electronegative components like SF6, freon or oxygen, the electrons are captured and there is a reduction in the standing current. The schematic arrangement of the detector is shown in Fig. 5. This method is simple and the equipment also is inexpensive and portable. The sensitivity is limited by the background current due to atmospheric oxygen.

2.5   Thermal Conductivity Leak Detector

This utilises the altered thermal conductivity of the environment when a suitable search gas like

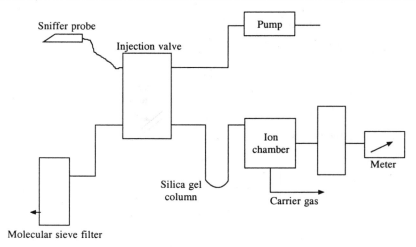

Fig. 5 **SF$_6$ detector**

hydrogen or helium from the leak is encountered. The heat is carried away from the thermistor. Thermistors are temperature dependent resistors with very large temperature coefficient of resistivity. Usually two identical thermistors are employed, one of them suitably isolated from the search gas entering the system and the other mounted in the path of sniffed air sample. Both the thermistors are electrically heated and form the two arms of a measuring bridge circuit. When the search gas coming out of the leak from a pressurised job is sampled by the sniffer, the bridge is unbalanced and the unbalanced voltage is amplified and indicated. The sensitivity of this detector is in the order of 10^{-6} Pa m^3/s. The advantages of these detectors are the simplicity of their construction, low cost, immunity to ambient temperature variations and small size. The disadvantages are the limited sensitivity and the hazards associated with the search gas.

2.6 Mass Spectrometer Leak Detection

The mass spectrometer helium leak detection (MSLD) is the most useful method in the accurate detection and quantification of minute leakage rates, of the order of 10^{-13} Pa m^3/s (10^{-12} std. cc per sec.). It is the most sensitive type of leak detector. MSLD systems consist of: (i) a mass spectrometer, (ii) a vacuum pumping system for pumping the spectrometer and associated accessories, (iii) a test inlet for connecting the test vessel or the calibrated leak, with provision for independent pumping and (iv) electronic control.

2.6.1 *Methods of Mass Spectrometer Leak Detection*

All methods of leak detection using a mass spectrometer leak detector involve passage of a tracer gas through a presumed leak from one side to the other side of a pressure boundary and subsequent detection of the tracer gas on this lower pressure side. The typical basic methods used in mass spectrometer leak testing include: tracer probe method (vacuum leak testing), detector probe method (sniffer testing), hood method, bell jar method, accumulation method, pressure-vacuum method etc.

2.6.1.1 Tracer Probe Method: This is one of the simplest methods of leak detection and is used to locate leaks. The mass spectrometer leak detector is connected to the internal volume of the evacuated test object (such as vessel or piping system) and a helium spray tracer probe is moved over the external surface to detect the specific location of leaks. The helium flow rate and the probe speed is so selected to avoid flooding the system. It is advisable to spray top joints first and then move to the lower joints. The schematic arrangement is shown in Fig. 6. This test is well suited for small volume components designed for vacuum and which can be evacuated by the vacuum system of the leak detector and systems having its own vacuum pumping arrangement.

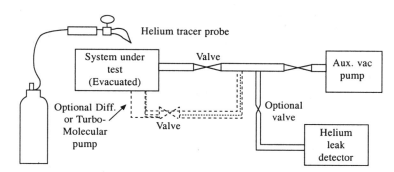

Fig. 6   Helium leak testing of evacuated vessel or system with tracer probe

2.6.1.2 Detector Probe Method: This method is useful when the test object is big and can withstand positive pressure. The test object is pressurized internally with helium or a gas mixture containing helium. The mass spectrometer leak detector is connected to the hose of a scanning probe that collects samples of gas leaking from the external surface into the surrounding atmosphere. The leaking helium from the test object along with surrounding air is sniffed into the detector and indicated. This method can be used to determine leak locations. The sensitivity of this method is generally less compared to the tracer probe method because of dilution of helium in the atmosphere. In practice, it is not possible to collect all the helium as the probe will be moving and the helium coming out will be always diffusing into air. It is therefore as a standard practice that all the welds will be covered with packets of polyethylene for a pre-determined period and probed with sniffer probe. The schematic arrangement is shown in Fig. 7.

2.6.1.3 Hood Method: In vacuum leak testing by hood method as shown in Fig. 8, the mass spectrometer leak detector is connected to the evacuated interior of the system under test. The test object or system is then placed under a hood or within a chamber containing helium gas or an air-helium mixture usually at atmospheric pressure. This method can be used to determine the total leakage rate of the system. However, it cannot be used to determine the specific location of leaks.

2.6.1.4 Bell Jar Method: In the Bell jar method of Fig. 9, sealed components filled with helium or a gas mixture containing helium are placed in an evacuated testing chamber. The mass

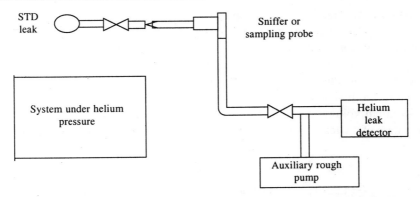

Fig. 7   Helium leak testing of pressurized vessel or system with detector probe

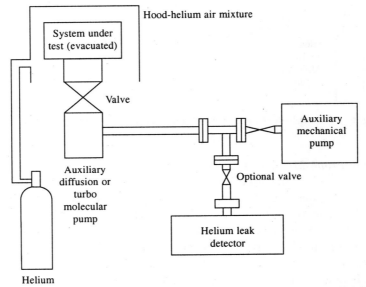

Fig. 8   Hood method for leak testing of evacuated components inserted into hood

spectrometer connected to this vacuum chamber detects helium leaking from any part of the surfaces of the sealed test objects in the vacuum chamber. This test does not permit location of leaks on the test object surfaces.

2.6.1.5   *Helium Bombing (Backfill) Method:* Leak tests are often required for small, hermetically sealed test objects that have an internal cavity, such as transistors, diodes, small relays, nuclear fuel elements etc. These components can be leak tested by subjecting them to an environment of high helium pressure prior to leak testing them in a small vacuum chamber connected to the detector. This method is usually referred to as bombing, or helium bombing, since the test objects are bombed with high helium pressure. The logic behind this method is as follows. If leaks are present in the test objects, the high pressure will force some helium into the part

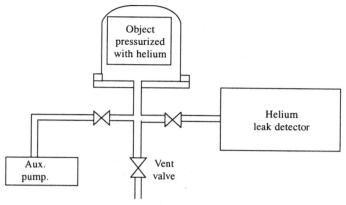

Fig. 9 **Leak testing of sealed components internally pressurized with helium tracer gas and enclosed in a bell jar**

through the leaks. When these parts are subsequently subjected to bell jar test, the helium will then flow from the leaks and be detected. The schematic arrangement is shown in Fig. 10.

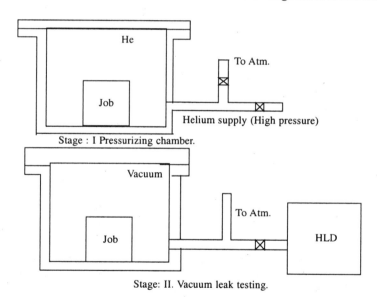

Stage : I Pressurizing chamber.

Stage: II. Vacuum leak testing.

Fig. 10   Helium bombing method

2.6.1.6   Accumulation Method: In the accumulation method of leak testing, the leaking helium tracer gas is allowed to collect for a period of time before being sampled by the leak detector. The device can be accommodated in a collection chamber as indicated in Fig. 11(a) or flexible shrouds fixed and collected over a small portion of the device as indicated by Fig. 11 (b). The accumulation method does not usually permit leak location. However, by sealing off small surface areas and accumulating tracer gas within the sealed volume, areas of leakage can be localized.

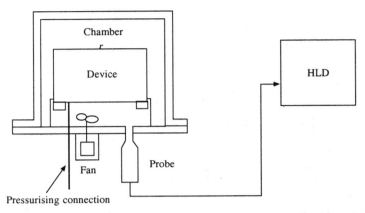

Fig. 11 **Accumulation Testing with sampling (Detector probe) probe. (a) Accumulation leak test, complete device in chamber**

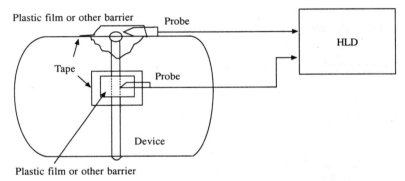

Fig. 11. (b) Accumulation Leak Test, flexible shroud over a small portion of device

2.6.2 Calibration

Calibration Leak Standards - The calibration leak standard may be either a permeation or a capillary type standard. Very small calibration leak standards are produced by flow through a capillary tube (capillary type) or by permeation through a membrane (normally glass, permeation type). The capillary tube may or may not have self-contained gas supply. A constant tracer-gas pressure must be maintained during calibration. Capillary tubes are available with leak rates ranging from about 10^{-3} to 10^{-8} Pa m^3/s (10^{-2} to 10^{-7} atm-cc per sec). Permeation type leak standards are supplied with their own self-contained gas supply usually helium filled at atmospheric pressure. Although the flow through the membrane is pressure dependant, typical helium loss is only 10% in 10 years. These standards have a flow in the range of 10^{-7} to 10^{-11} Pa m^3/s (10^{-6} to 10^{-10} atm-cc per sec).

Instrument Calibration - The instrument shall be calibrated, after the specified warm up time suggested by the manufacturers, using a permeation type calibration leak standard. Most of the

Codes stipulate that the sensitivity of the instrument shall be minimum of 1×10^{-10} Pa m^3/s (10^{-9} std. cc per sec.).

System Calibration - Calibration is done by introduction of a known size standard leak into a system with a leak detector. Calibration determines the smallest leakage rate of a particular gas at a specific pressure and temperature that the leak detector as part of the test system is capable of indicating per division on the leak indicator scale. The system calibration can be performed using either capillary type calibrated leak standard for technique like tracer probe technique or permeation type calibrated leak standard for hood technique (for example). The calibration leak (CL) standard with 100% helium shall be attached to the component as far as possible from the instrument connection to the component. The calibrated leak standard shall remain open during system calibration until response time is determined. The stable instrument reading shall be noted and recorded as M_1 in divisions. Background M_2 in divisions is to be noted after the calibration leak standard is closed and the instrument reading becomes stable.

System calibration Sensitivity $S = CL/(M_1 - M_2)$ in $Pa\ m^3/s$ per division

If a certain percentage of helium is used in the tracer gas mixture, then the actual leakage rate (corrected for tracer gas concentration used) can be calculated by

$$Q_2 = Q_1 \cdot 100/\%\text{He}$$

A comparison is made for all the methods discussed above and is presented in Table 1.

3 HYDROSTATIC PRESSURE TEST

Hydrostatic pressure testing is conducted for the pressure vessels by pressurising the vessel gradually using liquids like water to a known value above the design pressure and noting any leak which is given by reduction of pressure and also occurrence of any permanent deformation. This is also called as proof test as this gives (i) assurance to safe working of the pressure vessel in service, (ii) demonstration that the vessel is free from defects which permit leakage of its contents, (iii) confirmation of the intended margin of strength above that required to withstand the design working pressure or the working pressure with the factor of safety before the occurrence of any deformation and (iv) provides a means of reducing stress concentration in localised regions by causing plastic deformation to occur. Hydrostatic pressure testing is safer compared to pneumatic testing because the energy stored in the system during the pneumatic test is several times greater than in a hydrostatic test as the liquid medium is incompressible. In a hydrostatic test, if proper venting is not provided serious accidents are likely to happen.

Pneumatic testing is sometimes resorted to, when: (1) service of the vessel does not permit even smallest traces of moisture, (2) vessel design is impractical for filling with water, (3) static load imposed by water cannot be tolerated by the vessel or its supports.

Table 1   Leak Testing Methods

Method	Min. Detectable Leakage Rate (Pa m^3/s)	Comments
Pressure Change	Time Related	Gross Leak Detection only No information of leak location Quantitative
Bubbles	10^{-4} or smaller	Location only Clean up required
Halogen	10^{-10}	Simple & Portable Operates in air Clean up required Loses sensitivity with use Sensitive to ambient halide gases
Mass Spectrometer 1. Vacuum	10^{-12}	Most accurate Relatively Complex Needs Vacuum Pump
2. Pressure	10^{-7}	Less Sensitive Qualitative and Suitable for large volume components Not as portable as Halogen Detectors

4   FIELD EXPERIENCE ON LEAK TESTING

4.1   Helium Leak Testing of a Large Volume Pipeline

One of the systems designed to handle liquid sodium is the secondary sodium system of Fast Breeder Test Reactor which was required to be leak tested. The system was constructed with AISI 316 material consisting of vessels, tanks and pipelines of different sizes and lengths totalling about 700 m and weld joints numbering over 1300. Intermediate heat exchanger (IHX), expansion and surge tanks, steam generator modules and associated piping system, are the main components of the system. Sodium storage tank is used as part of the system for the storage. The general arrangement of the system is shown in figure 12. It was designed to handle liquid sodium at 773 K and all welds were to be 100% radiographed and helium leak tested under vacuum to a leak tightness of 2×10^{-8} Pa m^3/s for local leaks and 2×10^{-7} Pa m^3/s for global leaks. These components were manufactured with utmost care with stringent quality control measures as any micro-leak could develop into a large leak in service and the consequences are severe. Hence it was essential to use helium leak testing under vacuum. Helium leak testing using MSLD of large sized components such as pipelines and pressure vessels requires a vacuum of the order of 10^{-2} Pa or better in the component.

4.1.1   Sequence of Leak Testing

The following steps were considered essential and accordingly the test sequence planned. It was decided (1) to test wherever possible, in small spools of piping with reasonable numbers of weld joints in each spool, (2) avoid welding of major tanks and vessels prior to HLT of weld joints in the piping system and (3) to test individually the large volume vessels and tanks and after satisfactory testing, include these with terminal welds and test the terminal joints with the vacuum jacket method and then test and clear the complete system.

4.1.2   Testing of Major Tanks and Vessels

All the major vessels/tanks were helium leak tested under vacuum at shop and leak tightness ensured as required by the specification. The testing details of sodium storage tank are detailed below and the other vessels/tanks were tested in a similar way.

4.1.2.1   *Testing of Large Sized Storage Tank:* The storage tank of the secondary sodium system was about 3500 mm diameter, 3500 mm in height, fabricated using 14 mm AISI 316 plate, with a storage capacity of about 24 m^3 of sodium at 423 K. Fig. 13 illustrates the general assembly of the tank with the test set-up. The large volume of the tank forbade the direct use of any standard leak detector to test the tank under vacuum. Large capacity grouped high vacuum pumping system with a capacity of 2000 m^3 per hour at 10 Pa had to be employed to evacuate the tank to a vacuum of 5×10^{-2} Pa or better. A standard leak and a vacuum gauge were connected to a port at the far end from the pump with a bellow sealed valve. The tank was positioned in a pit and the pumping system was positioned at a higher level. It took about 80 h of continuous pumping to reach an equilibrium state of vacuum of 5×10^{-3} Pa in the system. The combined sensitivity and response time were obtained with the auxiliary vacuum pumps running serially. All the weld joints were suitably tested by jacketing each weld joint with a polythene hood. After completion of testing of each weld joint, a global leak test was conducted by enclosing the tank with a polythene envelope and filling the same with helium. The observations were made after an hour for global leak and found to be within the acceptable limits.

4.1.2.2   *Testing of Piping System:* As a large number of weld joints were involved at various lines involving different elevations, it was appropriate to subdivide the pipelines into different sections and locate the standard leak and vacuum gauges accordingly to ensure the sensitivity of testing in all areas. The system was planned for the first stage of leak testing with all the pipelines and tanks except expansion tank and steam generators. The total volume involved at this stage was around 18 m^3 which needed to be evacuated to a vacuum of 1×10^{-2} Pa to facilitate testing with a mass spectrometer leak dector.

4.1.2.3   *Evacuation and Testing:* The system was subjected to pneumatic test to identify and correct gross leaks, if any, including temporary connections. Then the system was evacuated by a high vacuum system. As the impedance of the pipes was high it took about 150 hours of continuous pumping to reach a steady vacuum of 5×10^{-3} Pa in the system. The general arrangement of leak testing is shown in Fig. 12.

After attainment of steady vacuum, calibration was attempted using three numbers of standard leaks located at different regions, opened one at a time. For each calibration the combined sensitivity and response time were noted. Appropriate test time was assigned for each region of

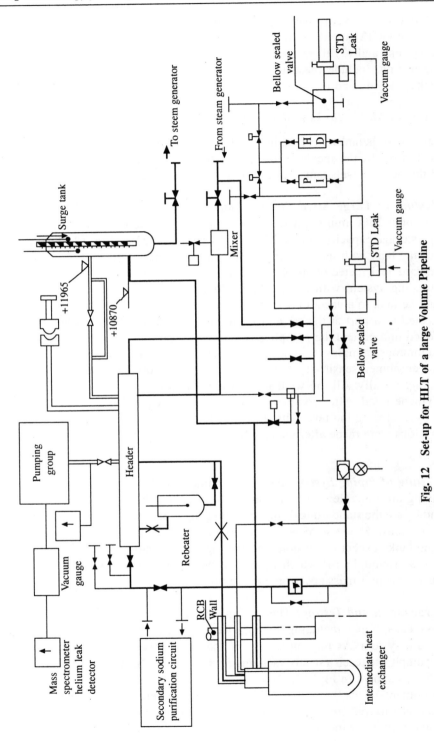

Fig. 12 Set-up for HLT of a large Volume Pipeline

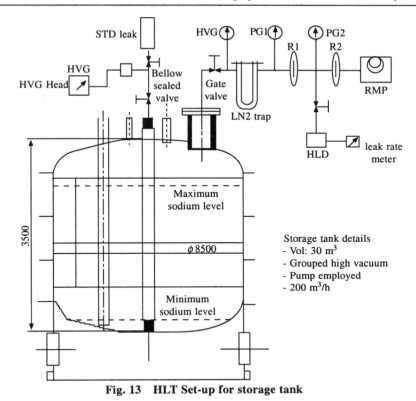

Fig. 13   HLT Set-up for storage tank

testing, based on the difference in the response time. The testing of the weld joints was started from the nearest point from the pumping unit. A polythene jacket was provided on each joint and helium gas was filled into it and observed for minimum of half an hour more than the response time. Only one or two weld joints were tested at a time. If any leak was noticed, it was marked and identified for rectification. Thus, all weld joints were leak tested sequentially.

After completion of the leak testing of the weld joints in the piping system, the large volume tanks which had been tested earlier were connected to the piping system with terminal joints numbering about twenty. Each joint was leak tested by suitable vacuum jacket and cleared.

5   FIELD EXPERIENCE ON NDE OF WELDS

5.1   Introduction

Quality requirements of components and systems vary according to the service demands. Stringent quality requirements are specified in nuclear, space and petrochemical industries. Therefore, a planned approach to improve and maintain the quality of the components for the pressure vessels and piping assumes a greater significance. Non-destructive evaluation (NDE) methods can be applied for evaluating the internal conditions which would guarantee satisfactory performance during service besides ensuring internal soundness during fabrication. The applications may be of any form of NDE. An attempt is made to highlight the different methods of applications of radiographic and ultrasonic examinations.

5.2   Radiographic Examination

Radiography is a volumetric non-destructive examination method and uses a beam of penetrating radiation, such as x-rays or gamma rays. When the beam passes through the specimen/component, some of the radiation energy is absorbed and the intensity of the beam reduced. Variations in the beam intensity are recorded on film and are seen as differences in shading that are typical of the type and size of any defect/discontinuity present.

It may be seen from the above that three basic elements, a radiation source, the test piece or the object being evaluated and the recording medium (usually film), combine to produce the radiograph. These elements are shown in Fig. 14, which also shows the general arrangement of the radiographic set up.

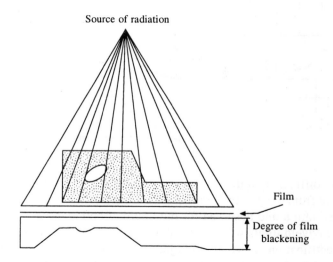

Fig. 14   Effect of radiation on radiographic film

5.2.1   *Radiographic Examination Techniques*

The choice of particular technique is generally based on the sensitivity requirement. The discerning of minute discontinuities in the test object is possible only when the proper technique is applied. The sensitivity of the radiographic technique is influenced by the following.

1. Radiation source
2. Film used
3. Source-to-film distance and
4. Radiation beam alignment

The selection of the particular technique is based on the knowledge about the following factors.

1. Test object - material, thickness and configuration
2. Fabrication - a. welds - edge preparation and welding process
   b. casting – foundry techniques including mould preparation, location of vents, gates etc
3. Anticipated location and nature of the discontinuities
4. Critical and vulnerable locations
5. Area of the inspection coverage
6. Sensitivity level required

5.2.2 Weld Inspection Techniques

The welds can be on flat plates or of cylindrical objects such as pipes. Also the welds can be of butt or fillet type with partial or full penetration. Depending on the type of the weld geometry a particular examination technique is selected, so as to get the optimum sensitivity. The techniques can be classified into two broad categories, namely single wall and double wall techniques.

5.2.2.1 Butt Welds

5.2.2.2 Single Wall Technique:
In the single wall technique the radiation passes through a single wall of the object and the image of the single wall is obtained in the recording medium, the radiographic film. The radiation source is located on one side of the object and the radiographic film on the other side. This technique is applicable whenever both top and bottom sides of the weld are accessible. This is followed for plate welds and large diameter vessels as shown in Fig. 15.

5.2.2.3 Double Wall Techniques:
In the double wal technique the radiation passes through two walls of the object and the image of one or both the walls are obtained in the recording medium, according to the case. The double wall image techniques are used mainly for pipe welds where both side accessibility is not available. In these techniques both the radiation source and the film will be kept outside. The double

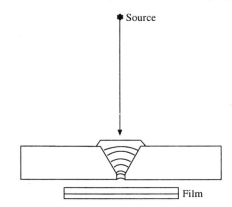

Fig. 15   Radiographic setup for butt weld

wall technique is further divided into two, namely double wall single image (DWSI) and double wall double image (DWDI) techniques, according to the size of the pipe to be radiographed. DWDI is used for the pipes below 89 mm OD and DWSI is used for above 89 mm OD. In the DWDI technique the source is kept inclined or offset to avoid the overlap of the top and bottom weld images. A minimum of two exposures are required to cover the weld length. In the case of DWSI the source is kept near one wall of the pipe and a number of exposures made to cover the full weld length. The examination set up for both the tyeps are given in Fig. 16.

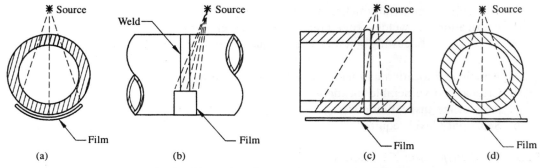

Fig. 16   Double-wall radiographic exposure techniques

5.2.2.4   *Fillet Welds:* All the fillet welds, nozzle tee joints and other types can be examined using the exposure techniques as given in the Fig. 17.

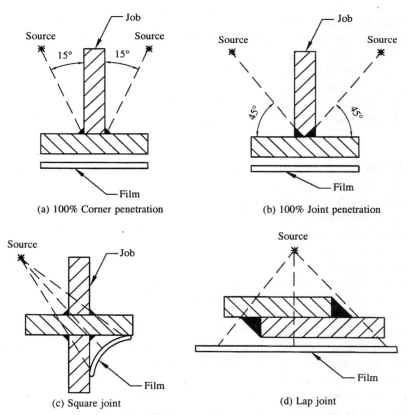

Fig. 17   Radiographic exposure techniques for fillet welds

5.2.3 Some Special Techniques

5.2.3.1 Radiographic Examination of Multi-Wall Configuration

5.2.3.2 Construction Details of The Components (Piping and Vessels):
In fast breeder reactors (FBRs) with liquid sodium as coolant, the major portion of the piping and vessels of the primary and the secondary systems are fabricated with a complex construction of core (pipe/vessel) positioned in a concentric double envelope (guard pipe or vessel) without any spacers between them. At times, a number of core pipes are assembled in a common double envelope. The concentricity of the double envelope with respect to the core also has to be maintained during the construction.

The double envelope configuration posed many problems during the welding of seams both at shop and at site conditions. Radiographic examination was found an appropriate technique in addition to ultrasonic examination for achieving stringent NDE requirements. The radiographic quality level stipulated for the core components were more stringent than that specified in the corresponding clauses of International Codes like ASME Sec. III.

5.2.3.3 Multi-Wall Image Technique:
The site welds of core pipes and the double envelopes of the system constitute a multi-wall configuration, being four walls minimum at any cross section. It was observed that the pipes were amenable to radiographic and ultrasonic examinations independently. The quality requirements stipulated for the core components demand the most stringent sensitivity levels. Achieving such a quality level mainly depends on the judicious selection of radiation source adoptable within the restricted site conditions. The core pipe welds were successfully radiographed by employing conventional double wall single or double image techniques according to the pipe size. The double envelope weld joint examination could be carried out by multi-wall exposures involving a minimum of four walls of the pipes using multi-wall image technique. The interpretable weld length per radiograph was arrived at by evaluating the radiographic density, within the acceptable range, taking density value 2.0 as optimum. It was essential to take more number of exposures to cover the entire weld circumference compared to the usual number of exposures with the conventional double wall techniques specified for the same pipe size. The multi-wall exposure techniques are illustrated in Figs. 18 and 19.

5.2.3.4 Measurement of Annular Gap in the Pipelines:
A uniform gap between the core and double envelope was a prime requisite for such configurations as explained earlier. Hence the necessity arises for proper assessemnt of annular gap after welding. In the absence of access for direct measurement, the only method available was radiography. The assessment of the gap being the main consideration over sensitivity, the gamma source was considered a better alternative, as it provides clear outer and inner wall edges, compared to an X Ray source. The pipes were exposed in two perpendicular directions, using the multi-wall image technique, directing the gamma ray beam normal to the expected annular gap as shown in Figs. 18 and 19. The actual annular gap was arrived at, by applying an appropriate correction factor corresponding to the radiographic set up. After studying the radiographs, it was noted that a non-uniform gap existed between the core and the envelope due to welding distortion. It was also observed that at some sectors of the piping system, the double envelope was touching the core pipe. Such sectors were

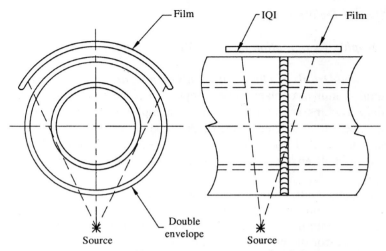

Fig. 18   Multi-wall radiographic expoure setup for defect assessment

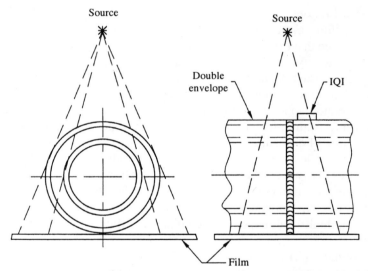

Fig. 19   Multi-wall radiographic setup for assessment of gap between pipes.

rectified by selective heating of the weld joint and the minimum gap was ascertained by radiographic examination.

5.3   Ultrasonic Examination

Ultrasonic examination is a volumetric NDE method that uses sound waves in the range of MHz (0.5 to 25). Ultrasonic examination can detect discontinuities oriented at different angles at various planes in the materials and welds. The sound wave is introduced into the material and the reflection from the discontinuity is analysed for detection and sizing.

5.3.1 *NDE for Typical Weld Geometry In Pressure Vessel*

Radiographic and ultrasonic examinations are complementary in nature for 100% volumetric examination of the weldments to detect both volumetric and planar type of defects. However, on one typical weld joint both the techniques could not be beneficially applied. The weld joint configuration as shown in Fig. 20, was encountered in the assembly of primary system of Prototype Fast Breeder Reactor (PFBR). In order to asses the feasibility of executing the welding and establishing the appropriate NDE procedure for ensuring the stringent quality requirements on the joint, a mock-up assembly in carbon steel was made. The actual material of construction is AISI 316LN and the operating temperature is approximately 823 K (550°C) with liquid sodium as coolant. A 30° segment of vessel having 6650 mm outer radius and 16 mm wall thickness was fabricated with the penetrating pipe of 2200 mm outer diameter and 16 mm wall thickness, through the tapered portion. The annular gap between the two was 130 mm.

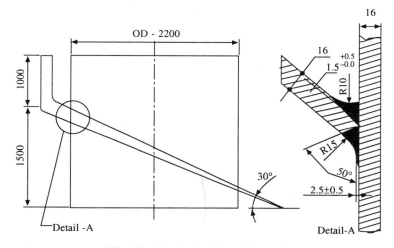

Fig. 20   Typical weld configuration

5.3.1.1   Radiographic Examination: From the joint configuration, it can be noted that the thickness range to be covered at the cross section, along with the axis of the vessel, is 25 mm to 45 mm. It was found that the ratio of the above will be in the order of 2 to 4 with steep variation. This forbids the use of uniform radiographic densities across the weld. Even the improvised radiographic exposure with X ray source failed to attain the required sensitivity. The radiograph thus produced had a wide variation in radiographic density and made the defect detection difficult.

5.3.1.2   Ultrasonic Examination: The non-amenability of the joint to radiographic examination necessitated a great emphasis on the ultrasonic examination to assure the volumetric NDE needs. As the base material of the mock-up assembly is of carbon steel, no appreciable problems were foreseen for conducting the examination. However, it was found that a minimum of three different directional scannings from three sides were essential to ensure the coverage of the entire volume of the weld. It was also recognised that a minimum of three reference blocks with 2 mm dia side drilled holes at different locations on the weld were needed to set the procedure and as reference for the examination. The scanning was also carefully planned as the beam path and the skip distances play an important role during the examination. The weld was scanned from three sides with four directions based on the possible orientation of the defects. The procedure was validated by detecting slag inclusions of varying lengths which were present in test welds.

5.3.2 *Measurement of Liquid Level and Annular Gap Measurement in Vessel*

5.3.2.1 *The Component and the Failure:* In one of the components of sodium purification system, liquid NaK was used in the annular gap between the inner vessel and the outer vessel, to maintain the system at particular temperature, for purifying sodium in the inner vessel. In an incident, the liquid NaK contained in the annular space, leaked out due to over heating. There was a posibility of differential pressure due to this leak, across the walls of inner and the outer vessel which might have caused the buckling of inner vessel. Hence, there was a need for checking the NaK level in the annular space.

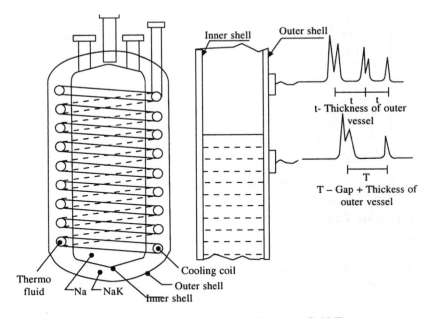

Fig. 21 General arrangement of Primary Cold Trap

5.3.2.2 *The measurement:* Ultrasonic examination was considered to be the best method, which would give the position of the inner vessel compared to the outer vessel. The principle of the examination was that the sound energy passing through the liquid NaK column would give the information of liquid NaK level. By measuring the thickness of liquid NaK in the annular space, the buckling, if any, on the inner vessel could be detected. During scanning on the outer vessel multiple echoes were observed indicating the absence of liquid NaK. The CRT pattern will get changed when the probe crosses the liquid column, which shows the level and the annular gap. The annular gap was arrived at from the thickness of liquid column revealed by CRT display and applying the velocity correction factor to the measured values.

Figure 21 shows the vessel and the CRT pattern. From the examination, the liquid NaK column level and the annular gap as well as the buckling, if any, could be measured. The analysis revealed the absence of buckling and it was decided the vessel can be used for its remaining design life.

15. Quality Control in Production Welding of Different Metals and their Alloys

M. Gopalakrishna and B.S.C. Rao
Quality Assurance Division, IGCAR, Kalpakkam 603 102

Any weldment should possess a sufficient level of quality or fitness for purpose to provide required reliability throughout its life. Weld quality relates directly to the integrity of the weldment. It underlines all of the fabrication and inspection steps necessary to ensure that welded product will be capable of serving the intended function for the design life.

Quality is a relative term. Specifying excessive quality can lead to high costs with no benefits, while low quality weldments lead to high maintenance costs and loss of service. Therefore the aim should be to specify the optimum level that leads to fitness for purpose.

For any job, optimum quality level requirements should be thought of at design stage itself. How do we strike the optimum level? As you know, with the increase in quality level, the cost of quality assurance increases but the loss due to scrap, rework or repair decreases. The point of intersection of these two curves on quality verses cost gives the optimum level as shown in Fig. 1. The curve of total costs descends gradually up to optimum level and there onwards it ascends. One should realise that it is difficult to maintain quality exactly at optimum point but to be economical, it should be maintained in optimum range, i.e. nearer to optimum level.

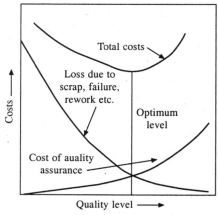

Fig. 1   Cost components in manufacturing as a function of quality level

As a practical approach, quality levels can be categorized as workmanship standard or quality control standard which is best possible by practice, and fitness for purpose (FFP) level, as shown in Fig. 2. If the quality level falls below the workmanship standard, i.e., the flaws present exceed the size of allowable flaws defined in the workmanship/ manufacturing code standard, the flaws may be evaluated for FFP using analytical procedures based on critical flaw size/critical applied stress intensity factor for consideration of design concession to avoid unnecessary repairs. If the quality level falls below FFP standard, the flaw calls for repair. But the FFP approach does not recommend relaxation of presently used workmanship standards for manufacture and inspection. It only gives assessment of any flaw for fitness for the intended service.

To maintain quality, stage inspection is an effective tool. The number of inspection stages required is a function of materials to be welded, welding processes and the criticality of the job with respect to end use. The selection of welding process for a particular application depends upon many factors such as materials, thickness, welding position, overall dimensions of the job, accessibility, quality and finally, cost.

Once the material to be welded and the welding process are selected, a quality assurance plan has to be drawn up indicating the number of quality assurance stages and the agency responsible for each stage, to ensure smooth functioning and flow of work with quality.

Weld quality is verified by non-destructive examination. All deviations are evaluated, and

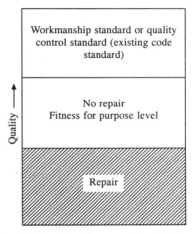

Fig. 2   The significance of quality level

the acceptance or rejection of a weld is usually based on well-defined criteria. Repair of unacceptable or defective condition is normally permitted so that the quality of the weld may be brought up to acceptance level.

Among non-destructive examinations, visual examination is the most crucial and important non-destructive examination in the field of welding. Visual examination is the most extensively used NDE on weldments. Without this, one can not assure the quality of the weld, whatever may be NDE technique one uses afterwards. Visual the examination is the primary evaluation method of any quality control programme. In addition to flaw detection, it can discover signs of possible fabrication problems in subsequent operations and therefore should be incorporated in process control programmes. Conscious visual inspection before, during and after welding can avoid or detect many of the discontinuities that would be found later by more expensive NDE methods. Even though it is simple NDE, it demands high skill, practical experience, theoretical knowledge and judgment from the inspectors. So, to carry out an effective visual examination, the inspectors engaged in this field are to be trained and qualified and their periodical performance should be monitored. If visual examination is carried out dedicatedly at every stage by the inspector and welder, the quality of the welds can be achieved, thereby making the other NDE techniques a mere formality for acceptance.

QUALITY CONTROL BEFORE WELDING

Examination of the base metal prior to fabrication can detect conditions that tend to cause weld defects. Scabs, seams, scale, or other harmful surface conditions may be found by visual examination. Plate laminations may be seen on cut edges. Base metal should be identified by type and grade. Corrections should be made before work proceeds.

Before the parts are assembled for welding, the edge preparations should be checked for root face, bevel angle and after the parts are assembled for welding, the fit-up should be checked for root opening and misalignment which affect the quality for the weld. The inspectors should check the following for conformity to the applicable specifications.

1. Materials
2. Edge preparation and cleanliness
3. Clearance dimensions of backing strips, rings or consumable inserts
4. Fit-up of the parts being welded
5. Welding process and consumables including baking requirements
6. Welding procedure and performance qualifications
7. Welding machine settings
8. Preheat temperature
9. Tack weld quality

QUALITY CONTROL DURING WELDING

During welding, visual examination is the primary method for controlling quality. The following aspects should be checked.

1. Treatment of tack welds
2. Quality of the root pass and the succeeding weld passes
3. Proper preheat and interpass temperature
4. Sequence of weld passes
5. Interpass cleaning
6. Root condition prior to welding on second side
7. Distortion
8. Conformance with the applicable procedure

The most critical part of any weld is the root pass because many weld discontinuities are associated with the root pass. Another critical root condition exists when second side treatment is required for a double welded joint. This includes removal of slag and other irregularities by chipping, arc gouging or grinding to sound metal. The root gap should be monitored as welding of the root pass progresses. Special emphasis should be placed on the adequacy of tack welds and clamps designed to maintain the specified root gap to assure proper weld penetration and alignment. Inspection of successive layers of weld metal usually concentrates on bead shape and interpass cleaning.

When preheat and interpass temperature are specified, they should be monitored at the proper time with a suitable temperature indicating crayon. The amount of heat input and also the sequence and placement of each weld pass should be monitored to maintain mechanical properties and to limit distortion. The weld parameters arc voltage, arc current and welding speed are to be recorded for each bead for competing heat input.

To ensure weld quality as work progresses, each weld layer should be visually checked, by the welder for surface irregularities and adequate interpass cleaning to avoid subsequent slag inclusions or porosity.

QUALITY CONTROL AFTER WELDING

The following are checked by visual inspection after welding

1. Final weld appearance.
2. Final weld size.
3. Dimensional conformance.
4. Amount of distortion.
5. Post weld heat treatment.

The following discontinuities on the surface of a completed weld can be found by visual inspection: (1) crack (2) undercut (3) overlap (4) surface porosity and slag inclusions, (5) unacceptable weld profile, (6) irregularities in the weld faces.

A fabrication standard may permit limited amounts of undercut, concavity and porosity but lack of penetration, cracks, incomplete fusion, and unfilled craters are generally not acceptable. Undercut, overlap and improper weld profile act as stress raisers under load and cracks may develop at these locations under cyclic loading.

The conformity of weld size and contour may be determined by the use of a suitable weld gauge. In general the weld surface appearance should meet the requirement of the specification.

When post weld heat treatment is specified the operation should be monitored and documented for conformity with approved written procedure. The items of importance in heat treatment may include the following: (1) area to be heated, (2) heating and cooling rates (3) holding temperature and time (4) temperature measurement and distribution (5) thermocouple and equipment calibration.

The other NDE applied in determining the quality of welds include PT, MT, RT and UT and also AE technique has potential to monitor the quality of weld during welding. These techniques are not discussed here.

ROLE OF JOINT DESIGN

Joint design plays a vital role in producing welds fit for the purpose. The following rules are generally applied for good design of weld joints.

1. Select the joint design that requires the least amount of weld metal.
2. Where design permits, use square-groove and partial penetration welds.
3. Use lap and fillet welds instead of groove welds if fatigue is not a design consideration

4. Use double 'V' or 'U' groove instead of single V or U groove welds on thick plates to reduce the amount of weld metal and to control distortion.

5. Give due consideration for fluidity of weld metal while selecting groove angles for easy manipulation of weld metal.

6. For corner joints in thick plates where fillet welds are not adequate, bevelling both members should be considered to reduce the tendency for lamellar tearing.

7. Design the assembly and the joints for good accessibility for welding and non-destructive testing.

CONTROLS SPECIFIC TO CARBON STEEL WELDING

Carbon steels are generally classified as per their carbon content as indicated in the following table.

Category	Carbon content %	Typical hardness	Weldability
Low carbon steel	0.15 Max.	60 HRB	Excellent
Mild steel	0.15–0.30	90 HRB	Good
Medium carbon steel	0.30–0.50	25 HRC	Fair (preheat and postweld heat treatment normally required. Low hydrogen welding process recommended)
High carbon steel	0.50–1.00	40 HRC	Poor (low-hydrogen welding process, preheat and post treatment required)

Carbon steels containing up to 0.30 percent carbon and relatively low manganese content have good weldability. As the carbon content of the steel is increased, the welding procedure must be planned to avoid the formation of large amounts of hard martensite to minimise or avoid the risk of hydrogen induced cracking.

Medium carbon steels should be preheated prior to welding to control the cooling rate and thereby the formation of martensite. Preheat temperature increases with higher carbon equivalent, greater joint thickness or increased hydrogen in the arc. The interpass temperature should be the same as the preheat temperature.

A stress relief heat treatment is recommended immediately after welding, particularly with thick sections. If possible, the welded joint should be heated to stress-relief temperature without intermediate cooling to ambient temperature. When immediate stress relief is impractical, the welded joint should be maintained at or slightly above the specified preheat temperature for 2 to 3 hours per 25 mm of joint thickness. This procedure promotes the diffusion of hydrogen from the weld zone and reduces the possibility of cold cracking during intermediate handling. However, it should not be considered as a substitute to stress-relief heat treatment.

Low hydrogen welding procedures are mandatory with these steels. Pick-up of carbon from a steel containing 0.5 percent carbon by dilution will usually result in high weld metal hardness and susceptibility to cracking. Dilution can be minimised by depositing small weld beads with shallow penetration.

CONTROLS SPECIFIC TO LOW ALLOY STEEL WELDING

Welding procedures must contain the necessary safeguards to prevent hydrogen induced cracking. Low hydrogen welding processes and procedures must be used.

Preheat is required to prevent hardening and cracking. Recommended minimum preheat and interpass temperature for various thicknesses and compositions are given in codes. They generally increase with alloy content and section thickness.

It is advisable to complete the weld without interruption of the welding cycle. However, based on industrial experience and specific job conditions, codes make certain general suggestions regarding the interruption of the heat cycle during welding.

If an interrupted procedure is followed in the welding of section thickness less than 25 mm, the weld deposit prior to interruption should be at least 33% of the thickness, but not less than two weld layers whichever is greater. For very thick sections, 33% may be very excessive, but a minimum weld thickness should be specified when immediate stress relief is not practicable, the temperature of the weld should be held at preheat temperature for one hour before cooling to room temperature to allow hydrogen to escape.

A stress relief heat treatment is used to reduce residual stresses and also to increase the ductility and toughness of the weld metal and heat affected zone. The stress-relief temperature should not exceed the tempering temperature of normalised and tempered or quenched and tempered steel. During heating and cooling period temperature variation over 4.5 mm should not exceed 140°C in order not to produce high stresses from differential expansion as per ASME code requirement.

CONTROLS SPECIFIC TO MARAGING STEELS

Maraging steels are a group of iron-nickel alloys that are strengthened by precipitation of one or more intermetallic compounds in a matrix of essentially carbon-free martensite. In addition to nickel, these steels generally contain either cobalt or chromium, molybdenum, titanium and aluminium. The carbon content is limited to a maximum of 0.03 percent. Maraging steels are characterised by high strength and excellent toughness. The strength is obtained as a result of age hardening of low carbon martensite. Maraging steels are used for aircraft, aerospace components where both high strength and weldability are important considerations.

In view of the low austenitie to martensite transformation temperature and low thermal conductivity, maraging steels should be welded without preheat and interpass temperature should be restricted to 120°C and also with minimum practical heat input to keep austenitic reversed zone very narrow in the heat affected zone so that the joint strength will be controlled by the weld metal properties.

To achieve good toughness at the high strength levels filler metals and welding procedures must be designed to ensure that impurities in welds are at very low levels. Prior to welding, joint surfaces should be cleaned with clean lint-free cloth and suitable solvent. Welding should be carried out in extremely clean environment. Cleanness of the filler wire is very important. Vacuum annealing and ultrasonic cleaning are recommended. Cleaned wire should be stored in dry inert gas-filled containers.

Each bead of multiple pass welds of even GTAW process should be cleaned before depositing the next bead using clean stainless steel brush. The most widely used welding process is GTAW process for these steels.

Maraging steels are less sensitive to hydrogen induced cracking than low alloy steels at the same strength levels. This is because the low carbon martensite formed is relatively soft in the as welded condition. The danger of cold cracking is also lessened because of the residual stress pattern which is compressive in nature rather than tensile due to martensitic transformation.

Hot cracking can be a potential problem in welding maraging steels and is related to impurity levels and low manganese in these steels. Hot cracking can take place with sulphur content as low as 0.005 percent when joint fit-up is poor. With good fit-up i.e. with minimum root opening and less joint restraint, sulphur levels up to 0.010% can be tolerated.

CONTROLS SPECIFIC TO STAINLESS STEELS

The high chromium content of stainless steels promotes the formation of tenacious oxides that must be removed for good welding practice. The surfaces to be welded must be completely cleansed of all hydrocarbon and other contaminants such as cutting fluids, grease, oil etc. by suitable solvents. General pre-weld cleaning methods are (1) pickling with 10 to 20 percent nitric acid solution and (2) cleaning with stainless steel wire brushes that have not been used for any other purpose.

Carbon contamination can adversely affect the metallurgical characteristics, the corrosion resistance or both of stainless steel. Pickup of carbon from surface contaminants or due to contact with carbon steel materials must be prevented.

Thorough post-weld cleaning is required. Objectionable surface discoloration from welding is best removed by wire brushing and local passivation treatment.

CONTROLS SPECIFIC TO AUSTENITIC STAINLESS STEEL

No preheating is required for welding of austenitic stainless steels. These steels are welded with interpass temperature not exceeding 120°C to keep the precipitation of intergranular chromium carbides to a minimum.

Low heat input welding techniques i.e. stringer bead technique or limited weaving technique where stringer bead technique is not possible, along with low current and possible high welding speed without sacrificing fusion are used for welding of these steels to keep sensitization to a minimum and to obtain better mechanical properties. A heat input of around 1 kJ/mm of weld pass is considered a low heat input.

Proper control of delta ferrite in the weld metal is needed to prevent or minimise microfissuring. A filler metal of suitable composition to yield 3 to 5% delta ferrite in the weld metal should be selected using Delong diagram or WRC – 1992 diagram.

CONTROLS SPECIFIC TO FERRITIC STAINLESS STEELS

The ferritic stainless steels are generally less weldable than the austenitic stainless steels and produce weld joints having lower toughness because of grain coarsening that occurs at the high welding temperature.

Variations in chemical composition within standard limits can result in the formation of small amounts of austenite during heating to elevated temperature. On cooling the austenite transforms to martensite, resulting in a duplex structure of ferrite and a small amount of martensite. The martensite reduces both ductility and toughness of the steels. Annealing transforms the martensite and restores normal ferritic properties.

The key to successful welding of low interstitial ferritic stainless steels is to prevent any carbon, nitrogen, or oxygen contamination during welding. Thus, the base and filler materials must be cleaned before welding and both the molten weld metal and hot weld metal area must be fully shielded from the atmosphere. All moisture must also be excluded from the weld area before and during welding.

The recommended preheating temperature range for these steels is 150 to 225°C. The need for preheating is determined largely by composition, mechanical properties and thickness of the steel being welded.

The temperature range for post heating or post weld annealing of these steels is 800 to 840°C which is safely below the temperatures for austenitic formations and grain coarsening. Annealing transforms a mixed structure to a wholly ferritic structure and restores the mechanical properties and corrosion resistance that may have been adversely encountered in welding. Annealing except for its inability to refine coarsened ferrite grains, is generally beneficial.

Cooling ferritic stainless steel from the annealing temperature may be done by air or water quenching. To minimise distortion from handling, weldments are often allowed to cool to about 300°C before they are removed from the furnace. Slow cooling through the temperature range of 560 to 400°C must be avoided because it produces brittleness in the steel. Susceptibility to this type of embrittlement known as 475°C embrittlement, normally increases as chromium content increases. Heavy sections may require forced cooling or a spray quench to bring them safely through this embrittlement range.

Both ferritic and austenitic stainless steel filler metals are used in the arc welding of these steels. Ferritic stainless steel filler metals offer the advantage of having the same coefficient of thermal expansion and the same corrosion resistance as the base metal. However, austenitic stainless steel filler metals are often used to obtain more ductile weld metal in the as welded condition.

Although austenitic stainless steel weld metal does not prevent grain growth and martensite formation in the HAZ, the ductility of austenitic weld metal improves the ductility of the welded joint.

For weldments that are to be annealed after welding, the use of austenitic filler metal can introduce several problems. The normal range of annealing temperature for ferritic stainless steels fall within the sensitizing temperature range for austenitic steels. Consequently unless the austenitic weld metal is of extra low carbon content or is stabilised with niobium or titanium, its corrosion resistance may be seriously impaired. If the annealing treatment is intended to relieve residual stress, it cannot be fully effective because of the difference in the coefficients of thermal expansion of the weld metal and the base metal.

CONTROLS SPECIFIC TO MARTENSITIC STAINLESS STEELS

The usual preheating temperature range of martensitic steels is 200 to 300°C. Carbon content of the steel is the most important factor in determining whether or not preheating is necessary.

The following can be used to correlate preheating and post weld heat-treating practice with carbon contents and welding characteristics of martensitic stainless steels.

1. Carbon below 0.10% : neither preheating nor post-weld annealing generally is required.
2. Carbon 0.10 to 0.20% : preheat to 250°C, weld at this temperature, cool slowly.
3 Carbon 0.20 to 0.50% : preheat to 250°C, weld at this temperature, and anneal.
4. Carbon over 0.5% : preheat to 250°C, weld with high heat input and anneal.

If the weld is to be hardened and tempered immediately after welding, annealing may be omitted. Otherwise the weld should be annealed immediately after welding, without cooling to room temperature.

CONTROLS SPECIFIC TO ALUMINUM AND ALUMINIUM ALLOYS

1. The tenacious, refractory oxide film on the joint surface prevents good wetting between it and the filler metal. The welding AC arc can remove this oxide film as the welding proceeds but for best results pre-cleaning by mechanical means is advisable. Suitable mechanical methods are wire brushing, scraping and filing. For brushing, stainless steel wire brushes must be used and they must be maintained scrupulously clean.
2. It is equally important to keep the joint surfaces free from moisture, grease, oils and paints. If present, they are decomposed by the welding arc and hydrogen released causes porosity. Degreasing by dipping in a suitable solvent or by steam cleaning is recommended for critical fabrications. Components are best cleaned before assembly and fit-up.
3. For fusion welding of aluminium and its alloys preheating is not necessary and should be avoided as far as possible. Only in case of thick sections preheat becomes necessary. Even then the duration of heating should be as short as possible and the preheating temperature should not exceed 150°C. In the case of alloys containing 3 to 5.5% Mg, the preheat temperature must not exceed 120°C and the interpass temperature must never rise above 150°C.
4. Weld metal cracking can occur in a specific aluminium alloy if the choice of filler metal is not correct and the result is that either the weld metal or the HAZ has low ductility or strength at elevated temperature. This phenomenon is referred to as hot shortness.

To reduce the tendency for intergranular cracking in the HAZ, it is advisable to use a filler metal whose melting point is equal to or below that of the base metal. In other words, one should use a filler metal of higher alloy content. For example, aluminium containing 0.6% Si is very likely to crack in the weld joint if a filler metal of matching composition is used. The cracking can be eliminated by using a filler metal containing 5% Si. Since the latter has a lower melting point, it remains more plastic than the base metal and yields during cooling to relieve the contraction stresses that might cause cracking.

In many applications, Al-5% Mg filler wire gives welds of good strength and crack resistance. Al-Mg alloys should never be welded with Al-Si alloy filler wires because of the formation of magnesium-silicide eutectic which decreases ductility and causes cracking. Similarly, Mg and Cu should not be allowed to be present together in an aluminium weld. This means that Al-Mg filler wires should never be used to weld Al-Cu alloys and Al-Cu filler wires should not be used to weld Al-Mg alloys. In welding an Al-Si alloy base metal with an Al-Si filler wire, their alloy contents must be so arranged that the weld metal has Si content either below 0.5% or above 2%. With Si content between these limits, the crack sensitivity increases markedly. In the case of Al-Mg alloys also, the Al-Mg weld metal must not have Mg content between 0.5 and 2% for a similar reason. In these examples, dilution must also be taken into account and properly controlled during welding.

CONTROLS SPECIFIC TO NICKEL ALLOYS

1. Molten nickel alloy weld metals do not flow and wet the base metal so readily as do carbon and stainless steel weld metals. The groove angle must be large enough to permit proper manipulation of the filler metal and deposition of stringer weld beads.

2. Cleanness is the single most important requirement for successful joining of nickel alloys. Nickel and nickel alloys are susceptible to embrittlement by sulphur, phosphorus and low melting point metals such as lead, zinc and tin. These detrimental elements are often present in oils, paints, marking crayons, cutting fluids and shop dust. Cracking from sulphur embrittlement of nickel sheet is often evident in the heat affected zone.

Oxides should be thoroughly removed from the surfaces to be welded because they can inhibit wetting and fusion of the base metal with the weld metal. Their presence can also cause subsurface inclusions and poor bead contour. They may be removed by grinding, machining, filing or pickling. Wire brushes used for cleaning should be made of austenitic stainless steel.

Preheat is not required for welding nickel and nickel alloys. The interpass temperature should be low to help minimise total heat input. A maximum temperature of 100°C is recommended for some corrosion resistant alloys; stringer beads must be used to fill the joint.

CONTROLS SPECIFIC TO TITANIUM WELDING

1. Titanium is highly reactive at the weld and HAZ in contact with air and most elements and compounds (excluding the inert gases) including refractories.

2. Titanium is subject to severe embrittlement by relatively minute amounts of impurities, especially nitrogen, oxygen, carbon and hydrogen. Titanium has a high affinity for these elements at the welding temperature.

Titanium must be carefully shielded to prevent the absorption of these impurities at welding temperatures. The weld puddle as well as all hot metal must be protected from atmosphere by shielding gas until the temperature of the metal comes down to 400°C. The general effect of these elements is to drastically reduce ductility while increasing strength and hardness. Gas shielded arc welding processes using the inert shielding gases, argon and helium are used for welding. Other gases such as carbon dioxide and nitrogen are not inert to titanium and cannot be used.

3. Pre-Weld Cleaning: Proper cleaning techniques before welding are essential and must be followed exactly. The weld joint and adjacent area should be degreased if they have been in

contact with grease or oil. All scales or other foreign materials must be removed from the surface. Cleaning of jigs and fixtures and clamping equipment is of equal importance. Titanium has little resistance to stress corrosion cracking when heated in the presence of chlorides, even in trace amounts. Titanium before heating in welding or heat treatment should be free of fingerprints, degrease residue, perspiration and even stains from high-chloride rinse water.

4. Post Weld Cleaning: Any color or film is cleaned from the weld and the heat affected zone. Mechanical cleaning techniques such as grinding or polishing are normally used.

REFERENCES

1. AWS Hand Book seventh edition volume 4 on Engineering Application—Materials.
2. ASM Metals Hand Book 8th edition Vol. 6 Welding and Brazing.
3. US Atomic Energy Commission Regulatory Guide 1.31.

16. Weld Joint Design

T.K. Mitra

Reactor Engineering Group
Indira Gandhi Centre for Atomic Research Kalpakkam

1 INTRODUCTION

Welding is one of the most important and versatile means of fabrication available to industry. Welding is used to join hundreds of different commercial alloys in many different shapes. Greater freedom in design is also made possible by the use of welding. The integrity and cost of welded fabrications depend ultimately on the details of the welded joints. The welded joint is designed to meet a certain combination of properties required by end use.

2 OBJECTIVE OF WELD JOINT DESIGN

The basic objectives of weld joint design are ideally to provide an assembly that

1. will perform its intended functions
2. will have required reliability and safety
3. is capable of being fabricated, inspected, transported and placed in service at minimum total cost

Total cost includes the cost of design, materials, fabrication, inspection, erection, operation, repair and product maintenance.

3 THE DESIGNER

Designer of weldments should have some knowledge and experience in the following areas in addition to the basic design concepts for the component/structure:

1. Cutting and shaping of metals
2. Assembly of components
3. Preparation and fabrication of welded joints
4. Weld acceptance criteria, inspection, mechanical testing, and evaluation

Designers also need general knowledge of the following subjects and their effects on the design of weldments:

1. Mechanical and physical properties of metals and weldments

2. Weldability of metals
3. Welding processes, costs, and variations in welding procedures
4. Filler metals and properties of weld metals
5. Thermal effects of welding
6. Effects of restraint and stress concentration
7. Control of distortion
8. Communication of weldment design to the shop, including the use of welding symbols
9. Applicable welding and safety standards

Several of these topics involve special areas of knowledge and experience. Therefore, designers should not rely entirely upon their own knowledge and experience, which may be limited but should consult the people who are experts in materials, corrosion and welding technology whenever appropriate.

While it is anticipated that designer would have correctly accounted for all the loading details, made proper choice of materials and assured acceptable level of quality during fabrication of welded components/structures, early failures can still occur as indicated in Fig. 1 due to lack of adequate knowledge about the behaviour of welded joints [1]. Therefore, it is essential to understand the factors influencing weld joint design.

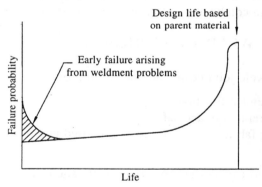

Fig. 1   Schematic representation of the probability of failure during the life of a welded component

4   JOINT DESIGN

Joint design is a general term for a group of variables, which includes thickness, arrangement of the members/parts, the geometry of the parts as prepared for welding, weld joint and finally the restraint of the weld joints.

The required thickness for the load carrying members is commonly determined by an 'allowable' design stress, usually based on a fraction of yield or tensile strength at room temperature and elevated temperature and stress-to-rupture for high temperature design. However, the design engineer might have unknowingly built in stress concentrations that grossly increase stresses and change the failure mode by

(a) locating abrupt changes of sections in highly stressed areas

(b) concentrating numerous heavy welds in small areas with no provision for relief of shrinkage forces and

(c) using unnecessarily larger welds

Under these conditions the integrity of the component/structure may be determined not by the design stress, but by the stresses developed in the weld joint due to above factors. These problems could be minimized if the designer would consult with fabricating shop personnel to take advantage of their experience with similar components/structures.

The first step in the joint design is to recognise different types of weld joints and various parameters commonly associated with them. The joint design should be selected primarily on the basis of load requirements. Both the type of joint and type of weld are specified by the designer. In fact, welds and joints are often confused in arc welding. Fig. 2 shows the joint and weld types. Specifying a joint does not describe the type of weld to be used. Thus, ten types of welds are

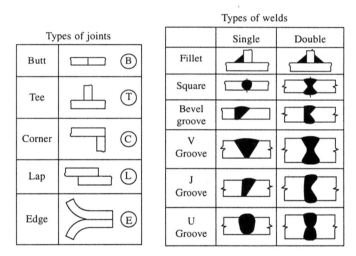

Fig. 2   Typical joint designs and weld grooves in engineering design

shown for making a butt joint. Although all but two welds are illustrated with butt joints here, some may also be used with other types of joints. Thus a single bevel weld may also be used in a T or corner joint (Fig. 3) and a single V weld may be used in a corner, T, or butt joint.

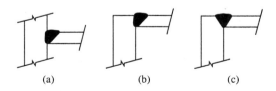

Fig. 3   Groove designs used in T and corner joints, (a) T joint, (b) single bevel corner joint and (c) single-V in corner joint

Generally the following rules apply for joint design.

1. Select the joint design that requires the least amount of weld metal. Over welding not only leads to distortion but also wastes time and money adding nothing to strength or performance of the joint.
2. Use lap and fillet welds instead of groove welds if fatigue is not a design consideration
3. Use double V or U groove instead of single V or U groove welds on thick plates to reduce the amount of weld metal and to control distortion. It makes possible alternating the weld passes on each side of the joint, again reducing distortion.
4. Use minimum root opening and included angle in order to reduce the amount of filler metal required.
5. For corner joints in thick plates where fillet welds are not adequate, beveling both members should be considered to reduce tendency for lamellar tearing.
6. Avoid joints that create extremely deep grooves
7. Design the joint for easy accessibility for welding.

Fig. 4 indicates the various parameters of weld joints and the associated nomenclature is given in Table 1[2]. It is clear that the parameters indicated are applicable for other joint types as well which are adopted by the industry during fabrication. While some of the parameters indicated are arrived at based on type of welding process, others like size of the weld are determined based on joint strength considerations. Distinction between the different welds is important because allowables stresses are often defined on the basis of weld types. Sizing of the butt weld is done based on throat thickness whereas for fillet weld, either leg length or throat thickness is used. The throat of full penetration butt weld is the same as the thickness of the part being joined, whether axial load, shear or bending, and if the design is checked for stress there is no need to do special calculations for the weld. The stresses induced in a fillet weld joint are complex because of eccentricity of applied load, weld shape and notch, and consist of shear, tension, compression etc. There are several methods of calculating the size or strength of fillet welds. But the simplest method assumes that the throat is in shear for all types of load and the shear-stress in the throat is the load divided by throat area. Estimation of size of the weld involves usage of stress-strain formulae based on mechanics of materials and various failure theories. This includes assessment of the allowable stress for the joint considering the working environment, selection of proper failure criteria and finally estimation of the weld size. The failure theories like 'maximum principal stress theory' are widely used for general purpose application. Fig. 5 lists some of the weld stress estimation formulae for different types of joints based on the above theories [3,4]. The approach adopted by design codes like ASME Sec VIII Div 1 [5] is based on 'maximum principal stress theory'. The following paragraphs explain the approach adopted in design codes.

4.1   JOINT DESIGN APPROACH IN CODES

Codes and specifications apply to weldments that are designed for certain types of service. The more widely used specifications are those covering areas such as structural work, pressure vessel and piping, etc. While it is out of place to discuss in detail all the above codes, the design aspects of weld joints as envisaged in ASME Boiler and Pressure Vessel Code Sec VIII Div. 1 are presented briefly.

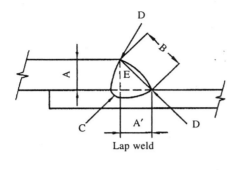

Lap weld

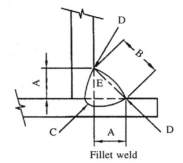

Fillet weld

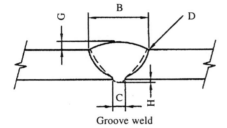

Groove weld

A : Leg
A' : Smaller leg size (equal to size of weld)
B : Face
C : Root
D : Toe
E : Throat
F : Penetration (equal to size of weld)
G : Face reinforcement
H : Root reinforcement

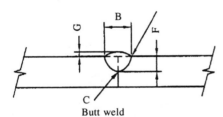

Butt weld

Fig. 4   Schematic diagram of joint configurations commonly used, showing critical dimensions and design parameters

Table 1   Nomenclature for fillet, lap, butt and groove welds

Feature	Definition
Face	Exposed surface of a weld on the side from which the welding was performed
Root	Points, as shown in cross section, at which the back of the weld intersects the base metal surface
Leg	Shortest distance from root to toe in a fillet weld
Toe	Junction between the weld face and the base metal
Throat	Shortest distance from root to face in a fillet weld
Penetration	Depth of a groove weld extends into the root of a joint, measured on the centerline of a root cross section
Reinforcement	Weld metal in excess of the specified weld size
Face reinforcement	Reinforcement at the side of the weld from which welding was performed
Size (groove weld)	Joint penetration (depth of root preparation) plus the root penetration (when specified)
Size (fillet weld)	Leg of the largest isosceles right triangle that can be inscribed within the fillet weld cross section

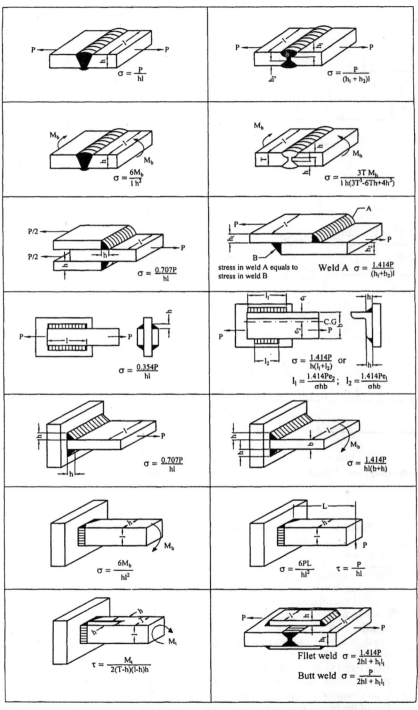

Fig. 5   **Weld stress formulae for typical weld configurations under various types of loading commonly encountered in practice**

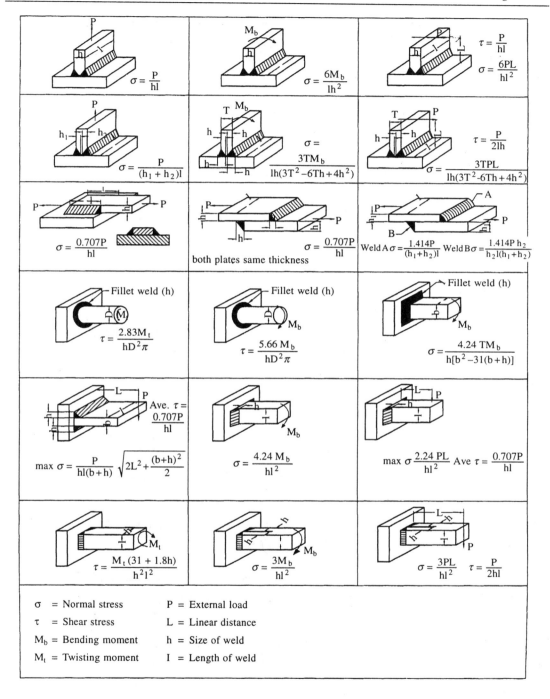

Fig. 5 **Weld stress formulae for typical weld configurations under various types of loading commonly encountered in practice** *(contd.)* **Source: Design Data Book, PSG Tech., Coimbatore, 1995.**

The ASME code recognises the significance of defects in welds and has attempted to overcome the reduction in strength by incorporating suitable joint efficiency factors depending on the type of weld and degree of its radiographic inspection carried out. The formulae for thickness evaluation are as follows:

Thickness based on

(a) Circumferential stress

$$t = \frac{PR}{SE - C1 \cdot P}$$

(b) Longitudinal stress

$$t = \frac{PR}{SE - C2 \cdot P}$$

where

t = minimum thickness of the section
P = design pressure
R = inside radius of the vessel
E = joint efficiency
$C1$ = 0.6 and $C2$ = 0.4
S = maximum allowable stress

$C1$ and $C2$ are constants in the ASME modified formula to achieve close agreement with the results of Lame's equation. The joint efficiency, E, for arc and gas welded joints is indicated in Table 2 [5, 6]

The majority of the codes specify the following for welded joints.

1. Types of joints generally permitted
2. Joint details
3. An allowable design stress based on material properties at service temperatures.
4. Manufacturing and testing requirements.

However, there is in general, no mention about detailed requirements for specific environmental conditions. Hence the designer has to look into this aspect carefully.

4.2 INFLUENCE OF DEFECTS AND GEOMETRY ON FATIGUE PERFORMANCE OF WELD JOINTS

It is widely recognised that welded joints almost always contain some discontinuities, and this places the designer using joints in a dilemma. The designer plans joints that are essentially free from discontinuities but this is not realistic. Weld defects/discontinuities are obviously, undesirable by definition but the complexity of the technology of welding means that it is not usually a worthwhile aim to expect total freedom from all defects. The practical approach is to recognise that discontinuities are present and to place a reasonable limit on their existence. The problem is how to determine the types and extent of discontinuities that are acceptable.

Welded components/structures are invariably subject to cyclic loadings during service. This leads to fatigue loading and fatigue failure of weld joints has been the main concern for designers. Apart from nature and frequency of loading, the strength of the joints in fatigue is dependent also on such things as physical shape and surface contours. All kinds of discontinuities, such as sharp

Table 2   Maximum allowable joint efficiencies for arc and gas welded joints

No.	Type of joint Description	Limitations	Degree of Examination		
			(a) Fully Radio-graphed	(b) Spot Examined	(c) Not Spot Examined
(1)	Butt joints as attained by welding or by other means which will obtain the same quality of deposited weld metal on the inside and outside weld surfaces to agree with the requirements of UW–35. Welds using metal backing strips which remain in place are excluded	None	1.00	0.85	0.70
(2)	Single—welded butt joint with backing strip other than those included under (1)	(a) None except as in (b) below (b) Butt weld with one plate offset-for circumferential joints only	0.90	0.80	0.65
(3)	Single—welded butt joint without use of backing strip	Circumferential joints only not over 16 mm thick not over 610 mm outside diameter	. . .	. . .	0.60
(4)	Double full fillet lap joint	Londitudinal joints not over 610 mm thick. Circumferential joints not over 16 mm thick	. . .	. . .	0.55
(5)	Single full fillet lap joints with plug welds conforming to UW–17	(a) Circumferential joints for attachment of heads not over 610 mm outside diameter to shells not over 12.7 mm thick	. . .	. . .	0.50
		(b) Circumferential joints for the attachment to shells of jackets not over 16 mm in nominal thickness where the distance from the center of the plug weld to the edge of the plate is not less than $1\frac{1}{2}$ times the diameter of the hole for the plug	. . .	. . .	0.50
(6)	Single full fillet lap joints without plug welds	(a) For the attachment of heads convex to pressure to shells not over 16 mm required thickness, only with use of fillet weld on inside of shell; or	. . .	. . .	0.45
		(b) for attachment of heads having pressure on either side, to shells not over 610 mm inside diameter and not over 6.4 mm required thickness with fillet weld on outside of head flange only	. . .	. . .	0.45

corners, notches, angles, and weld beads, cause obstruction to flow of stresses and can create stress intensities of greater magnitude than design values. These peak stresses, or stress concentrations, can gradually develop into small cracks. These discontinuities are called "stress raisers". Thus, it is most important that in initial design the engineer make every effort to eliminate or at least keep to minimum, all possible discontinuities. Welding introduces flaws/defects that act like pre-existing cracks, which influence the fatigue behaviour of weld joints. A comprehensive list of defects/discontinuities in welds is given in Table 3. It is noticed that, while some of the defects are of metallurgical origin, some owe their origin to design and fabrication deficiencies. We will restrict our discussion in the following paragraphs to the defects that are related to design and fabrication deficiencies.

Table 3   Characterization of weld discontinuities/defects

Weld Process and Procedures Related	Metallurgical
A Geometric	A Cracks or Fissures
Misalignment	Hot
Undercut	Cold or delayed
Concavity or convexity	Reheat, stress–relief or strainage
Excessive refinforcement	Lamellar tearing
Poor refinforcement	
Poor refinforcement angle	B Porosity
Overlap	Spherical
Burn through	Worm–hole
Backing ring–lack of penetration	
Insert ring–lack of fusion	C Heat–affected zone, microstructure alteration
Backing–left on	
Incomplete penetration	D Weld metal and heat–affected zone segregation
Lack of fusion	
Shrinkage	E Base plate delamination
Surface irregularity–ripples	
B Other	Design
Arc strikes	
Slag inclusions	A Changes in section/stress concentration
Oxide films	
Weld dressing	B Weld Joint Type
Spotter	
Arc crater	

Fatigue failure at normal working stresses is invariably associated with stress concentrations. Fatigue is probably the most common cause of failure in welded construction. The discontinuities most significant in promoting fatigue failures, except for the obvious defect of gross cracking or extensive incomplete fusion, are those, which affect the weld faces. The combination of excessive weld reinforcement and slight undercutting is one of the most serious discontinuities affecting fatigue life. Contrary to popular belief that reinforcement increases the joint strength, it is seen from Fig. 6 that joint strength is adversely affected by reinforcement [7]. The strength of flush weld joints are higher than those with reinforcements. Fabrication codes usually specify the

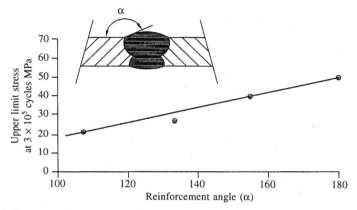

Fig. 6 **Effect of reinforcement bead angle on fatigue strength of transverse butt welds (after Rogerson [7])**

maximum permissible height of reinforcement, for example, as shown in Fig. 7, the reinforcement may meet the code requirement for maximum height [8] but actually it does not improve the fatigue life. In fact, the reinforcement should blend smoothly into the base metal as shown in

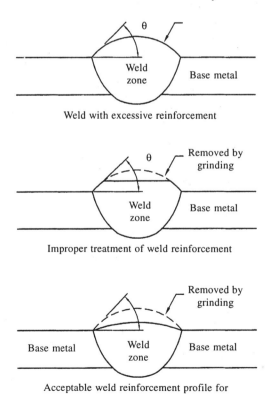

Weld with excessive reinforcement

Improper treatment of weld reinforcement

Acceptable weld reinforcement profile for
fatigue applications

Fig. 7 **Schematic showing (a) weld with excessive reinforcement, (b) improper removal of weld reinforcement and (c) acceptable weld profile for fatigue applications [8]**

Fig. 8. As a general recommendation for design where repetitive loading can be expected, full penetration welded joints should be used, and where possible, surfaces should be machined or ground smooth to eliminate possible minute discontinuities.

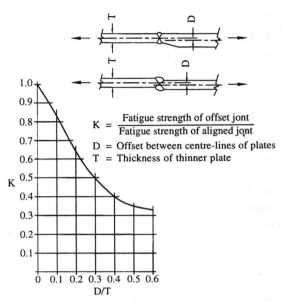

Fig. 8   Effect of offset ratio on the fatigue strength of misaligned butt-welded joints (after Harvey [9])

Misalignment of weld joints is often noticed due to improper fit-up, fixuring, tack welding or a combination of these factors. The misalignment increases the direct stress by introducing a secondary bending stress, Sb, given as below:

$$Sb = \frac{3e}{B} Sa$$

The total stress = Sa + Sb = Sa × Km
where, e = axial misalignment
    Sa = nominal applied stress
    Km = Stress magnification factor $Km = 1 + \frac{3e}{B}$
    B = thickness of the section
    Sb = secondary bending stress

A chance presence of angular misalignment, another type of defect, at the same location will further increase the total stress in the junction. Fig. 8 indicates the fatigue strength of offset or misaligned butt welded joints [9].

Undercut also acts as a flaw and influences the fatigue performance of weld joints by aiding crack initiation. It creates a mechanical notch at the weld interface.

Clearly, all the above examples indicate that defects are the source of stress concentration. The design codes also have recognised the perilous effects of these defects on the weld performance and have specified certain acceptance criteria for defects in order to mitigate their influence. As an example, the acceptance criteria for pressure vessel weld joint as specified by ASME Sec VIII Div 1 for weld reinforcement and offset is given in Table 4. The stress concentration effects due to abrupt changes in cross section have been taken care of in the code by specifying a transition slope of more than 1 in 3 (Fig. 9) during joining of plates with unequal thickness.

Table 4   Acceptance criteria for some defects in circumferential and longitudinal weld joints

Reduction in thickness
⊁ 0/8 mm or 10%

Reinforcement (mm)	
Material Thickness inch	Thickness of Reinforcement
< 2.4	0.8
> 2.4 to 8.4 incl	1.6
> 4.8 to 25 incl	2.4
> 25 to 50 incl	3.2
> 50 to 75 incl	4.0
> 75 to 100 incl	5.6
> 100 to 125 incl	6.4
> 125	8.0

Maximum offset		
Section Thickness (mm)	Joint Categories	
	A	B, C, & D
up to 12.7 incl	1/4t	1/4 t
> 12.7 to 19 incl	3.2 mm	1/4 t
> 19 to 38 incl	3.2 mm	4.8 mm
> 38 to 50 incl	3.2 mm	1/8 t
Over 50	1/16 t or 9.5 mm	1/8 t or 19 mm

The other area of structural discontinuity often encountered by the designers is the nozzle-shell junction. The design codes provide guidelines for area compensation by way of material reinforcement from strength considerations (Fig. 10). In addition to the above, features like shell pullout, forged shell nozzle and rounding the sharp edges (Fig. 11) or providing re-entrant nozzles further reduces the stresses in the junction.

Though all the aspects discussed above are applicable for dissimilar metal weld joint as well, additional care must be exercised in selection of electrodes as it is noticed that failure in such joints primarily stems from mismatch between the coefficients of thermal expansion (CTE) apart from other metallurgical considerations. The electrode chosen must have compatible characteristics and possess matching CTE to minimise thermal stresses on either side of the weld. For critical

Butt welded joints of plates of unequal thicknesses	
Joining plates of unequal thicknesses with butt weld, the thicker plate shall be tapered if the difference in thickness is more than 1/8 in. or one-fourth of the thiner plate code UW-9(c), UW-13. The length of the tapered transition shall be minimum 3 times the offset between the adjacent surfaces. The weld may be partly or entirely in the tapered section or adjacent to it.	
	$1 \geq 3y$
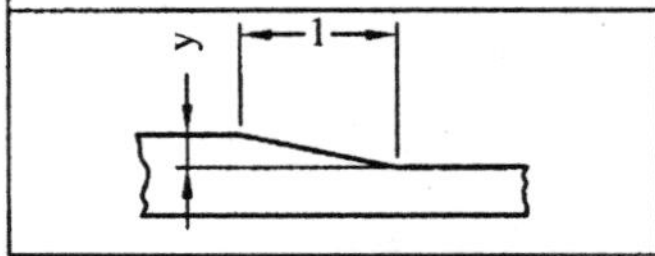	$1 \geq 3y$ Taper either inside or outside of vessel
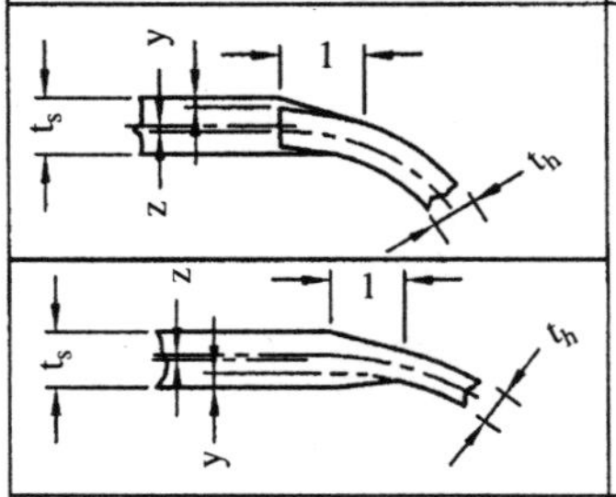	Heads to shells attachment $1 \geq 3y \quad z \leq 1/2\,(t_s - t_h)$ The shell plate centerline may be on either side of the head plate centerline.
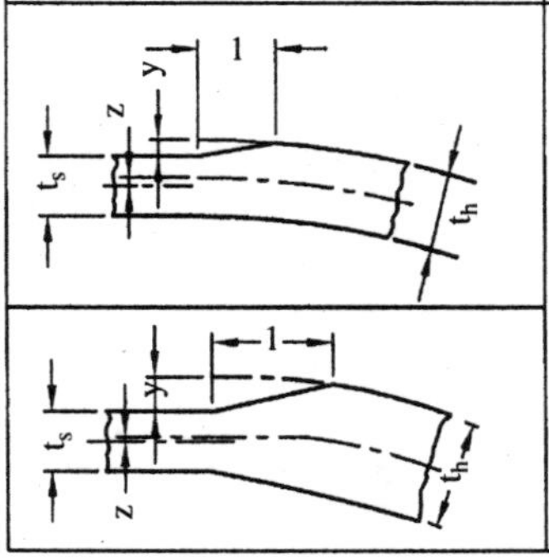	Heads to shells attachment $1 \geq 3y \quad z \leq 1/2\,(t_h - t_s)$ When t_h exceeds t_s, the minimum length of straigth flange is $3t_h$, but need not exceed 1-1/2in. except when necessary to provide required length of taper. when t_h is equal to or less than $1.25i_s$, the length of straight flange shall be sufficient for any required taper. The shell plate centerline may be on either side of the head plate centerline.

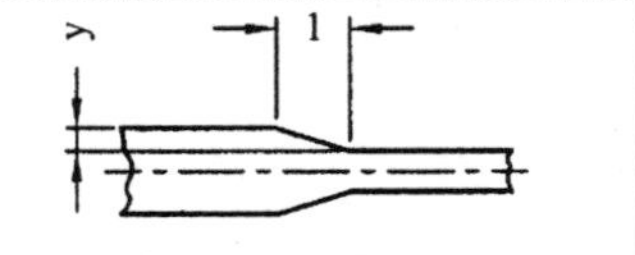

Fig. 9   Acceptable tapered transition for butt-welded joints between plates of unequal thickness [5]

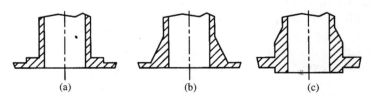

Fig. 10   Typical designs of nozzle opening reinforcement

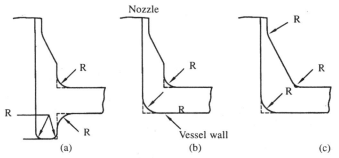

Fig. 11   Some configurations of nozzle reinforcement designed to reduce stress concentration

application a trimetallic transition joint configuration (Fig. 12) instead of direct (bimetallic) configuration shall be preferred.

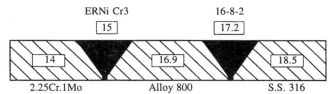

Fig. 12   Design of dissimilar metal joint with transition piece welded using appropriate filer materials for providing graded coefficient of thermal expansion; the numbers indicated within squares are thermal expansion coefficients, in $\mu m\ m^{-1}$

5   CONCLUSION

An attempt has been made to bring out the salient aspects of weld joint design. In conclusion, the integrity of welded fabrication depends ultimately on proper designing of welded joints.

REFERENCES

1. Coleman, M.C., in "Physical Metallurgy and Failure Phenomena", Proc. Fifth Bolton Landings Conference, Lake George, August 1978, Christoffel (RJ) Ed, Schenectady, NY, General Electric, 1979, pp. 408–420.
2. Metals Handbook, vol. 6, "Welding Brazing and Soldering", 9th Edition, American Society for Metals, Metals Park, OH, 1983.
3. Cary, H.B., "Modern Welding Technology", Prentice Hall, Englewood Cliffs, NJ, 1989.
4. "Design Data Book", PSG College of Technology, Coimbatore, Kalaikathir, 1995.
5. ASME Section VIII Division I, Boiler and Pressure Vessel Code, American Society for Mechanical Engineers,
6. Brownell, L.E. and Young, E.H., "Process Equipment design", Wiley Eastern, New Delhi.
7. Rogerson, J.H., In "Significance of Defects in Welds" Second Conf. London 1968, Welding Institute, Cambridge, 1969.
8. Welding Handbook, 8th Edition, vol. 1, Welding Technology, American Welding Society, Miami, 1991.
9. Harvey, J.F., "theory and design of Pressure Vessels", CBS Publishers and Distributors, New Delhi.
10. Hicks, J.G., "Welded Joint Design", Granada, London, 1979.
11. Pfluger A R and Lewis R E eds., Weld Imperfections, Proce. of Symp. At Lockheed Palo Alto, California, Addison Wesley, Reading, UK, 1968.
12. Schwalbe, KH and Kocak, M., "Mis-matching of Welds", Mech. Engg. Publications Ltd., London, 1994.

17. Challenges in Meeting Reliability Requirements in Welding

Baldev Raj and T. Jayakumar

Metallurgy and Materials Group Indira Gandhi Centre for Atomic Research
Kalpakkam 603 102, India

Welding technology is an essential ingredient of the industrial world. It is impossible to imagine the industrial scenario without this technology. While it is necessary to use the already established welding technology in the conventional materials and components with more and more stringent control on quality and reliability, it is also necessary that conventional and modern welding technologies are used in advanced materials and in newer component designs that are undertaken for critical applications, and for improving the economics. A good welding technology and practice must ensure that, whatever may be the innovations introduced, there must not be any sacrifice on safety and reliability that are expected from the components. All the efforts made to design a good weld and to fabricate one may simply be wasted if it is not ascertained and known beforehand that the joint is indeed fit for the purpose. Failure of many of the components which occurs in-service could be avoided if well known engineering practices in materials selection, design and welding technology and quality assurance were respected.

In its infancy, welding was confined at the technicians level and survived the initial period of uncertainty primarily on the strength of the skills of the welders. However, a few incidences made the industry realise that to extract the most from this exciting technology, multidisciplinary efforts are needed and wide ranging R&D activities must be initiated. New materials, new welding processes and stringent requirements of performance have strengthened the need for multidisciplinary efforts in an inter-related way. In India, the situation is better as the welding fraternity has always been active with modern outlook having the correct attitude of mixing R & D with practical applications.

The stringent requirements in the Indian nuclear industry had led to rapid progress in welding technology. It is this industry that laid the foundations and set the pace for total quality management and the concept like 'fitness for purpose' has to be built into the component. The ISO-9000 concepts that are sweeping the industry were in fact started in the nuclear industry a few decades ago. An important philosophy preached and adhered to by the nuclear industry is that cost-effectiveness and quality are inseparable partners for obtaining long term benefits from any industrial endeavor of mankind. These objectives of nuclear industry set the trends for significant progress in welding science and technology. Today, the concepts, developed by the nuclear industry, are practiced by many forward looking industries. Indeed, the space, defence, power, petrochemical and transport industries follow these concepts to their advantage for healthy growth. Many refinements and specific developments have been brought by these industries to suit to specific needs.

Fitness for purpose for much of even the most stringent applications tolerates (though not desirable) a certain rate of failures, repair and maintenance even though there are always some elements of reluctance in such tolerances. Tolerance for the minimum failure incidents is accepted from the realisation that the market for quality components depends on cost-effectiveness that cannot be forgotten. These are certain situations in nuclear, aerospace and a few strategic components of conventional plants where design, manufacture and quality assurance work in unison to bring the failure incidence to near zero. This necessity may be imposed on account of hazards associated with the consequences of failures, and/or inaccessibility of the component for replacement or repair. Strictly speaking, there are no codes or standards available to ensure absolutely safe welds. In very stringent situations, the user is required to develop his own design and safety criteria and requirements to enhance the reliability so that failures can be minimised and the backup actions are available in the event of the unavoidable failure. Keeping aside such extraordinary situations, it is common to refer to national and/or international standards or codes to lay down the basis for good welding engineering practice. Indeed, even in the demanding situations of near zero failure, international codes and standards are the basic building blocks and these are carefully modified to enhance reliability with an eye for cost competitiveness.

Many industrial failures are weld related. Analysis of failures clearly demonstrate the shortcomings in weld design, fabrication and quality assurance aspects. Therefore the information on systematic analysis of failures and lessons learnt from the analysis are channeled back to the designers and operators, it goes a long way to contribute to the reliability and safety by way of reduced incidences of failures in future.

In this paper, the experiences and the perception of the authors on various above mentioned aspects with respect to the advancements in inspection, testing and quality control of weldmets for success of welding technology and practice are discussed. The developments of suitable specifications, codes and standards are discussed for high technology strategic areas where the presently available specifications, codes and standards do not cover such high technology practices. This would be discussed in the paper by taking a few examples from nuclear industry. A few techniques developed at the authors' laboratory for high sensitive defect detection in welded components are discussed. These include application of signal analysis, pattern recognition and neural network methodologies on ultrasonic signals, microfocal radiography, image processing and enhancement of radiographs. The procedures developed at the author's laboratory for assessment of microstructures and residual stresses in welded components are also discussed in this paper. These include use of magnetic Barkhausen noise analysis and XRD measurements for assessment of post weld heat treatment (microstructure and residual stresses) in tube to tube-sheet weld joints. In spite of adopting various procedures and practices for reliable welded components, defects in welds (formed during fabrication or developed in service) are inevitable and suitable repair procedures are to be developed and qualified. The programme undertaken at the authors' laboratory to assess the repair welding procedures is also discussed in this paper. As mentioned, the majority of industrial failures are weld related. It becomes an absolute necessity to analyse the causes of these failures and recommend corrective actions, thus improving the welding technology and practice on a continuous basis. The experience of the authors in the area of failure analysis of welded components has shown that the failures are due to non-adherence to specified fabrication procedures and inadequacy in quality assurance procedures, deficiency in weld design, human factor (inspection related) etc. Development of mainiature specimen testing methodologies at the authors' laboratory, for obtaining mechanical properties of weld and HAZ regions (with different microstructures and compositions) is also discussed. The miniature specimen technology is essential to obtain the properties of weld and HAZ regions separately. It is also possible to test the actual welded components as these tests require only specimens of size 3 mm diameter X 500 micron thick, which can be scooped out from the actual components.

The current practice is to make the welds and then check the quality. Any rejection of final product leads to economic penalty. On-line monitoring of weld quality during welding itself is the current thinking. Two potential techniques that make this possible are acoustic emission technique and thermography. This allows immediate detection of unacceptable welds thus allowing for repair/rejection. The future is the intelligent welding practice. In this case, the quality of weld is continuously monitored as the welding progresses (as in the case of on-line weld monitoring) using NDT techniques. However, the superiority of the intelligent welding procedure is that it uses the NDE parameters in a feedback loop to control the welding procedure, thus giving 100% quality weldments. These developments are also discussed in this paper. The expert systems developed at the authors' laboratory for deciding the procedures for nondestructive inspection of weldments by X-radiography and ultrasonic testing for defect detection and assessment are also discussed in this paper. The authors' views on human resource development with respect to welding education, refresher courses, training and certification of welding technologists and development of welding technology related standards are also brought out in the paper.

CODES AND STANDARDS

It is important to recognize that codes and standards for non-destructive testing and evaluation are evolved by multidisciplinary inputs from experts having rich experiences and insight in the particular field. Codes, standards and specifications are constantly evolving in line with the progress and developments in the industry. At any point of time, the codes and standards reflect the level of technological expertise available. However, there is always a gap between the codes and standards and the level of available technology. The technology may be at a higher level than that implied in a standard. However, it may not be proven. Only proven technology (materials, manufacturing process, inspection techniques, in service inspection) gets incorporated into standards and codes so as to benefit a given industry or industries. The utility company can always ask for higher level of technology available at that time but not included in the codes and standards, if it is felt that this is necessary for enhanced quality and reliability (even if this may entail additional costs). But for that, it must ensure that a special code/standard is made specific to the application at hand. A few examples given below would explain the observations mentioned above in quantitative engineering terms.

Fast Breeder Test Reactor (FBTR), at India Gandhi Centre for Atomic Research, Kalpakkam, Tamil Nadu uses sodium as coolant at approximately 823 K outlet temperature for the purpose of removing the fissile heat. The high temperature and the high neutron fluence (10^{23} n/cm², Energy: > 0.1 MeV) seen by the components, coupled with the performance requirements due to the exposure to liquid metal sodium coolant have imposed certain stringent specifications for the properties of the austenitic stainless steel welded joints. These have necessitated the following:

(i) stringent control on local and volumetric content of ferrite, (ii) measures to achieve adequate tensile properties at high temperature and ensuring minimum of 40% elongation on all welded and transverse tensile specimens, (iii) control on heat input during welding and heat treatment (to avoid sensitization), (iv) undertaking the fabrication and assembly work in a nuclear clean hall by effectively controlling the air borne dust and particulate matters, (v) minimising the mismatch of the joint between dished end and shell, (vi) preventing carbon steel contamination and restricting the halogen and sulphur contents on all the stainless steel surfaces. The specifications made for FBTR components include the above requirements and they have been stringently followed. It was also seen that in any fabrication shop, stainless steel work area was exclusive and away from carbon steel work area. Stainless steel wire brushes were insisted upon for cleaning austenitic stainless steel components. Care was also exercised to ensure that only aluminium oxide grinding wheels were used. The teams working on stainless steel nuclear components were adequately trained and disciplined to respect the work requirements during fabrication. Even walking on stainless steel plates was considered a lapse as per specifications.

The dished ends for the various pressure vessels were made with the dimensional tolerances in accordance with IS 4049 (1971). Special care was taken and instructions were issued to the manufacturer to start rolling and manufacture of shells, only after obtaining the dished ends and taking the circumference of the flanged portion as a reference dimension. As an example, we know that for a dished end with outer diameter between 1200 mm and 2400 mm and thickness of 25 mm, a standard tolerance in circumference was specified as ± 12 mm. In such a case, there is every possibility that gross mismatch may occur between shells and dished end if the shell has already been made. This mismatch will finally lead to indiscriminate and heavy cold work and residual stresses during the efforts to match the dimensions of the shell and the dished end prior to welding of the dished end with the shell. Such situations were avoided in the case of fabrication of vessels for FBTR.

During the design and construction phase of FBTR, a set of specifications, under the title FBTR specifications was finalised. These specifications took into account the appropriate clauses and provisions from ASME, ASTM, AFNOR (French standards) with supplementary requirements, based on the experience and expertise of the FBTR engineers as well as the experience gained by French nuclear industry during the construction, operation and maintenance of Rapsodie (a reactor similar to FBTR) and by the nuclear industry in other countries where fast breeder technology was being pursued. The database thus prepared was used at different stages of procurement of raw materials, fabrication of components and final inspection, testing and commissioning. The acceptance criteria for the welding consumables and welded constructions were required to be more stringent and exacting than the criteria spelt out in ASME or AWS. The scopes of acceptance criteria for the various non-destructive testing techniques i.e. liquid penetrant examination, magnetic particle testing, radiography and ultrasonic testing have been more stringent as compared to those available in ASME. To give an example, in a radiography situation where the detection of 4T hole in an ASTM 5 penetrameter may be considered adequate under the normal circumstances, the requirement for FBTR has been the detection of 1T hole in ASTM 5 penetrameter. In certain cases, multi-wall radiography technique was adopted with stringent sensitivity requirements. Special attention was paid to ensuring dimensions to close tolerances. Helium leak testing under vacuum was used for all components in primary and secondary sodium circuits to achieve high degree of leak tightness in large sized vessels and systems (for example vessels with 40 m^3 capacity). The leak testing was carried out using specially designed combinations of vacuum systems using roots-blower and mechanical vacuum pumping system with the capacity of 2000 m^3/hr at 0.132 Pa for achieving the vacuum condition in the large vessels of the order of 10^{-2} Pa (a prerequisite for helium leak testing).

It is essential to appreciate that updating of specifications is an essential feature of quality management in any system. Specifications are modified to take care of deficiencies noticed in service or to effect improvements called upon by advances in technology. As the level of technology improves, to remain competitive in business as well as to ensure safe and reliable performance of components, it is essential that design, manufacturing and inspection specifications are updated. Improvement of quality by one or a few of the industries is not sufficient to improve quality of finished products since total quality depends on overall quality of many components which go into a product and all industries cannot be hundred percent self-sufficient to produce all the parts of a finished product. Thus, effort should be made to inculcate the quality concept and ensure their adoption by all industries (small and big) to earn competitive edge in the international market. It is pertinent to point out here that many small industries often feel that quality management concepts are uneconomical and are only needed in large scale setups. This is a very wrong notion because it is a small scale setup which often collapses due to heavy rejections which could have been easily avoided if proper management concepts for quality at all the stages of manufacture were followed. ISO-9000 accreditation is well within the reach of many welding industries in India. Total commitment of management is however, a prerequisite if the concepts are to be absorbed by the industries. Strict and honest adherence to the system specifications laid down is a must for ISO-accreditation. The crux of the matter lies in defining realistic system specifications and creating the discipline from the workers in the bottom rungs to the topmost person in the organisation hierarchy to respect the system. The summary of the above arguments and descriptions is aimed at to convey that no standard is static, not even ISO-9000. The survival of the industry depends on evolution and improvement. This concept well known as Deming (the quality Guru) rule has emphasised that quality improvement and not the present quality should be the end objective. The realistic engineering inspection of some of the critical welded components for enhanced reliability is often not possible with the present NDT standards. The standards specify the use of artificial defects. Strictly speaking, use of artificial defects to simulate the natural defects is basically invalid and illusory. This observation is based on the fact that the equivalence of a natural defect and an artificial defect is not achievable. Again, the standards are often silent on the microstructure of the parent metals and the weld metals that may significantly influence the defect detection capability of a NDT technique. An important example is the ultrasonic testing of large grained and textured austenitic stainless steel weldments. In such cases, sophisticated methods often are required to extract desired information from the noise signals. Thus standards are required on advanced signal and image analysis, pattern and cluster analysis and artificial intelligence to give clear and reliable evaluation of defects in welded components made of thick austenitic stainless steel materials.

GOOD ENGINEERING PRACTICES FOR ENHANCED RELIABILITY

The design, manufacture and construction should employ proven techniques and it should be possible to conduct such analysis of the design as may be necessary for the purpose of demonstrating adequate integrity at any specified time throughout plant life. Every effort should be made in the design, manufacture, construction and operation to avoid the occurrence of defects in the structure. Analyses should be provided to demonstrate the following at any specified time in the life of the plant: (a) that an adequate margin exists between the capability of defect detecting equipment and dangerous defects, and (b) where defects are detected, they can be accepted or an adequate repair can be made. All materials employed in the manufacture and construction should be demonstrated to be suitable in all respects for the purpose of enabling an adequate design to be constructed, operated, inspected and maintained at all specific times throughout the life of the component.

Fabrication Rules

The important fabrication rules are the following

(a) use of high standards of materials, (b) use of high quality welding during all the stages of manufacture supported by a quality assurance programme which ensures full approval of procedures and provides verification of compliance with the procedures and practices, and (c) use of pre-service and in-service inspections to detect subcritical defects which have the potential for developing into critical sizes in future and leading to failures.

A good fabrication practice should consider the three main areas of materials, welding and inspection assessments carefully to achieve high reliability.

Inspection Assessment

During manufacturing, inspection has three principal objectives: (a) to provide an assurance that there are no unacceptable defects by which it is ensured that the manufacturer has satisfied the standard required in the contract specification, (b) to provide assurance that subsequent inspections can be carried out, and (c) to provide assurance that no defects are present in the completed component which could be of safety concern. To meet these objectives, components are subjected to a number of inspections during fabrication. The product form, i.e. plate, forging or casting, is important. For example, inspection of cast austenitic steel is difficult due to the coarse, columnar grains and is often limited to relatively thin surface layers. As the various welds joints are completed, inspections are carried out to ensure that no significant defects are present and that the required quality standards have been met. Finally, after stress relief heat treatment (where appropriate), the welds are reinspected to confirm that no defects of concern to safety and reliability are present. Subsequently, during service, inspections are carried out to find: (a) new defects, which may include small sized pre-existing defects that have grown and become detectable as a result of service exposure, and (b) defects that have grown in service from below the reporting threshold. The processes available for volumetric examination are restricted in practice to radiography and ultrasonics. Of these, only ultrasonic inspections are able to characterise the through thickness size and location of crack-like defects. However, there is no single ultrasonic technique that is capable of detecting and sizing all defects equally, regardless of size, location and orientation. Various different inspection techniques are therefore required. These inspections should be repeated to give confidence in their reliability and must be validated such that the procedures, techniques, equipment and operators are capable of performing the inspection conforming to the required standard. Therefore, diverse and redundant inspections, in terms of both operator and technique, are required for components where incredibility and impossibility of failure is desired and claimed. There are also a number of practical considerations which can degrade the inspections, such as component geometry, access and surface finish. These can be overcome if they are addressed at the design stage, consistent with a "design for inspection" philosophy.

A few case studies emphasising the use of advanced NDT methods and signal analysis in ultrasonic testing (UT) and evaluation of some difficult to inspect welded components are described below:

DEFECT DETECTION WITH HIGH SENSITIVITY AND RELIABILITY IN WELDMENTS USING ADVANCED SIGNAL ANALYSIS CONCEPTS IN ULTRASONIC TESTING

Maraging and Austenitic Stainless Steel Welds—Defect Detection and Characterisation using Pattern and Cluster Analysis

High sensitivity defect detection and characterisation in weldments in these materials continues to be of sustained interest. This is due to the fact that these weldments are used in large numbers in critical and heavy industry applications. Dendritic (hence anisotropic) microstructures of these weldments, especially in the thickness range of 10 to 40 mm pose problems for ultrasonic testing. Considering these facts, the ASME boiler and presser vessel code has recommended that in the case of austenitic stainless steel weldments, any defect that is 10% of thickness should be recorded and monitored. In some cases, it may be desirable to detect defects of much less than 10% of the thickness. In this connection, signal analysis (SA) procedures, by using effective cluster and pattern analysis algorithms have been developed, in the authors' laboratory. These enable detection and characterisation of defects down to 1% of weld thickness (14.0 mm weld thickness) in austenitic stainless steel welds [1]. The complexity of the problem is an excellent area for the development of an expert system, for offering advice in order to carry out effective NDE on these weldments. Such an expert system developed in the authors' laboratory would be described later in this paper. In the case of maraging steel weldments used in the rocket motor casings by the aerospace industry, tight cracks (3 mm × 1 mm) produced by fatigue loading were detected and characterised in the authors' laboratory using cluster and pattern analysis principles [2]. Detection of such small defects for this application, enhances the payload capacity of the rocket, resulting in significant economic and technological gains.

In both the above cases, the cluster and pattern analysis methods use the crosspower spectrum (between signals from weld noise and those from the defects), to obtain the cluster elements. The pattern analysis method generates a pattern called demodulated autocorrelogram (DMAC) pattern from the autocorrelation function of a signal. Features of DMAC are studied for interpretation and evaluation. Figures 1 (a) and (b) show the DMAC patterns for a typical noise and the defect signal from a 1% of the wall thickness notch in an austenitic stainless steel weldment [1]. It may be seen that the noise pattern has more number of lobes as compared to the pattern of the defect signal. Figure 2 shows the clusters for a cross power data for maraging steel weldment [2]. The coordinates of centroids for the noise-defect signals are higher than those for the noise-noise signals.

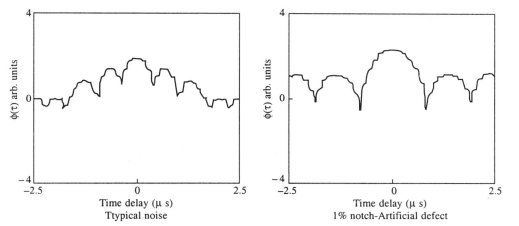

Fig. 1(a) **DMAC pattern for noise in an austenitic stainless steel weld**

Fig. 1(b) **DMAC pattern for a 1% notch in an austenitic stainless steel weld**

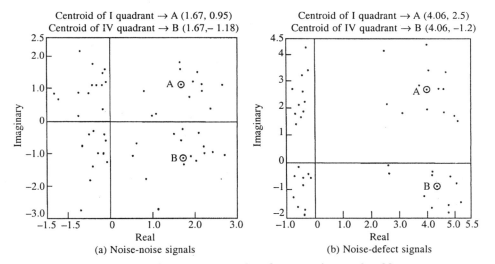

Fig. 2 Clusters for cross power data for maraging steel weldment

During the inspection of one of the rocket motor casings, a defect was noticed by ultrasonic testing. In order to assess the integrity of this casing on the basis of fracture mechanics principles, quantitative assessment and characterisation of type of the defect was necessary. The information needed in this case includes type, location (surface/subsurface) and size of the defect. It can be understood that linear defects which are present right on the surface are more harmful as compared to volumetric defects inside the material. Spectral analysis of the ultrasonic signals recorded from the defect locations has been carried out. In this connection, a systematic study made has shown clear differences in the auto-power spectra of the signals recorded for (a) noise (defect free region), (b) linear defect (single planar crack), (c) multiple planar cracks (SCC) and (d) corrosion pit (Fig. 3 (a-d) [3]. Based on this information and the auto-power spectrum of the

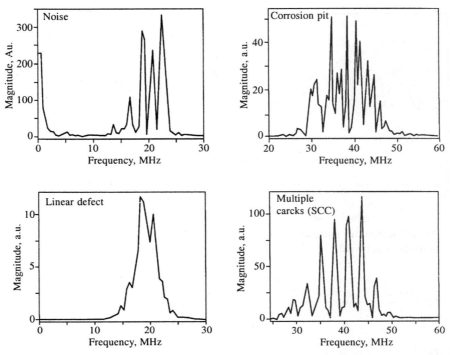

Fig. 3   **Autopower spectra of general noise and signals received from regions of defects viz. linear defect (single planar crack), multiple planar cracks (stress corrosion cracking) and corrosion pit.**

signal obtained from the defect in one of the segments of rocket motor casings, it has been concluded that the defect is of planar type. The depth analysis indicated that the defect is located 2 mm below the surface. The size of the defect was estimated to be 3.5 mm deep and 3.0 mm length.

Subsequently, the radiographic image of this defect has been processed (averaging and contrast stretching) and found to be made up of interconnected porosities appearing as a linear defect (Fig. 4). The size of the defect as measured from radiographic image matched well with that obtained by ultrasonic testing, thus enhancing the reliability of size estimation. Such a systematic study provided all the information needed for assessing the acceptability of the casing.

End-cap Weld Joints in Fuel Elements of Pressurised Heavy Water Reactors (PHWR)

In PHWRs, uranium oxide fuel pellets are encapsulated in Zircaloy-2 cladding tubes of 0.37 mm thickness and sealed with end caps. Resistance welding of the end caps of cladding tubes leaves a material upset both inside and outside on the joint. The outside upset is machined off leaving only a tiny step between the end cap and the cladding tube, but the inside upset remains. Figure 5 shows the cross-section of a typical end cap weld, with these upsets and ultrasonic ray propagation path. So far, helium leak test on all the weld joints and destructive metallographic tests on a sampling basis have been carried out to ensure the integrity of the weld joints. These

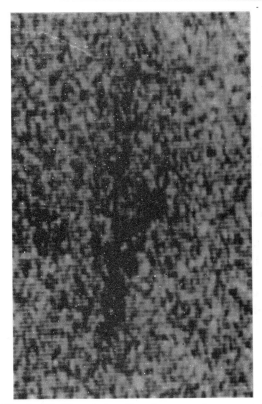

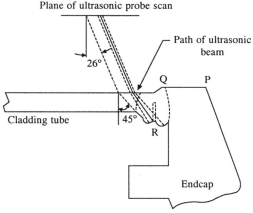

Fig. 4 Radiograph after image enhancement showing inter-connected porosities (appears as a linear defect

Fig. 5 Cross-section of typical end plug weld joint and ultrasonic ray propagation path in the end cap weld of the fuel element of a pressurized heavy water reactor-water immersion ultrasonic testing

techniques have their own limitations. Helium leak test detects only those defects which have passed 'through' the tube wall thickness. Metallography is a destructive test and reveals only the cut section, and cannot be carried out on all the joints. The quality assurance procedures do not give enough confidence when the target is zero failure rate with the objective of keeping the coolant of nuclear reactors as less radioactive as possible. In the authors' laboratory, a solution has been found in this regard by developing ultrasonic testing aided by digital signal analysis [4].

UT of the end-cap weld joints poses several significant difficulties. These are due to: (i) small dimensions (diameter of the tube and the wall thickness etc.) involved, (ii) abnormal weld contours and (iii) stringent sensitivity requirements. The use of signal analysis technique on the ultrasonic echoes was expected to overcome these difficulties. In order to simulate ideal conditions, reference defects (holes) of 0.1 mm dia. and 5, 10, and 20% of the wall thickness depth were introduced at the ID region and also on the OD region of the weld joint using spark erosion machining (standardised at the authors' laboratory). The above reference defects were selected in order to find the level of detection sensitivity achievable and extract information on the defect sizes. The ultrasonic testing of the weld region is based on angle beam with shear wave using immersion pulse echo methods.

Since the signals from the geometrical features of the weld joints were found to vary between 17–35% full scale height (FSH), only OD defects of 20% wt. and above could be detected reliably using conventional UT technique. In the case of 10% and 5% wt. defects, the signals from the defects were fully masked by the signals due to geometrical features. Hence, in order to increase the sensitivity of defect detection down to 10% wt. or less, digital signals analysis technique, particularly autopower spectral analysis, was explored. The autopower spectra of signals from the defects have a broad envelope pattern with or without small fluctuations in the spectrum envelopes. In the case of autopower spectra of signals due to the geometrical upset, the spectrum envelope has large flucturations in its power (a number of narrow packets), often attaining zero or near zero values, which is not observed in the case of defect signal autopower spectra. Figure 6(a) shows the autopower spectrum of a signal from a geometrical upset, whereas Figure 6(b) shows that from a defect. After establishing this approach with the help of fine artificial defects, a large number of production end cap welds which passed helium leak testing were subjected to digital ultrasonic signal analysis tests. The results from these studies were confirmatory of the earlier studies on artificial defects, thus establishing the validity of the signal analysis approach for defect detection in these weldments. This approach also paved way for the design and use of an automated workstation through which probe scanning, signal acquisition, digitisation and analysis, and classification can be performed.

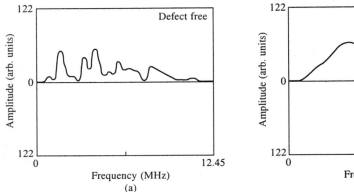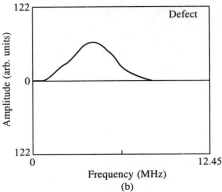

Fig. 6   (a) Auto spectrum of UT signal from the geometrical upset of end plug, (b) Auto spectrum of UT signal from a defect in the end plug

UT of Weld Joints in Thin Walled Hastelloy Tubes

This example again demonstrates the use of digital signal analysis for the discrimination between the ultrasonic signals due to geometrical features and those due to defects during UT. The test object is the longitudinal weld joint in a thin tube (0.4 mm wall thickness and 78 mm OD) of hastelloy [5]. In the weld seam, undercut type weld defects and porosities were earlier observed by radiography. Difficulties were encountered in evaluating the weld quality from the radiographs due to the small tube wall thickness. Ultrasonic immersion testing was carried out with 10 MHz transducer. Suitable test parameters were selected based on the experience gained in testing the thin walled PHWR fuel clad end-cap weld, discussed earlier. Weld geometry was found to give an echo amplitude of about 20–40% FSH, and at the same sensitivity, porosities (0.05 – 0.1 mm) gave an amplitude of about 50–80% FSH. Weld undercut was also found to give prominent echo amplitude. In addition to the defects detected by radiography, additional defect indications were detected by UT. In order to confirm the additional UT indications, destructive metallography was carried out. Analysis of each of these signals was carried out to study the demodulated autocorrelograms (DMAC) for the porosities observed in metallographic analysis. Figure 7(a) shows the DMAC pattern for a signal from a defect free region and Fig. 7(b) shows the DMAC pattern from porosity. The DMAC patterns of porosities showed non-overlapping lobes and distinct differences in the number of lobes, as compared to those from the good regions of the weld. The height of the central lobe for the patterns of porosities could also be used as a distinguishing parameter, since they were higher in amplitude. The total spectral energy of the signals were also computed. It was found that the total spectral energy varied from 300 to 400 units for the signals from the good region of the weld, and from 400 to 800 units for the porosities depending on their size.

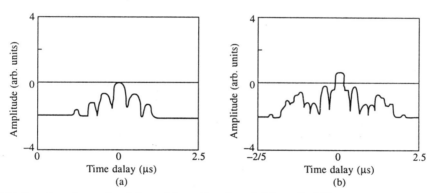

Fig. 7 **DMAC pattern for a signal from (a) good region of thin walled Hastelloy tube, (b) from a region with porosity**

QUALITY ASSURANCE OF TUBE TO TUBESHEET WELD JOINTS OF STEAM GENERATOR ASSEMBLY OF PROTOTYPE FAST BREEDER REACTORS—NEW INSPECTION TECHNIQUES, THEIR RELEVANCE AND STANDARDISATION METHODOLOGIES

The Problem and the Requirement

The tube materials of steam generators of fast breeder reactors are mainly Cr-Mo steels. The basis for the selection of these steels is well known [6–8]. The importance of high integrity welds in steam generators is due to risks arising out of sodium water reaction [9]. Hot liquid sodium flows in the shell region outside the tubes and water flows inside the tubes. A leak in a tube leads to the generation of hydrogen due to reaction of sodium and water with undesirable consequences. Tube to tube weld joints (Fig. 8) are the regions of a tube where the possibility of a leakage path is highest. Thus extreme care is taken in the quality assurance of the joints. In this regard, two aspects are important: (a) control of weld defects, (b). use of proper post weld heat treatment (PWHT) to get a heat treated weld with good resistance to caustic stress corrosion cracking and acceptable long term mechanical properties.

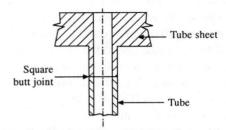

Fig. 8 Sketch showing tube to tubesheet joint of steam generator assembly of Prototype Fast Breeder Reactor

The main defects in the weld joints are porosities. Standards stricter than ASME code are used for acceptable porosity levels in the weld. In is expected that the radiography technique should be able to detect single porosities of size at least of the order of 50 μm [10]. In the entire weld (i.e. for an outer diameter 17.2 mm, thickness 2.3 mm, and width 5–6 mm) of the weld, the total pore count must be such that the sum of diameters of all the pores visible is less than 2.54 mm. This leads to the necessity of high sensitivity defect detection in these welded joints.

Microfocal Radiography of Tube to Tubesheet Weld Joint

The configuration of the weld joint is such that conventional radiography is not possible as the desired position for the X-ray source to carry out single wall high sensitivity radiography is not accessible. Gamma radiography using thulium 170 has been attempted. However, resolutions are poor due to finite size of the radiation source. Hence, microfocal radiography with rod anode is the only solution for the NDT examination of such welds.

Microfocal radiography technique with rod anode configuration has been standardized in the authors' laboratory for the evaluation of the weld joints [10, 11]. The first step in the technique was to characterize the focal spot size of the microfocal radiography system. This is the most important parameter which contributes to radiographic resolutions. The knowledge of focal spot size and shape also enables quantitative interpretation. Only if the focal spot size is sufficiently small, the porosities of the order of 25–30 μm in the weld can be reliably detected. There is always a doubt on the focal spot size that is quoted by the manufacturers. Pinhole imaging is used in conventional radiography for the sizing of the focal spot. However, for microfocal radiography, this is difficult due to the small size of the focal spot and the very low contrast of the pinhole image. Digital image processing was developed in the authors' laboratory to overcome the problem of low contrast image [9]. The focal spot size delineated by this technique was 44 $\mu m \times 29$ μm (the major and minor axes of an ellipse of the image of backward throw probe at 90 kV and 20 μA ratings.

More than 100 trial weld joints were radiographed to establish the procedure for quality assurance. The weld joint specimens were prepared by butt welding of 2.25 Cr–1 Mo tubes of 17.2 mm OD and 2.3 mm wall thickness. Autogenous GTAW process was used from the bore side. A backward throw probe with a diameter of 10 mm and with a beam spread of −5 × 55 × 360 was inserted from the tubesheet side and the radiography of the weld was carried out with a projective magnification of 3X. A special radiographic cassette was designed and developed for this purpose.

Results on the trial welds of these tubes have shown that it is possible to resolve a 30–40 micron diameter steel wire placed on the inside of the tube. This corresponds to 1.3%–1.6% of the wall thickness of the tube. Radiographs taken during the developmental stage of the welding have revealed the following:

(i) Too many minute gas porosities, the extent of which needs to be reduced
(ii) Weld joint line was found to be wavy due to non-perfect tie-up.
(iii) Uneven reinforcements
(iv) Significant weld ripple

Figure 9 shows a typical microfocal radiograph of weld joint with porosities of the order of 100–300 microns. The penetramenter wires can also be seen clearly in the radiograph. The feedback information from the microfocal radiography studies was helpful to arrive at the correct weld parameters for an optimum weld joint. This work has shown how the microfocal radiography technique can be effectively used in coordination with the welding method for ensuring quality of heat exchanger assembly.

Fig. 9 **Typical microfocal radiograph of weld joint with porosities of the order of 100–300 microns. The penetrameter wires can also be seen clearly.**

Post Weld Heat Treatment of Tube to Tubesheet Weld Joint

Apart from the requirement in the quality control procedure that the weld joints should be free from unacceptable defects that may lead to leakage paths, it is also considered essential that post weld heat treatment (PWHT) should be used for removing most of the residual stresses whose presence, may lead to the failure of the tube to tube—sheet weld joint. Although preventive measures during welding to eliminate or minimize tensile residual stress by controlled heating and cooling have been suggested [12], PWHT is considered a necessity for preventing the problem mentioned above. In the authors' laboratory, the adequacy of the PWHT has been assessed by the measurement of residual stresses and by measurement of microhardness profiles before and after PWHT. A new technique called Magnetic Barkhausen Noise analysis has also been developed and used for the assessment of residual stresses in the weld joint [13]. The results of Barkhausen Noise analysis have been correlated with those obtained by microhardness measurements. This is the first time that an assessment of the residual stresses before and after PWHT in such a joint has been done.

Magnetic Barkhausen Noise Analysis of Tube to Tubesheet Weld Joints

It is often felt necessary to use a field worthy NDT technique to check the adequacy of the

PWHT employed. It is all the more necessary for this application in view of the large number of tube to tube sheet weld joints involved. For example, the total numbers of tube to tubesheet weld joints in the steam generator modules (42 Nos) of the proposed Prototype Fast Breeder Reactor (500 MWe) in India are: evaporator: 7084, reheater: 1708, superheater: 2380. A technique based on Magnetic Barkhausen Noise (MBN) signal analysis developed in the authors' laboratory has shown good promise for assessment of residual stresses. This work is the first to use MBN for the characterisation of PWHT in the weld joint. Magnetic flux perturbation and acoustic emissions are generated when an induced magnetic field in ferromagnetic materials is swept in a hysteresis loop. The former is referred to either as MBN (magnetic Barkhausen noise) or BN (Barkhausen Noise). MBN signals are produced as a result of discrete changes in magnetisation caused mainly by the motion of the 180 degree domain walls as the magnetic field is varied. The signals are detected by a search coil. Since MBN is related to the nucleation and movement of magnetic domain walls which get influenced by presence of residual stresses in addition to different microstructural features, MBN measurements can be used to assess residual stresses and for characterisation of microstructural features. MBN measurements were made at the weld centre, 5, 15, and 25 mm from the weld centre on both sides of the weldment. Figure 10 shows the schematic of the weld joint with positions on actual scale at which MBN measurements have been made. The measurement positions were selected in such a way as to cover weld, HAZ and base metal regions. Microhardness measurements were made at these positions using a Vicker's hardness tester with a load of 5 kg for the purpose of correlating the MBN data. After the measurements in the as welded condition, the tubes were post weld heat treated at 973 K for 1 h followed by air cooling. Again the measurements were repeated at the same locations after removing the oxide layer.

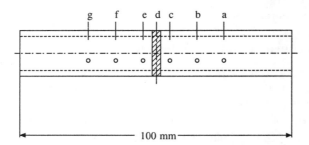

Fig. 10   Schematic diagram of the weld joint drawn to scale indicating the positions at which MBE measurements were carried out

Figure 11 shows the typical variation in RMS voltage of the MBN signal as function of applied magnetic field at different locations of the tube joint in the as welded condition. Figure 12 shows the same after PWHT. Figure 13 shows the MBN peak height at different locations before and after PWHT for three tubes. It is very clear from Fig. 11 that there is maximum MBN peak height at both ends (parents metal region and there is gradual reduction in peak height with decreasing distance from weld. The weld shows the minimum MBN peak height. The difference in the peak height and peak position at the two ends (a, f) is attributed to the difference in the heat transfer during welding due to the presence of thick carbon steel support block on one side

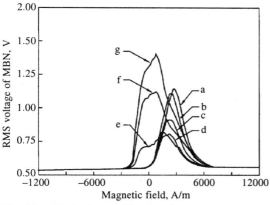

Fig. 11 Typical variation in the rms voltage of the MBE signal as a function of applied magnetic field for half of the magnetization cycle in the as-welded condition at different positions (a to g in Fig. 10)

Fig. 12 Typical variation in the rms voltage of the MBE signal as a function of applied magnetic field for half of the magnetization cycle after PWHT at different positions (a to g in Fig. 10)

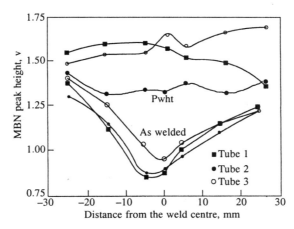

Fig. 13 Peak height value of the MBE signal at different positions before and after post-weld heat treatment

and the free end on the other side (Fig. 10). The carbon steel block acts as a heat sink in one side and the free end is subjected to slow cooling. The large variation in MBN peak height indicates a significant difference in the hardness in the weld, HAZ and base metal regions. This is supported by the hardness measurements as evident from Fig. 14 which shows the hardness values at these regions for the same three tubes before and after PWHT. It can be seen from Figure 13 that, after PWHT, the MBN peak height becomes more or less same at all locations. This is also supported by the narrow variations in the hardness values after PWHT as shown in Figure 14. Figure 15 derived from Figures 13 and 14 shows the relationship between MBN peak height and hardness values before and after PWHT obtained from different locations for all the three tubes. In the as welded condition, it can be observed that an inverse linear relationship between MBN and hardness exists. There is a large increase in the MBN peak height in the weld

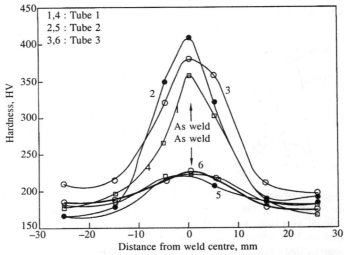

Fig. 14 Hardness values at different positions before and after post-weld heat treatment

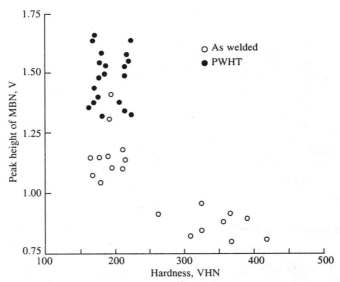

Fig. 15 Relationship between MBE peak height and hardness values before and after post weld heat treatment at different positions

and HAZ regions after PWHT as compared to base metal regions. This is attributed to the removal of residual stresses and reduction in dislocation density in the weld and HAZ during PWHT. The MBN peak height values in the weld and HAZ regions significantly differ before and after PWHT and found to be complementary to the hardness values. It is possible to evolve an acceptance criterion based on MBN peak height values to ensure the effectiveness of PWHT. A few case studies pertaining to failure investigations which have led to enhanced reliability of welded components are described further.

Imaging and Assessment of Post Weld Heat Treatment in Cr-Mo Ferritic Steel Weldments by Ultrasonic Velocity Measurements

At elevated temperatures, the performance of Cr-Mo steel weldments is considered to be a life limiting factor and a high percentage of failures have been reported to be weld related. As the microstructure in the as-welded condition is predominantly martensitic in both heat affected zone (HAZ) and weld metal, proper post weld heat treatment (PWHT) is required to be carried out to temper the microstructure and thus improve the toughness of the weld. To ensure acceptable microstructure and mechanical properties after PWHT, a non-destructive technique based evaluation is required. Ultrasonic velocity measurements have been carried out to get the weld profile and to assess the adequacy of PWHT in modified 9Cr-1Mo ferritic steel weldments (Fig. 16) [14]. Ultrasonic velocity measurements across the weld in the as-welded condition revealed that ultrasonic velocity was maximum in the parent metal and minimum in the weld metal. As the amount for weld metal increased in the propagation direction of ultrasonic beam, ultrasonic velocity decreased and hence the amount of weld metal and parent metal could be determined in the propagation direction of ultrasonic beam, which could be used in-turn to get the weld profile. The ultrasonic velocity plot was found to almost replicate the weld profile. The lower velocity in the weld metal is due to the presence of martensitic structure with lower ultrasonic velocity.

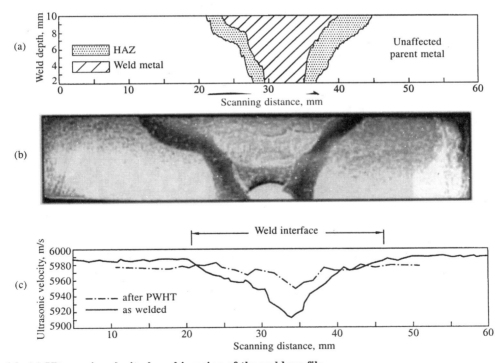

Fig. 16 (a) Ultrasonic velocity-based imaging of the weld profile
   (b) Microphotograph of the etched weldment
   (c) Variation in ultrasonic longitudinal wave velocity with scanning distance across the weldline in as-welded and PWHT conditions

After PWHT (1033 K for 1 h), ultrasonic velocity in the weld metal was found to be slightly lower than that in parent metal but was higher than that in the weld metal in the as welded condition. Hence the adequacy of PWHT can be assessed using ultrasonic velocity and the weld profile can be determined even in the PWHT condition.

Identification of Different Zones in Cr-Mo Ferritic Steel Weldments by Magnetic Barkhausen Emission Technique

Magnetic Barkhausen emission measurements have been used to characterize different microstructural regions such as coarse grain region, fine grain region, intercritical region (composed of retained austenite and tempered ferrite) within the heat affected zone (HAZ) of 2.25Cr-1Mo steel and 9Cr-1Mo steel weldments using specimens with simulated HAZ microstructural features [15]. It is observed that the MBE level decreases with increase in hardness corresponding to different microstructures. The behaviour has been confirmed by the measurements on the actual weldments of 2.25Cr-1Mo steel and 9Cr-1Mo steel [15]. To find out the extent of different microstructural regions, a miniature MBE probe has been used with prior calibration. Figures 17(a) and (b) show the typical variation in the rms voltage value of the MBE signal as a function of current applied to the yoke for different microstructural regions of actual weldments of 2.25Cr-1Mo steel and 9Cr-1Mo steel respectively. It is clear from Figures 17(a) and (b) that the weld metal region, coarse-grain bainite, fine-grain bainite, intercritical region and base metal

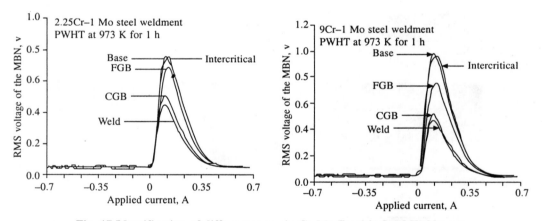

Fig. 17 Identification of different zones in Cr-Mo Ferritic Steel Weldments

region in 2.25Cr-1Mo steel weldment and weld metal region, coarse-grain martensite, fine-grain martensite, intercritical region and base metal region in the 9Cr-1Mo steel weldment could be clearly identified. In weldments of both steels, the MBE amplitude is found to be similar for the intercritical region and the base metal region, however, the field corresponding to the peak position is different. Hence, the intercritical region and the base metal region can be distinguished from the peak position of MBE. In the case of 9Cr-1Mo steel weldments, the CGM with δ-ferrite and CGM without δ-ferrite could not be distinguished, while this was possible in the simulated specimens. This is attributed to the limitation on the spatial resolution of the probe.

FAILURE ANALYSIS OF STAINLESS STEEL DISHED END JOINTS RESULT IN RECOMMENDATIONS FOR ENHANCED RELIABILITY OF PRESSURE VESSELS

Dished ends are common in industrial vessels. In applications where corrosion resistance is needed, a suitable variety of stainless steel is the choice for the vessel. The dished ends which can be torispherical or hemispherical in shape are joined with the cylindrical shells of the vessels by butt welding. The dished ends are commonly fabricated either by cold pressing or by cold spinning. Both these fabrication techniques give rise to high levels of residual stresses [16]. The residual stresses in austentic stainless steel dished ends give rise to problems in two ways: (a) When the dished ends are weld joined with the shells, there is a possibility of sensitisation at the HAZ region. The sensitisation (in some cases termed as weld decay) is strongly enhanced by the presence of residual stresses. (b) In the presence of residual stresses, the sensitised microstructure is highly prone to stress corrosion cracking. A judicious combination of approaches as indicated below can be used to avoid the above problems: (i) Use of very low carbon varieties of steel, (ii) Use of steels with very low contents of deleterious elements like P, S, Sb, etc., (iii) Reduction of the propensity of sensitisation by stress relief annealing of the dished ends, (iv) Reduction or avoidance of chloride or other deleterious ions from the ambience, (v) Avoidance of contact with carbon steel implements.

It was reported [17] that typical temperature distribution during welding of AISI 304 stainless steel shows that in a narrow range in the HAZ, the sensitisation temperature range is present for a considerable amount of time leading to the possibility of sensitisation. Figure 18 (a) shows typical cracking in a U-bend specimen taken from the HAZ region of an AISI 316 SS hemispherical dished end—tested as per ASTM A 562 – practice E for the assessment of sensitization [18–20]. This particular dished end failed during storage, by intergranular stress corrosion cracking at the HAZ of the circumferential weld joint (Fig. 18(b)) [18–20].

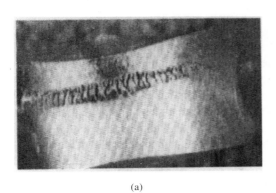

(a)

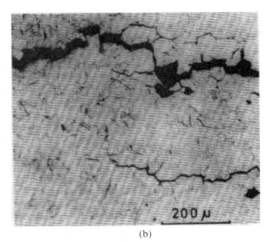

(b)

Fig. 18(a) Typical cracking in a U-bend specimen taken from the heat affected zone region of an AISI type 316 stainless steel dished end (tested as per ASTM A262 practice E). (b) Intergranual crack in an AISI type 316 stainless steel specimen

Residual Stresses in Dished Ends

Theoretical calculations have shown that very large levels of tensile and compressive stress may be present in cold formed dished end. Measurements by X-ray diffraction technique in dished ends have confirmed presence of high residual stress. In a typical case of an AISI 316 SS dished end, the maximum tensile residual stress levels before stress relieving are as follows:

(i) Straight end outside : 85 Mpa
(ii) Straight end inside : 106 Mpa
(iii) Crown inside : 250 Mpa
(iv) Row outside : 270 Mpa

However, it must be remembered that the residual stress pattern in a dished end is very complex and the values of stress often fluctuate in sign both on the inside and outside surface. Our extensive experience shows that in order to have reliable austenitic stainless steel dished ends and the vessels, one important option is to relieve the residual stresses of the cold formed dished ends. The necessity of stress relieving is often not appreciated by the designers, fabricators, and users of austenitic stainless steel process vessels with dished ends.

Attention is paid more to the control of ambient conditions, and the control of the material composition. While these two factors are definitely important, no less is the importance of stress relieving.

FAILURE ANALYSIS OF METALLIC BELLOWS LEADS TO CHANGES IN FABRICATION AND QUALITY ASSURANCE PROCEDURES RESULTING IN ENHANCED RELIABILITY

Metallic bellows are used in engineering industry in a wide range of applications such as vibration isolation, transmission of linear/rotary motions, accommodation of thermal expansion, etc. Leak tightness of operations is very critical in these operations. Welding constitutes the most critical operation in the manufacture and installation of these components. Most commonly used welding techniques in the manufacture are pulsed gas tungsten arc welding (GTAW) and microplasma welding processes. However, special welding processes like electron beam welding or laser welding are also employed in a few specialized cases. Even though various non-destructive evaluation (NDE) techniques like liquid penetrant testing (LPT), X-radiography and helium leak testing (HLT) are used to ensure quality during various stages of manufacture, at present there is no suitable NDE methodology for assuring that the finished bellows would meet fitness for purpose criteria. The worldwide experience shows that the life of welded type bellow is highly unpredictable in spite of various advancements in design, manufacture and quality control procedures. Thus, there is a need for continuous evolution of design, specifications, manufacturing and quality assurance procedures for improving their reliability in operation. A major source of inputs for effecting such changes has been detailed failure analysis of a few weld related failures undertaken by us, on critical bellows used in the Fast Breeder Test Reactor (FBTR), where these bellows are required to experience very demanding service requirements [21].

Welded disc type bellows of the type shown in Fig. 19 are used in the control rod drive mechanism (CRDM) of FBTR. CRDM is an operational and safety device used for start up and

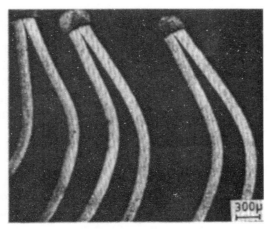

Fig. 19 Photomicrograph showing a section of disc to disc welds

fast shut down of the reactor. It is used to control the nuclear fission reaction in the nuclear core. In addition, it is used to adjust the power levels of the reactor. These thin bellows made out of 0.15 mm thick preformed annular discs (material of construction–AM 350) are welded as shown in Fig. 20 and are used to isolate moving parts of CRDM from molten sodium at 823 K. Optical metallographic examination of cut sections of the disc to disc weld zones (taken at the sites indicated by helium leak testing) revealed unexpected result [12]. It was found that the weld bead profile was non-uniform. There was also considerable variation in the fusion zones (0.150 mm to 0.275 mm). Some sharp crack like openings almost to the extent of opening up of the weld bead were also noticed. All these observations can be appreciated by close examination of Figures 20(a) to (c). The good welds showed uniform weld bead profile and penetration (Fig. 20(a)). The detailed specifications did not include specification for the weld bead profile and penetration. Absence of an adequate NDE method to check the welds (because of complex geometry) resulted in acceptance of these defective welds during manufacturing stage. These

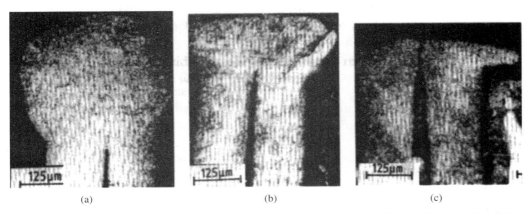

(a) (b) (c)

Fig. 20 Photomicrographs showing bead profiles and extent of fusion of disc to disc weld in different segments of the failed bellow

failure analyses resulted in evolution of specifications for the weld bead profile and depth of penetration. Destructive metallography on a statistical basis to check the weld quality was also specified to ensure the fitness-for-purpose of the fabricated bellow. Even though this quality control check is expensive, in view of the the critical nature of application and cost of replacement of an entire sub-assembly in the event of a failure, such an examination proves to be cost effective and thus fully justified. In addition, metallographic evaluations are incorporated at the stage of manufacturing for optimisation of welding parameters and qualifications of welding fixtures and manipulators.

There have been other instances of metallic bellows failures, like in the case of a few convoluted bellows used in bellow sealed globe valves for sodium service. In this failure incident, opening had occurred in the region of weld metal joining the bellow to the end fitting. It was observed that failures had primarily resulted from the use of wrong material (AISI 316 instead of AISI 316L) which in combination with high heat inputs during welding had led to sensitization in the heat affected zone. Intergranular corrosion during storage (in a coastal climate) claimed the life of these bellows prematurely. This clearly brings out the need for strict compliance of material specification and use of optimum welding parameters in ensuring reliability in service. A few failures have also been noticed in welded disc type bellows made of AISI 347 during storage in coastal, humid and saline climate, due to the presence of residual stresses in the material. The presence of residual stresses were confirmed by microstructures and hardness evaluations. These failures have shown the necessity for not only specifying stress relieving of finished product, but also procedures for safe storage of the metallic bellows. Thus, we have learned to use metallic bellows in a reliable manner by making modifications in the design, specification, manufacturing, quality assurance and storage. The modifications have resulted in enhanced reliability. The lessons have been learnt through meticulous failure analyses.

EVALUATION OF REPAIR WELDING PROCEDURES

Repair welding of engineering components is a technology which has several important implications for industries in today's economic scenario. It would help in extending the life of the components. ASME Section III and XI recommend half bead and butter bead temper bead methods for repair welding as these methods do not require post weld heat treatment. It is reported that the microstructure and microhardness in the weld and HAZ are acceptable and hence no PWHT is necessary. However, no studies have been made on the residual stress distribution after repair welding to ensure that the stresses are also within acceptable limits. Therefore, studies have been carried out at the authors' laboratory by making X-ray residual stress measurements in repair welded samples of 9Cr-1Mo steel, to assess the different repair weld methods [22].

Four repair welded samples made by different methods were taken for this purpose. In the conventional method (specimen A), repair welding was carried out by simply filling the defective portion by depositing layers of molten metal. In the ASME recommended half-bead method (specimen B), a layer of molten metal was first deposited on the defective portion. Then after cooling the first layer, half thickness of the first layer was removed mechanically and then second layer of molten metal was deposited over this. In the other ASME recommended butter bead temper bead method, after depositing the first layer, the second layer was deposited with higher heat input, using higher current (specimen C) or higher diameter electrode (specimen D). In all the three ASME methods, the microstructure of the HAZ formed during first layer deposition gets transformed to an acceptable structure. Figure 21 shows the distribution of residual stresses across the weld (the direction) of residual stress is perpendicular to the weld line) for the four specimens. It is clear from Fig. 21 that, in all the methods, the stresses in the weld centre are tensile with the values in the range 260 to 300 MPa. The specimen D shows the compressive stresses in the HAZ (5 mm from the weld centre line) as compared to tensile stresses seen in the HAZ region in the case of other specimens. Since HAZ is weak in the case of 9Cr-1Mo steel and prone to failure, the method used for making specimen D i.e. butter bead temper bead method using higher diameter electrode is most suitable as it avoids tensile stresses in the HAZ region. This study also pointed out that if high tensile stresses are to be avoided in the weld region, post weld heat treatment becomes necessary even if the ASME recommended methods are used for repair welding.

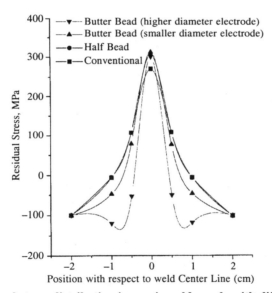

Fig. 21 Residual stress distribution in repair welds made with different methods

MINIATURE DISC BEND TESTING (MDBT)—A NEW TECHNIQUE TO DETERMINE THE MECHANICAL PROPERTIES OF WELD JOINTS

This innovation is a spin off from the nuclear technology where experimental irradiation programmes require the use of very small specimens. The technique can be used very effectively in aged components to find out the accumulated damages and for life extension. Mechanical property assessment of weldment and heat affected zone (HAZ) of a given material is essential in assessing the quality of the weld. However, in many cases, like in the case of thin weldments or weldments of costly materials, it may not be possible to carry out mechanical testing using specimens of size and geometry as per standards/codes, because the volume of material available is not adequate. Again, in the case of service-exposed components, when it is necessary to find out the strength of welded joints without jeopardising the functional capabilities of the components, it is only possible to extract very small specimens of weldment/parent metal from the components. Hence there is a need for the development of miniature specimens and test methods to ensure reliability in a cost effective way. Miniature disc bend test (MDBT) is a technique developed to satisfy these requirements.

MDBT employs a 3 mm diameter and 0.2 to 0.3 mm thick circular disc, similar to a transmission electron microscopy specimen. The volume of such a specimen is over 500 times smaller than that of a conventional tensile test specimen. The testing involves the axisymmetric bending of disc specimens, using a hemispherical punch and test fixture as shown in Figure 22. The figure also shows the positioning of an acoustic emission (AE) probe which is used to determine the desired mechanical properties correctly. The test is carried out in the compression mode using

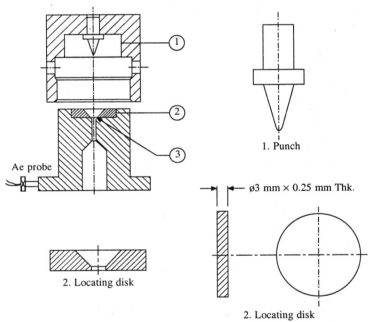

Fig. 22   Fixture for miniatue disk bend test (MDBT) along with acoustic emission probe

a standard tensile testing machine and the resultant load-deflection curve is analysed to obtain mechanical behaviour of the material. Figure 23 shows a typical load-deflection curve obtained by MDBT. The whole curve can be divided into 5 regions as marked in the Figure. Region 1 is the initial linear elastic region and region 2 represents behaviour when the specimen undergoes plastic deformation. The load at measurable deviation from linearity (transition from region 1 to region 2) is a reasonable indicator of yield strength (YS). Region 3 marks the transition from bending to membrane stretching, while in the region 4 the membrane stretching regime spreads to most parts of the specimen volume. Region 5 indicates fracture of the disc specimen. Total

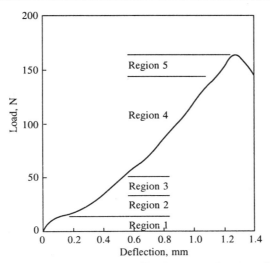

Fig. 23 **Qualitative interpretation of load-deflection curve from a miniature disc bend test**

deflection till failure and total area under the curve are measures of material ductility and toughness respectively. The load vs deflection data can be further analysed using simple plate bending theory and yield strength of the material could be calculated with reasonable accuracy. It is possible to use finite element modelling technique to generate complete mechanical test data.

MDBT test fixture and yield strength calculation methods were developed and used for a variety of specimens in the authors' laboratory. The results have shown good correlation between the yield strength data obtained using conventional test specimens of the same material. One of the important applications where MDBT has been used relates to failure analysis of an aluminium vessel weldment, which had failed in service. The sample sizes available for analysis were small and conventional test methods could not be employed. However, MDBT could clearly bring out the deficiency in a defective weldment that had led to premature failure of the components (weld no. 2 in fig. 24). The defective weld region in the failed piece is seen to have higher YS, reduced ductility and toughness. Acoustic emission (AE) monitoring during MDBT has been employed in order to detect the yield point reliably (Fig. 25) [23]. Yielding leads to unique AE activity that is easily identifiable. AE r.m.s. voltage pattern, superimposed on a load deflection curve obtained using MDBT recognised yield point in an unambiguous manner. Thus, AE monitoring during MDBT provides an authoritative way to determine onset of yielding.

We have not only developed the miniature specimen testing methodology to determine mechanical properties of interest to the designer but contributed by way of enhancing the reliability of test data with AE monitoring. The approach, so developed, has a significant practical value in failure investigation, life prediction studies and generating data where availability of material or test environment is restricted.

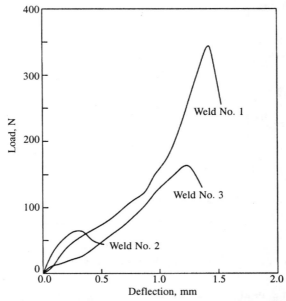

Fig. 24   Load-deflection curves obtained from miniature disc bend tests of different specimens

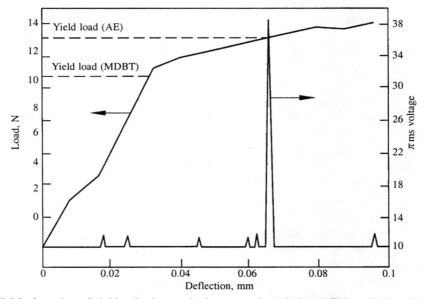

Fig. 25   Reliable detection of yield point by employing acoustic emission (AE) monitoring during MDBT

ON-LINE MONITORING OF WELDS TOWARDS ACHIEVING COST EFFECTIVE RELIABILITY

The reliability and consistency of welds produced can be enhanced through the use of real time (in-time) monitoring. This approach enables assessment and control of the welding process.

Presently, success of automatic/robotic welding systems have been confined to repetitive and large scale fabrication jobs. The present day automatic welding systems do not have the adaptive features of welding process control unlike manual welding wherein the welder alters the welding parameters utilizing his experience and depending on his visual observations during welding. An approach to the adaptable and automatic welding systems lies in the development of on-line sensing techniques capable of giving precise information about the appearance of defects. Two such techniques for on-line sensing are discussed. They are thermography and acoustic emission (AE). On-line techniques are particularly useful and cost effective for high technology industries like nuclear, aerospace etc. where welds with stringent specification for defect acceptance are a must for higher reliability.

Thermography and AE techniques give real time information regarding weld quality and defect formation thus offering on-line possibility of rectification of the welding procedure resulting in reduced scrap and repairs. Thus the need for post weld NDT techniques for examination is reduced. This helps in timely completion and also reduces financial and man-hour requirements. The advantage is particularly important for thicker weldments as rectification and repair costs are significantly reduced by on-line monitoring approach. On-line monitoring can be utilized for welders qualification/training for specialized jobs as the welder gets additional information about his capabilities and inadequacies. In the case of resistance spot welding, weld quality can be immediately known without the necessity for destructive testing of samples.

Thermography to Monitor Welding Process

Thermography refers to the mapping of temperature profiles on the surface of an object. This technique utilizes the infrared spectral band of the electromagnetic spectrum. With the aid of a suitable detector, infrared radiation (IR) can be converted into an image and visualized for interpretations [24]. The temperature distribution over plate surface and weld profile are monitored. For a good weld, these gradients should show repeatable and regular patterns. However, imperfections arising due to weld perturbations are expected to cause a discernible change in the thermal profiles. Experiments were conducted in the authors' laboratory on the possibility of the use of thermal imaging as a real time device for monitoring the defects arising during the welding process [25]. A set of experiments were conducted in which six plates were butt welded by manual metal arc welding process and gas tungsten arc welding process. The plate material used in all the cases were austenitic stainless steel (AISI 316). Four plates were welded in the 1G position while two plates were welded in the 3G position. Surface temperature distributions were measured using the infrared scanning camera placed both at the front side (i.e. the same side as the welding torch) and at the rear of the plate. One of the objectives of the investigations was the detection of arc misalignment during the welding process. It was observed that with the arc being aligned with the centre of the weld, the heat input to the plate by the welding torch is equally distributed on either side of the joint. This balanced thermal distribution results in isotherms that are symmetric about the weld torch centre. In the case of off-seam weld, where the torch has been offset from its centre, the heat input is unequally distributed on either side of the joint resulting in the asymmetry of thermal profiles. A variety of defects were introduced during the welding process. The thermal profiles were recorded and analysed so as to identify the presence and nature of the defects. The defects introduced included porosities, lack of side wall fusion, lack of root penetration, undercut and blow holes. Thermal images were recorded for each pass of the weld. The results obtained from thermography were then correlated with those obtained by radiographing the plates subsequently after welding. It was observed that thermography can be used for on-line detection of lack of penetration, lack of fusion and undercuts. Thermal profiles obtained during on-line weld monitoring are an excellent data bank to model residual stresses in the weldments. Thus, stresses and defects, determined with the help of thermographic technique can pave the way for reliable welds.

Acoustic Emission Studies for Monitoring Welding Process

Acoustic emission technique (AET) can be utilised for detection and location of dynamic defects (i.e. as and when they form or grow) as a welding process progresses. The generation of elastic waves due to strain energy released during the formation of above defects and consequent detection of these elastic waves using piezoelectric based transducers is the main principle of AET. The defects that can be detected, located and qualitatively evaluated by AET are (i) nucleation and growths of cracks during welding and cooling (delayed cracking), (ii) slag inclusion (iii) micro fissuring (iv) cold and hot cracking and (v) reheat cracks and (vi) weld cracking associated with phase transformations. Once these defects are detected and located by AET, other NDT methods can be used for detailed analysis, if needed. AET has been successfully used for on-line monitoring of welds prepared by TIG, submerged arc, electroslag welding, etc. However, non slag forming welding processes are particularly suitable for AE monitoring. The main problem in AE monitoring of welding process is the elimination of unwanted signals due to slag cracking and electromagnetic influence from the arc [26]. The methodologies have been developed to eliminate noise by proper signal conditioning and advanced digital signal processing techniques.

INTELLIGENT WELDING PROCESSES

A real time ultrasonic system (Fig. 26) is being developed for on-line monitoring and control of multipass arc welding process [27]. Experimental results show that it is possible to detect and

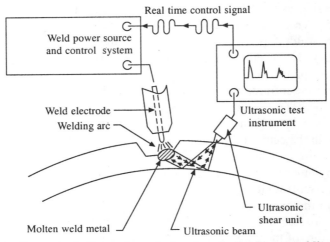

Fig. 26 Conceptual ultrasonic control system for intelligent welding process

locate the liquid/solid weld pool interface. The measurements enable understanding of the influence of high temperature gradients near the molten zones on the ultrasonic wave propagation. Artificial defects are introduced in the already completed weld pass. Detection and location of these defects during welding of subsequent passes by accounting for the beam propagation behaviour in the complex weld pool zone is in progress. The ultimate aim is detection of formation of defects during welding itself so that corrective action can be taken immediately by feed back control using intelligent algorithms.

As part of the previously mentioned DST project on Intelligent Procesing of Materials, work has been carried out on the use of NDT techniques such as acoustic emission and thermography for the study of resistance spot welding and narrow gap welding, and also for end cap welding, spacer pad welding and bearing pad welding processes employed for critical nuclear fuel sub-assembly components, in collaboration with Welding Research Institute (WRI) Tiruchirapalli and NFC Hyderabad [28–30].

Narrow Gap Welding

In this study, carbon steel plates of length 1000 mm, width 100 mm and thickness 40 mm were machined to have a "U" groove. CO_2 welding was carried out inside the groove. Acoustic emission and thermography techniques have been used to monitor the process. Analysis of the AE signals during the three phases of welding indicated that it should be possible to monitor the welding process. Analysis of thermal images indicated that it is feasible to map the thermal wave fronts from isothermal contour movements as the arc moves along the gap. The thermal distribution and its variation with time provides the required input for model based evaluation of residual stresses, which in turn helps in optimising the welding process for obtaining weldments with minimum residual stresses.

Evaluation of Resistance Spot Welds by Acoustic Emission, Thermography and Fuzzy Logic Assessment

In this study, acoustic emission and thermography techniques were used for on-line monitoring of resistance spot welding process. In addition, other on-line approaches such as the use of variations in dynamic resistance with fuzzy logic approach have been attempted on the data of resistance spot welding generated at WRI, Tiruchirapalli.

A number of carbon steel sheets of 1.6 mm thickness were spot welded by making use of 45-kVA capacity portable spot welding machine. Spot welding trials were carried out at different welding conditions (representing stuck weld, good weld and splash weld conditions) by adjusting the phase shift setting and the weld time. Figure 27 shows the variation of RMS voltage of the AE signal with time for good weld and bad weld. Figure 28 shows the thermal image of a good weld and that of a weld made with reduced current. Analysis of a number of welds indicated that the heat distribution in a good weld is uniformly and symmetrically distributed about the centre of the weld, whereas bad welds have irregular thermal pattern.

For implementation of the fuzzy logic control, both nugget diameter and dynamic resistance were graded as small, medium and large with triangular membership function. The quality is graded as very poor, poor, good and very good. Based on the software developed at Indian Institute of Technology, Madras (Chennai) fuzzy estimator for the above experimental data has

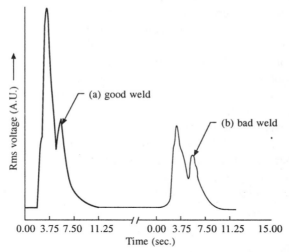

Fig. 27   Variation in AE RMS voltage with time for (a) good weld and (b) bad weld

Fig. 28   Infrared thermograms of resistance spot welds, (a) good weld and (b) bad weld

been arrived at. Systematic studies showed that the experimental value of quality index is in agreement with that predicted by the fuzzy estimator.

Artificial Neural Networks applied to Evaluation of Resistance Spot Welding Process

The process variables considered are the dynamic resistance, nugget diameter and the percentage load. From the data generated, a database of 20 points has been screened during the training process. The first 15 points were used for training and the rest were used to predict. The optimum network architecture has been arrived at with 20 hidden nodes. The number of cycles required was 30000. The optimum value of learning rate is 0.00013 and momentum rate is 0.5. The maximum deviation in the percentage error is about 5% for the trained data and 3.23% for the predicted data.

Weld Monitoring of Nuclear Fuel Element Components

End Cap Welding

End cap welding is used for welding of nuclear fuel elements. The AE signals generated during the welding stage as well as during the post-weld stage were also found successful to discriminate normal welds from welds with presence of defects. Higher acoustic activity was generated for tubes welded with presence of various defects as compared to the AE generated during welding of tubes without any defects i.e. normal weld (Fig. 29) The AE signals generated during welding stage as well as during the post-weld stage were also found successful to discriminate normal welds from welds with defects. It has been observed that two separate clusters (normal welds

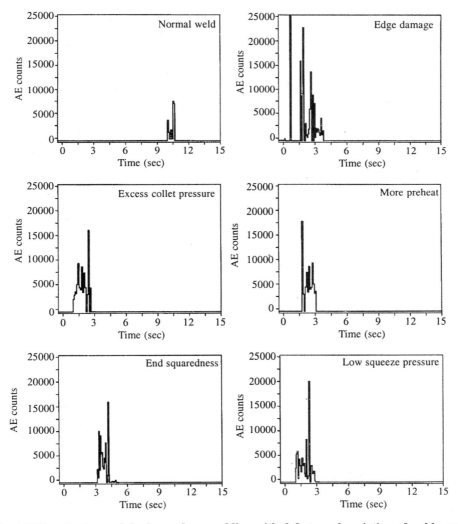

Fig. 29   AE Counts observed during end cap welding with defects and variation of weld parameters

and welds with defects) are formed corresponding to the two weld categories. Thermal imaging carried out on these elements after the welding process indicated that it is possible to detect most of the imperfections very confidently. In general good welds are characterised by uniform isothermal widths and symmetrical isothermal patterns (Fig. 30(a)) while bad welds are characterised by uneven isothermal widths and patterns (Fig. 30(b)). By thermography, the circumferential location where the defect had occurred could also be indicated.

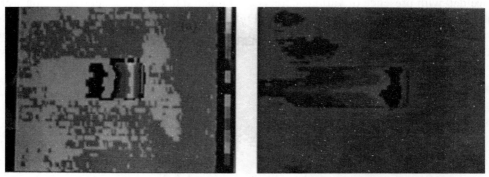

Fig. 30 (a) Thermal image of normal weld, (b) Thermal image of weld with excess graphite coating

Spacer Pad Welding

AE generated during the spacer pad welding was correlated with weld quality. A combination of AE parameters such as (a) initial counts and energy upon start of welding (b) cumulative counts and energy for the complete weld cycle including their values; and (c) counts and energy generated only during the welding stage, were identified. Figure 31 shows the master plot

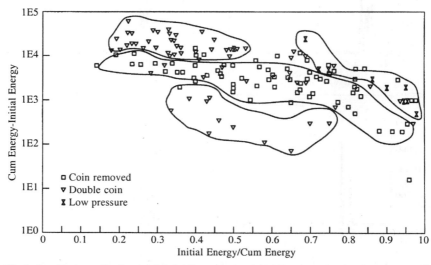

Fig. 31   Variation in (cumulative—initial AE energy) with AE energy ratio for spacer pad welding

((cumulative energy — initial energy) vs. (initial energy/cumulative energy)) for different types of welds. It can be seen that normal double coin welds form clusters in both the upper and lower regions of the plot while the single coin welds fall in the central region. The low pressure welds cluster in the central region. It is also seen that the defective welds comprising both single coin welds and welds made with low-pressure fall in the high side of the energy ratio. Thus, the different categories of welds namely normal double coin weld, single coin welds and welds made with low pressure can be clearly distinguished using different parameters of the AE signals.

Bearing Pad Welding

AE activity generated during bearing pad welding of the normal welds and welds with high current have shown that higher AE counts are generated during welding of the bearing pads with high current as compared to normal weld. Variation of total counts generated with total strength values of the welds has also indicated the feasibility of distinguishing normal welds and welds with high current (Fig. 32).

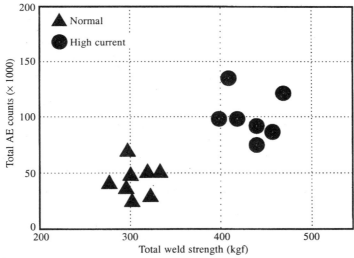

Fig. 32   AE during bearing pad welding

USE OF ARTIFICIAL INTELLIGENCE TOWARDS ENHANCED RELIABILITY OF WELDMENTS

One of the emerging possibilities to effectively utilise the knowledge explosion is to explore the concepts of artificial intelligence (AI) wherever applicable. Successful implementations of AI concepts, in the form of verified and validated expert systems (ES) and knowledge based inference mechanisms have been realised. An ES is ideally suited (a) when problems cannot be well defined analytically, and the number of alternative solutions is large, (b) the domain of knowledge is vast and (c) relevant knowledge needs to be identified rapidly, as it is to be used selectively. Large number of welded austenitic stainless steel components (ASS) are being used in the power industry, both thermal and nuclear. ASS welds having complex geometries, that require periodic NDE, are frequently encountered in these industries. Early detection of fine defects in these welds before and during service, using ultrasonic testing (UT) is mandatory. The problem of defect detection and characterisation in these welds, using UT, is complex and difficult when thickness of weldment is more than 10 mm. Also, there is still no standardised procedure concerning the ultrasonic inspection technique to be applied. The test method must be optimised specifically for each individual object to be examined. Apart from the problem due to the dendritic microstructure of these weldments, other factors such as the weld dimensions, geometry, joint type, welding procedures used, metallurgical history of the weld, reflective characteristics of various types of defects and the UT procedure, probe and scanning method used, the ultrasonic equipments used are some factors that affect the reliability of defect detection and characterisation in these weldments. It is also well known that a wealth of knowledge has been published in each of the areas mentioned above. Undoubtedly, due consideration must be given to all the above factors before deciding on the ultrasonic method to be adopted for the NDE of these welds.

The knowledge and databases pertaining to these aspects is very large, but the expertise to assimilate and apply this large amount of knowledge is scarce. Intelligent and timely application of this knowledge is the key for improving the efficiency of UT of ASS welds. Human experts have expertise in specific areas; the complete problem of ultrasonic testing of ASS welds requires the right combination of expertise. In this respect, there is an acute and growing shortage of human experts capable of performing reliable UT of thick ASS weldments.

Proper organisation and effective use of the available knowledge, in the form of an integrated expert system (ES), will help in taking quick and reliable decisions regarding ultrasonic procedures and techniques (conventional/signal analysis) to be adopted for efficient NDE of these welds. Such an integrated prototype rule based expert system (ES), has been developed in the authors' laboratory, to be used as an advisor for UT of ASS welds.

The performance of the expert system have been assessed by judging the flexibility of the design, the user friendly nature of the ES, the number of constructive rule firings (number of rules successful out of the total number of rules present in the ES) per second, the maximum and the average time taken by the ES to arrive at a solution are some of the criteria used for evaluating the ES. Another way is to study the effect of the absence of the ES, for the same type of problem solving; i.e., is there any difference with and without the ES.

General Performance Factors

The most important performance factor among these is the time taken by the ES to generate and display the advice, after the user has stated his/her problem. This time is now approximately only 20 seconds. The other important performance factor is the time taken by the ES to offer help/reasoning/suggest possible literature sources for further references by the user. This operation is very quick.

Specific Performance Factors

The major specific components to be evaluated in the ES are the user interface, correctness and consistency checking segment, advice generation segment and explanation generation segment (both together can be called the inference engine). The user interface is quite user friendly, and is the interactive module that performs the initial dialogue with the user. It allows a lot of flexibility to the user like random selection of entry modules, help menus, reasoning for each of the questions asked, literature support, facility for correcting user input (for changing the scope of advice) and so on. Since the entire user interface is menu driven, its performance level is good. The correctness and consistency checking segment performs in the background and is capable of detecting errors and incompleteness in the user input knowledge base (UKB), correcting them. The inference engine is very simple and compact. This is the reason for its speed of 20 seconds in generating both the advice and the explanation. The inference engine offers advice on twelve issues that are critical for the inspection of any ASS weld. They are (a) UT technique to be used (A-scan, B-scan, etc.), (b) mode of contact to be used (contact, immersion or noncontact), (c) wave mode to be used (longitudinal, shear, etc.), (d) size of the probe to be used, (e) angle (f) frequency, (g) skip, (h) speed of testing, (i) directions to be tested, (j) overlap of probe movements, (k) necessity for zoning of the welds, (l) necessity for contouring the probes, etc. Whenever multiple solutions exist for an issue, the ES will grade these solutions in the order of priority, to give the complete advise to the user.

The model and the architecture of the ES has been so designed, that it will be easy to use the same architecture for other related NDE problems also. An expert system has also been developed for radiography and another system is being developed for eddy current testing.

CONCLUDING REMARKS

Enhanced reliability of welded components can be achieved mainly through quality assurance procedures in addition to adequate appreciation of materials and their weldabilities, properties of welding consumables, characteristics of welding processes, and the conditions that would be present during performance of the component, and the possible failure mechanisms. Scientists and technologists are always on the look out for ways and means to increase reliability to acceptable levels on cost-effective basis. Advanced NDT&E play a significant role in reaching through objects. Efforts in the coming years would be focused in the areas of preparing relevant specifications and standards in advanced NDE techniques especially where no standards exist as on today, training and certification of personnel in new NDE techniques, so that professionals capable of working with modern relevant concepts are available to the nation and developing NDE methodologies for life prediction and extension of welded components. These are inter-related areas and are of great significance to the national economy and vital to the growth of welding technology in India.

ACKNOWLEDGMENT

The contributions from many colleagues of Division for PIE & NDT Development are gratefully acknowledged.

REFERENCES

1. Baldev Raj and T. Jayakumar, Trends in Advanced Non-destructive Evaluation Techniques for Comprehensive Assessment of Engineering Materials and Components, J. Inst. Engineers (India), 80, 1999, pp. 1–23.

2. P. Kalyanasundaram, Baldev Raj, P. Barat and T. Jayakumar, Reliability of Detection of small Defects in Noisy Weldments by Advanced Signal Processing and Pattern Recognition Techniques, J. Pressure Vessel and Piping, 36, 1989, p. 103.

3. Baldev Raj and T. Jayakumar, Advances in NDT Techniques for Space and Defence Applications, Proc. Seminar on Engineering Materials (SEM-2000), MRSI, Thiruvananthapuram, April 1999.

4. C.V. Subramanian, M. Thavasimuthu, C. Rajagopalan, P. Kalyanasundaram, and Baldev Raj, Ultrasonic Testing for Quality Assurance of End Plug Weld Joints of Fuel Elements of pressurised Heat Water Nuclear Reactors, Proc. 13th World Conf. on NDT, Sao Paulo, Brazil, Eds. Challai and P. Kulcsar, Elsevier Publishers, 1992, Vol. 2, pp. 1065–1070.

5. M. Thavasimuthu, C.V. Subamanian, C. Rajagopalan, P. Kalyanasundaram, and Baldev Raj, Ultrasonic Evaluation of Longitudinal Seam Welded Thin Walled Hastelloy Tube, National Seminar on NDT, December 3–5, Tiruchirapalli.

6. C.N. Spalaris, K.D. Challenger, D. Kutina and P.J. Ring, Sodium Heated Steam Generators: Near Term and Projected Information Needs of Ferritic Steels, Proc. BNES Conference on Ferritic Steels for Fast Reactor Steam Generators, British Nuclear Energy Society, May–June 1977, Paper No. 9.

7. J.C. Whipple and C.N. Spalaris, Design of the Clinch River Breeder Reactor Plant Steam Generators, J. Nuclear Technology, 3, 1976, p. 305.

8. H.P. Offer, J.L. Krankota and P.J. Ring, Properties of Remelted 2.25 Cr-1 Mo Steels for Nuclear Steam Generators, Ref. 6, Paper 24.

9. The Under Sodium Leak in the PER Superheater 2, Nuclear energy, Vol. 31, No. 3. February 1987, p. 221.

10. E.C. Lopez, C.B. Rao, D.K. Bhattacharya, and Baldev Raj, Measurement of Focal Spot in Microfocal Radiography, British Journal of NDT, September, 1986. pp. 299–300.

11. B. Venkatraman, V.K Sethi, T. Jayakumar and Baldev Raj, High-Definition Radiography of Tube to Tube Sheet Welds of Steam Generator of Prototype Fast Breeder Reactor, INSIGHT, 37, 1995, pp. 189–192.

12. C.H. Popeler, T. Barber, J. Groom, A Method for Determining Residual Stress in Pipes, J. of Pressure Vessel Technology, August 1982, Vol. 104, pp 223–228.

13. V. Moorthy, S. Vaidyanathan, T. Jayakumar and Baldev Raj, Evaluation of Post Weld Heat Treatment in 2.25 Cr-1Mo Steel Tube to Tube Sheet Weld Joints using Magnetic Barkhausen Noise Measurements, Materials Science and Technology, 13, 1997, pp. 614–617.

14. Anish Kumar, K. Laha, T. Jayakumar, K. Bhanu Sankara Rao and Baldev Raj, Imaging of Modified 9Cr-1Mo Ferritic Steel Weldment by Ultrasonic Velocity Measurements, Science and Technology of Welding and Joining, 6, 2001, pp. 383–386.

15. V. Moorthy, S. Vaidyanathan, K. Laha, T. Jayakumar, K. Bhanu Sankara Rao and Baldev Raj, Evaluation of Microstructures in 2.25Cr-1Mo and 9Cr-1Mo Steel Weldments using Magnetic, Barkhausen Noise, Materials Science and Engineering, A231, 1997, pp. 98–104.

16. J.C. Gerdeen, Residual Ductility and Residual Stresses in Formed Heads, J. Pressure Vessels Technology, Nov. 1977. pp 593–599.

17. M.G. Fontana, and N.D. Greene, Corrosion Engineering (Book). McGraw Hill International Book Company. 1982. p. 62.

18. P. Rodriguez, Baldev Raj and T. Jayakumar, Failure Analysis in Nuclear Industry-Specialties and Ensuing Strategies, Trans. Ind. Inst. Metals, 46, 1993, 111–126.

19. D.K. Bhattacharya, T. Jayakumar and Baldev Raj, Intergranular Stress Corrosion Cracking Failure in AISI 316 Stainless Steel Dished Ends near Weld Joints, ASM Metals Handbook on Failure Analysis, Vol. 2, 1992.

20. D.K. Bhattacharya, Baldev Raj, E.C. Lopez and T. Jayakumar, Failure in Austenitic Stainless Steel Dished Ends, Int. Conf. on Fracture, (ICF6) New Delhi. Dec. 1984.

21. T. Jayakumar, D.K. Bhattacharya and Baldev Raj, Failure of AM350 Stainless Steel Bellows, ASM Metals Handbook on Failure Analysis, Vol. 2, 1992.

22. A.K. Bhaduri, Sanjay K. Rai, T.P.S. Gill, S. Sujith and T. Jayakumar, Evaluation of Repair Welding Procedure for 2.25 Cr-1Mo and 9Cr-1Mo Steel Welds, Science and Technology of Welding and Joining, 6, 2001, pp. 89–93.

23. N. G. Muralidharan, T. Jayakumar, Rakesh Kaul, A. Ramabathiran, K. V. Kasiviswanathan, D.K. Bhattacharya and Baldev Raj, Acoustic Emission Monitoring during Miniaturised Disk Bend Testing of Stainless Steel and Aluminum Alloy, Seventh Asian-Pacific Conference on Non-Destructive Testing, Shanghai, China, Sept. 1993, 768–785.

24. L.H. Loh, J.A. Johnson and H.B. Smartt, in NDE: Application to Materials Processing, ed. O. Buck and S.M. Wolf, ASM, Mars, Pennsylvania, USA, 1984, p. 13.

25. S. Nagarajan, W.H. Chen, and B.A. Chin, Infrared Sensing for Adaptive Arc Welding, Welding Journal. Nov. 1989. pp 462S–466S.

26. B. Venkatraman, S. Kanmani, C. Babu Rao, D.K. Bhattacharya, and Baldev Raj, On-Line Monitoring of Welds by Infrared Imaging, 7th Asian-Pacific Conference on Non-Destructive Testing. October 1993, China.

27. P. McIntire, and R.K. Miller, Non-Destructive Testing Handbook. Vol. 5 on Acoustic Emission Testing. American Society for Testing and Material. 2nd Edition. (1987), p. 276.

28. Baldev Raj, T. Jayakumar and B. Venkatraman, Intelligent Welding, Proc. Int. Conf. Recent Advances in Metallurgical Processes, IISc, Bangalore, eds. D.H. Sastry, E.S. Dwarakadasa, G.N.K. Iyengar and S. Subramanian, New Age International Publ., New Delhi, Vol. 2, 1997, pp. 1035–1046.

29. Baldev Raj, B. Venkatraman, T.P.S. Gill and T. Jayakumar, Reliable Quality through Intelligent Welding Methodologies, Proc. Int Conf. IMACS-IEEE 99, Athens, Greece, June 1999.

30. Baldev Raj, B. Venkatraman, C.K. Mukhopadhyay, T. Jayakumar, A. Lakshminarayana, N. Saratchandran and Ashok Kumar, Intelligent Welding using NDE Sensors, Proc. European Conference on NDT, Copenhagen, May, 1998, pp. 1244–1250.

18. Selection of Welding Consumables

R.D. Pennathur

Mailam India Limited, Pondicherry

1 INTRODUCTION

The term "welding consumables" refers to the filler metals employed in different forms in various welding processes. The selection of the most appropriate welding consumable is of paramount importance to achieve quality most economically and selection involves study of metallurgy of base material, service conditions as also ready availability of consumables.

Globalization and rapid industrialization has brought about major changes in design and selection of base materials for fabrication. The emphasis is mainly in cost reduction by using improved base materials. The advancement in welding technology has made it possible to meet this challenge by developing new consumables to meet specific requirements. Advances made by consumable manufacturers in terms of products and processes are required to be understood by fabricator to achieve quality welded products at minimum cost.

2 CRITERIA FOR SELECTION

For a given application, the filler metal selection with compatible prccess is to be done taking the following factors into consideration.

2.1 Metallurgical

- Base materials
- Mechanical properties
- Chemical composition
- Corrosion requirements
- Physical properties
- Soundness and structural stability
- Heat treatment

2.2 Mechanical

- Thickness of material
- Dimension and number of components

2.3 Process

- Available forms of consumables
- Adaptability for the job
- Welding process selected

2.1.1 Base Material

The single important factor determining the selection of filler metal and process is the base materials being joined. The base materials are classified as per ASTM specification.

In general the base metals are broadly classified as carbon steel, low alloystal stainless steel and high alloy steels. In addition there are other steels for low temperature application, quenched and tempered steels etc., for specific applications.

Even though consumable selection steps are the same for various materials, in this presentation consumable selection for carbon and stainless steels are highlighted.

2.1.2 Mechanical Properties

Mechanical property of the weld metal basically covers the aspects of

(i) Soundness
(ii) Strength
(iii) Toughness

The welding consumable should be so designed, so as to be compatible metallurgically with the base material and produce a sound weld to give radiographic quality deposits.

As the weld metal has a cast structure as compared to the rolled structure of the base metal and the weld zone is likely to contain defects like porosity and slag, the weld metal tensile strength is required to be higher than that of base material or at least equal to it.

The weld metal should also have adequate toughness at given design temperature taking into account fabrication practices.

2.1.3 Chemical Composition

The weld metal chemistry, in general, matches the composition of the base metal for similar metal joining. In case dissimilar base metals are being welded, care should be taken to see that diluted weld metal will not result in formation of brittle intermetallics.

2.1.4 Corrosion Properties

The weld metal corrosion properties are to be equal or superior to that of base metal. This is to avoid preferential attack on the weld joint.

2.1.5 Physical Properties

The physical properties of the weld metal should be compatible with that of the base metal. These include properties like thermal expansion co-efficient, thermal and electrical conductivities, magnetic permeability etc.

2.1.6   Soundness and Structural Stability

The weld metal should be capable of resisting some amount of dilution of the base metal without forming a crack sensitive weld metal and the weld microstructure should be stable under the expected service conditions.

2.1.7   Heat Treatment

The consumables selected for joining should be capable of giving the desired test results in as welded condition as well as heat-treated condition. When heat treatment is not specified in design/code, it is very essential to identify various heat-treatment stages during fabrication and ensure that consumable selected does meet these requirements. The general heat-treatment cycles encountered during fabrication are normalizing and stress relieving.

2.2.1   Thickness of Material

For selection of proper consumable and process, thickness of material plays a vital role. The selection of semi-automatic and process comes into picture only if base metal thickness normally exceeds 10 mm and joint configurations are adaptable for automation.

2.2.2   Dimension and Number Components

While thickness, in principle decides the selection of process, the dimensions of the job and number of components to be welded also play an important role. In case of heavy sub-assembles even though length of the joint may be too small for automation, if the operation is repetitive in nature, the same can be considered for automation. The automation not only reduces cost but also improves the quality of jobs.

2.3.1   Available Forms of Consumables

This is the single most important factor for selection of process. Once the technical details are worked out and suitable consumable specifications are identified, it is essential to find out whether consumables are readily available for SMAW, GMAW, FCAW and/or SAW before process selection could be started. In general, for all common materials SMAW, SAW and FCAW consumables are readily available.

2.3.2   Adaptability for The Job

Before finalization of the type of consumable to be used, it is essential to study whether the job is being done in the workshop, site or sub-contractor's premises, so as to ascertain availability of suitable equipment and also take into consideration environmental conditions.

3   CONSUMABLE SELECTION

The welding consumables for welding of carbon, low alloy and stainless steels are selected based on guidelines provided in ASME II C. The relevant specifications are indicated here:

SFA 5.1	Carbon Steel Electrodes for Shielded Metal Arc Welding
SFA 5.4	Stainess Steel Electrodes for Shielded Metal Arc Welding
SFA 5.5	Low-Alloy Steel Electrodes for Shielded Metal Arc Welding
SFA 5.9	Bare Stainless Steel Welding Electrodes and Rods
SFA 5.17	Carbon Steel Electrodes and Fluxes for Submerged Arc Welding
SFA 5.18	Carbon Steel Electrodes and Rods for Gas Shielding Arc Welding
SFA 5.20	Carbon Steel Electrodes for Flux Cored Arc Welding
SFA 5.22	Stainless Steel Electrodes for Flux Cored Arc Welding and Stainless Steel Flux Cored Rod for Gas Tungsten Arc Welding
SFA 5.23	Low Alloy Steel Electrodes and Fluxes for Submergd Arc Welding
SFA 5.29	Low Alloy Electrodes for Flux Cored Arc Welding
SFA 5.01	Filler Metal Procurement Guidelines

3.1 Consumable Selection for Carbon Steels

Suggested welding consumables for welding carbon steel are indicted in Table 1. For welding of carbon steels the additional metallurgical factors to be taken into consideration are discussed below:

Table 1 Suggested consumables for welding carbon steel for structures

ASTM Steel	Welding process			
	Shielded Metal arc	Submerged Arc	Gas metal Arc	Flux cored Arc
A 242 A 441 A 572 Grade 42 A 588 (100 mm and under) A515 GR 60/70	E 7015 E7016 E7018 E7028	F7XX-EXXX	ER 70S-X	E7XT-1 E7XT-4, 5, 6, 7 or 8 E7XT-11 E7XT-G
A572 Grade 60, 65 A 633 Grade E A 515 GR 70	E 8015-XX E 8016-XX E 8018-XX	F8XX-EXXXb	ER80S-XXb	E8XTX-XXb

(i) *Base Material*: As per ASTM specification

(ii) *Mechnical Properties*: For achieving mechanical properties with regard to strength, there are not many problems as matching consumables are readily available.

Wherever toughness requirements are specified for weld metal, particularly for low temperature application, it is essential to keep in view variables like specification of elctrodes used, heat input, inter-pass temperature, position of welding, heat treatment and specify higher impact acceptance value than required for the job.

(iii) *Chemical Composition:* In most cases, the consumables selected are of matching composition with lower percentage of carbon and higher percentage of manganese to compensate for strength. The silicon percentage is so controlled as to achieve full deoxidation without seriously affecting the ductility.

(iv) *Corrosion Requirements*: For carbon steel material, this requirement is not generally applicable. However, for specific cases like weathering steel, atmospheric corrosion tests may be specified which has to be taken into account and weld metal should meet the requirements.

(v) *Physical Properties*: As matching consumables are used, the physical properties match quite well.

(vi) *Soundness and Structural Stabilitiy*: For carbon steel consumable, no metallurgical transformation takes place at the operating temperature. Hence, this requirement does not pose any serious problems, provided the weldment is sound at room temperature.

(vii) *Heat Treatment*: This is a critical area that requires study of fabrication sequence. Even though heat treatment may not be called for in many carbon steel applications, the components like dished end blanks, petal dished end assembly may undergo normalizing treatment due to process requirement. If matching consumable is used, there may be drastic reduction in the strength values of the weld. Also in case of components having toughness requirements specified, the heat treatment cycle may alter the values.

Hence, the consumable selected has to be duly tested for operational heat treatment cycles whether final heat treatment cycle is involved or not. Table 2 highlights the properties of consumables with typical HT cycles. Also, a typical case study of fabrication of dished end brings to fore the problems involved.

Table 2   Properties of consumables with typical heat treatment cycle

Sl. No	Consumable	Technical Condition UTS (MPa)		
	Type	As Welded	SR	Normalized
1.	E 7018	530	525	480
2.	E 7018–A1	540	535	530
3.	E 8018	550	540	500

3.2   Consumable Selection for Stainless Steel

Table 3 indicates the selection of consumables for austenitic stainless steel. In addition, for welding of stainless steel the metallurgical factors to be considered are as indicated below.

(i) *Base Material*: As per ASTM specification

(ii) *Mechanical Properties*: In general, for welding of stainless steel, matching composition consumables are used. Hence, the strength properties are easily achieved.

Whenever stainless steel is selected for cryogenic servce say −196°C application, special emphasis on selection of consumable is to be considered vis-à-vis micro fissuring. It is true for severely corrosive applications also.

(iii) *Chemical Composition*: In most cases matching composition consumables are selected.

(iv) *Corrosion Requirement*: For stainless steel application, the corrosion requirement becomes the most important factor. For many applications, control of delta ferrite in the weld becomes critical to achieve the desired corrosion rates. Even though the control of delta ferrite to near zero percentage gives excellent corrosion results, this in turn results in micro fissuring of welds. Hence, such consumables are not particularly suitable for restraint joint welding. The solution lies in selecting suitable consumables having excellent

Table 3 Suggested consumables for austenitic stainless steel

Base Metal Wrought	Cast	SMAW	GMAW/GTAW PAW, SAW	FCAW
AISI	ACI	AWS A 5.4	AWS A 5.9	AWS A 5.22
		E 209	ER 209	
201		E 219	ER 219	E 308T-X
202		E 308	ER 308	
301	CF-20	E 308	ER 308	E 308T-X
302	CF-8			
304				
304L	CF-3	E 308L	ER 308L	E 308LT-X
		E 347	ER 347	E347T-X
303		E 312	ER 312	E312T-X
309	CH-20	E 309	ER 309	E309T-X
310	CK-20	E 310	ER 310	E 310-X
314				
316	CF-8M	E 316	ER 316	E 316T-X
316L	CF-3M	E 316L	ER 316L	E 316LT-X
317		E 317	ER 317	E 317T-X
321		E 347	ER 321	E 321T-X
347		E 347	ER 347	E 347T-X

crack resistance behavior and also controlled ferrite. This is possible by selecting consumables by subjecting them to Thomas and Schaeffler crack resistivity test in addition to standard corrosion test.

(v) *Physical Properties*: As matching consumables are used, no appreciable change is noticed.

(vi) *Soundness and Structural Stability*: For application below 450°C there is no metallurgical transformation and stable structure is guaranteed. However, whenever operating temperature is in the range of 530°C – 750°C carbide precipitation occurs along the grain boundaries and corrosion resistance is drastically reduced in HAZ area. This leads to a typical failure known as "knife line attack" and subsequent failure. Their failure can be minimized with use of either extra low carbon consumable or by using stabilized grade depending on the specific application.

(vii) *Heat Treatment*: SS fabricated components are not normally subjected to heat-treatment operations, except solution annealing treatment which only improves corrosion properties without impairing mechanical properties.

3.3 Selection of Process

The process selection of course is based on availability of suitable consumables in addition to taking into consideration thickness of components, dimensions, number of components also adaptability of the process for the job.

We will now look at various process options available such as SMAW, SAW, GMAW and FCAW—advantages and limitations of each of the above.

3.3.1   Shielded Metal Arc Welding (SMAW)

Advantages

(a) Variety of electrodes with different features
(b) Most versatile in use—all-position joints/joints with limited access
(c) Suitable for most alloys
(d) Equipment simple, inexpensive and portable

Disadvantages

(a) Finite length
(b) High dependence on welder skill
(c) Not amenable to automation

3.3.2   Submerged Arc Welding (SAW)

Advantages

(a) Highest deposition rate
(b) Most suited for automation
(c) Consumables can be contomised
(d) Lowest operator fatigue

Disadvantages

(a) Not versatile – no positional capability
(b) Generally not used for thin sections
(c) Joint fitup very critical
(d) Arc not visible. Hence joint or seam tracking may be necessary

3.3.3   Gas Metal Arc Welding (GMAW)

Advantages

(a) Continuous electrode
(b) Higher current possible
(c) Minimal post-weld cleaning required
(d) Highly amenable to automation

Disadvantages

(a) Equipment more complex and costlier their SMAW

(b) Welder skill dependence still high, especially for out-of-position welding
(c) Not amenable to customization

3.3.4 *Flux Cored Arc Welding (FCAW)*

Advantages

(a) High productivity of continuous wire welding
(b) Metallurgical benefits of flux
(c) Higher current density than solid wires
(d) Versatile use—all-positional, wide thickness range
(e) Visible arc – easy to use

Disadvantages

(a) Equipment more complex and costlier than SMAW, same as GMAW
(b) FCAW wires more expensive on weight basis but compensated by higher productivity

As for welding of CS/LAS and SS in most cases as all the process consumables are readily available, the process limitation is finally dictated by the following criteria.

Criteria	SMAW	SAW	GMAW	FCAW
Dep. Rates	Low	Very good	Satisfactory	Good
Geo. Symmetry	Low	Very good	Satisfactory	Good
Positional welds	Good	–	–	Very good
Field joints	Good	–	–	Very good
Difficult field joints	Very good	–	–	Good

3.5 *Cost of Weld Metal*

Another important factor to be considered by welding engineer in selecting appropriate welding consumable is cost of weld deposition.
The cost of weld metal consists of following factors.

(i) Consumable cost
(ii) Gas cost for GMAW and FCAW
(iii) Flux cost for SAW
(iv) Power cost
(v) Labour and overheads
(vi) Rework cost

It is a well-established fact that cost of labour and overheads will decide the economic level of operation. Hence reduction in fabrication cost is possible only with increase in productivity. Fig. 1 indicates the productivity of various processes and table 4 indicates typical cost calculation for SMAW and FCAW processes.

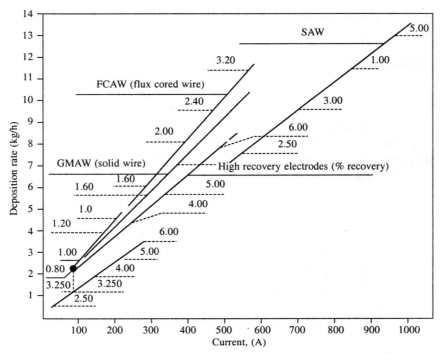

Fig. 1 **Comparison of the deposition rates of various welding processes, numbers in the graph indicate wire diameter in mm**

Table 4 Weld metal cost formulas

1. Labor & overhead = $\dfrac{\text{Labor \& Overhead Cost/h}}{\text{Deposition Rate (kg/h)} \times \text{Operating Factor}}$

2. Electrode = $\dfrac{\text{Electrode cost/kg}}{\text{Deposition Efficiency}}$

3. Gas = $\dfrac{\text{Gas Flow Rate (l/min)} \times \text{Gas cost/l}}{\text{Deposition Rate (kg/h)}}$

4. Flux = $\dfrac{\text{Flux cost/kg} \times 1.4}{\text{Deposition Efficiency}}$

5. Power = $\dfrac{\text{Cost perkWh} \times \text{Volts} \times \text{Amps}}{1000 \times \text{Deposition Rate}}$

Total cost per kg of Deposited weld metal = Sum of 1 – 5 above

From this it is clear that even though unit cost of consumable is high, the deposited weld metal cost is lower beyond particular labour and overhead cost. This factor becomes of prime importance while selecting process for fabrication using available consumables.

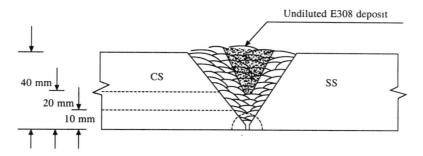

Fig. 2   CS to SS welding with E 308 type consumables

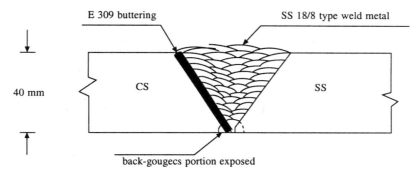

Fig. 3   CS to SS welding with CS side buttered

4   TYPICAL CASE STUDIES

Keeping in view selection of consumables as per guideline given in ASME Sec IIC and establishing procedure as per Sec IX, some typical industrial applications where failure occurred are highlighted further with analysis of likely cause.

4.1   Manufacture of CS Dished end

Description

Formation of dished end can be done by one of the following methods.

   (a) Petal construction
   (b) Hot forming
   (c) Spinning

Problem: In petal construction, the weld metal does not undergo any heat-treatment. In case of hot forming even though normalizing cycle is known, many a times blank made with weld is not specified in drawing. In case of spinning the fabricator may use intermediate normalizing for ease of forming.

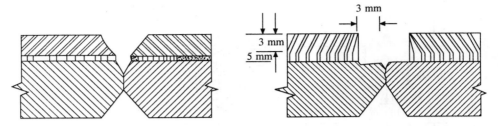

Fig. 4   Common types of edge preparation for clad joints

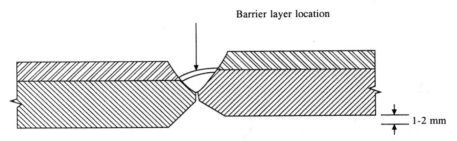

Fig. 5   Mismatch of 1-2 mm in conventional edge preparation

Hence, in case of hot forming with welded blank/spinning the weld may undergo normalizing operation which is not planned.

Analysis: Considering CS of 515 Gr 70 as base material & E 7018 or E 71T-1 as welding consumable, the UTS drop of 50–70 N/mm^2 is common with normalizing operation. Hence, the UTS of weld metal will drop to 470 N/mm^2, which is below acceptable level and results in a failure.

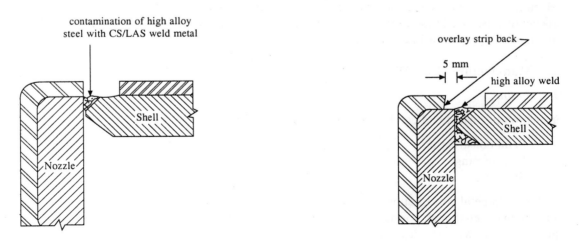

Fig. 6   Nozzle to shell welding edge preparation

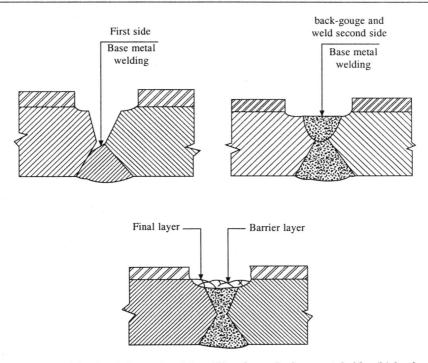

Fig. 7 **Sequence of welding in clad repairs, (a) welding from the lase metal side, (b) back-gouging and welding from the clad side (c) barrier layer welding**

Solution: It is recommended to use E708-Al or E70-TAl as welding consumable which does not show any significant drop in UTS with normalizing heat treatment also.

4.2 316 LF with Nil Ferrite

Description: 316 LF consumables with nil ferrite for butt welds and overlay for used reactor application.

Problem: These types of consumables were required to be used for fabrication of urea reactor.

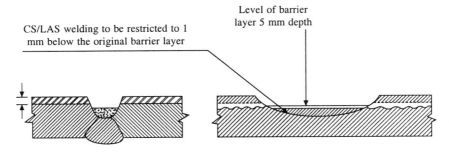

Fig. 8 **Repair from clad side**

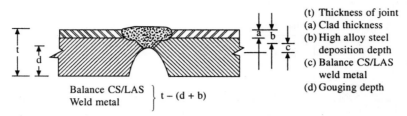

Fig. 9   Repair from CS/LAS side

During qualification of consumable, no problems were encountered and corrosion results were excellent.

However, on actual job condition, particularly on C-seams and nozzle to shell joints serious micro fissuring problems were encountered.

Analysis: Even though problem was controlled by grinding off all crater points, still micro fissuring were noticed at regular intervals which shattered the confidence of the fabricator.

After detailed study, an additional "Thomas Schaeffler" crack sensivity test was introduced for evaluation of consumables. The consumables, which gave satisfactory results in this test, were found to give excellent weld performance or actual job also.

Solution: Use modified 316 LF with crack sensitivity test qualified consumables.

5   CONCLUSION

1. Even though "Selection of Welding Consumables" are based on guidelines specified in ASME Sec II C and procedures have to be established as per ASME Sec IX, in actual fabrication, metallurgical factors affecting the weldment have to be given due recognition.
2. The process of welding is dictated by availability of suitable consumables. When available, due improtance is to be given for productivity.
3. Whenever weld contour and location makes SAW process not easily adaptable, FCAW plays an important role as most adaptable process without unduly sacrificing productivity.
4. "Quality" and "Productivity" being main tools for minimizing fabrication cost, the adaptability of processes like SAW and FCAW are to be fully explored and utilized.

19. Mechanical Testing of Weldments

S.K. Ray

Materials Technology Division, IGCAR, Kalpakkam

1 INTRODUCTION

The direct way to assess the performance of a welded joint in service would be to test it in actual service conditions. However, this in most cases is impractical, and therefore standardized tests and testing procedures become necessary. It is important to realize that any mechanical testing reflect interplay of two basic processes in the material, deformation and fracture. These processes are differently influenced by the internal variable, namely material microstructure, and external variables, namely, (I) type of loading (II) temperature, and (III) environment. Deformation may be elastic or elastic+plastic, and the dominant plastic deformation mechanism varies with the internal and external variables. Similarly, depending upon these variables, fracture may be brittle (low energy) or ductile (high energy), slow (quasi-static) or fast (dynamic), inter-or trans-granular, due to growth of one or more major cracks or due to microvoid nucleation, growth and coalescence. The dominant mode of plastic deformation, and the mode of fracture may vary during the course of a single test. For the case of weldments, with graded microstructure, there is the additional complication of the specific regions of microsructures of the specimen that are being sampled by these processes. Each laboratory test is an idealization, providing a limited amount of information on the properties of the welded joints. Thus, translating laboratory test results to the expected performance of components in service must rely upon relating to results for metals and structures that have performed satisfactorily in service. Also, most weldments are evaluated by several tests, each test providing specific information on the serviceability of the weldments. Specifically, such tests are used (I) for welding procedure qualification, to establish properties of welded assembly (including filler material), and to determine that the weldment is capable of providing required properties for the intended application; and (II) for welder qualification to establish the ability of the welder to deposit sound weld metal.

In this article, the following common mechanical tests for welds are introduced: (I) Tension test, (II) Hardness test, (III) Bend test, (IV) Charpy V-notch impact test, (V) Plane strain fracture toughness test, (VI) Drop weight test, (VII) Fatigue test, and (VIII) Creep test. The emphasis is on the basic principle involved and utility. No efforts have been made to be comprehensive as to the testing procedure, for which the following standards may be consulted:

1. ANS/AWS B4.0, Standard Methods of Mechanical Testing of Welds

2. ASTM A 370, Standard Methods and Definitions for Mechanical Testing of Steel Products, and other testing standards.

2   TENSION TESTS

2.1   Uniaxial Tension Tests

The uniaxial tension test is a very popular method for evaluating strength and ductility. The test procedure involves pulling a smooth tensile specimen of uniform cross section, usually at constant displacement rate, to fracture; the load—displacement plot is recorded. Longitudinal specimens have axes along the direction of rolling, while transverse specimens are oriented perpendicular to this direction. Figure 1 schematically shows the nominal stress (load divided by initial cross section area) vs. nominal strain (elongation divided by original gauge length) plot for a ductile material like mild steel. The initial linear segment reflects elastic deformation. The subsequent regime leading to the maximum load (tensile instability) is dominated by plastic deformation, at around the maximum load a neck initiates. In the post-necking regime, plastic deformation is increasingly concentrated in the neck; this regime is dominated by microvoid nucleation, coalescence and fracture, which are accentuated by localized deformation at the neck. Ultimately, the specimen fractures, and the fractured halves usually have typical cup-and-cone appearance. The engineering parameters that are commonly measured are the yield and the ultimate tensile strengths, percentage uniform (i.e., up to the point of maximum load) and total elongations and the percent reduction in cross sectional area (measured at the minimum, fractured section).

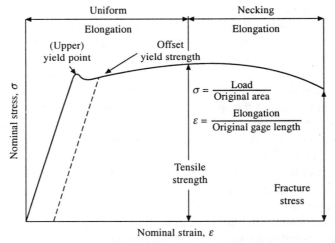

Fig. 1   Schematic engineering stress-strain curve for a ductile material showing yield point elongation

In planning tensile tests on weld joints, it is necessary to consider the heterogeneity of weld test section. The base metal tension test can be with either longitudinal or transverse specimens (ASTM A370). For weld joints, two different tests are required:

1. All-weld-metal tests use specimens machined entirely out of the weld metal. For filler metal testing, melting of base metal should be minimized (AWS A5.1), and for testing weld metal of a specific weldment, welding process and procedure should be identical to that used in fabrication.

2. Longitudinal Weld Test is a variant of the above. The specimen orientation is identical, but test section contains weld metal, HAZ and base metal loaded to identical strain levels. Low weld or HAZ ductility may initiate ffacture at strength levels below that of base metals. Normally only tensile strength is reported; elongation may be measured as an indication of the minimum ductility of the joint.

3. Transverse Weld Test-specimens contain base metal, HAZ and weld metal in the gauge section. These sections are loaded to identical stress levels; failure takes place in the section with the lowest toughness. Therefore usually tensile strength and the failure locations are noted for these tests. These are used to qualify weld process, and *can not* be used for quantitative comparison of weld metals because of property variation along the gauge length. Figure 2 shows the typical tension test specimen orientations for evaluation of welded joints.

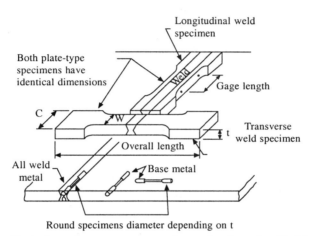

Figure 2   Typical tension test specimens for evaluation of welded joints

2.2   Tension-Shear Tests

Fillet Weld Shear Test is carried out to determine the shear strength of fillet welds prepared using production procedure. Figure 3 schematically shows the longitudinal and transverse fillet weld shear stress specimen configurations. Double lap joints are used to avoid rotation and bending stresses during testing in transverse shear test specimens. The report normally indicates shear strength of weld = $P/(I \times a)$ (Figure 4) where P = load, I = length of fillet weld sheared and a = theoretical throat dimension, and also the location of failure. The longitudinal shear test measures the shear strength of the fillet weld when the specimen is loaded perpendicular to the axis of the weld. The specimen preparation, illustrated in Figure 5 avoids bending during testing.

The results from these tests are sensitive to specimen preparation procedures. Variation in root opening in the transverse fillet welds can give inconsistent results. Test specimens are sensitive to HAZ cracking, undercut, and bead surface contour. Longitudinal edges of transverse specimens should be machined to eliminate crater effects and to provide smooth surfaces; corners should be slightly rounded.

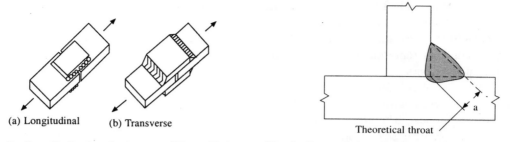

Fig. 3 **Longitudinal and transverse fillet weld shear stress specimens**   **Fig. 4** **Determining shear strength of fillet welds**

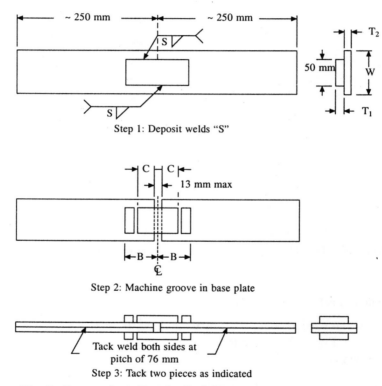

Fig. 5 **Preparation of longitudinal fillet weld shear test specimen**

2.3 Strength Tests for Spot Welds

For this purpose, three different types of tests are used. Tension-Shear Test is used to determine strength of arc and resistance spot welds (AWS) C1.1 for resistance welding). This test is easy to perform and inexpensive, and is used for quality assurance testing of production welds. The specimen essentially is two overlapping coupons of suitable size, with a spot weld in the center (Figure 6). The test is carried out in standard tensile testing machine, For < 1 mm thick sheets,

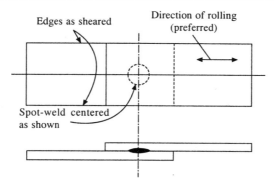

Fig. 6   Tension-shear test specimen

eccentric load on weld causes bending and rotation, and results in failure around edge of nugget. For thicker sheets, base metal tends to resist bending, and weld may fail through/around nugget. For specimen thickness of 4.8 mm or more, wedge grips should be offset to reduce eccentric loading on weld.

Direct-Tension Test measures strength of welds for loads applied normal to the spot weld interface. It is used also to determine relative notch sensitivity of spot welds. Both cross-tension (Figure 7) and V-test (Figure 8) specimens are in use. The specimens are tested in tension using suitable jigs. Weld may fail either by pulling a plug (tearing around the edge of the spot weld) or tensile failure across the weld metal. The maximum load (causing failure) is reported. The direct tension load is normally less than the tension shear load for the same size weld and alloy; their ratio, varies from the range 0.6 to 0.99 for low carbon steels to about 0.2 for medium carbon

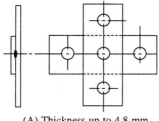

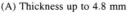

(A) Thickness up to 4.8 mm

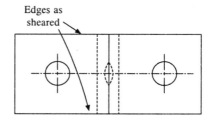

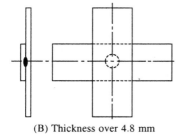

(B) Thickness over 4.8 mm

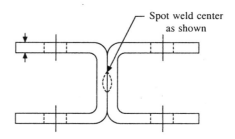

Fig. 7   Cross-tension test specimen   **Fig. 8   U-test specimen**

steels. This ratio, frequently referred to as the ductility of the weld, and is a measure of notch sensitivity of the weld; a ratio of > 0.5 is considered ductile while a ratio < 0.3 indicate notch sensitive welds.

The Peel Test is a variation of direct-tension test; it is fast and inexpensive, and is used for quality control of production welds. Figure 9 schematically illustrates the principle; the dimensions vary according to sheet thickness (AWS C1.1). The nugget size is measured, and compared with a standard size determined by the tension shear and direct tension tests; a nugget size greater than or equal to the standard size for design indicates that the welds are acceptable.

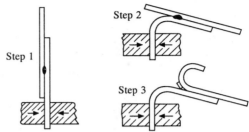

Fig. 9   Steps in peel test: 1: grip in a suitable device, 2: bend specimen, 3: peel pieces apart with pincers or other suitable tool

3   HARDNESS TEST

This is a very common testing method, and essentially characterizes the strength properties of the material. The test consists in applying a standard load on a standard indentor placed on a ground, polished/polished and etched surface of the specimen for a specified period. The specimen undergoes localized plastic deformation in the immediate vicinity of the indentor. A variety of indentor geometry and material, and corresponding loads have been standardized. In Brinell, Vickers, and Knoop hardness testing, the area of indentation under load is used to define hardness; in Rockwell hardness depth of indentation under load is used as measure of hardness. Correlations are available for hardness values and strength for various grades of steel, but should be used with caution for welds because the structure is heterogeneous. The most important feature of this test is that the hardness measured pertains to the region below the indentor undergoing plastic deformation. While tests that make large indentations relate more to bulk properties, those with small indentations (e.g., Vickers) can be used to characterize gradual variation of strength properties of a weld joint with microstructure, e.g. by making hardness traverse (Figure 10).

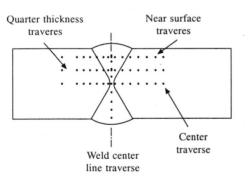

Fig. 10   Typical hardness traverse for a double-V groove welded joint

Indeed, the same principle has been incorporated, and can be analogously used, in microhardness testing which has also proven to be a most widely used tool in R&D. More recent advances in this direction utilize nano-indentation techniques.

4   BEND TESTS

The Guided Bend Test (AWS B4.0) evaluates ductility and soundness of welded joints, and is most commonly used in welding procedure and welder performance qualification. The specimens are bent in tensile test machine or wrap-around bend test jigs (Figure 11).

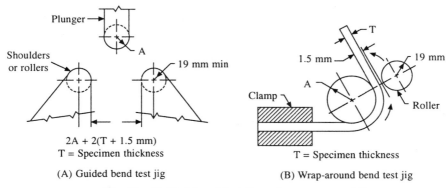

2A + 2(T + 1.5 mm)
T = Specimen thickness

(A) Guided bend test jig

T = Specimen thickness

(B) Wrap-around bend test jig

Fig. 11   Guided bend test jig and wrap-around jig

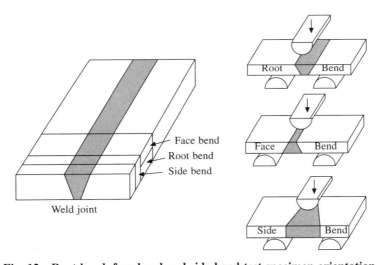

Fig. 12   Root bend, face bend and side bend test specimen orientation.

The variants of the test are root-bend (weld root in tension), face-band (weld face in tension) or side-bend (weld cross section in tension) tests (Figure 12), and the parameter that is measured is % strain on the outer fiber = $100T/(2R + T)$ where T is the bend specimen thickness and R the inside bend radius. The parameter reflects ductility and soundness of welded joints. For sound mild steel welds, outer fiber strain of 20% can be easily achieved, but presence of weld defects will drastically reduce this ductility. Non-uniform properties along the length of the specimen can cause non-uniform bending.

The bend test is sensitive to relative strengths of the various section of the weld joint. In transverse bend tests, with overmatched welds base metal may deform to a smaller radius and desired elongation of weld may not be achieved. On the other hand with under-matched weld, failure may result from exhaustion of weld metal ductility and not because of defect in weld metal. Problems of weld mismatch can be avoided by using longitudinal bend specimens with weld running full length of the specimen and bend axis perpendicular to the weld axis; in this geometry all zones are equally and simultaneously deformed. This test is generally used for evaluating dissimilar weld joints; however, weld flaws which run parallel to the weld axis (incomplete fusion, inadequate joint preparation) may not cause failure under moderate strain. Side bend tests strain the entire weld cross section and are useful for exposing defects near mid-thickness that might not contribute to failure in root and face bend tests. These are usually adopted for relatively thick sections (> 19 mm). Codes (AWS, ASME) generally specify a maximum allowable size of crack in bend tests made for weld procedure qualification.

A characteristic feature of ferritic steels (that is not found in austenitic steels) is the ductile-to-brittle transition behavior. In simple terms, in ferritic steels at low temperatures, the stress for brittle cleavage fracture is lower than that for gross plastic deformation, while at higher temperatures the trend reverses. As a results, these materials show brittle behavior at low temperatures, but with increasing temperature, the behavior changes via a relatively narrow transition regime to fully ductile behavior at high temperatures. The brittle to ductile transition temperature increases with decreasing toughness of the material, and also with increasing restraint to plastic deformation (e.g., presence of a notch, or worse, presence of a crack; larger specimens/components) and strain rate. Brittle fracture, once initiated, tends to propagate with increasing speed (as increasing quantities of stored elastic energy is released), leading to catastrophic failure. This assumes special significance in weld joints, as weld metals/HAZ generally have inherently lower toughness than the base metals. Indeed, historically, this was one of the major limitations of welded constructions (at low temperatures, weld metal provides a continuous path for propagation of brittle fracture) that led to rapid R&D in the area of fracture mechanics and mechanism.

5   CHARPY V-NOTCH IMPACT TEST

Charpy V-notch impact tests (ASTM A370 and AWS B4.0) is one of the early tests devised to characterize the transition behavior; however, because of its simplicity, it continues to be the most common testing method. The specimen design is shown in Figure 13. The specimen is tested in a pendulum impact tester. Brittle fracture is promoted (propensity to plastic deformation is reduced) by the introduction of a notch leading to a triaxial state of stress at its tip, and also by the high deformation rate that is used. Test results are most usefully presented as plot of absorbed energy and % shear fracture vs. test temp, see Figure 14 for an example. Specifications usually call for a minimum absorbed energy (plus possibly a minimum notch-root-contraction, which is a measure of ductility) at a given temperature. For weldments, fabrication code may require Charpy tests to be conducted on both weld metal and HAZ (notch tip and crack paths located in these regions). The use of Charpy test data in design typically would be to specify a minimum service temperature to avoid possibility of brittle fracture. Current practice however is to use data from both Charpy and drop-weight tests to arrive at this temperature.

The Charpy test has the following limitations: (I) it is highly dependent on specimen size, (II) the toughness is function of loading rate, (III) the specimen notch is relatively blunt and most

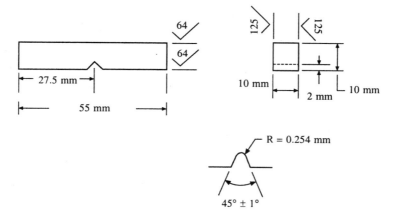

Fig. 13   Charpy V-notch impact specimen

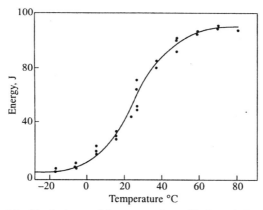

Fig. 14   Typical transition curve for milled steel ship plate

often does not simulate a sharp crack, (IV) it does not distinguish between crack initiation and propagation phases, and thus (V) cannot be used for calculating load bearing capacity of a flawed component.

We may note here the for austenitic steels (which do not show ductile to brittle transition) also, the Charpy test is sometimes used; the parameter of interest then is the energy absorbed (more specifically energy absorbed per unit ligament area) in causing fracture (this would correspond to the upper shelf regime for a ferritic steel), as a measure of toughness. Such tests have proven useful in developing welding consumables for austenitic steels.

6   PLANE STRAIN FRACTURE TOUGHNESS K_{IC}

K_{Ic} is the resistance to crack extension under conditions of plane strain (highest restraint to plastic flow) at a crack tip. The testing procedure (ASTM E 399) allows for several standard geometries, but for welded material, compact tension (CT) specimen, as per Figure 15 is recommended (AWS B4.0). The initial crack is obtained by fatigue pre-cracking a machined notch. Once desired crack length is obtained the specimen is tested in tension and the load corresponding to "failure" (see the standards for details) is determined. Then standard equations are used to determine the value of K_{Ic}. An interesting feature of this test is that for the specified geometries only the relative dimensions, and not the absolute sizes, for the specimens are specified. Whether the specimen size used is adequate (that is, plane strain condition obtains at crack tip, and crack tip plastic zone size is small relative to the specimen dimensions) can be verified only after the test, by ensuring

$$a, B, W \geq 2.5 \, (K_{Ic}/\sigma_{ys})^2$$

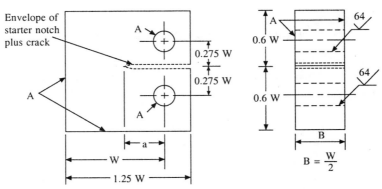

Notes:
1. Dimensions a, B, and W are to be determined in acccordance with ASTM E 399.
2. Surfaces marked A shall be perpendicular and parallel as applicable to within 0.002W total indicator reading (TIR).
3. The intersection of the crack starter tips with the two specimen faces shall be equally distant from the top and bottom edges of the specimen within 0.005W.
4. Integral or attachable knife edges for clip gage attachment to the crack mouth may be used.

Fig. 15   Compact tension specimen to determine K_{Ic}

σ_{ys} is the yield strength. Only if plane strain condition obtains can the fracture toughness determined be considered as material property, independent of size and geometry of the specimen. The use of such data is straightforward: once plane strain condition obtains in a flawed structure, the material property K_{Ic} determined in the laboratory and the proper K_{Ic} expressions relevant for the component geometry can be used to determine its load bearing capacity. Codes (e.g., CEGB/R6 from Central Electricity Generating Board, UK) address this issue in detail. So far as testing weld specimens is concerned, to determine toughness properties of weld metal, HAZ or base metal, it is necessary to ensure that crack tip and crack extension path lie in the corresponding region of the microstructure. Since K_{Ic} corresponds to very limited plasticity at crack tip, the variation of plastic flow properties over the crack tip plastic region, if any, can be ignored.

7   DROP WEIGHT TESTS

This test (ASTM E208 and AWS B4.0) determines the nil-ductility transition temperature, the temperature above which a dynamic crack will be arrested for gross elastic deformation of the specimen. A "crack starter" bead is welded on a rectangular test specimen, which is then notched (leaving a margin between the notch root and the specimen plate). The specimen is chilled to test temperature and tested with notched bead in tension by applying a load from a falling weight. A brittle crack initiates in the bead and propagates through the specimen. The "break" or "on break" performance is noted. Figure 16 shows a typical example, For an all meld material. NDT (Nil Ductility Temperature) is the highost temperature for "break", with "no break" being obtained for NDT + 5°C. The current practice is to define a "Reference

Fig. 16   Typical "break" and "no-break" performances in drop-weight specimens

Temperature–NDT" (RT-NDT) combining results from Charpy V and drop weight test, that ensures fully ductile behaviour at RT-NDT + 33°C under severest constraints.

8   FATIGUE TEST

Fatigue testing of weldments is performed (ANSI/AWS D1.1) primarily to develop design data. Fatigue refers to damage in a material subjected to cyclic loading. The mechanism of failure in general consists of development of a crack, which then extends with each load cycle till failure occurs. Fatigue properties depend very much upon the specimen/component design, and the state of stress, mean stress and stress range. In particular, crack initiation depends very much upon surface conditions (including smoothness), and any stress concentrations (e.g. presence of a notch). For example, in base material while about 90% of fatigue life may be spent in crack initiation, for weld joints with propensity to inherent defects, this phase may be only a very small fraction of the total life. Crack propagation may be accelerated in a region containing defects and thus internal soundness. The data are presented in the form of a S-N plot, i.e a double logarithmic plot of stress range to cycles to failure, Figure 17 shows an example. In design it is necessary to consider the large statistical scatter shown by high cycle fatigue properties.

9   CREEP TEST

Creep is a *time-temperature* phenomenon, and refers to permanent deformation under sustained loading at levels lower than those required for rapid failure to metal at the test temperature. This is a crucial property for structural applications at high temperatures. Creep and stress rupture tests are carried out following ASTM E 139. Basically it consists in taking a specimen with cylindrical gauge section and applying a uniaxial load. Figure 18 shows a typical creep curve, i.e., variation of strain with time under constant applied stress (more commonly, load) and

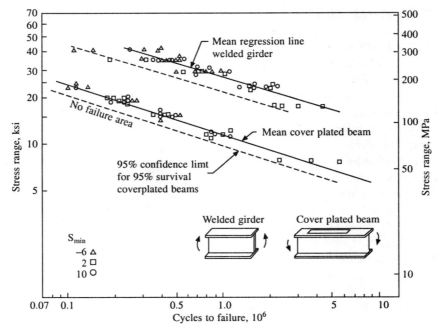

Fig. 17   Example *of* **S-N curves for fatigue**

temperature. Increasing load and/or temperature reduces the time for completion of each stage. The important parameters for design are time for onset of secondary stage and extent of primary creep, secondary (more precisely, minimum) creep rate, and time to rupture.

Since it is impractical to simulate service conditions in creep testing, accelerated tests are carried out. Application of test data thus generated to design involves extrapolation of by suitable time-temperature parametric formulations. A plethora of such formulations have been proposed in literature; this essentially reflects the complexity of creep deformation and fracture processes, modulated by evolving microstructure. For example, a popular parameter is the well-known Larson-Miller parameter:

$$P = T(C + \log t_r)$$

with T absolute temperature, t_r the rupture life and C a material constant; P is considered to be a function of stress alone. In view of the essentially empirical nature of such correlations, care is required to be exercised in using these to extrapolate to long service lives. For testing of welds, both all weld and transverse weld specimens are used, The interpretation of data vis-à-vis base metal however is not straight forward, because of the interplay of deformation and fracture with time-dependent evolution of

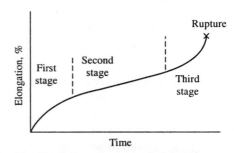

Fig. 18   Typical creep curve showing three stages

microstructure, which become compounded in a transverse weld specimen because of the gradient in creep deformations properties and the corresponding restraining effects between adjacent sections of the specimen.

10   CONCLUDING REMARKS

In this brief article, it has been possible only to introduce the variety of mechanical testing of weldments. While the issue of mechanical properties evaluation in corrosive environments has not been covered, the importance of such tests in appropriate cases, and the necessary extensions of experimental facilities can be readily envisaged. However, it is hoped that the above description amply bear out the points made in the Introduction: each type of test is aimed at elucidating some particular feature of deformation and/or fracture. Therefore, often a number of complementary tests are needed, and usefulness of data must depend heavily upon experience, as embodied in the various codes.

20. Advanced Non-destructive Testing Techniques for Inspection of Weldments

T. Jayakumar, G.K. Sharma and Baldev Raj

Metallurgy and Materials Group
Indira Gandhi Centre for Atomic Research
Kalpakkam - 603102

1 INTRODUCTION

Welding is widely used in the fabrication of industrial components. In spite of best efforts taken to design, fabricate and inspect the welded components for their high quality and reliable performance, many of the industrial failures are related to weld and heat affected zones. These failures can be attributed to improper design of weld joint, selection of base materials and filler materials, welding processes, inspection procedures and/or operating parameters. One major factor that would help in minimising the failures is inspection of welded components using non destructive testing (NDT) techniques immediately after fabrication and also during service to ensure that no unacceptable defects are present [1]. In order to improve the sensitivity for defect detection and for quantitative characterisation of defects that would help in reducing the failures, use of advanced NDT techniques is resorted to. In this way, it is also possible to make economic design of weld joints. Signal and image processing methodologies are also being increasingly employed to meet these objectives. In fact, some of the advancements in conventional techniques are related to development of imaging based methodologies. Fracture mechanics based analysis of the welded components is the driving force for developments in the science and technology of NDT. In this paper, the advancements made in radiographic, eddy current and ultrasonic techniques are discussed. Also use of acoustic emission technique for on-line monitoring and control of welding processes and for integrity assessment of welded pressure vessels are also discussed. A few case studies have been given to demonstrate the usefulness of these NDT techniques for evaluation of welded components. The techniques used for evaluation of residual stresses are also discussed.

2 VISUAL TECHNIQUES

Visual techniques play an important role in quick assessment of the quality of welds and to identify various defects like undercut, lack of penetration etc. Geometrical imperfections such as improper weld ripples, convexity and concavity can be detected even in inaccessible regions by using videoimagescopy and replica techniques. One typical example of tube to tube-sheet weld joint is discussed here. [2]

One of the imperfections that could occur due to improper internal shield gas flow and weld parameters is weld concavity and convexity. Depending on the geometry of the weld, the presence of such convexity and concavity can result in concentration of stresses in and around the region. Under the presence of thermal, hydraulic and other pressures such regions are prone to creep and fatigue damage and have been the cause for many failures. Thus codes of practice always place an upper limit on the maximum permissible values of convexity and concavity.

In the case of the tube to tube sheet weld joints of the steam generators of the prototype fast breeder reactor (PFBR), it is specified that the maximum permissible values for the convexity and concavity are 0.2 mm (both for internal and external concavity and convexity). It is easy to determine the external convexity and concavity due to availability of access for replica based measurements. In the case of internal concavity and convexity, the technique of replica using dental compounds is quite difficult. Procedures for measurement of internal concavity and convexity by replication using silicone rubber compound and special hardware and also by videoimagescopy have been developed at the author's laboratory.

2.1 Replica Technique

The hardware for the replica technique essentially consists of manual injection device, mixing guns, injection head, spring loaded CRS plugs and recovery cork screw head. The consumable is a silicone rubber compound of the type RTV-FA 877 with a pot life of 2 months and a curing time of 4 hours. Horizontal injection technique was adopted. Initial calibration was carried out on tube to tube sheet weld samples with grooves and notches. For concavity measurement, notches and grooves of two different depths (0.35 mm and 0.25 mm) were made internally by electro discharge machining in a standard tube of OD 31.2 mm and ID 27.8 mm. The profile of the groove was then replicated using silicone rubber compound. The dimensions of the groove were then measured from the replica using a profile projector having a measurement accuracy of ±5 microns. Dial gages were used to measure the actual concavity in the tubes. It was observed that an overall accuracy of ±20 microns could be obtained for concavity and convexity measurements. This procedure has been subsequently adopted for examination of a number of joints in the reheater of PFBR. A typical silicone replica of the weld is shown in Fig. 1.

2.2 Videoimagescopy

The videoimagescope is an advanced version of the flexible fiberscope in which a CCD chip is used for imaging. Compard to fiberscopes, videoimagescopes provide high resolution and brighter images. With the introduction of advanced image management functions and measurement capabilities,accurate measurements of internal profiles of tubes is possible. The use of videoimagescopy for profiling of reheater tube joints is described below:

The Olympus videoimagescope model IVC-6 used for this application has a diameter of 6 mm and working length of 7 m with a field of view of 60 degree convertible by tip. A variety of viewing tips with varying fields of view are available which can be used depending on the

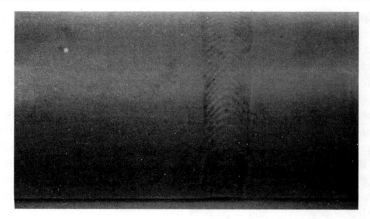

Fig. 1 Typical silicone compound replica of tube to tubesheet weld joint. The weld ripples can be discerned clearly.

nature and type of application. In the present experimental campaign, the 80 degree forward viewing and side viewing tip were used. The light source used was ILV-2 with a 300 W xenon lamp. The unit is linked to IW-2 industrial video analyzer equipped with a built-in hard disk for the storage of images. About 400 images can be stored. Each image can be tagged with characters for easy identification and further reference. The images can also be suitably enhanced through image processing functions such as contrast stretching and edge enhancement. Using the 3-D graphic measurement system, it is possible to measure the length, width etc. of the images very accurately.

Before the actual work was undertaken, the feasibility of using videoimage scope for quantitative weld profiling and also the accuracy of the method were established. A tube identical in dimensions (OD and ID but of shorter length) to the actual tube was selected. Internal convexity was simulated by placing steel wires of known diameter (0.4 mm and 0.2 mm) both longitudinally and circumferentially at a distance equivalent to the distance of weld from the face of the tube sheet. Measurements of the wire diameter were taken at a number of points by placing the videoimagescope in line with the wire. Comparison of the diameters estimated using videoimagescope with the actual diameters measured using a micrometer indicated an accuracy of the order of 20 microns.

For concavity measurement, notches and grooves of two different depths (0.35 mm and 0.25 mm) made internally by electro discharge machining in a standard tube of OD 31.2 mm ID 27.8 mm, were made on calibration standards. The methodology based on video image has been adopted for concavity and convexity measurement of a number of joints of the Reheater. Images of good weld, weld with convexity and weld with concavity are shown in Figs. 2–4 respectively.

3   ADVANCES IN RADIOGRAPHY

3.1   High Resolution Radiography

High resolution X-radiography has been developed to offer an edge over conventional radiography

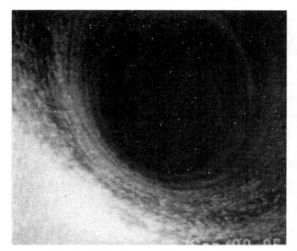

Fig. 2   Videoimage of a good weld.

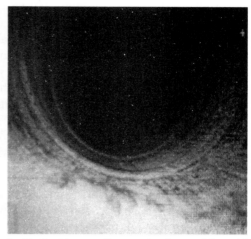

Fig. 3   Typical image of convexity detected in weld Joint. The convexity is 0.437 mm.

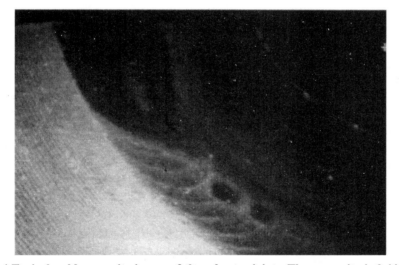

Fig. 4 Typical weld concavity in one of the reheater joints. The concavity is 0.44 mm

for better definition of defects and detectability of small defects like microcracks in components having thin sections and complex geometries [3]. This is more so in the present context of the use of high technology manufacturing processes like laser welding and electron beam welding which has led to drastic reduction in component sizes and have consequently necessitated detection of smaller defects.

Advancement in electron-optical systems, vacuum technology and computer controlled parameter optimisation and monitoring techniques have made X-ray generators of very fine focus and smaller sizes of anode tubes available for industrial radiography. Advantages of such systems compared to conventional radiographic systems are:

(a) Fine focal spots (15 microns) give advantages like higher resolution, higher contrast and possibility of large magnifications.

(b) Rod anode X-ray heads are available with small sizes (diameter 6mm onwards and lengths between 100mm to 1000 mm) which facilitate panoramic radiography of smaller diameter pipe welds and radiography of complex joints like tube to tube sheet weld joints.

(c) High resolution of the defect of the order of 25 microns using direct enlargement is possible which facilitates radiography of thin objects and use of large film to object distances.

(d) Specially shaped anodes give a variety of X-ray emission modes for panoramic, radial backward or forward throw of X-rays and directional throw of X-rays for varied applications.

(e) Easy adaptability for on-line fluoroscopy.

Main limitations of this technique are the maximum voltage (max. 225 kV) and maximum current (3 mA) which restrict thickness of objects to be radiographed to 3mm of steel equivalent. The equipment is not portable like conventional X-ray equipment and thus restricted in its use for in-service applications. One of the applications of microfocal radiography is evaluation of tube to tube sheet weld joints made by welding between pull out of tube sheet and the tube.

3.2 Real Time Radiography

Real time radiography or fluoroscopy differs from conventional radiography in that the X-ray image is observed on a fluorescent screen rather than recorded on a film [3, 4]. Fluoroscopy has the advantages of high speed and low cost of inspection. Present day real time systems use image intensifiers, video camera and monitor. The image intensifier tube converts photons to electrons, accelerates the electrons and then reconverts them to light (Fig. 5). Intensifiers typically operate in the range of 30-10, 000 light amplification factors. Improvements in electronic gain, fluorescent and photo cathode layer efficiency and electron optics have made modern X-ray image intensifiers very useful in medical and industrial applications. Modern tubes are available with 10 to 40 cm input diameters and trifield configuration. A typical 21 cm tube performs with resolution of the order of 40 line pairs per mm and gain of the order of 14,000. The overall geometric distortion at the centre is less than 2%. The use of microfocal units in conjunction with image intensifying system greatly enhances the versatility and sensitivity of the real time radiographic set up. The inherent unsharpness of the fluorescent screens would be compensated by the focal spot size (<100 microns) of the microfocal units.

With X-ray energies greater than 400 kV and with gamma rays, a computer aided real time radiography system can match the performance of film radiography. If a slightly poorer sensitivity can be accepted, a conventional minifocus X-ray set with 0.3/0.4 mm focal spot size can be used with some projective magnification and computer digital image processing. If high flaw sensitivity is not needed, the advantage of computerised image processing coupled with an equipment with X-ray intensifier and a television camera with a digital output would reduce operating costs and provide high inspection speed. An advantage of real time microfocal radiography is that of zooming or projection magnification by dynamically positioning the object with the manipulators between the X-ray tube and the image receptor. Real time radiography is finding increasing applications in industries where speed in testing is a primary consideration. Direct examination of the welds in real time saves film costs and the associated processing time and is found to be

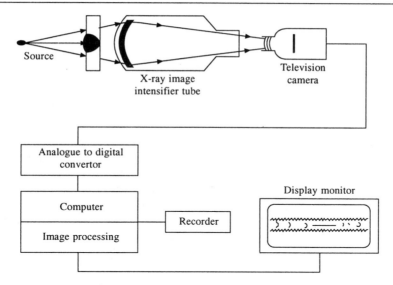

Fig. 5 Schematic of real time radiography system

cost effective in the long run. With the advent of image processing systems, the sensitivity that can be achieved is comparable to film sensitivity. Figures 6(a) and 6(b) show typical radiograph of a weld joint. Figure 6(a) gives the raw image wherein penetrameter wires are not clearly seen. After contrast stretching and image enhancement (Fig. 6(b)), the lack of penetration can be seen and the wire penetrameters can be identified thereby increasing the sensitivity. On-line monitoring of welding is another possibility by real time radiography.

Fig. 6(a) Positive print of a radiograph of a weld before image encahantment

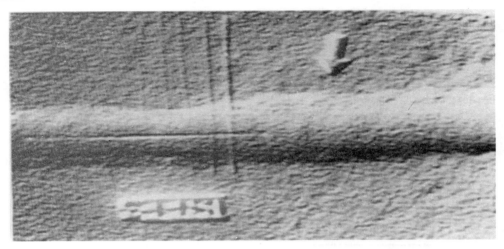

Fig. 6(b) Positive print of the radiograph of the weld given in Fig. 6(a), after image enchantment

3.3 Image Processing

Any image on a film or a screen can be scanned with a CCD television camera with a digital output and stored on a magnetic tape or disk as a number of pixels. A pixel array of 512×512 elements with 256 brightness levels on each pixel is quite common and can be handled through a personal computer. Once stored as digital pixel data, the image is available for computer enhancement techniques such as contrast stretching, edge enhancement, special filtering, differentiation, averaging and pattern recognition. The versatility of image processing is that this can be performed in real time as well as on film images. This technique suffers from the following limitations:

1. Enhancement of the image noise as well to some extent and radiographs are inherently noisy.
2. The limited dynamic range and contrast characteristics of conventional TV cameras result in a loss of image quality during its acquisition from the film/screen.

3.4 Real time radiography of Welds of Ti-alloy Fuel Tanks of Indian Satellites

One of the welds of the indigenously built Ti-alloy fuel tanks of an Indian satellite had been found to contain porosity (Fig. 7 (a)). In order to assess the suitability of the tank for its use, it was necessary to obtain reliable quantitative information about the pores for fracture mechanics based integrity evaluation. Real time radiography was carried out on the weld for obtaining quantitative information [5]. The radiographic parameters (voltage and current) were optimised to get a reasonably good quality image of the weld. The images were processed using an image processor and stored in a video casette recorder. The processed images (Fig. 7 (b)) were subsequently analysed for quantitative evaluation as per the specifications given for aceptance of the welds. As per the specifications, pores of diameter equal to or more than 0.9mm are to be reported. The closely spaced pores whose total diameter exceeds 0.9mm as per the standard ARP1317 have also been analysed. For this purpose, number of pores exceeding 0.9mm diameter, total pore

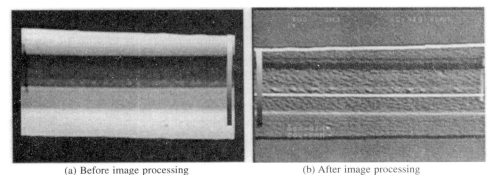

|(a) Before image processing| (b) After image processing |

Fig. 7 Real time radiographic image of porosities seen in the welds of fuel tanks.

diameter and distance between pores in the case of closely spaced pores, maximum size of the pore in each segment of the weld have been quantitatively obtained from the image analysis. In order to ascertain the depth at which the pores were present in the thickness direction, radiography at different orientations has also been carried out and analysed. The quantitative information provided by these procedures has been used for fracture mechanics based assessement of acceptance of the fuel tank.

4 ADVANCED EDDY CURRENT TESTING TECHNIQUES

4.1 Eddy Current Imaging

By generating a two dimensional C-scan of the eddy current data in the form of an image and viewing, it is possible to substantially enhance the defect detection capability. Compared to conventional ECT, this gives a global perspective and allows balanced interpretation of the results [6, 7].

Imaging based techniques are playing an important role in non-destructive evaluation. Eddy current imaging (ECI) is a recently emerging trend in the field of eddy current testing. In this ECI technique, images are formed by scanning the surface of an object in a raster fashion, measuring impedance point by point and converting these data into gray levels. The images represent complete information about the extent of discontinuities in two dimensions. Images of welds, notches, corrosion pits and cracks are generated using this approach for quantitative evaluation. Imaging techniques have the potential for automating the measurement process, providing estimates of defect sizes from the image data and improving the probability of detection.

Humans are generally comfortable in interpreting images or pictures or two dimensional representation of objects. By generating two dimensional "C - scan" of NDT data in the form of an image and viewing, one can substantially enhance the defect detection and the characterisation capability. It is stated that in NDE, an image is worth a thousand signals. Imaging techniques have been routinely applied for visual, X-ray and ultrasonic applications. However, they are relatively new to eddy current NDT. Also, it would be possible to extract the information regarding the depth of the features from the gray level variations in the images.

4.2 Eddy Current Imaging System

An ECI system has been built around a PC at the author's laboratory to scan the object surface and create impedance changes in a laboratory environment. This consists of a PC controlled X-Y scanner which scans the object surface, point by point with an eddy current probe. The analog signals from the eddy current tester (EM - 3300, Automation Sperry Inc., USA) are acquired using a 12 bit Analog to Digital Converter (ADC) card. At each probe position, ADC acquires data 10 times and the average impedance value is stored as an array on the hard disk of the PC. This averaging is performed to increase the signal to noise ratio. These data are normalised with respect to lower and upper gray values to construct the impedance image. Since the probe impedance is a vector quantity, both in-phase and quadrature components have to be considered while formatting the impedance image. With these data, four types of images can be created: in-phase images, quadrature images, amplitude images and phase angle images. The images thus generated can be displayed using: (i) color code, (ii) 3-D (X-Y impedance) graphics of (iii) gray level images. Gray level images can be displayed by transferring the data to video memory of an image processor. However, in this case, since the studies are on laboratory scale and resolution and gray level range requirements are minimal, the PC screen itself was used to view the image for convenience. For this purpose, point clusters proportional to the gray levels are used. Figure 8.1 shows the schematic sketch of the eddy current imaging system developed at the authors' laboratory.

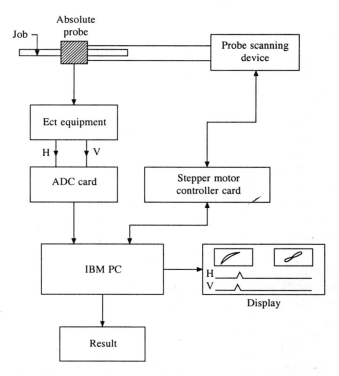

Fig. 8.1 Schematic sketch of eddy current impedance imaging system

4.3 Imaging and Characterization of Defects

Using the above ECI system, fatigue cracks of 15 microns and 23 microns wide in aluminium compact tension (CT) specimens and 0.5mm deep and 2mm diameter corrosion pit in a 4mm thick AISI type 316 steel plate were imaged. A ferrite cored probe of 0.8 mm diameter was used for imaging. The test frequencies used are 200 kHz for stainless steel plate and 100 kHz for the aluminium CT specimens. Close observation of the images clearly indicated that each image has a definite symmetry. The symmetry of the image is directly related to the defect/feature shape. Circular corrosion pit has produced a circular image and linear defects like fatigue cracks have produced images with a line of symmetry along the length of the defect. Hence from the images, it was possible to know the exact shape of the defect/feature. In the case of fatigue cracks, imaging is found to be capable of revealing the direction of growth of crack, a useful information for fracture mechanics studies. Also, when proper calibration procedures are followed, it would be possible to arrive at the exact defect size from the gray level information. Thus, from the above discussions, it is clear that ECI is an effective tool for detecting and characterising surface defects in metallic plates. The system has also been used for imaging austenitic stainless steel welds to identify weld centre line.

4.4 Detection of Weld Centre Line in Austenitic Stainless Steel Welds

Many a time, it would be necessary to remotely inspect welds by ultrasonic testing. Identification of weld centre line is necessary for fixing the required skip distance ranges for ultrasonic testing. In the case of austenitic stainless steel welds, by making use of the presence of delta ferrite in the weld metal, eddy current inspection can be employed for identification of the weld centre line. An example is given here. The precise location of the weld centre line, in the inner vessel of Prototype Fast Breeder Reactor (PFBR), is required as feedback information for remote operation of robots for detailed inspection of the weld by other NDT techniques. Feasibility studies have been carried out to precisely locate the weld centre line [6]. Butt weld joints of 2mm thick AISI type 316 stainless steel plates were studied to accurately locate the weld centre line. A ferrite cored probe was used at a test frequency of 100 kHz. The filtering techniques can be employed if the image data are of reasonable length (i.e. if the scanned area is limited). These techiques are generally employed after acquiring the data. However, in the test object envisaged, the surface of the reactor vessel of a few meters in diameter is proposed to be scanned remotely with a crawler fixed with a probe scanner. Thus, continuous data is generated which is enormous. In such a case, employing filtering techniques may not be easy. Therefore in this study, improved probe design was adopted to get better point spread function and image processing techniques were confined to those that could be implemented on-line/real time. Ferrite cored probe was used to get better point spread function giving reasonably resolvable images without filtering.

Figure 8.2 shows the gray level impedance image of the weldment and the corresponding 3-D plot of the impedance along X and Y axes. Due to predominant variations in the electrical conductivity and magnetic permeability (due to the presence of delta ferrite) of the weld metal, this region is distinctly brought out. The changes in the material properties affect the probe impedance. The change in the impedance varies from the base metal - weld interface to the weld - base metal interface and reaches a peak at the centre of the weld. This peak is clearly observed in the 3D plot (Fig. 8.2). Thus the precise location of the weld centre line can be found from this plot by measuring the distance along Y axis from the origin i.e. the starting point for scanning. The accuracy of detection of the weld centre line is found to be ± 0.1 mm. The above studies clearly reveal the capability of ECl system for the detection and characterization of surface defects in metallic plates and also for precise location of the weld centre line in austenitic stainless steel weldments.

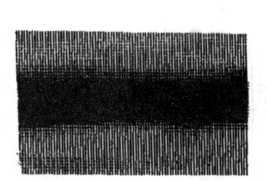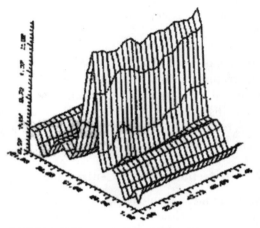

Fig. 8.2   Eddy current impedance imaging of SS 316 weldment and its 3D profile

4.5   Artificial Neural Network for On-line Eddy Current Testing

Eddy current test (ECT) is affected by a large number of influencing variables such as lift-off, variations in geometry, electrical conductivity, magnetic permeability and surface condition. To carry out meaningful ECT and evaluation, it is essential to eliminate or reduce the influence of unwanted variables. When the number of unwanted variables is one, its effect can be eliminated using single frequency eddy current, for example, by rotating the phase of the signal along one of the impedance axes, the abscissa in general and taking measurement along the other axis, i.e. the ordinate. However, in actual practice, the influencing variables are more than one, defect detection and characterization in their presence becomes rather difficult using single frequency. In the present study, a new methodology has been proposed for on-line eddy current test [7]. This uses a feed forward and error back propagation Artificial Neural Network (ANN) in conjunction with an on-line data acquisition system. This methodology, implemented in a PC, digitizes the in-phase and quadrature components of the eddy current signals and uses them directly as the input vectors (e.g. four nodes for a two-frequency ECT) of the network and displays the network output on-line.

The digitized in-phase and quadrature data is directly used as input to the ANN. The experimental procedure involves two steps. In the first step i.e. on-line training, the eddy current probe is placed on locations of unwanted and desirable parameters. The digitized in-phase and quadrature data from various frequencies thus chosen, along with the desired outputs (e.g. zero for all unwanted parameters and defect size for desirable parameters) is subjected to the ANN.

Interconnecting weights are adjusted till relationship between the input and the output nodes is established for a desired level of performance. In the second step, i.e. on-line evaluation, the digitized in-phase and quadrature data from various frequencies is fed on-line to the ANN and the resulting 'computed output' is directly displayed on the PC screen with distance and 'computed output' as absicca and ordinate respectively.

Experimental studies have also been carried out on AISI type 304 austenitic stainless steel welds (6 mm thick) with continuously varying surface roughness and δ ferrite using a two frequency eddy current tester. EDM notches (width 0.3 mm and length 6 mm) with different depth ranging from 0.2 mm to 1.5 mm have been machined and used for studies. Eddy current signal amplitude or phase increases monotonically with increasing variable of interest.

Neural network requires training prior to evaluation. During training phase, in the present case, when the parameters from two frequencies (4 input parameters viz. X_1, Y_1, X_2 and Y_2) and defect depth ('desired output') are fed to the network, moving forward with arbitrary weights, the network generates 'computed output'. Then, using the difference between the 'computed output' and 'desired output', moving backwards into the network, the weights are adjusted till the error is minimized and the process is iterated.

The number of nodes in the hidden layer and the number of iterations for convergence, learning rate and momentum parameters have been optimized. Three or four nodes are used in the hidden layer, depending on the complexity of the situation. For the applications considered in the paper, convergence has been achieved in about 600 iterations and high probability of detection and accurate evaluation has been observed. Further, in order to enhance the performance of the network with respect to sizing, a higher order polynomial fit is made between the 'actual output' and the 'computed output' after the training phase.

In the case of SS welds, in order to detect and size machined notches, measurements have been carried out with a specially designed surface probe. Since defect detection is affected by surface roughness, variations in delta ferrite and electrical conductivity in the weld region, two test frequencies are chosen. Experimentally optimized test frequencies are 35 kHz and 60 kHz. The real and imaginary components from these three frequencies have been digitized continuously. Sets of 4 representative inputs and the corresponding desired outputs of unwanted and desirable variables have been stored. In the present case, surface roughness, delta ferrite and conductivity variation are unwanted variables and a desired output of 'zero' has been assigned to them. On the other hand, when measurements are taken on defects, their depths have been considered as the 'desired output'. A total of 60 independent sets of measurements have been taken and subjected to a 4-5-1 ANN. Figure 9 shows the typical eddy current signals and the ANN output. As can be seen in Fig. 9, the proposed method has successfully detected 0.4 mm deep machined notch in the weld region and has accurately sized all the defects with good repeatability.

5 ADVANCED ULTRASONIC TECHNIQUES

A number of advanced ultrasonic techniques have been developed to meet specific demands of the industry [8]. In weldments made of stainless steel, the defect detection sensitivity is low. Also for imaging and quantitative sizing of defects, advanced ultrasonic techniques like synthetic aperture focusing technique (SAFT) and time of flight diffraction technique (TOFD) are increasingly employed. The principles of these techniques and their applications to inspection of weldments

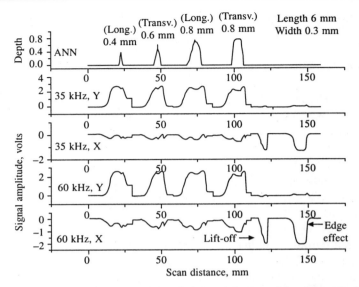

Fig. 9   **The real and imaginary components of signals formed during eddy current testing of an austenitic steel weld consisting of 2 longitudinal and 2 transverse notches (length 6 mm, width 0.3 mm and depths 0.4, and 0.8 mm) and the results of application of the artificial neural network method. The network eliminated all the weld variations, lift-off and edge effects and successfully detected all the 4 notches and accurately evaluated their depth on-line.**

are discussed. use of advanced transducers such as electromagnetic acoustic transducers (EMATs) is also discussed.

5.1   Synthetic Aperture Focusing Technique (SAFT)

A major application of this technique is to characterise the defect for quantitative evaluation and also to enable application of fracture mechanics based concepts for estimation of the remaining life of a welded component [9, 10]. In this method, analysis of the received ultrasonic signals is carried out either by stationary methods, where at fixed probe positions, all the echoes from a defect - direct as well as satellite echoes - are compared with the results of calculated or measured echoes of typical defects (modeling) or by moving the probe along the surface picking up the echoes for all probe positions thus synthesising an aperture. The basic idea of a synthetic aperture is to measure the complete sound field scattered by a defect on an orbit S_m around the defect as shown in Fig. 10.1 During re-construction, this sound field is calculated back into that region where the scattering occurred making use of well known scalar wave propagation formulae. The result is the three dimensional amplitude distribution of the sound field inside the orbit. In an ideal case, this will be non-zero only on the surface of the scatterer, thus enabling an image of the defect by describing its surface. Since a 360° scanning around a defect may be possible only in a few cases like rods or turbine rotors, one is forced to reduce the aperture to that part of the surface which is accessible. Therefore only that part of the defect may be imaged which could be insonified during scanning of the aperture. This is explained further in the following way.

    This technique is based on the idea that the more often the discontinuity is encountered by the

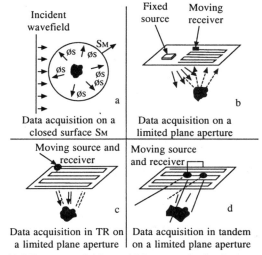

Fig. 10.1 Data acquisition within a synthesized aperture

beam, the more precisely the discontinuity can be viewed. The principle of SAFT is schematically shown in Fig. 10.2. When the transducer is located directly above the discontinuity, the time delay to receive the defect echo is minimal. As the transducer moves away from this position, the time delay increases in a non-linear fashion. The curve defined by tracing the peak amplitude (in each aperture element) as the transducer moves parallel to the surface is a function of the speed of sound in the material and the geometry of the transducer and target. The first synthetic aperture processing step is to choose a collection of aperture elements to be processed as a unit,

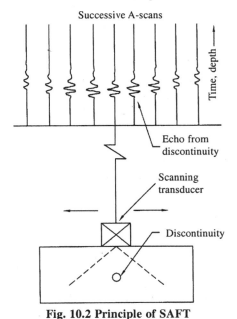

Fig. 10.2 Principle of SAFT

hereinafter referred to as the 'aperture'. The essence of SAFT processing is to introduce a time shift to each individual A-scans which varies with time delay introduced by the test system geometry, to sum these individual aperture elements point by point across their length, and then to place the result at the center of the chosen aperture. This process is shown schematically in Fig. 10.3, where the aperture is chosen to be five elements wide. If the aperture is centered over the target, as in the case of Fig. 10.3a, then the shift and sum operation will produce a strong signal (constructive interference). If the aperture is located off center of the target as in Fig. 10.3b, then the shift and sum operation will produce a weak signal (destructive interference). Reflections coming from the defect are constructively added and other signals such as grain noise and electronic noise are destructively summed, resulting in good signal to noise ratio for the defect. Enhanced signal to noise ratio is obtained due to spatial averaging, which is inherent in SAFT.

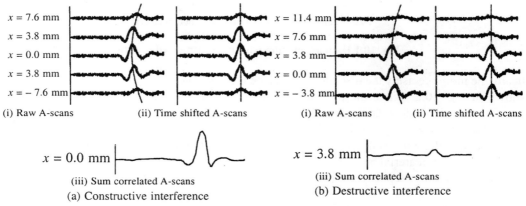

Fig. 10.3 The process of time shift in SAFT

To maximize the illuminated area of the defect, probes with large beam opening angle have to be used, that is small probes or the defocussed part of the farfield of focus probes. In addition, it is possible to synthesise the scanning around the defect using different insonification angles and different inspection techniques like pitch-catch or tandem. Data acquisition involves scanning of the probe on the surface and recording complete rf-echo signals coming back from the specimen. That is, for each probe position (X, Y) inside the scanned aperture, the complete received ultrasonic signals are stored as an input for the SAFT - algorithm as shown schematically in Fig. 10.4. By using suitable algorithms, three dimensional amplitude distribution inside the specimen (D-Scan) is obtained. When scanning is done in one direction (X), we get only two dimensional amplitude distribution corresponding to the area below the scanned line and perpendicular to the scanned surface thus performing a side view (B-Scan).

Case studies

A study was carried out in the authors' laboratory on a calibration block to understand the feasibility of ultrasonic testing of a carbon steel 'TEE' joint with stainless steel weldment (Fig. 10.5). The calibration block contained four side drilled holes at different depths in the stainless

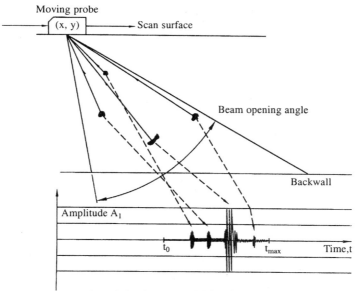

Fig. 10.4   Data acquisition for SAFT

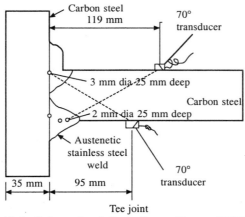

Tee joint

Fig. 10.5   Schematic of dissimilar weldment (TEE Joint)

steel weld metal. Conventional ultrasonic angle beam examination could not be carried out successfully due to poor signal to noise ratio. Strong echo from the carbon steel/stainless steel weld overlay interface was obtained thereby reducing the sensitivity of detection of the holes. The hole of 3mm dia could not be detected using conventional technique (Fig. 10.6). Using SAFT with a 2.25 MHz frequency longitudinal probe, a clear image of the reference holes could be obtained at the expected depth. Angle beam examination using shear wave probes of 45 and 70 degrees gave better results in terms of better image contrast and with less gain in noise. Based on the standardized test parameters, actual testing was carried out on a 'TEE' joint using 45 and 70 degree angle beam probes using a manual scanner. Figure 10.7 shows the SAFT pattern obtained from a 3 mm diameter hole in the SS weldment.

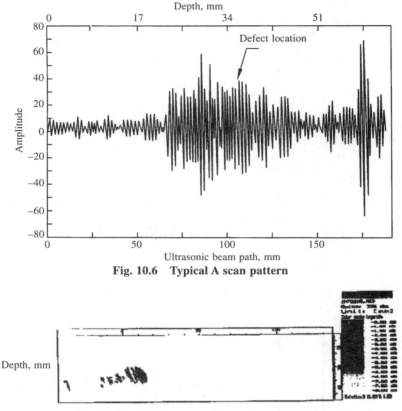

Fig. 10.6   Typical A scan pattern

Fig. 10.7   SAFT pattern from a 3mm dia. hole

In another case, it was necessary to carry out examination of resistance welded joints of fuel clad tubes used in Pressurised Heavy Water Reactor. The required test sensitivity of 10% WT could not be obtained by conventional immersion testing due to noise signals from tube ID surface weld upset. SAFT was employed to test the endcap weld joints [11]. To set the sensitivity, 10% ID defect was introduced in the weld upset of the endcap clad tube. Immersion testing was carried out using 4 MHz probe on these endcap weld joints. Scanning was done with an incident angle of 22.5° with respect to the axis of the tube so that the beam enters the tube material at an optimum angle of 45°. which is ideal for detecting defects of unknown orientation.

The SAFT image obtained from the upset of the endcap weld is shown in Fig. 10.8. The image from a defect of 10% WT is shown in Figure 10.9. The image revealed very clearly the presence of defect at the ID side of the weld upset. The same defect could not be detected using ultrasonic A-scan.

5.2   Time of Flight Diffraction Technique (TOFD)

This has the ability to capture high resolution, low amplitude signals and perform real-time processing to carry out crack tip diffraction examination using the acclaimed time of flight

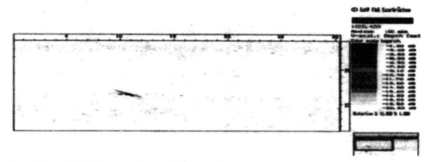

Fig. 10.8   SAFT image of a weld upset from an end cap weld of 14.7 dia. tube

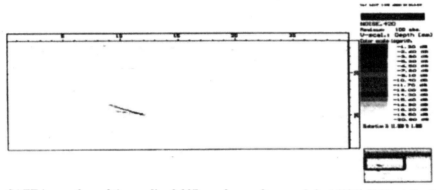

Fig. 10.9   SAFT image from 0.1 mm dia, 0.037mm deep reference defect (10% WT) at the ID in an end cap weld

diffraction (TOFD) technique [12]. It lends itself ideally to fast volumetric detection applications where inspection results need to be of sufficient quality to enable decisive on-line action. This speed is achieved by virtue of the fact that a wide beam, tandem array of transducers and scanned parallel to the weld, are usually sufficient to achieve full coverage and scan rates upto 50 mm/s. This approach overcomes the need for comprehensive raster scanning and probe skewing to optimise signal responses and thus massive reduction in the amount of data generated.

As TOFD technique relies solely on the time separation between signals diffracted only from the edges of the defects (Fig. 11.1) – rather than conventionally reflected energy - it can be

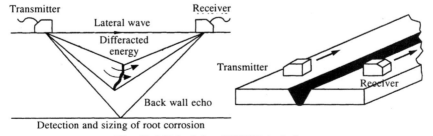

Fig. 11.1 Principle of TOFD technique

performed almost independently of amplitude response and thus the coupling quality, material attenuation and defect orientation are much less critical than with conventional pulse-echo methods. The interaction of an ultrasonic beam with a crack like defect gives rise not only to a specular reflection from the face of the crack but also to two cylindrical diffracted waves from the crack tips. Since these waves effectively have their origin at the defect extremities, it is clear that their time delay or phase relationsip can provide data on the separation of the crack tips and thus on the size of the crack. Single probe and two probe examination using both compressional and shear wave ultrasound have been carried out and the data were analysed directly in the time domain or by the use of spectrographic techniques.

It is for this reason that the TOFD method of inspection is now recognised as one of the reliable and accurate means of defect detection and sizing. One possibility for improving the decision making capability based upon the size of the defect in the depth direction, is to move away from techniques based upon the amplitude of reflected signals towards such concepts as the time of flight diffraction techniques.

A typical TOFD image is shown in Fig. 11.2. The major advantage of the TOFD made of operation is the on-line graphic (D-Scan) display of inspection data. This presents the operator with a real-time radiographic-type image, representing a through wall section along the weld axis with defects shown in their true length and accurate sectional location and size.

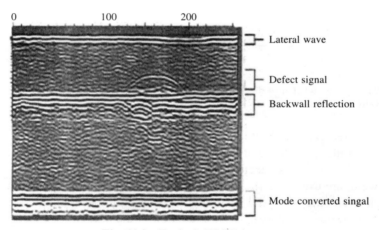

Fig. 11.2   Typical TOFD image

Single Probe Time-of-flight Techniques: This approach, irrespective of use of compressional wave or shear wave, works well for the nearer (upper) crack tip but less well for the most distant tip. Normally the crack tip location is calculated from the time of diffraction between the tip echoes and the angle of the probe. To gain sufficient accuracy, the beam spread must be limited so that angle is well defined. This means that the probe should be scanned in two dimensions which makes the technique more useful for hand scanning work than for automated studies.

Two Probe Shear Wave Time-of-flight Techniques: In the two probe approach, the relative times-of-flight to the echoes from the defect extremities provides an indication of the defect depth. Since only time delay is used in the analysis, broad beam probes can be used to cover greater depths of material. With shear waves, no greater efficiency is obtained with steeply angled probes and close separations between the probes. This gives rise to two practical problems; firstly the energy diffracted from the lower extremity of the crack may interact again with the crack producing a weak or misplaced signal; and secondly lateral scanning is again required in order to accurately define the crack depth. An additional problem is that mode converted energy can produce interfering pulses which arrive earlier than the pulses of interest. This could be a serious limitation if the technique is used to locate defects.

Two Probe Compressional Wave Time-of-flight Techniques: This approach utilises the earliest arrival of pulses thus minimising problems due to mode conversion. In addition, the probes can be more widely spaced which allows a single linear scan to be used to accurately size defects in the through-thickness direction. This mode of operation has been the most commonly used among the various alternatives mentioned above.

Data Analysis: Broadly, the analysis of the data in the time domain is favoured since information on the order of arrival of the pulses in retained. This informaton is lost in frequency domain analysis. In addition, it is generally true that the resolution is not improved by frequency domain analysis because there is an underlying link between bandwidth and pulse length. However, spectral analysis in conjunction with these probes could provide additional information on defect characterisation.

In terms of defect sizing, the time-of-flight technique has been used to examine specimens, containing both crack-like and volumetric defects. There is also a development in AERE-Harwell of using multi-probe system (instead of two probe system) capable of inspecting the given weld region of the pressure vessel as well as building a prototype nozzle scanner based on the same technique. The multiprobe system is capable of detecting and locating defects in the given weld region throughout the full depth of the pressure vessel and to a width of t/L on either side of the weld region. It uses sixteen probes controlled by a computer with automated data acquisition and processing. It is intended to size defects within $\pm$ 2mm and size all defects greater than 5mm in depth below the interface between the stainless steel cladding and the carbon steel plate.

5.3   EMAT Generated Shear Horizontal Waves for NDE

Ultrasonic waves generated by EMATs are gaining importance in many industrial applications [13]. One ultrasonic wave mode that has provided solutions to many inspection problems is SH wave. SH waves can be generated by using conventional PZTs as well as by using EMATs. In the former case, though it is possible in principle, practice PZTs are not effective due to coupling problems. In the latter case, it is quite easy and the transduction is effective enough to use these waves for practical applications. Different EMAT configurations are used to launch SH waves in non-ferromagnetic and ferromagnetic materials, as the interaction is different. In non-ferromagnetic electrically conducting materials, the EMAT configuration consists of an arrangement of Periodic Permanent Magnets (PPM) and the SH waves are excited by Lorentz forces. For ferromagnetic material, EMAT configuration consists of an rf coil arrangement in a meander fashion and a U-shaped electromagnet is used and the SH waves are excited by magnetostriction. The angle of incidence α is varied by suitably changing the frequency f, shear wave velocity C_t and the wavelength λ_s. However, the non-segmented permanent magnet based EMATs of the end-fire type suffer from inadequate side lobe suppression and have the disadvantage of bidirectional radiation and narrow band waveforms. Beam steering can only be performed by changing the frequency of the transmitted wave and therefore also the wavelength. To overcome these diasdvantages, angle beam EMATs are designed as phased arrays by dividing the whole transducer aperture into multiple segments which are excited with appropriate time delay. Essentially, phased array EMATs consist of several small, discrete elements rather than the series connected meander, multi-period radio-frequency coils that excite narrow band, obliquely propagating bulk waves. When the discrete elements are appropriately driven, the EMAT phased arrays exhibit a unidirectional directivity pattern and produce broad band signals of controlled direction and focusing. The phased array EMATs provide a greater flexibility in both the selection of wave modes and angles of propagation. The time delayed transmitted signals interfere constructively in the far-field under a pre-selected angle α given by the relation

$$\alpha = \sin^{-1}(C_t \Delta t / D)$$

where Δt is the time delay, D is the spacing between the segments and C_t is the shear wave velocity of sound in the material. Due to the smaller aperture of the array-elements, shorter ultrasonic pulses are radiated, yielding a short pulse of the interfered signal in the far field. This phased array principle helps to enlarge the beam width, furthermore it improves the signal-to-noise ratio. Further, given the ability to operate when the test object is moving past the EMAT at production speeds, it would be possible with phased arrays to be able to rapidly change the characteristics of the interrogating radiation, to obtain as much information as possible.

5.4   Defect Characterisation using EMAT Generated SH Waves

Considering the many advantageous features of SH waves over Longitudinal and Shear Vertical (SV) waves, experimental studies were carried out to detect and charcterise defects in materials. Sizing of defects using reflected signal amplitude based methods such as 6 dB and 20 dB drop methods is most common. However, in many situations under or over sizing is reported. On the other hand, the time-of-flight based methods are found to size the defects more accurately. As discussed earlier, one such method is the TOFD method. Experimental investigations were carried out using the SH waves generated by EMATs for defect sizing by TOFD method [14]. Two 8-segmented EMATs were designed for their use as transmitter and receiver in pitch-catch mode (Fig. 12.1). Test and instrument parameters were optimised for high sensitive detection of diffracted signals. The following optimum parameters were arrived at: distance between EMATs 40 mm, angle of insonification 52°, pulse length 2 and number of segments 4. Besides signal averaging, cross-correlation and analytical signal processing using Hilbert transform were adopted to enhance SNR and to improve accuracy in the transit time measurements and in turn the defect sizing. Experimental studies were carried out on fatigue cracks and machined notches in carbon steel and stainless steel specimens. Typical rf signal from a 28 mm deep fatigue crack in 56 mm thick carbon steel sample is shown in Fig. 12.2. The back wall and diffracted echoes are clearly seen. The beam entry point was determined by the back-wall echo arrival time and analytic signal method was implemented for precise transit time measurements. From the transit time measurements, using distance between EMATs and angle of insonification, defect depths were calculated and a correlation coefficient of 0.99 was observed between actual and calculated

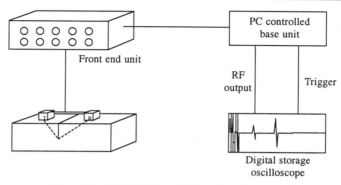

Fig. 12.1   EMATs based Pitch-Catch method

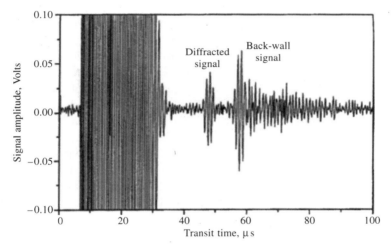

Fig. 12.2   Typical RF signal from a fatigue crack

defect depths. The studies confirmed the feasibility of using diffracted SH waves for sizing defects. Due to large initial leakage pulse, only defects with depth exceeding 12 mm could be detected.

Another study pertains to detection and characterisation of fatigue cracks and machined notches in anisotropic stainless steel welds, which is rather difficult using L or SV waves due to beam skewing and mode conversion problems. However, the situation is different for SH waves. Experimental studies were carried out using SH waves. Four segment *T/R* EMATs operating at 1 MHz were scanned along the length of the weld at a predetermined distance from the weld center line. The rf signals from defect locations were digitised and stored in a personal computer. Signal envelopes were generated using analytic signal method. Considering the variations in the envelopes of the analytic signals from defects at top and bottom locations, a set of representitative parameters were computed and processed by a feed-forward error back propagation Artificial Neural Network (ANN) methodology to characterise defects. The parameter chosen are: rise time, fall time, peak height, full- width-at-half-maximum, mean, standard deviation and skewness.

During the training phase of the ANN, the interconnecting weights of the network were adjusted in such a way that the network learned the relationship between the eight parameters generated from the envelopes and the desired output i.e. defect top (0) or bottom (1). With a mere 50 iterations convergence was observed and a success rate of 100% was achieved, confirming the exactness of the chosen parameters. This methodology is particularly attractive for high temperature and radioactive components and also for components with limited access, primarily due to the fact that EMATs do not need couplant to transfer ultrasonic energy. Further, when the experimental conditions are fixed, it would be possible to implement this methodology on-line and to find location and size of the defects precisely.

5.5   Limitations of EMATs

Two major limitations in using EMATs for a number of practical applications are the physical size of the source of magnetic field (a few tens of millimeters) and the low transduction efficiency (due to weak Lorenz and magnetostrictive driving forces) as compared to piezoelectric transducers. However, with the availability of high 'energy product' rare-earth magnets, it is now possible to construct small and high by sensitive EMATs. Due to low transduction efficiency (commonly quoted as about 50 dB), only a small part of the rf energy entering the metal will be converted into acoustic energy, the rest being normally dissipated as Joule heat in the metal. The problem of low transduction efficiency can be overcome by the use of high transmitting currents, low noise receivers and careful electrical matching. Though EMATs can be used in non-contact manner, higher lift-off values drastically reduce the EMAT's efficiency and alter the directivity characteristics. Also, EMATs exhibit lower driving point impedances than PZTs and are inductive rather than capacitive in character. Because of these differences, most commercially available ultrasonic instruments designed primarily for PZTs will produce dynamic responses which are far-from-optimum when used in conjunction with EMATs. However, with simple redesign or augmentation, the same instruments can be adapted for use with EMATs with near-optimum results.

6   ACOUSTIC EMISSION TECHNIQUE

Acoustic emission technique (AET) has potential for many important applications and has already become an important non-destructive testing technique [15]. Its origination lies in the phenomenon of rapid release of energy within a material/component in the form of a transient elastic wave resulting from dynamic changes like deformation, crack initiation and propagation, leakage etc. It is a real time technique which can detect initiation and growth of cracks, plastic deformation, fatigue failure, leaks etc. which are not amenable for detection by ultrasonics and other NDT methods, due to access considerations and very small sizes of the early stage cracks.

AET is used during hydrotesting of as-fabricated welded vessels and also in service during their hydrotesting. AET is also used for on-line inspection of welded vessels and pipe lines for monitoring their structural integrity. In addition to this, of late AET is being considered for on-line weld monitoring during fabrication. It is used as a helpful complementary technique for inspection of critical areas in important installations. During in-service inspection and hydrotest of welded vessels used in petrochemical, nuclear and allied industries, welded zones are generally weaker, particularly the nozzle areas. Many defects that come to light through AE inspection/

hydro test are most likely to be detected in the welded and surrounding regions and AET to this extent is very useful in monitoring of welds in vessels when employed under such conditions.

6.1 On-Line Monitoring of Welds by Acoustic Emission

AET can be adopted for simultaneous detection of defects as the welding progresses in real time [15]. The defects so found can be immediately rectified thus avoiding the completion of defective weld and then carrying out conventional NDT techniques to find out the defects and repairing the weld, resulting in loss of time and resources. AET has been successfully used for on-line monitoring of welds prepared by GTAW, SAW, ESW etc. However, non-slag forming welding methods are most suitable for AE monitoring.

The main problem of AE monitoring of welding process is elimination of unwanted signals generated during welding. The unwanted signals may be generated due to welding process like metal transfer, slag cracking and detachment and noise caused by operator and electrical interference due to high frequency starter pulses. But these noises can be eliminated by proper signal conditioning and processing techniques. Limitations of these techniques include interpretation of wrong signals and extensive calibration for different applications. The defects that can be detected, located and quantitatively evaluated by AE monitoring during welding are:

(1) Weld cracking associated with phase transformation, (2) Nucleation and growth of cracks during welding and subsequent cooling e.g., delayed cracking, (3) Porosity and slag inclusions, (4) Microfissuring, (5) Hot and cold cracking and (6) Reheat cracks.

Once these defects are located, these regions are further probed using other NDT techniques for in-depth analysis. AE occurs only under the influence of a normal or applied stimulus due to constraints, temperature gradient, phase transformation etc. that cause deformation, crack initiation and propagation. This indicates that AE source is the site of dynamic change in a material to the stimulus generated during welding which responds by releasing part of the energy in the form of elastic stress waves. This dynamic nature of AET makes it a high-potential technique for monitoring of welding processes. The above said sources may also be present in welding during weld bead solidification and further cooling.

One of the important factors that is to be considered is calibration of the AE system. This is carried out after adopting the system to the welding procedure to make sure that the system collects the signal properly and locates the source of AE correctly. Simulation sources are used for this purpose.

6.2 Advantage of AET for Weld Monitoring

In addition to AET's superiority over RT and UT, there are many other added advantages:

1. AET is particularly useful for high technology industries like nuclear, aerospace etc., where defect free welds are a must for high reliability.
2. AET is best and economical since defects are found during welding and immediate repair of weld and also feedback for changing the process parameters are possible based on AE results.
3. In resistance spot welding, weld quality can be immediately known by AE monitoring without going in for many samples being destructively tested.
4. In very big offshore structures where several metres of welds are made, total ultrasonic

testing is costly. First AE monitoring during welding is carried out and only defect indications identified by AET are further probed by UT.

5. This method is particularly sensitive for detection of cracks which are the most serious flaws in welds.

6. In most cases, AE monitoring of welding is cheaper and simple to apply compared to other NDT methods.

6.3   Resistance Spot Welding (RSW)

Figure 13.1 shows the typical experimental set up for the AE monitoring during resistance spot welding. Figure 13.2 shows the typical pattern of AE signals generated during resistance spot welding. By judicious analysis of the signals generated during different periods of the welding cycle, it is possible to identify good and bad welds and also the shear strength of the nugget can be estimated using AE parameters. The AE generated can be related to the weld quality parameters such as strength and size of the nugget, the amount of expulsion and the amount of cracking. Therefore, in-process AE monitoring can be used both as an examination method and as a means for providing feedback control. The various stages in RSW are: set down of the electrodes, squeeze, current flow, forging, hold time and lift off. Various types of AE signals are produced during each of these stages. Using time and amplitude or energy discrimination or both, the AE

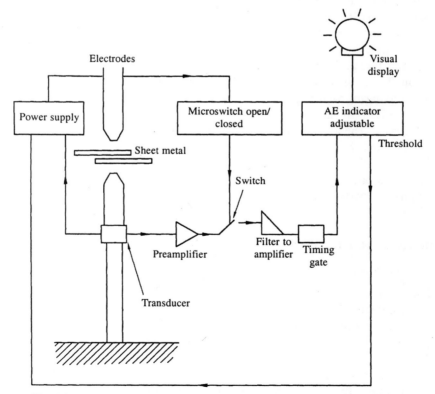

Fig. 13.1   Experimental set-up for AE monitoring during spot welding

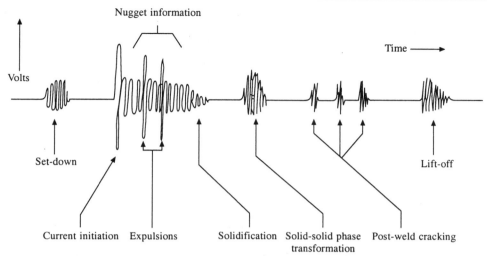

Fig. 13.2 Typical Acoustic Emission response signals during Resistance Spot Welding

response corresponding to each stage can be separately detected and analysed. AE during nugget formation and expansion can be used to correlate with the strength of the weld.

The sensors normally used have a frequency response in the range of 100 kHz to 1 MHz. The sensor is normally fixed to the lower (grounded) electrode. The instrument should have provision for detection of AE within a certain time interval or energy/amplitude range. ASTM standard E751 describes the procedure for the measurement of the AE response associated with selected stages of the resistance spot welding process. This standard also provides guidelines for feedback control by utilizing the measured AE response signals during spot welding process.

6.4 On-Line Monitoring of Chemical Vessel using AET

There are two ways of monitoring the integrity of welded structure: (1) Proof testing initially and then periodically at regular intervals and monitoring AE generated during these tests and (2) Continuous monitoring of structures by AET. The success of the structural integrity monitoring using AET depends on the calibration of the test set up and the methods used for processing and analysing the signals.

Many simulation experiments are carried out by introducing flaws into the structure and monitoring AE response during growth of these flaws. Some of the conclusions obtained are as follows: (1) Flaw growth was successfully detected in time to prevent failure, (2) Good correlation was obtained between the crack growth measured by pitch-catch ultrasonic method and the AE generated, (3) The sensitivity of AET can be judged by the fact that flaw growth as small as 25 μm can be detected with transducers spaced 1.25 metres apart in a particular test, and (4) Fluid leaks can also be detected. Figure 13.3 gives the statistical location map for defects on a cylindrical portion of a reactor vessel during a hydrotest. most of the defects were small and were located either in or adjacent to weld area or at the nozzle to vessel interface.

On-line AE monitoring has been used to monitor the integrity of carbon dioxide absorber unit (Fig. 13.4) in a fertiliser industry [16, 17]. During periodic inspection of the vessel it was

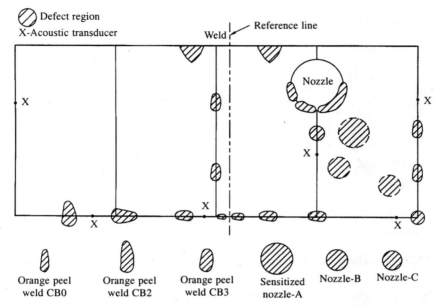

Fig. 13.3 **Typical layout showing the locations of AE sensors and regions of growing defects**

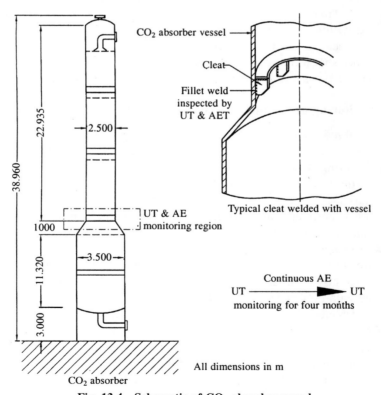

Fig. 13.4 **Schematic of CO_2 absorber vessel**

observed that the vessel had suffered severe chemical corrosion. Cracks were also detected in the fillet welds of the cleats of the internal support structure. It was proposed to carry out acoustic emission monitoring to assess the status of the detected cracks as also to detect any nucleating cracks in the welds of the cleats. AE monitoring was carried out continuously for a period of several months and it was observed that propagation of the defects had occurred at some locations. Subsequently using ultrasonic technique, it was confirmed that none of the defects observed earlier had extended into the surface of the vessel. Based on the recommendations made from the acoustic emission results, the operation of the vessel was continued.

6.5 AE Monitoring of Oxyacetylene Welded Gas Distribution Pipelines

Acoustic emission technique was used to inspect oxyacetylene welded gas distribution pipelines. 5 km of 10 cm diameter pipeline was inspected during flexural stress created by heavy vehicle loading. A test vehicle (for application of load) weighing 32 tonnes would run back and forth on a pipeline segment at approximately 3 km/h for 20 minutes and the AE sensors were mounted at every 61 meters along the pipe line. Using radiography, it was found that, locations with emitter level below 700 did not have cracks. The emitter level was defined as the ratio of total number of detected events from a location to the average total count of a sensor segment. Based on the above investigation, a correlation between AE and radiography results of the weld seams on the pipe line was established.

6.6 Hydro Testing of Horton Sphere

For AE monitoring during hydro testing of the 17 m LPG Horton sphere, a total of twenty four sensors were used in four different groups and in four different configurations to cover the whole structure [18]. In group I, 12 sensors of 150 kHz resonant frequency each were used in 1-5-5-1 configuration to cover the whole sphere in a triangular location mode. In group II, three sensors of same frequency were mounted in a triangular location mode to cover a specific region where an indication was observed from the ultrasonic testing carried out earlier. In group III, one broadband (100 kHz to 2 MHz) sensor was mounted near the suspected region to characterise the deformation and crack growth signals generated, if any during hydro test. In group IV, eight sensors of 150 kHz resonant frequency each were placed in 1-3-3-1 configuration to cover one half of the vessel including the suspected region. The Group IV sensors were connected to a different AE system and used as a backup in case of malfunction of the system used for the Groups, I, II and III sensors.

In groups I and IV, one sensor each was placed at the bottom and top of the vessel. Based on the response of the sensors to simulated pencil break source, the inter-sensor distance of 9.5 m was optimized. Groups I, II and III sensors were connected to the sixteen channel Spartan 2000 acoustic emission testing system. Group IV sensors were connected to the eight channel Spartan AET system. By this, the entire vessel could be covered to detect and locate any AE source associated with local plastic deformation and/or growing discontinuities from any part of the sphere.

The hydro test of the vessel was carried out to a pressure of 22 kg/cm^2, with periodic holds at different pressures. A reloading cycle from 20 kg/cm^2 to 22 kg/cm^2 was immediately carried out following the first cycle of hydro test. During the hydro test, it was observed that acoustic emission signals were generated only during the pressure rise. With increase in pressure, AE signals were generated in the newer areas and the areas where AE occurred in the previous pressure steps did not generate AE in the subsequent pressure steps. These signals were attributed to local micro-plastic deformation of the material. A few signals have also been generated from specific regions, particularly throughout the circumference at an elevation corresponding to the concrete supports. Subsequent inspection of the vessel and simulation pencil break study after the hydro test indicated that the AE signals were generated from the cracks in the concrete columns which were supporting the vessel. Some of the signals could also be confirmed to be due to fracture of oxide scale or paint layer. The results obtained from the broadband sensor were analysed in terms of the spectral energy in different frequency bands. The overall spectral energy was found to increase with pressure rise and this increase was predominantly concentrated in the low frequency band up to 200 kHz. This was attributed to the micro-yielding taking place in the sphere. This was also confirmed from the fact that, during the repressurisation stage (20-22 kg/cm^2), the energy of the signals were at the background level, and is attributed to Kaiser effect.

7 ASSESSMENT OF RESIDUAL STRESSES

Residual stresses are introduced in industrial components during fabrication (including welding process) and in service due to loading conditions. For example, the stresses are introduced during welding process due to nonuniform heat distribution taking place during the welding process. Several destructive and nondestructive techniques are presently available for the residual stress measurements. Destructive techniques cannot be applied on finished components and are time consuming and uneconomical. Therefore nondestructive techniques are preferred for residual stress measurements [19–20]. Some of these techniques include: (i) Ultrasonic (ii) X-Ray Diffraction (XRD), (iii) Acoustic Barkhausen Noise (ABN) and (IV) Magnetic Barkhausen Noise (MBN). Additionally, semi-destructive hole-drilling strain gauge technique is also employed for measurement of residual stresses.

Ultrasonic technique of evaluating residual stresses is based on the measurement of changes in the velocity of ultrasonic waves due to stress and by establishing the acousto-elastic constant. Several methods using ultrasonic waves of various types such as longitudinal, transverse and surface waves have been tried with varying degree of success for weldments.

XRD technique measures the change in the interplanar spacing of the lattice in the presence of stresses in a material. It is well known that peak intensity of diffracted X-ray beam occurs when Bragg's law is satisfied. In the presence of elastic macro stresses, there is a shift in the diffraction peak positions. The magnitude of the shift gives a measure of the stress and the direction of the shift depends on the nature of the stresses i.e. whether they are tensile or compressive.

MBN and ABN techniques are based on Barkhausen effect and are applicable only to ferromagnetic metals and alloys. Barkhausen effect takes place when a magnetic field is swept through the material along a hysteresis loop. MBN is due to irreversible change in magnetic domain movements during hysteresis and ABN is due to elastic deformation associated with magnetic domain rotation during irreversible changes in magnetization. MBN signals can be acquired by sensor coil or by Hall type probe and ABN signals are acquired by piezoelectric transducers. Both MBN and ABN signals are strong functions of stress condition and hence stresses can be assessed by analysing the MBN and ABN signals.

In the hole-drilling strain gauge technique, a specially configured three element rosette is bonded to the component and a small hole is drilled into the component through rosette centre. The measured (relieved) strains in three directions are useful in determining the magnitude of maximum and minimum principal stresses and their directions. Usually, a small hole of 1.6mm diameter drilled to a depth of 2mm is involved in relieving the stresses and this may not impair the structural integrity of industrial components and hence this technique is considered as semi-destructive technique. It is also possible to repair weld the hole, if necessary.

7.1   X-Ray Diffraction Method

This is a very commonly used method. With the help of portable equipments, it is also possible to apply the technique on large objects and carry out the measurements in field and quickly. It can be used for quantitative analysis of macro and micro residual stresses separately.

Principle of diffraction: A monochromatic X-ray beam of sufficient intensity is made incident in the direction AB on the atomic planes as shown in Fig. 14. The reflected beams from successive planes of atoms are observed in the direction BC. Bragg's law defines the condition for diffraction through the following equation:

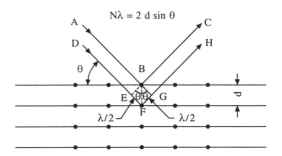

Fig. 14 Principle of diffraction

$$n\lambda = 2d \sin \theta \qquad (12.1)$$

λ – the wavelength of incident X-rays
θ – the angle between incident or reflected beams and surface reflecting planes
d – the interplaner spacing
n – the order of reflection (n = 1, 2, 3 ....)

The above equation shows that, if the wavelength of X-rays is known, the interplanar spacing can be determined by measuring the angle θ. The first order stresses or macrostresses cause a shift in the X-ray diffraction peaks. Measurement of the peak shift is the first requirement in such methods. The techniques generally used for residual stress measurement are: (i) Single exposure method (ii) Double exposure method and (iii) $\mathrm{Sin}^2\psi$ method.

Residual stress measurement in ferritic steel tube welds using X-ray diffraction technique: X-ray diffraction (XRD) technique has been used to measure the residual stresses before and after post weld heat treatment, in autogenous butt weld joints in 2.25 Cr-1 Mo steel tubes [21]. The tubes are used in the steam generator assemblies of fast breeder reactors.

Hot liquid sodium flows in the shell region (outside the tubes) and water inside the tubes. A leak in the tube will lead to the generation of hydrogen due to the reaction of sodium with water with dangerous consequences. Tube to tube sheet weld joints are the weakest regions where a leakage path can be formed with relative ease. Apart from the requirement in the quality control procedures that the weld joints should be free from unacceptable defects that may lead to leak paths, it is also considered essential to use a NDT technique to assess the residual stress (RS) pattern and to evaluate the post weld heat treatment (PWHT) to be used for removing the residual stresses whose presence, otherwise, may lead to failure of the tube to tube sheet weld joint.

The typical dimensions of the tubes and tube sheets of various steam generator modules in the case of a fast breeder reactor are as follows. (a) Evaporator: tube outside diameter 16mm, tube wall thickness 2mm, and tube sheet thickness 150mm, (b) Superheater: tube outside diameter 21.3, tube wall thickness 2.9mm, and tube sheet thickness 135mm, (c) Reheater: tube outside diameter 35 mm, tube wall thickness 2.5mm, and tube sheet thickness 80mm. The weld joints are prepared from the bore side of the tubes by internal bore welding technique from the tube sheet side by GTAW process. The joint is square butt. The welding of the full thickness is done in a single pass without adding filler metal. Preheat is done at 523K. Pre purging and post purging are done to avoid oxidation. Pulse current is varied from 95A to 80A. Rotation is done at a rate of 2.2 revolutions per minute.

The weld joints in the 2.25 Cr - 1 Mo steel tubes are individually post weld heat treated by split type external, and rod type internal electric heaters at 988 K (715°C) for 30 minutes. The joints are then subjected to micro focal rod anode X-radiography, and helium leak testing under vacuum. For the purpose of the investigation, the tube sheet constraint was simulated using a special set up. A total of 9 tube to tube weld specimens have been prepared each about 200mm long, six with preheat and 3 without preheat. For the experiments, the tube to tube joints thus obtained were trimmed to get a length of 140mm with the weld joint at the centre. The selection of the tube specimens was made after carrying out visual and microfocal radiography ensuring that weld joints satisfied the requirements for steam generators of fast breeder reactors in terms of weld penetration, weld width and internal defects like porosities.

The equipment used for the measurement of the residual stresses is a portable X-ray stress analyzer (Rigaku Strainflex MSF) and $\sin^2\Psi$ multiplex method was used for the stress measurements. The conditions used for XRD measurements are given in Table 1. The ψ angles used were 0, 10, 20, and 30 degrees.

Table 1   X - ray diffraction conditions

Characteristic X-ray	Cr Kα
Diffraction plane	{211}
Diffraction angle (degrees)	156.5
Filter	Vanadium
Tube voltage	30 kV
Tube current	8 mA
Irradiated area	2 x2 mm
X - ray fixed time	5 sec

Figure 15 shows the residual stress variations across the weld joints prepared with pre heat. The variations on both the outside surface and the inside surface are shown. The tensile stress maximum occurs at the weld center line both on the outside and the inside surface. On the inside surface, the zero crossing of RS from tensile to compressive occurs about 2 cm away from the weld center line, as compared to 1 cm on the outside surface. The maximum compressive stress level on the inside surface is also much higher than that on the outside surface. The asymmetry in the variation of RS both on the outside and the inside surfaces is attributed to the restraint offered by the tube sheet block on one side where the compressive stresses were found to be higher.

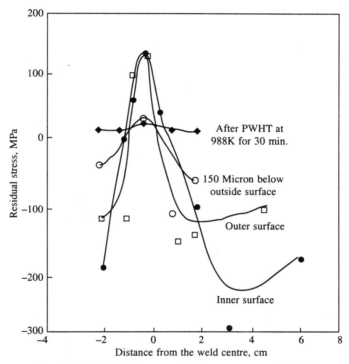

Fig. 15   Residual stress variation across a weld joint

Variation of stress distribution at different depths below the top surface is also shown in Figure 15. These measurements were done after removing 50 to 150 micron layers on the outside surface. Surface removal was done by electropolishing only at the point of measurement so as to avoid any stress relaxation due to layer removal . It is seen that, within a depth of only 150 microns, the stresses approach zero value. This shows that the RS is restricted only to a thin layer at the top.

7.2   Ultrasonic measurements

Ultrasonic technique of evaluating residual stresses is based on the measurement of changes in the velocity of ultrasonic waves due to stress and by establishing the acoustoelastic constant for the material. For precise ultrasonic transit time measurements, pulse-echo-overlap technique is employed. Following are the basic steps involved in the residual stress measurements using ultrasonics: (i) Determination of acoustoelastic constant (AEC) of the material, (ii) Ultrasonic transit time measurements across the weld joint and (iii) Estimation of residual stresses using AEC.

Ultrasonic measurements were carried out across 15mm and 47mm single "*V*" weld joints of AISI type 304 stainless steel using a 2 MHz longitudinal wave transducer [22]. At each position, on an average, five measurements were carried out. Relative changes in the velocities were converted into respective residual stress values by using AEC. Finally, semidestructive hole-drilling strain gauge technique was employed on these weld joints, at these same positions where ultrasonic measuremnets were made. Measurements were also carried out on 8mm and 15mm joints of carbon steel, before and after the PWHT at 873 K for 2 hr.

Figure 16(a) shows the residual stress measurements made using ultrasonic technique in 15mm thick AISI type 304 stainless steel weldment. Stresses at the weld are tensile in nature and change over to compressive at the HAZ. The stresses again become tensile further away i.e. in the parent metal region. The results of the ultrasonic technique have been supplemented by hole drilling strain gauge technique (Fig. 16 (b)). A similar trend was also observed in the case of 47mm thick SS weldment except at the weld centre line, where ultrasonic technique could not be used due to intense scattering taking place due to the textured weld structure. Similarity in the stress distribution pattern was observed for both the methods. However, the absolute values could not be compared since the strain gauge method gives only the subsurface stress distribution, whereas the ultrasonic method gives the stress distribution averaged over the thickness of the plate.

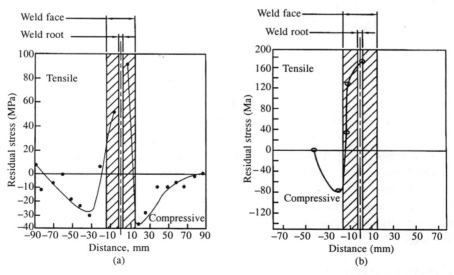

Fig. 16 Comparison of residual stress assenments across an austenitic stainless steel weld joint by (a) ultrasonic and (b) hole drilling method

8 CONCLUSION

In this paper, advanced NDT techniques used for quality assessment with improved sensitivity and quantitative characterisation of defects and for evaluation of residual stresses in welded components are highlighted. A few case studies have been given to demonstrate the usefulness of these techiques for evaluation of welded components.

9 ACKNOWLEDGEMENTS

We wish to convey our sincere thanks to many colleagues in the Division for PIE and NDT Development of Indira Gandhi Centre for Atomic Research, Kalpakkam, for their contributions.

REFERENCES

1. Baldev Raj, C.V. Subramanian, T. Jayakumar, Non Destructive Testing of Welds, Narosa Publishing House, New Delhi, 2000
2. B. Venkatraman, V. Manoharan, T. Jayakumar and P. Kalyanasundaram, Quantitative Profiling of Internal Weld Contours through Videoimagescopy, Proc. of 15th World Conference on NDT, Rome, Oct. 2000.
3. Baldev Raj and B. Venkatraman, Applications of IonisingRadiations for NDE, ISRP Technical Monograph, ISRP (K)/TD-1, Sept. 1989.
4. B. Venkatraman, S. Saravanan, T. Jayakumar, P. Kalyanasundaram and Baldev Raj, performance Evaluation of Real Time Radiographic Systems, Proc. of 14th World Conf. on Non Destructive Testing (14th WCNDT), New Delhi, India, 1996, Ed. C.G. Krishnadas Nair, Baldev Raj, C. R. L. Murthy and T. Jayakumar, Vol. 3, pp. 1401–1404.
5. Baldev Raj and T. Jayakumar, Advances in NDT Techniques for Space and Defence Applications, Proc. Seminar on Engineering Materials (SEM-2000), MRSI, Thiruvananthapuram, April 1999.
6. Baldev Raj and T. Jayakumar, Trends in Advanced Non-destructive Evaluation Techniques for Comprehensive Assessment of Engineering Materials and Components, J. Inst. Engineers (India), 80, 1999, pp. 1–23.
7. B.P.C. Rao, Baldev Raj, T. Jayakumar and P. Kalyansundaram, An Artificial Neural Network for on-line Eddy Current Testing, Materials Evaluation, 60, 2002, pp. 84–88.
8. T. Jayakumar and K. V. Rajkumar, Advanced Ultrasonic Techniques for Evaluation of Materials, j. Pure and Applied Ultrasonics, 22, 2000, pp. 89–105.
9. L. J. Busse, H. D. Collins and S. R. Doctor, Review and Discussion of the Development of Synthetic Aperture Focusing Technique for Ultrasonic Testing (SAFT-UT), *US Nuclear Regulatory Commission Report NUREG/CR-3625*, PNL-4957, 1984.
10. J.A. Seydel, Ultrasonic Synthetic Aperture Focusing Techiques in NDT, Research Technique in Non destructive Testing, Ed. R.S. Sharpe, *Academic Press,* London, 6, 1982, pp. 1–47. M.
11. M. Thavasimuthu, K. V. Rajkumar, T. Jayakumar, P. Kalyanasundaram and Baldev Raj, Ultrasonic Examination of Thin Walled Stainless Steel Tubes by Synthetic Aperture Focusing Technique, *Review of progress in Quantitative NDE,* Plenum Publ. Corp., New York, Vol. 18B, pp. 1987–1993.
12. Vekooijen TOFD Used to Replace Radiography, *Insight,* 37, 1995, p. 433.
13. M. Frost, Electromagnetic ultrasound Transducer Principles Practice and Applications, *Physical Acoustics,* vol. XIV, 1979, pp. 179–275.
14. B. P. C. Rao, T. Jayakumar, P. Kayanasundaram and Baldev Raj, Ultrasonic Detection and Characterisation of Defects using Electromagnetic Acoustic Transducers (EMATs) *Journal of Non destructive Evaluation,* 19, 1999, pp. 32–39.
15. Acoustic Emission Testing, Nondestructive Testing Handbook, Vol. 5, American Soc. for Nondestructive Testing, 1987.

16. P. D. Patel, K. N. Parikh, N.S. Shah, M. R. Bhat, U. K. Vaidya, C. R. L. Murthy, J. Philip, D.S. Pande, T. Jayakumar, Baldev Raj and D. K. Bhattacharya, On-Line Monitoring of a Chemical Vessel by Acoustic Emission Technique, First Natl. Workshop on Acoustic Emission, Sriharikota, June 1990.

17. C. V. Subramanian, M. T. Muthu, T. Jayakumar, Baldev Raj, C. R. L. Murthy, M. R. Bhat and N. S. Shah, On-Line Structural Integrity Assessment of a Carbon Dioxide Absorber Vessel in an Ammonia Unit of a Fertilizer Plant, National Welding Seminar, New Delhi, Dec. 1989.

18. N. Parida, B. Ravikumar, Parvesh Kumar, D. K. Bhattacharya, T. Jayakumar, C. K. Mukhopadhyay, V. Moorthy, S. Devagan, Baldev Raj, D. C. Patel, S. P. Hariharan and A. Joseph, Acoustic Emission Testing of LPG Horton Sphere, in Fourth National Workshop on Acoustic Emission (NAWACE-97), Aug. 22–23, 1997, BARC, Bombay.

19. P. Palanichamy, A. J.oseph, D. K. Bhattachary and Baldev Raj, Residual Stresses and Their Evaluation in Welds, Welding Engineering Hand Book, Eds. S. Soundararajan S. Vijaya Bhaskar and G. C. Amaranath Kumar, Radiant Publications Pvt. Ltd., Secundrabad, India, 1992, Vol. 1, pp. 269–296.

20. P. Palanichamy, A. Joseph, Sanjay K. Rai, T. Jayakumar and Baldev Raj, Evaluation of Residual Stresses in Weldments using NDT Techniques, Proc. Symp. Joining of Metals (SOJOM 96), Tiruchirapalli, India, Sept. 1996, pp. H021-H028.

21. Sanjay K. Rai, T. J. Jayakumar, C. Babu Rao, D. K. Bhattacharya and Baldev Raj, Residual Stress Measurement in Ferritic Steel Tube Welds using X-ray Diffraction Technique, Science and Technology of Welding and Joining 3, 1998, pp. 204–207.

22. Baldev Raj, T. Jayakumar and P. Palanichamy, Ultrasonic Non-destructive Evaluation for Defects, Microstructures and Residual Stresses, Proc. National Symposium on Ultrasonics (NSU-96), Sivakasi, Sept. 1996.

Index

acoustic emission 328, 391
    bearing pad welds 337
    detection of yield point 330
    end cap welding 335
    miniature disc bend test 328
    monitoring of hydrotesting 390, 395
    on-line monitoring 330, 331, 332, 391, 393
    resistance spot welding 392
    spacer pad welding 336
advanced eddy current techniques 374
    characterization of defects 377
    eddy current imaging 375
    impedance imaging 377, 378
    impedance imaging system 376
    weld centre line 377
alloy 718 84
    transformation (TTT) diagram 84
aluminium and alloys 67, 286
    AC welding 286
    Al-Mg fillers 286, 287
    composition 69
    electron beam welding 71
    GMAW 71
    GTAW 70
    hot shortness cracking 286
    intergranular cracking 286
    mechanical properties 69
    physical properties 67
    preheating 286
    pressure welding 71
    pre-weld cleaning 286
    types and grades 68
aluminium base alloys to steels 109
    solid state welding 110
aluminium bronze 91
    hot cracking 91
    martensitic transformation 92
austenitic stainless steel 37, 284, 346
    Cr_{eq}/Ni_{eq} ratio 37
    delta-ferrite control 284
    fully austenitic grades 44
    interpass temperature 284

    nitrogen-added grades 44
    post-weld heat treatment 46
    stress relief cracking 44
    welding process selection 348, 349
    welding stabilized grades 43

bend tests 360
    face bend 361
    guided bend test jig 361
    root bend 361
    side bend 361
    wrap-around jig 361
bonding 2
    Coulombic force 1, 3
    covalent 2
    ionic 2
    metallic 2
brass and nickel silver 92
    hot shortness cracking 93
    zinc fuming 93
butt weld configurations 237
    joint terminology 237

carbon steels 32, 282, 345, 346
    heat treatment cycle 346
    low hydrogen procedures 282
    post-weld stress relieving 282
    stress relieving 32
    weldability and carbon content 282
    welding consumables 345, 346
cast iron 30
    electrodes for 31
Charpy V-notch impact test 362
    test specimen 363
    transition curve 363
C-Mn steels 32
    effect of steelmaking process 32
    cooling time $(t_{8/5})$ 24
    t_{100} 26
coated electrodes 125, 128
    cast iron 131
    cellulosic 129

coating materials 126
  development 125, 126
  iron powder 129
  rutile 129
  stainless steel 131
  storage and handling 132
cobalt base alloys to steel joints 109
code design approach 292, 306
  ASME Section VIII Div. 1 292
  joining unequal thickness 301
  joint efficiency 296, 297
  nozzle-shell junction 301, 302, 303
  section thickness 295
  weld stress formulae 294, 295
copper 90
  oxygen free (OFHC) 90
  phosphorus deoxidised 90
  steam reaction 90
  tough pitch copper (ETP) 90
copper alloys, age-hardenable 93
  beryllium oxide toxicity 94
copper base alloys 87
  classification 87
  joint designs 95
  PWHT 95
  shielding gases 94
  themit welding 94
  welding characteristics 88, 89
  welding practice 94
copper base alloys to steels 109
  filler metals 109
  preheat temperatures for GTAW 109
copper-nickel 93
  hot cracking 93
corrosion 183
  corrosion cell 184
  electrochemical reactions 183
  factors influencing 184
  manifestations 184
corrosion of weldments 192
  austenitic stainless steel welds 199, 200
  effect of microsegregation 196
  effect of microsegregation 196
  effect of residual stresses 209
  effect of secondary phases 205, 206
  effect of transformation in SS weld metal 208, 210
  effect of weld defects 194
  HAZ corrosion in Cr-Mo steels 211
  preferential attack in multiphase weld metal 198
  unmixed zone 192, 193

creep test 365
  ASTM E 139 366
  creep test curve 366
Cr-Mo steels 33–36
  delta-ferrite 33
  reheat cracking 33
  temper embrittlement 33
  type IV cracking 34

diffusion welding 169
  variables 170
dished ends 324
  intergranular SCC 323
  residual stresses in 324
dissimilar metal welding 97, 302, 303
  buttering 102
  carbon migration 104
  coefficient of thermal expansion (CTE) 100, 302, 303
  corrosion resistance 105
  dilution 98
  effects of residual stresses 105
  filler metal selection 101
  joint design 103
  joint integrity 97
  melting temperatures 99
  oxide notches 105
  preheat and PWHT 103
  problems in 97
  service considerations 103
  thermal conductivity 100
  welding processes 100
dissipation of welding heat 10
  conduction 10
  peak temperature 10
  thermal cycles 10
drop weight test 365
  ASTM E 208 364
  RT-NDT 364
duplex stainless steels 55
  austenite reversion 62
  CCT diagram 61
  compositions 55
  corrosion resistance 56
  chromium nitride precipitation 65
  ferrite control 62
  ferrite-austenite balance 60
  pitting resistance equivalent 64
  preheat and interpass temperature 61
  PWHT 63
  welding consumables 63

welding procedures 60
welding processes 63

eddy current testing 232
   ANN analysis 378
   discontinuities detected 234
   exciting current 233
   on-line 378
   principle and procedure 233
   sorting of welding consumables 235
   test coil 233
   variables influencing, 234
edge preparation 352, 353
   clad repairs 353
   nozzle to shell welds 352
effect of magnetic field 7
   arc deflection, arc blow 7
   residual magnetism 8
electrode polarity 6
   DCEP, DCEN 6, 7
embrittlement of SS welds 45
   effect of weld composition 45
   sigma phase 45
energy input and distribution 8, 9
   energy loss 8
   transfer (arc) efficiency 9
environment-sensitive cracking 188
   corrosion fatigue 191
   effect of applied potential on SCC 203
   effect of delta ferrite on SCC 203
   effect of heat input on SCC 206
   effect of media on SCC of austenitic SS 221
   factors influencing SCC 189
   hydrogen damage 191
   hydrogen embrittlement (HE) 190
   mitigation of HE 191
   stress corrosion cracking (SCC) 189

failure analysis 324, 325
   dished ends 324
   metallic bellows 325, 326
fatigue performance 296
   acceptable weld profile 299
   effect of offset ratio 299
   effect of reinforcement bead angle 299
fatigue test 365
   S-N plot 366
ferritic stainless steels 48, 284
   475°C embrittlement 50, 285
   austenitic filler (use of) 285
   compositions 49

filler material selection 52
   gaseous contamination 285
   impact transition temperature 50
   intergranular corrosion 52
   notch toughness 52
   phase diagram 49
   post-weld annealing 52, 285
   sigma phase 51
field NDE of components 269
   angular T-joint 275
   annular gap measurement 273, 276
   measurement of liquid level 276
   multi-wall image techniques 273
fitness-for-purpose 225, 304
flash butt welding 163
   variables 164
flux coating 128
   functions 128
foil butt seam welding 163
friction welded products 165
   dissimilar metal joining 167, 168
   similar metal joints 165
friction welding 164
   applications 164, 166

gas metal arc welding (GMAW) 116
   arc self-regulation 119
   equipment and current source 117
   power source characteristic 118
   wire melting characteristics 117, 118
gas tungsten arc welding (GTAW) 134, 135
   AC waveforms 144
   AC welding 143
   back purging 146
   DC pulsed welding 141
   effect of polarity 142
   high frequency start 146
   power source characteristics 140
   shielding gases 145
   tungsten electrodes 137
   welding torches 136
good engineering practices 306
   fabrication rules 306
   inspection assessment 306
GTAW variables 146
   arc current 147
   arc voltage 147
   automatic welding 148
   defects 150
   machine welding 148
   manual welding 148

travel speed 148
  weld preparation 149
  wire feed 148

halogen leak detectors 257
  halide torch 258, 259
  heated anode 258, 259
  SF6 detectors 257, 260
  thermal conductivity detector 259, 260
hardness test 360
  hardness traverse 360
heat affected zone 19
  hardenability 21
  lower/upper critical temperature 19
  microstructure 19
  prior austenite grain size 21
  sub-zones 19
heat-treatable aluminium alloys 72
  aging, natural and artificial 72
  Al-Zn-Mg 72
hot cracking 15
  interfacial energy ratio 16
  shrinkage stresses 15
  wetting angle 16
hot cracking in duplex SS 64
  effect of Cu and P 64
hot cracking in Ni alloys 83
  constitutional liquation of NbC 83, 84
  gamma-Laves eutectic 83
hot cracking in stainless steels 40
  evaluation criteria 43
  ferrite number 41
  mechanisms 40
  relation to Cr_{eq}/Ni_{eq} ratio 41
  relation to P+S content 41
  self-restraint tests 43
  tests for 42
  types 40
  Varestraint test 42
hot cracking in steels 22
  HCS, UCS parameters 23
HSLA steels 32, 33
  local brittle zones 33
  softening of the HAZ 33
hydrogen-assisted cracking 23
  carbon equivalent 24
  diffusible hydrogen 24
  Graville Diagram 26
  hardness control approach 24
  hydrogen control approach 25
  minimum preheat temperature 26

  restraint factor 26
  sources of hydrogen 23
  tests for 27
  weld metal 33
hydrostatic pressure test 265
  pneumatic testing 265
  venting 265

infrared thermography 331
  end cap welds 336
  resistance spot welds 334
  temperature profiles 331
intelligent welding system 332
  expert systems 337
  narrow gap welding 333
interfaces in welding 2
  adsorbed layers 4
  contaminants 4
  theoretical strength 3

joining methods 1

lamellar tearing 27
  through-thickness ductility 28
leak test methods 254
  bubble emission techniques 255
  minimum detectable leakage rates 266
  ultrasonic leak detection 257
  vacuum box technique 257
  vacuum retention test 256
leak testing of systems 266
  major tanks and vessels 267
leak test methods 254
  pressure change method 254
leak testing 253, 264
  calibration standards 264
  instrument calibration 264
  leak 253
  leak rate 253
  system calibration 265
  test sensitivity 253
  units 253, 254
leak testing of systems 266
  large volume piping system 266
leak types 254
  real leak 254
  virtual leak 254
liquation cracking 17
  grain boundary migration 17
  partially melted zone 17
liquid penetrant inspection 227

developer, types 228
    fluorescent penetrant systems 228, 229
    fluorescent penetrants 228
    penetrant, types 227
    types of developers 228
    types of penetrants 227
    variables 228
localised corrosion 187
    crevice corrosion 187
    effect of heat input 204
    effect of nitrogen content 205
    intergranular corrosion 192
    pitting corrosion 187
low alloy steel welding 283
    post-weld stress relieving 283
    preheat 283
low hydrogen electrodes 130, 133
    coating properties 133
    mechanical properties 134
    rebaking 134
    running properties 133

magnetic Barkhausen noise analysis 317
    assessment of PWHT 317, 318, 319
    identification of weld zones 323
magnetic particle testing 229
    circular magnetization 230
    continuous magnetisation 230
    demagnetisation methods 232
    demagnetization 232
    leakage field 229
    magnetisation current 230
    magnetisation methods 230
    magnetization current 230
    magnetization methods 230
    prod contact method 231
    prod contacts 231
    residual magnetisation method 230
    skin effect 230
    use of yoke 231
    weld inspection 231
    yoke, positioning 231
maraging steels 283
    cleaning procedures 283
    role of fit-up 284
    post-weld ageing 35
martensitic stainless steels 286
    preheat temperatures 286
    compositions 53
    filler materials 54
    preheat and PWHT 55

    transformation temperatures 54
    welding procedures 54
mass spectrometer leak detection 260, 261
    accumulation testing 263, 264
    bell jar method 261, 263
    detector probe 261
    helium bombing 262, 263
    hood method 261, 262
    tracer probe 261
mechanical tests 355
    ANSI/AWS B4.0 355
    ASTM A 370 355
    bend tests 361
    Charpy V-notch impact test 362, 363
    creep test 366
    drop weight test 365
    fatigue test 365
    hardness test 360
    plain strain fracture toughness test 363
    spot welds (for) 359
    tension shear test 357, 358
    tension test 356
metal transfer modes in GMAW 119
    globular transfer 121, 122
    short circuit transfer 120
    spray transfer 122, 123
metallic bellows 325
    stress relieving 326
microsegregation 14
    effect of convective mixing on 15
    effect of solid diffusion on 15
    equilibrium phase diagram 14
    growth morphologies 14, 15
    partition coefficient 14
    partitioning 14
miniature disc bend test 328
    load-deflection curve 329
    offset ratio 299
    secondary bending stress 299
    stress magnification factor 299

NDT of welded components 224
    defects 224
    fitness for purpose 225
    imperfections 224
nickel base alloys 79
    classification 79
    filler metals for 81
    joint designs 86
    oxide removal 287
    precipitation-hardenable 82

process selection 85
PWHT 86
shielding gases 85
solid solution alloys 80
weld defects 86
welding practice 85
nickel base alloys to steel joints 107
filler metals 108
nickel steels 34
consumables for 34
non-destructive tests 225

on-line monitoring 330, 331, 332
acoustic emission 330
ANN analysis 333
end cap welding 335
infrared thermography 331, 332
resistance spot welds 333
ultrasonic measurements 332

phosphor (tin) bronze 92
hot cracking 92
plane strain fracture toughness 363
ASTM E 399 364
compact tension test 364
prediction of delta-ferrite 39
DeLong diagram 39
Schaeffler diagram 39
WRC-92 diagram 39
process variables in GMAW 123
arc voltage 124
cold lapping 124
electrode extension 124
shielding gas 125
welding current 123
welding speed 124
projection welding 162
products 162
testing 162

quality and reliability 304, 306
quality assurance 224, 248
QA programme 248
quality 248
quality control 278
after welding 281
before welding 280
during welding 280
fitness for purpose 279
role of joint design 281, 282
workmanship standard 279

radiographic exposure techniques 244–247
double wall penetration 245, 247
single wall penetration 244, 246
radiographic testing 238
ASTM E-142 242
ASTM E-99 242
butt welds 244
corner joints 245
defect evaluation 243
defect evaluation 243
double wall penetration 245, 247
encapsulated source 241
fillet welds 244, 245
film viewing 243
film viewing 243
geometric factors 240
geometric factors 240
industrial X-ray film 242
industrial X-ray films 242
lap joints 245
penetrameters 242
principle and procedure 238, 239
radiographic sensitivity 242
radiographic sensitivity 242
radioisotope camera 241
single wall penetration 244, 246
sources 241
sources in radiography 241
various joint configurations 244
radiography, high resolution 370
detection of porosity 374
image processing 374
on-line fluoroscopy 372
radiography system 373
radiography, real time 372
resolution 372
rod anode X-ray head 372
reheat cracking 28
susceptibility parameters 29
methods to reduce 29
butter-bead temper bead technique 325
half-bead technique 326
residual stress assessment 396
acoustic Barkhausen noise 396
hole drilling technique 397, 400
magnetic Barkhausen noise 396
ultrasonic velocity 396, 399, 400
X-ray diffraction 397
non-destructive techniques 396
residual stresses in welds 172
basic mechanism 172

effect on fracture 178
effects on fatigue strength 178
effects on performance 178
environmental effects 178
measurement 182
types 173
typical stress distributions in plates 174
weld residual stresses, origin 173
residual stresses, factors influencing 174
component dimensions 175
differential cooling 176
material properties 174
phase transformations 176
shrinkage 175
sources of 175
residual stresses, methods to reduce 179
mechanical methods 179
monotonic overload 180
thermal stress relief 181
vibratory stress relief 180
resistance welding 157
heat generation 157
resistance welding machines 157
classification 158
flash butt welding 158
machine selection 158
projection welding 158
seam welding 158
spot welding 158
resistance welding process 159
automation 160
sequence timers 160
synchronous controls 160

safety in GTAW 150
fume hazard 150
radiant energy hazard 151
seam welding 162
testing 163
sensitisation in the HAZ 212
carbide precipitation in SS 213, 214
CCS diagram 215
effect of heat input 212
effect of thermal cycles 212
elemental effects on kinetics 219
EPR technique 217
mitigation techniques 220
TTS diagrams 214
silicon bronze 91
hot cracking 91
solidification mode 38

relation to Cr_{eq}/Ni_{eq} ratio 39
spot welding of sheets 160
dial indexing table 160
quality control 161
spot welded products 161
testing 161, 358, 359
stainless steel to carbon steel joints 106
difference in CTE 106
filler metal selection 106
use of transition piece 107
stainless steels 284
carbon pickup 284
steel welds 22
cold cracking 23
hot cracking 22, 23
liquation cracking 22
strain age embrittlement 30
Al content 30
strain-age cracking in Ni alloys 83
effect of Al and Ti content 83
submerged arc welding, SAW 151
flux feed and recovery systems 154
power sources 153
weld defects 156
welding head mounting 152, 153
welding set-up 152
welding variables 154
wire feed system 152
super-austenitic grades 46

temper embrittlement 30
J factor 30
tension tests 356
all-weld-metal test 356
cross-tension test 359
for spot welds 358
longitudinal weld test 357
peel test 360
tension-shear test 357, 359
transverse weld test 357
titanium alloys 73–75, 287
basket weave alpha 78
CCT diagram 77
classification by strength 74
classification by structure 74
effect of impurities 73
embrittlement 287
hot cracking 78
normalised strength 75
phase diagram 76
post-weld cleaning 288

precautions in welding 75
pre-weld cleaning 287
PWHT 77
side-plate alpha 78
tube-tubesheet weld joints 315, 316
microfocal radiography 316

ultrasonic examination 235–240, 307
acoustic anisotropy 237
advanced signal analysis 307–9
angle beam examination 238, 239, 240
autopower spectra 312, 314
characteristics of ultrasonic waves 236
demodulated autocorrelogram 310
digital signal analysis 313
end plug weld 313
fuel pin 312, 313
inspection system 235
normal beam examination 240
scanning techniques 237
spectral analysis 311
tandem technique 238
test techniques 237
transducers 235
transducers and probes 236
typical defect patterns 239
ultrasonic techniques 379
EMAT 387
EMATs for fatigue cracks 389
SAFT 380, 381
SAFT for tee joint 382, 383
synthetic aperture focusing technique 380, 381
time of flight diffraction 384
TOFD 384
TOFD compression wave 387
TOFD for end cap weld 385
TOFD shear wave 386
TOFD single probe 386
ultrasonic testing of welds 237
detecting the weld centre line 238
double probe technique 238
joint configurations 237
single probe technique 238
single vee joint 239
various joint configurations 240
ultrasonic velocity measurement 321
for assessment of PWHT 322
ultrasonic imaging 322
weld profile 322
ultrasonic wave characteristics 235
longitudinal waves 235

surface waves 235
transverse waves 235
ultrasonic waves 236
longitudinal waves 236
Rayleigh waves 236
transverse waves 236
ultrasonic welding 169
applications 169
uniform corrosion 184
corrosion rate 185
erosion corrosion 188
galvanic corrosion 185
galvanic series 186
leaching or dealloying 188
unmixed zone 192, 193, 202, 204
effect of welding process 193
in multipass welds 193
preferential attack 204

visual inspection 225
borescope 226
borescope 226
CCD camera 225
endoscope 226
endoscope 227
flexible borescope 227
flexible fibre-optic borescope 227
microscope 226
microscope 226
optical aids 226
optical aids for 226
visual techniques 368
internal curvature of tubes 369
replica 369
videoimagescopy 369

weld cladding 110
application considerations 111
composition control in overlays 111
dilution 112
stainless steel filler metals 111
weld cladding processes 113
alloy addition through flux 113
electroslag overlaying 114
flux-cored wire 114
metal powder addition in SAW 113
other nonferrous overlays 115
plasma hot wire process 114
SAW 113
solid state cladding 115
tubular wire in SAW 113

weld defects 224
weld discontinuities 297
    classification 297
weld imperfections 224
weld joint design 289
    design rules 292
    joint and groove designs 291
    objectives 289
    role of designer 289
weld joint zones 11
weld penetration 17
    convective flow mechanisms 17, 18
    effect of surface active elements 17, 18
    improvement 17, 18
weld puddle shape 11, 12
    effect of welding speed 12
weldability 30
welder performance qualification 251
    renewal of 252
welding arc 5
    regions 5
    temperature distribution 5

voltage distribution across 5
volt-ampere characteristic 6
welding consumable qualification 249
    qualification tests 249, 250
welding consumables 342
    ASME Section IIC 345
    dissimilar welds 351
    selection criteria 342
    urea reactor 353
    welded dished ends 351
welding cost formulae 350
    deposition rates 351
welding procedure qualification 249
    essential variables 251
welding procedure qualification 249
    supplementary essential variables 251
welding processes 2
    classification 2

X-ray residual stress measurement
    dished ends 324
    repair welding procedure 326